Extending Art of Illusion

Scripting for 3D Artists

Extending Art of Illusion

Scripting for 3D Artists

Second Edition

Timothy Fish

Extending Art of Illusion
by Timothy Fish

Published by Timothy Fish, Fort Worth, Texas 76134
timothy@timothyfish.com

Printing History:
First Edition: 2011
Second Edition: 2019 - updated to AOI 3.0.3, increased scripting info, introduced ClothMaker Plugin (beta)

ISBN: 978-1-61295-003-7

Table of Contents

Preface

Have you ever been working in Art of Illusion and said:

I wish I didn't have to do this so many times?
I wish it would stick that object where I want it?
I wish that object would react to other objects?
I wish I had a menu item that would do that?
I wish there were a cloth simulator?

Then this book is for you.

And yes, I did say cloth simulator. One of the criticisms of Art of Illusion has lone been that it doesn't have a cloth simulator. New for the second edition of this book is the introduction of a cloth simulator in Chapter 10. It doesn't have the maturity of the cloth simulators in other 3D graphics tools but it did produce the cloth used for the cover of this book. It is good enough to be a good starting point for others. With a book like this, I could wish for nothing better than for a reader to use the information in the book to modify some of the projects and produce something better.

Another change from the first edition is that I have moved the information on writing scripts to the front of the book and lengthened it. From the e-mails I've received since the book was first published, it is my assessment that people are more interested in writing scripts for Art of Illusion than they are in developing plugins.

One reader contacted me concerning converting BeanShell scripts to Groovy. While there's no reason why someone must convert to Groovy, part of the new material is in reference to that, though there were very few changes required.

The plugins are largely unchanged from the first edition. The reference material at the back of the book required significant changes. Nearly every class changed, but far fewer had interface changes. In most cases the changes involved adding functions and not taking any away. Some of the class hierarchy changed and some new classes were added. Some don't have an obvious purpose. But I included them all so that anyone who is writing scripts can look them up. One of the things that makes Art of Illusion scripting so powerful is that the vast majority of the members of Art of Illusion classes are public. There is very little in Art of Illusion that can't be controlled via a script. The reference at the back of this book gives you the information you need to access those classes.

I have tried to include example plugins that you will find useful in using Art of Illusion, but more so, I hope that they will inspire you to develop even better scripts that you can use for you own work and make available for other people to use. Though I believe you will learn more if you type the code in manually, the code for all of the examples is available in a github repository at:

https://github.com/TimothyFish/Extending-Art-of-Illusion/archive/master.zip

Or clone the repository at:
https://github.com/TimothyFish/Extending-Art-of-Illusion.git

Should either of those fail, there is also a zip file on my website:
http://www.timothyfish.com/Extending_AOI_source_2.zip

If you have questions beyond what is covered in this book, you may want to visit the Art of Illusion forums. These forums are frequented by the people who developed Art of Illusion. Links to these forums are listed at:

http://www.artofillusion.org/forums

Timothy Fish
timothy@timothyfish.com

Chapter 1

An Introduction to Art of Illusion Scripting and Development

Art of Illusion (AOI) is a 3D graphics program originally developed by Peter Eastman. According to an undated interview, Dr. Eastman states that he began the project after taking a Computer Graphics class in which they had to use "truly horrible modeling tools". After trying commercial versions of modeling tools, he still thought the user interfaces left something to be desired, so he wrote his own. At the time of the interview, he reported that Art of Illusion had been downloaded over 130,000 times at a rate of 200-300 downloads per day. (http://aoi.sourceforge.net/temp/interview.txt)

Since the time of its initial release, Art of Illusion has matured significantly, but the user interface has retained its simplicity. Unlike some of its peers, Art of Illusion has a very small learning curve for first time users. Much of the user interface is just what one would expect, so in the time it takes first time users of some programs to learn how to reposition objects in a scene, a first time user of Art of Illusion can be rendering his first image.

But while Art of Illusion has a lot going for it, it isn't without its critics. One of the more frequent criticisms is that it doesn't do what some of the other tools do. In some cases, Art of Illusion has the capability to do what the other tool does, but it requires the user to accomplish the task in a somewhat different way. In other cases, there may not be a simple means of accomplishing the task in Art of Illusion. When that's the case, there are a number of options. One is to put Art of Illusion aside and use the other tool, then either complete the rendering in the other tool or import objects from the other tool. The image shown here is one example. While Art of Illusion has some capability to develop characters, it is much quicker to use Poser to create a human figure, export the figure as an OBJ file and import it into Art of Illusion. While that may seem like a waste of time, since Poser has many of the features that Art of Illusion has, the better rendering engine belongs to Art of Illusion.

Figure 1-1: Render of Imported Object

But it's not always possible to transition from one tool to another. You could contact the developers. In 2016 Peter Eastman transitioned to a less hands-on role and passed much of the responsibility to Lucas Stanik. The stated reason for this was that because of less development happening they were looking for a more self-sustaining organization of the project. My translation of this is that they are primarily doing bug fixes and not new features. The other option is that you can write a script or plugin that implements the feature you need.

Plugins or Scripts?

In the years following the first edition of Extending Art of Illusion readers have expressed more interest in scripting than they have in developing plugins. I did not anticipate this. My purpose in writing the book was to address what I felt was a shortfall in the plugin development documentation that was available at the time. I felt that there was sufficient documentation on scripting but the learning curve for developing plugins was steep and not documented properly. Based on e-mails I have received from readers it is now my view that the typical user will delve into writing a script to make it easier to create a scene and will create plugins only after much repeated use of the script or out of a desire to provide refinements that are not possible through scripting.

Art of Illusion currently uses the Groovy scripting language (a scripting language based on Java), but it also provides backwards compatibility to the BeanShell scripting language. If you have scripts written for a previous version of Art of Illusion using BeanShell it is likely that they will still work. There is no plan to remove that capability. The scripting examples are all written in Groovy. For those that were converted from BeanShell examples appearing in the first edition the differences in the scripts will be identified to help you if you decide to convert a BeanShell script to Groovy.

Why Use Scripts

In using Art of Illusion you have probably already seen that from the Tools menu you can access a number of script related functions and call a few scripts that are included with the install package. The oldest of these is the Distribute script which takes two scene objects as input and will distribute copies of one over the surface of the other, attempting to place the objects on the vertexes. You might, for example, want to place several cylinders in a circle in a scene. You could draw a cylinder, copy it several times, and then reposition each copy, or you could draw a circle and have the script copy the cylinder and place the copies on the circle.

You might want to write your own script for a scene if you have tasks that are tedious or you have objects that must change with respect to time or with respect to other objects in the scene. Some objects are impractical to draw by hand. With scripts you can automate the process, freeing yourself up to do the creative work.

Types of Scripts

There are three types of scripts in Art of Illusion, *Scripted Objects*, *Tool Scripts*, and *Startup Scripts*. Each type serves a different purpose and are executed at different times.

Writing Scripts for Scripted Objects
A Very Simple Object

A *scripted object* is a scene object. In every window that displays scene objects the script for the object will be called. To create a very basic scripted object do the following:

Select "Create Scripted Object..." from the Tools menu.

Enter a name for your object and select "New Script", then click OK.

Enter the following script into the window that appears:

```
sphere = new Sphere(0.25, 0.25, 0.25);
pos = new Vec3(0.0, 0.0, 0.0);
script.addObject(sphere, new CoordinateSystem(pos,0,0,0));
```
Click OK.

You should now have an object in the scene list with the name you provided and you should see a sphere drawn at the origin of the scene. While this is about as simple as any script can be there are a number of things going on for which an explanation may be helpful.

On the first line we create an instance of the Sphere class and we assign it to a variable. The parameters of the constructor are the radius of the Sphere given in the X, Y, and Z directions respectively. To display the object in the scene we need to add it to the scene. Because this is a Scripted Object we don't add the Sphere directly to the scene but we add the object to the script which will be a part of the scene. When the script receives the command to draw, it will send the draw command to its members.

The **script** variable is a special variable that exists for Scripted Objects. This variable is of type artofillusion.script.ScriptedObjectController. The full public interface is documented in the artofillusion.script package in the back of the book (page 428) .

In addition to the object we are adding to the scene, the second parameter to addObject() is a CoordinateSystem. CoordinateSystem is in the artofillusion.math package (page 364). A CoordinateSystem specifies position and rotation with respect to an object. In this case, the object it is with respect to is the scripted object. We are placing the Sphere at the origin of the scripted object, but if we were to move the scripted object within our scene then the Sphere would also be placed at that new location.

The second line of our script just creates a variable to hold the XYZ location to be passed to the constructor of the CoordinateSystem.

It is also worth noting that even through we have called *new* for three different classes we haven't specified the namespace for any of them. Sphere is in the artofillusion.object package. CoordinateSystem and Vec3 are both in the artofillusion.math package. It isn't necessary to specify those namespaces in our scripts because the scripting interface automatically imports the following packages:

artofillusion.*
artofillusion.image.*
artofillusion.material.*
artofillusion.math.*
artofillusion.object.*
artofillusion.texture.*
artofillusion.ui.*
buoy.event.*
buoy.widget.*
java.awt.*
java.awt.event.*
java.io.*
java.lang.*
java.net.*
java.util.*
javax.swing.*
javax.swing.event.*

The artofillusion and buoy packages are documented in the quick reference in the back of this book. For information on the java packages you will need to consult information on the Java programming language.

If you need additional packages in your script you will need to add the appropriate import statement. Also, if you should decide to convert a script to a plugin you will need to include import statements in the plugin code for any of these packages that you use.

Building on the Simple Object

To modify the code of our very simple object we need only double-click the Scripted Object name in the scene list. Right-clicking and selecting "Edit Object…" is another way to bring up the script edit window for the object.

We can add another Sphere by repeating the same code, but let's position the second Sphere in another location and make it smaller than the first.

```
sphere = new Sphere(0.25, 0.25, 0.25);
pos = new Vec3(0.0, 0.0, 0.0);
script.addObject(sphere, new CoordinateSystem(pos, 0, 0,
0));
sphere2 = new Sphere(0.05, 0.05, 0.05);
pos = new Vec3(0.5, 0.0, 0.0);
script.addObject(sphere2, new CoordinateSystem(pos, 0,
0,0));
```

This is likely to seem obvious. What may not be so obvious is how to deal with changes to the object over time or with respect to other changing conditions. For the purposes of this example, let's say we want the smaller sphere to be visible five seconds into the animation and disappear after another ten seconds. Your first thought might be that you want to set a visibility flag for the second sphere. While it is possible to do that, doing so complicates things. An easier way is to change the code to the following:

```
sphere = new Sphere(0.25, 0.25, 0.25);
pos = new Vec3(0.0, 0.0, 0.0);
script.addObject(sphere, new CoordinateSystem(pos, 0, 0,
0));
time = script.getTime()
if(time >= 5.0 && time <= 15.0){
  sphere2 = new Sphere(0.05, 0.05, 0.05);
  pos = new Vec3(0.5, 0.0, 0.0);
  script.addObject(sphere2, new CoordinateSystem(pos, 0,
0,0));
}
```

Now play the animation and you will see that the second sphere is invisible for five seconds and then it disappears a few seconds after it becomes visible. This demonstrates that the code for the scripted object is called each time a different frame is displayed. If you are familiar with the graphics library OpenGL then this is a concept with which you are familiar, but I don't assume that all Art of Illusion users are familiar with OpenGL. The objects we create exist only for long enough for them to be drawn once. When they must be drawn again they must be created again. The advantage of this approach is that we aren't going through some complicated process of finding certain objects and modifying them before each draw. But at the same time we have the Art of Illusion scene which has a set of objects defined that remain in the scene until we remove them.

Parameters

Scripted objects can have parameters. These are set by selecting the parameters button on the script editing window. For the Axis object in the example that follows the parameters

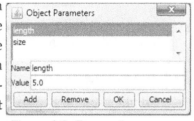

Figure 1-2: Parameters

need to be length and size. When you create the scripted object, you will need to add these, as is shown in Figure 1-2. Within the script we get the value of the parameter by calling script.getParameter(). So for the length value we would have the following statement:

```
length = script.getParameter("length");
```

Unfortunately, parameters aren't particularly user friendly. While the parameters will stay with the object in the scene, if you attempt to create another scripted object from a saved script that relies on parameters you will have to manually add the parameters to the scripted object before the script will function properly. One way people get around this shortcoming is by specifying any values they need at the top of the script rather than using parameters.

Hacking the Script Parameters

Having just said that Art of Illusion won't store the parameter information with the script, let me show you a hack that gets around the issue. One of the great things about Art of Illusion is that nearly everything is reachable using scripts and plugins. Since we can call the same code that is used by the GUI to add parameters to the Scripted Object our Scripted Object can add parameters to itself. The following code (from the Axis Example) does exactly that:

```
scene = script.getScene();
count = 0;
for(candidate in scene.getAllObjects()){
  obj = candidate.getObject();
  if(obj in ScriptedObject){
        if(obj.getScript().indexOf("<name>Axes</name>") != -
1){
      if(obj.getNumParameters() == 0){
        String[] names = ["length", "size"]
        Double[] values = [5.0, 0.01];
        obj.setParameters(names, values);
      }
    }
  }
}

// Retrieve parameter values
try{
  length = script.getParameter("length");
  size = script.getParameter("size");
}
catch(Exception ex){
  return;
}
```

In this code we get the scene from the script and then we step through all of the objects in the scene looking for the ScriptedObjects. Each ScriptedObject contains a copy of its code. To determine if the ScriptedObject is the one we want to add parameters to we look for the string "<name>Axes</name>" in the script. It doesn't matter what string we use because any string we search for will be in the script we are looking for, but it should be a string that only occurs in that script or we risk adding parameters to other ScriptedObjects. We also need to limit our search to objects that don't already have parameters. This keeps us from overwriting our own parameter values each time the script is called.

This code should be placed before any calls to get-Parameter() but even then it is necessary to put try-catch blocks around the getParameter() call because the ScriptedObject isn't actually part of the scene until after this code executes the first time. I will reiterate that this hack isn't required for scripted objects that you create in a scene and add parameters to by hand. It is only when you store the code in a separate file with the intent to load that code into a scripted object that you need this hack.

The Axis Example

To demonstrate another simple scripted object we'll create an object that can be used to represent a coordinate system. The scripted object will consist of three cylinders, each lying along a separate axis. The length and diameter of the cylinders are determined by the parameters. I used length=5.0 and size=0.01 as the initial values. The idea is to have three long thin lines in the scene.

The first few lines of code are XML that is provided to the Art of Illusion Scripts & Plugin Manager. The Scripts & Plugin Manger is one of the tools available from the Tools menu. The purpose of this tool is to provide a way to manage the scripts and plugins that are in the Art of Illusion folder. It provides a way to add or remove scripts and plugins (non-startup scripts) without restarting Art of Illusion. By including the XML information at the beginning of your scripts you provide the Scripts and Plugins Manager with the information displays.

```
/*
<?xml version='1.0' standalone='yes' ?>
<!-- xml header for scripts & plugin manager -->
<script>
  <name>Axes</name>
  <author>Timothy Fish</author>
  <version>0.1</version>
  <date>04/06/2019</date>
  <description>
This script creates an object that can be used to provide a
visual representation of the coordinate system.
    </description>
</script>
*/

// Add the parameters to the ScriptedObject
scene = script.getScene();
count = 0;
for(candidate in scene.getAllObjects()){
  obj = candidate.getObject();
  if(obj in ScriptedObject){
    if(obj.getScript().indexOf("<name>Axes</name>") != -1){
      if(obj.getNumParameters() == 0){
        String[] names = ["length", "size"]
        Double[] values = [5.0, 0.01];
        obj.setParameters(names, values);
      }
    }
  }
}

// Retrieve parameter values
try{
  length = script.getParameter("length");
  size = script.getParameter("size");
}
catch(Exception ex){
  return;
}

// Define the object
ObjectInfo createAxis(double length, double diameter){
  axis = new Cylinder(length, diameter, diameter, 1.0);
  return new ObjectInfo(axis, new CoordinateSystem(), "");
}

ObjectInfo obj = createAxis(length, size);
if (obj != null)
  script.addObject(obj);

obj = createAxis(length, size);
obj.getCoords().setOrientation(90.0, 0.0, 0.0);
if (obj != null)
  script.addObject(obj);
```

Example 1-2a: Axes.groovy

```
obj = createAxis(length, size);
obj.getCoords().setOrientation(0.0, 0.0, 90.0);
if (obj != null)
  script.addObject(obj);
```

Example 1-2b: Axes.groovy

In the next section of the script you see the code that adds parameters to the Scripted Object. We need not discuss this farther.

In the final section there is a function defined to create one axis. This function is then called three times and the object that is created each time is added to the scene.

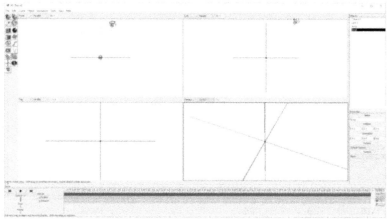

Figure 1-3: Axes.groovy Object

Writing Scripts for Tool Scripts

The second of the three types of scripts in Art of Illusion is the Tool Script. Tool scripts carry out a single action and are only executed when they are evoked. The existing scripts are located on the Tools menu under the Scripts submenu. The Distribute script that was mentioned earlier is one of the tool scripts that is installed with Art of Illusion.

Art of Illusion builds this list from the listing of files in the Scripts/Tools folder that is located within the Art of Illusion installation folder. Any scripts that you want to have access to from the menu must be

Figure 1-4: Script Editing Window

placed in that folder.

You can create or edit one of these scripts from within Art of Illusion by selecting "Edit Script..." from the Tools menu. This displays the window shown in Figure 1-4. This is the same window as was used for the Scripted Objects but it has an additional "Execute" button. This gives you the option to execute a script that isn't on the menu or to execute the script as soon as you are finished with editing.

Room Tool Script

One of the things you might need a Tool Script for is to add frequently used objects to the scene. The Room Tool Script that is provided as an example here adds the four walls, the floor, and the ceiling of a room to the scene. This is a quick way to provide reflective surfaces on all sides of your scene while giving you the ability to disable some of those sides or to use different textures.

This same tool is implemented in Chapter 9 as well, but there it is implemented as a plugin. The purpose of including it both as a script and as a plugin is to demonstrate the similarity between scripts and plugins. This is covered with more detail in the sections on plugins but it is interesting to note that Tool Scripts execute at the same level as the code inside of the commandSelected method of a ModellingTool. The commandSelected method for the Room plugin looks like the following:

```
public void commandSelected(LayoutWindow window) {
    // Create a new UndoRecord. This will be built as we
    // make changes, so we can go back to the previous state
    // of anything we changed.
    UndoRecord undo = new UndoRecord(window, true);

    layout = window;
    if(setRoomSizeAndOptions()){

        buildRoom(undo);
        window.updateImage();

        // Tell the layout window that it can store what we've
        // said is the previous state of the object.
        window.setUndoRecord(undo);
    }
}
```

Compare the two code segments and you will see that they are the same, with the exception that the script has an implied *window* variable while the ModellingTool has it as a parameter to the method. What this means for us is that we can write a Tool Script and then with little trouble copy and paste most of the code from the Room.groovy file into the Java file that defines the plugin. Any script that you create can be turned into a plugin. However, it isn't always the case that you can convert a plugin into a script. You might find some code in a plugin that you would like to include in one of your scripts and be unable to do so.

The next few pages are a listing of the Room.groovy Tool Script.

```
/*
<?xml version='1.0' standalone='yes' ?>

<script>
  <name>Room</name>
  <author>Timothy Fish</author>
  <version>0.1</version>
  <date>04-06-2019</date>
  <description>
Creates a room with four walls a ceiling and a floor. The
sides of the room can be hidden using the normal Art of Il-
lusion user interface. Is meant to work in the same way that
the Room plugin that is described in Extending Art of
Illusion does.
  </description>
</script>
*/
  class RoomDialogPanel extends ColumnContainer {

    ValueSelector widthSelector;
    ValueSelector depthSelector;
    ValueSelector heightSelector;
    BCheckBox ceilingCheckBox;
    BCheckBox floorCheckBox;
    BCheckBox frontCheckBox;
    BCheckBox backCheckBox;
    BCheckBox leftCheckBox;
    BCheckBox rightCheckBox;
    private static final double defaultValue = 25.0;
    private static final double minSize = 0.0;
    private static final double maxSize = 1000.0;
```

Example 1-3a: Room.groovy

```
private static final double increment = 0.1;
private static final boolean defaultVisibility = true;

public RoomDialogPanel(){
  add(new BLabel("Width"));
  widthSelector = new ValueSelector(defaultValue,
                          minSize, maxSize, increment);
  add(widthSelector);

  add(new BLabel("Depth"));
  depthSelector = new ValueSelector(defaultValue,
                          minSize, maxSize, increment);
  add(depthSelector);

  add(new BLabel("Height"));
  heightSelector = new ValueSelector(defaultValue,
                          minSize, maxSize, increment);
  add(heightSelector);

  ceilingCheckBox = new BCheckBox("Ceiling Visible",
                              defaultVisibility);
  add(ceilingCheckBox);

  floorCheckBox = new BCheckBox("Floor Visible",
                              defaultVisibility);
  add(floorCheckBox);

  frontCheckBox = new BCheckBox("Front Visible",
                              defaultVisibility);
  add(frontCheckBox);

  backCheckBox = new BCheckBox("Back Visible",
                              defaultVisibility);
  add(backCheckBox);

  leftCheckBox = new BCheckBox("Left Visible",
                              defaultVisibility);
  add(leftCheckBox);

  rightCheckBox = new BCheckBox("Right Visible",
                              defaultVisibility);
  add(rightCheckBox);
}

public double getWidth() {
  return widthSelector.getValue();
}

public double getDepth() {
  return depthSelector.getValue();
}

public double getHeight() {
  return heightSelector.getValue();
}
```

Example 1-3b: Room.groovy

```groovy
  public boolean getCeilingVisible() {
    return ceilingCheckBox.getState();
  }

  public boolean getFloorVisible() {
    return floorCheckBox.getState();
  }

  public boolean getFrontVisible() {
    return frontCheckBox.getState();
  }

  public boolean getBackVisible() {
    return backCheckBox.getState();
  }

  public boolean getLeftVisible() {
    return leftCheckBox.getState();
  }

  public boolean getRightVisible() {
    return rightCheckBox.getState();
  }

}

windowTitle = "Room Setup";
double width;
double depth;
double height;
boolean ceilingVisible;
boolean floorVisible;
boolean frontVisible;
boolean backVisible;
boolean leftVisible;
boolean rightVisible;
roomCount = 0;

 /**
  * Create the walls of the room based on the class
  * variables.
  * @param undo
  */
void buildRoom(UndoRecord undo) {
  // Add a null object to the scene
  ObjectInfo roomInfo = new ObjectInfo(new NullObject(),
      new CoordinateSystem(),
      "Room "+nextRoomCount() );

  float[] roomSmoothness;
  roomSmoothness = [0.0f, 0.0f, 0.0f, 0.0f];

  // Add ceiling
  Vec3[] ceilingVertices = new Vec3[4];
  ceilingVertices[0] = new Vec3(-(width/2.0), height,
                                -(depth/2.0)));
```

Example 1-3c: Room.groovy

```
ceilingVertices[1] = new Vec3((width/2.0), height,
                            -(depth/2.0));
ceilingVertices[2] = new Vec3((width/2.0), height,
                            (depth/2.0));
ceilingVertices[3] = new Vec3(-(width/2.0), height,
                            (depth/2.0));
createSide(undo, roomInfo, roomSmoothness, "Ceiling",
          ceilingVertices, ceilingVisible);

// Add floor
Vec3[] floorVertices = new Vec3[4];
floorVertices[0] = new Vec3(-(width/2.0), 0.0,
                            -(depth/2.0));
floorVertices[1] = new Vec3((width/2.0), 0.0,
                            -(depth/2.0));
floorVertices[2] = new Vec3((width/2.0), 0.0,
                            (depth/2.0));
floorVertices[3] = new Vec3(-(width/2.0), 0.0,
                            (depth/2.0));
createSide(undo, roomInfo, roomSmoothness, "Floor",
          floorVertices, floorVisible);

// Add front
Vec3[] frontVertices = new Vec3[4];
frontVertices[0] = new Vec3(-(width/2.0), 0.0,
                            (depth/2.0));
frontVertices[1] = new Vec3((width/2.0), 0.0,
                            (depth/2.0));
frontVertices[2] = new Vec3((width/2.0), height,
                            (depth/2.0));
frontVertices[3] = new Vec3(-(width/2.0), height,
                            (depth/2.0));
createSide(undo, roomInfo, roomSmoothness, "Front",
          frontVertices, frontVisible);

// Add back
Vec3[] backVertices = new Vec3[4];
backVertices[0] = new Vec3(-(width/2.0), 0.0,
                            -(depth/2.0));
backVertices[1] = new Vec3((width/2.0), 0.0,
                            -(depth/2.0));
backVertices[2] = new Vec3((width/2.0), height,
                            -(depth/2.0));
backVertices[3] = new Vec3(-(width/2.0), height,
                            -(depth/2.0));
createSide(undo, roomInfo, roomSmoothness, "Back",
          backVertices, backVisible);

// Add left
Vec3[] leftVertices = new Vec3[4];
leftVertices[0] = new Vec3(-(width/2.0), 0.0,
                            (depth/2.0));
leftVertices[1] = new Vec3(-(width/2.0), 0.0,
                            -(depth/2.0));
leftVertices[2] = new Vec3(-(width/2.0), height,
                            -(depth/2.0));
```

Example 1-3d: Room.groovy

```
    leftVertices[3] = new Vec3(-(width/2.0), height,
                                (depth/2.0)));
    createSide(undo, roomInfo, roomSmoothness, "Left",
            leftVertices, leftVisible);

    // Add right
    Vec3[] rightVertices = new Vec3[4];
    rightVertices[0] = new Vec3((width/2.0), 0.0,
                                (depth/2.0)));
    rightVertices[1] = new Vec3((width/2.0), 0.0,
                                -(depth/2.0)));
    rightVertices[2] = new Vec3((width/2.0), height,
                                -(depth/2.0)));
    rightVertices[3] = new Vec3((width/2.0), height,
                                (depth/2.0)));
    createSide(undo, roomInfo, roomSmoothness, "Right",
            rightVertices, rightVisible);

    layout.addObject(roomInfo, undo);

}

/**
 * Creates a side of the room and adds it to the scene.
 * @param undo
 * @param roomInfo
 * @param roomSmoothness
 * @param sideName
 * @param sideVertices
 */
void createSide(UndoRecord undo, ObjectInfo roomInfo,
    float[] roomSmoothness, String sideName,
    Vec3[] sideVertices,
    boolean visible) {
  Curve side = new Curve(sideVertices, roomSmoothness,
                        Curve.NO_SMOOTHING, true);
  TriangleMesh sideMesh = side.convertToTriangleMesh(1.0);
  ObjectInfo sideInfo = new ObjectInfo(
      sideMesh,
      new CoordinateSystem(new Vec3(0,0,0),
                        0.0, 0.0, 0.0), sideName);
  sideInfo.setVisible(visible);
  roomInfo.addChild(sideInfo,
                    roomInfo.getChildren().length);
  layout.getScene().addObject(sideInfo, undo);
}

/**
 * Returns next number for the room.
 * @return
 */
int nextRoomCount() {
  return roomCount++;
}

/**
```

Example 1-3e: Room.groovy

```
     * Displays dialog for user to select room options.
     * @return true if ok select, false if canceled
     */
    boolean setRoomSizeAndOptions() {
      RoomDialogPanel thePanel = new RoomDialogPanel();

      PanelDialog dlg = new PanelDialog(layout, windowTitle,
                                        thePanel);

      if (dlg.clickedOk()){
        // User clicked ok, so store the selected value.
        width = thePanel.getWidth();
        depth = thePanel.getDepth();
        height = thePanel.getHeight();
        ceilingVisible = thePanel.getCeilingVisible();
        floorVisible = thePanel.getFloorVisible();
        frontVisible = thePanel.getFrontVisible();
        backVisible = thePanel.getBackVisible();
        leftVisible = thePanel.getLeftVisible();
        rightVisible = thePanel.getRightVisible();

        return true;
      }
      else{
        // User clicked cancel, so everything should remain
        // unchanged.
        return false;
      }
    }

    /**
     * Return the menu item name.
     */
    String getName() {
      return "Create Room...";
    }

    /* Begin like commandSelected().*/
    // Create a new UndoRecord. This will be built as we
    // make changes, so we can go back to the previous state
    // of anything we changed.
    UndoRecord undo = new UndoRecord(window, true);

    layout = window;
    if(setRoomSizeAndOptions()){

      buildRoom(undo);
      window.updateImage();

      // Tell the layout window that it can store what we've
      // said is the previous state of the object.
      window.setUndoRecord(undo);
    }
    /* End like commandSelected().*/
```

Example 1-3f: Room.groovy

As we look at the code, we see in *Example 1-3a, 1-3b* and *1-3c* that we are declaring a class called RoomDialogPanel. This is for a popup window that will allow us to change size and visibility values. For each of the numeric values we have code like the following in the constructor:

```
add(new BLabel("Width"));
widthSelector = new ValueSelector(defaultValue, minSize,
                                  maxSize, increment);
add(widthSelector);
```

For each of the checkboxes we have code like the following in the constructor:

```
ceilingCheckBox = new BCheckBox("Ceiling Visible",
                                defaultVisibility);
add(ceilingCheckBox)
```

We also declare accessors for the values:

```
public double getWidth() {
  return widthSelector.getValue();
}
```

The class is instantiated in the setRoomSizeAndOptions() function with the following code:

```
RoomDialogPanel thePanel = new RoomDialogPanel();
PanelDialog dlg = new PanelDialog(layout, windowTitle,
                                  thePanel);
```

In *Example 1-3f* you can see the code for the main body of the script. It calls setRoomSizeAndOptions() and if the user clicks OK it calls the buildRoom() function which has all the details of how each of the objects are added to the scene.

There is also some overhead here. Following the call to buildRoom() is a call to updateImage(). This is to tell the layout window that something has changed and it needs to refresh something. There is also an UndoRecord that is created. UndoRecords are used by the undo system to save the current state of the scene to give us a place to go back to. Many of the details of this are also in buildRoom(). Effectively, what you are attempting to do with undo is to define a set of steps that must be followed to go from our current state back to the previous state. This is relatively easy in a script like this, but it can be more difficult if a lot of data or steps are involved.

Aside from that, buildRoom() simply creates a null object (an invisible object used for placement of other objects) and creates six cubes that have the dimensions specified by the dialog box. These objects are all added to the scene.

Room.groovy vs Room.bsh

There were a number of changes that I made to the script that appears in the first edition as a result of moving from BeanShell to Groovy. The first appears at the class declaration. I removed the **private** keyword.

BeanShell:
```
private class RoomDialogPanel extends ColumnContainer {
```
Groovy:
```
class RoomDialogPanel extends ColumnContainer {
```
Below the class declaration is a list of variables. Here, there are three changes. The first is to get rid of the declaration of Layout and simply assign the **layout** variable to **window**. You will recall that in Scripted Objects we have a special predefined property called **script**. We do not have that variable in Tool Scripts but we do have the predefined property called **window**, which is the layout window.

BeanShell:
```
LayoutWindow layout;
layout = window;
```
Groovy:
```
layout = window;
```
On the next line I removed "final String" and simply set the variable to the initial values, as is legal with Groovy.

BeanShell:
```
final String windowTitle = "Room Setup";
```
Groovy:
```
windowTitle = "Room Setup";
```

Similarly, I did the same with the initialization of roomCount.

BeanShell:

```
int roomCount = 0;
```

Groovy:

```
roomCount = 0;
```

Arrays are handled differently with Groovy, so I changed the declaration and initialization of the roomSmoothness array.

BeanShell:

```
roomSmoothness = new float[]{0.0f, 0.0f, 0.0f, 0.0f};
```

Groovy:

```
float[] roomSmoothness;
roomSmoothness = [0.0f, 0.0f, 0.0f, 0.0f];
```

Writing Scripts for Startup Scripts

Startup Scripts are called when Art of Illusion first loads. They must be stored in the Scripts/Startup folder in the Art of Illusion installation area. They can be edited using the Edit Script menu option on the Tools menu.

These scripts can be used for anything that you might want to do before you get started on work each time. In the documentation for Art of Illusion, Peter Eastman suggested a couple of reasons people might want to use a startup script.

First, he suggested that a user might want to open a particular scene file each time they run Art of Illusion, as would be the case if they have been working on the same scene for a long time. I don't find the reason to be compelling, but the script he suggested is worth looking at. He called the script "OpenMyScene.groovy" and the code is as follows:

```
scene = new Scene(new File("/Users/peter/aoi/MyScene.aoi"),
                  true);
ArtOfIllusion.newWindow(scene);
```

The second thing he suggested is to write "plugins" in Groovy. He is the one who put quotes around "plugins". As you will see as we get into plugins, the plugin code he shows is very lightweight in comparison to normal plugins:

```
PluginRegistry.registerPlugin(new Plugin() {
 void processMessage(int message, Object[] args)
 {
   if (message == Plugin.SCENE_WINDOW_CREATED)
   {
     args[0].setScoreVisible(true);
     args[0].setSplitView(false);
   }
 }
});
```

This is a function call to registerPlugin() with a Plugin passed as a parameter but with processMessage overridden. When the SCENE_WINDOW_CREATED message is received the Score is made visible and the view is unsplit.

Another reason you might need a startup script is if you have several sets of tools that you work with on different projects. You may not want all of them cluttering your workspace all the time, but you might not want to remove them from the folders by hand. You could have a window that pops up and allows you to select checkboxes next to the tools that you want available. It could copy in the files before the load process occurs.

Having looked at scripts, we will now look at plugins. There is significant carryover between the two, so even if you don't think you will ever need to write a plugin, many of the techniques that are used for plugins will work for scripts as well.

Overcoming the Learning Curve

Never underestimate the value of Hello World. Back in the days of Windows 3.1 I purchased the book *Programming Windows 3.1* by Charles Petzold. Having written the Hello World program in thirty or forty different languages and each time finding it required no more than a few lines of code, it surprised me to find that HelloWin.c was two pages long. Most of it had to do with setting various styles to create a window in which the words "Hello, Windows!" could be drawn. Fortunately, most of the other programs in the book used the same framework and few were much larger in size than that first program. Without that first Hello World program, it would've been difficult to understand all of the settings required to display that simple line of text.

The good news is that a plugin for Art of Illusion doesn't require as many lines of code as a Windows 3.1 program. But Art of Illusion plugins have their own share of details that can cause problems. Plugins must be registered with the Art of Illusion tool so that it knows what to do with them. There is also a message handling infrastructure that is similar to the one Charles Petzold had to explain to his readers.

The Workflow

The end product of a plugin development effort is a JAR file that must be placed in the Art of Illusion Plugins installation directory. Art of Illusion loads each JAR file it finds in the Plugins directory. For development work, it can be helpful to have two installations of Art of Illusion. If you are using Windows and installed Art of Illusion to the Program Files directory, you may receive warnings when you try to copy a plugin into the Plugins directory. Whatever operating sytem you are using, you should install Art of Illusion in a work location that the operating system considers safe for user modification.

At a minimum, an Art of Illusion JAR file consists of two files. One is the .class file that is generated when the .java file is compiled. This is the file that contains the executable code. The second file is the *extensions.xml* file. This file provides Art of Illusion with a description of what it will find in the JAR file. It also provides an area for human readable documentation of the plugin, such as a description and version information.

I use Eclipse as my development environment. Eclipse is another open source program. If you wish to use another IDE or a console based Java compiler, that's up to you. As long as you have a Java development setup that will allow you to create JAR files with the required files in them, you can use whatever environment you're the most comfortable with. It is worth noting, however, that you can install a plugin to Eclipse that has a Groovy editor, making it easier to edit the scripts that you create for Art of Illusion.

Extensions.xml

I usually start with the *extensions.xml* file because it requires the least amount of work and it is more like design work than it is coding. If you are using Eclipse, you have the option of editing the file in either the XML editor or the text editor. I find it easier to

```xml
<?xml version="1.0" standalone="yes"?>

<extension name="Hello World" version="0.1" >
  <author>Timothy Fish</author>
  <date>July 2011</date>

  <plugin class="extending.aoi.hello.FirstPlugin" />

  <description>First project for extending Art of Illusion</description>

  <comments>This is an example of a very simple project for Art of Illusion.</comments>

  <history>
    <log version="0.1" date="July 2011" author="Timothy Fish" >- Initial Version</log>
  </history>

</extension>
```

Example 1-4: extensions.xml

use the text editor because I typically copy the text of this file from an existing file and paste it into the new *extensions.xml* file.

While the *extensions.xml* file shown in Example 1-4 is somewhat typical of what you will see other people creating, it includes some XML tags that aren't required and it is missing some of the tags that you may need for other plugins. Let's look at the file tag by tag.

?xml

The first line is the XML definition. The purpose of this line is to describe the XML file and is helpful if you are using an XML editor but it has no meaning to Art of Illusion.

Extension

Every *extensions.xml* file must have the **extension** tag as the root tag. If Art of Illusion doesn't find this tag, the rest of the file will not be processed.

Two attributes are shown in the example, **name** and **version**. Only the **name** attribute is read by Art of Illusion. The **version** attribute is for humans reading the XML file.

The value of **name** can be any string. It is used for identification purposes by Art of Illusion. The value should be distinct from that of other plugins so that you'll recognize it if you see the string displayed in an error log.

Author

The **author** tag is not one that Art of Illusion needs but it is useful information for people looking at this file later. It is also some of the information that is displayed in the plugin manager.

Date

The **date** tag is another tag that isn't required but putting it here provides a form of documentation. It is also displayed in the plugin manager.

Plugin

The **plugin** tag is required. In this example, the **plugin** tag provides Art of Illusion with the name of the class, "extending.aoi.hello.FirstPlugin". Remember this name because you'll see it again. When we create the source code for this project, we'll create a class named FirstPlugin in the package "extending.aoi.hello". These names must match or your plugin will not work.

Export

Between the **plugin** opening and closing tags, you will sometimes see **export** tags. They aren't used here because Hello World doesn't export anything.

The **export** tag describes the export of a method from the plugin and the attributes are *method* and *id*. The purpose is to allow external code to invoke methods of the plugin. The *method* attribute is the name of the method and the *id* should be a unique identifier that can be passed to **invokeExportedMethod**.

Import

Another tag that isn't shown in our example is the **import** tag. It belongs inside the **extension** body. Possible attributes are *name* and *url*. If *name* is used, a plugin with the specified name will be added to the import list. For example, if another plugin is dependent on our Hello World plugin, we could include an **import** tag with *name*="Hello World".

The *url* attribute specifies a filename. If a plugin is located on a network, we might wish to tell Art of Illusion where to find it by setting the value in this attribute rather than copying the file into the Plugins directory.

Description

The **description** tag is documentation only and is not required by Art of Illusion. The information defined for this tag is displayed in the description field of the plugin manager.

Comments

The comments tag is documentation only and is not required by Art of Illusion. This information is included in the description field of the plugin manager.

History

The **history** tag as well as the **log** tag is ignored by Art of Illusion, but some people use these tags to document version information. As changes are made, they will add log entries to the history. If you are using a version control tool, this log may not be needed other than to provide other people with information about what you've done.

Resource

The **resource** tag is another tag that Hello World doesn't need, but Art of Illusion recognizes it. The attributes are *type*, *id*, *name*, and *locale*. You will see this tag used later in this book when we must work with icons for the tool palette. *type* is the type of resource. *id* is a unique identifier. *name* is a fully qualified name from which to load the resource. *locale* is optional, but it would be used if we might need a different resource for different locations. For example, if a resource has text of some kind, the text might need to be different for different locations.

FirstPlugin.java

For anyone who is familiar with Java, most of the example source file is self explanatory. As we defined in the *extensions.xml* file we are placing our plugin in the *extending.aoi.hello* package. Any package name will work, as long as it remains consistent between the two files.

```
package extending.aoi.hello;

import artofillusion.LayoutWindow;
import artofillusion.Plugin;
import artofillusion.ui.MessageDialog;

public class FirstPlugin implements Plugin {
  @Override
  public void processMessage(int msg, Object[] args) {
    switch (msg) {
    case Plugin.SCENE_WINDOW_CREATED:
      LayoutWindow layout = (LayoutWindow) args[0];
      new MessageDialog(layout, "Hello World!");
      break;
    }
  }
}
```

Example 1-5: FirstPlugin.java

We are importing three things from the artofillusion package. These are all defined in the *artofillusion.jar* file, which is located in the directory where Art of Illusion is installed. We'll look more at that in the discussion of how to setup the project in Eclipse. The LayoutWindow and the Plugin classes will appear in many plugins. The MessageDialog will appear less frequently. In this example, it will serve as the means by which we display the text "Hello World!"

Plugin Categories

For this class, we are implementing the Plugin interface. Art of Illusion has ten categories of plugins. The Plugin category is the most generic. When Art of Illusion loads the plugins, it checks each to see if it is an instance of a category. If it is, it adds it to the list of plugins in that category. A list of the plugin categories is included in Table 1-1.

Message Processing

The Plugin interface has one method, processMessage. Art of Illusion calls this method when it reaches various states. The *msg* parameter identifies which

Table 1-1: Plugin Categories

Plugin Type	Purpose
Plugin	General plugin type used for all plugins that don't fit in one of the other categories.
Renderer	Defines the methods used to render a scene. A plugin of this type would be used if a special ray tracer or another type of renderer were needed.
Translator	Used for a class that imports/exports a scene to another file format.
ModellingTool	For plugins that will appear on the Tools menu. Typically, these tools manipulate objects in a scene.
Texture	Defines a texture that can be applied to an object.
Material	Defines the internal physical properties, such as the transparency and index of refraction.
TextureMapping	Describes how a texture is mapped to an object.
MaterialMapping	Describes how the material is mapped to an object.
ImageFilter	An image filter is a type of post processing for rendered images.
Module	Describes a module in a procedure. Modules are used for user defined 2D and 3D textures.

state Art of Illusion has reached. The *args* parameter passes in additional information. The type of information is dependent on which state is being handled. For the Hello World example, all we care about is handling the SCENE_WINDOW_CREATED message. Art of Illusion sends this message when a new scene window has been created and is initialized, but just before the window is displayed. The *args* parameter points to a LayoutWindow, which is the main Art of Illusion window.

There are currently seven messages that Art of Illusion passes into the processMessage method. The *args* parameter has a different meaning for each one. Example 1-6 demonstrates how to handle each of the seven messages in processMessage.

While the set of messages is well defined, write your plugins in such a way that, if Art of Illusion were to pass processMessage a message that isn't defined, it will ignore the message. This allows for the future growth of Art of Illusion. By doing this, if a new message is added in future versions, your plugins will continue to work.

```
public void processMessage(int msg, Object[] args) {
  switch (msg) {
  case Plugin.APPLICATION_STARTING:
    // No Arguments
    // TODO: Add code for when program first starts here.
    break;
  case Plugin.APPLICATION_STOPPING:
    // No Arguments
    // TODO: Add code to do resource cleanup here.
    Break;
  case Plugin.SCENE_WINDOW_CREATED:
    LayoutWindow layout = (LayoutWindow) args[0];
    // TODO: Add code for when scene window created here.
    break;
  case Plugin.SCENE_WINDOW_CLOSING:
    LayoutWindow layout = (LayoutWindow) args[0];
    // TODO: Add code for when scene window closes here.
    break;
  case Plugin.SCENE_SAVED:
    java.io.File sceneFile = (java.io.File) args[0];
    LayoutWindow layout = (LayoutWindow) args[1];
    // TODO: Add code for when scene saved here.
    break;
  case Plugin.OBJECT_WINDOW_CREATED:
    ObjectEditorWindow editor = (ObjectEditorWindow) args
[0];
    // TODO: Add code for when object editor created here.
    break;
  case Plugin.OBJECT_WINDOW_CLOSING:
    ObjectEditorWindow editor = (ObjectEditorWindow) args
[0];
    // Add code for when object editor closes here.
    break;
  }
}
```

Example 1-6: processMessage for all messages

MessageDialog

For the Hello World example, the heart of the program is the one line call to MessageDialog. It is simple enough that it hardly needs explanation. The call allocates a new MessageDialog object and passes a reference to the layout window and a string literal to the constructor. The result of this call is that a window will be drawn as a child of the layout window with the message "Hello World!" and an okay button for the user to press.

Adding Your Work to the Tool

So far, you've seen what you need for an *extensions.xml* file (Example 1-4) and the code for a Hello World plugin (Example 1-5). While you can read the code and see that it will display a message when Art of Illusion starts, nothing will happen until you compile the code and bundle the files into a JAR file that goes in the Art of Illusion Plugins directory.

I'll be using Eclipse to demonstrate how to setup a plugin development workflow that will allow you to build and test your Art of Illusion plugins. If you prefer using another tool, it may work just as well or better, but you will need to adjust the instructions accordingly.

Create a Project

To create a project in Eclipse, select New | Java Project from the file menu. You will see a window similar

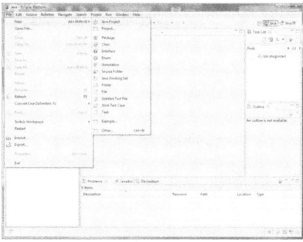

Figure 1-5: Eclipse Project Creation

to the one shown in Figure 1-6. Give the project a name and select Next >.

Figure 1-6: New Project

Figure 1-7: Project Options

This will bring up the window shown in Figure 1-7. There are several tabs here, but we can ignore all except for the Libraries tab.

Select the Libraries tab.

Figure 1-8: Libraries Tab

On this tab we need to add an external JAR to the project. Click the Add External JARs button.

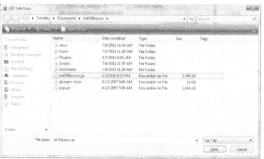

Figure 1-9: Eclipse Project Creation

Locate the *ArtOfIllusion.jar* file where you have installed Art of Illusion. Also add the *Bouy.jar* file from the lib directory.

Click Open and then click Finish to complete the project setup.

Right click the project name and select New | File. Give the file the name "extensions.xml" and click the Finish button.

Select the Source tab on the editor and type the text for the *extensions.xml* file into the editor. Save the file.

Right click the src directory in the project and select New | Package. Give the package the same name as is defined in the *extensions.xml* file. For this example it is "extending.aoi.hello". Click Finish.

Figure 1-10: Initial Project Structure

Figure 1-11: Create Class

Right click the new package and select New | Class. Type the class name in the name field.

Figure 1-12: Select Interface

To cause our new class to implement the Plugin interface, click the Add button and type "Plugin" into the top field. Select the Plugin interface and click OK. Click Finish. This will cause the Eclipse to add "implements Plugin" to the class we're creating. We could do this by simply typing the code. Using the GUI makes it easier to find the correct class name if we aren't sure which one we need.

The resulting code is shown in Example 1-7. Notice that the only different between this code and the code in Example 1-4 is that some of the imports are

```
package extending.aoi.hello;

import artofillusion.Plugin;

public class FirstPlugin implements Plugin {

  @Override
  public void processMessage(int arg0, Object[] arg1) {
    // TODO Auto-generated method stub

  }

}
```

Example 1-7: FirstPlugin.java

missing and we need to add code for processMessage. Replace the TODO comment with the code shown in Example 1-4. Also, change **arg0** to **msg** and **arg1** to **args**. Eclipse will give errors because of the missing imports. Either use the quick fixes to have Eclipse add the required imports or type the imports by hand.

Save the file.

Export the Plugin

At this point, we have all we need to create the JAR file for our plugin. Eclipse compiles automatically, so once the errors are resolved, we need only export the plugin as a JAR file.

Right click the Hello World project name and select Export.

Select Java | JAR File.

Click Next.

Click Browse to select the export location. Find and choose the Plugins folder of the Art of Illusion installation.

Type the file name, FirstPlugin.jar.

Click Save.

Figure 1-13: Plugin Export

Click Finish.

Now that the JAR file is in the correct place, you can run Art of Illusion and you will see the dialog box shown in Figure 1-14.

Figure 1-14: Hello Dialog

Call Art of Illusion from Eclipse

One of the conveniences of using an IDE like Eclipse is that we can set it up to run Art of Illusion at the click of a button, so that each time we modify a plugin it is a simple process of exporting the JAR file and clicking the run button.

Eclipse has three run buttons. They are shown in Figure 1-15. The third button

Figure 1-15: Run Buttons

is for running external programs like Eclipse, but the Debug button on the left is also useful because calling Art of Illusion in debug mode will allow us to use break points in our plugin when we need to see what the plugin is doing.

To use these buttons with Art of Illusion, we must first configure them. We can start with the button on the right.

Click the little triangle next to the image.

Select External Tools Configurations.

Right click Program and select New.

Give the Configuration a name, such as "Art of Illusion".

Browse or type the location of the Art of Illusion executable.

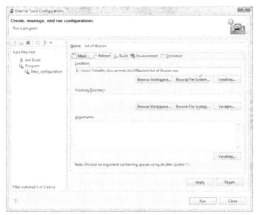

Figure 1-15: Run Configuration

Click Apply.

Click Run.

Art of Illusion will run. You may see warnings or errors in the Eclipse Console window. These are not necessarily errors that you created. While working with plugins, it is always a good idea to look through these errors to see if something you did caused an error, but some of these errors may have been caused by plugins other people developed or even Art of Illusion

Figure 1-16: Eclipse Debug Configuration

itself. If you didn't cause the error, you can probably ignore it.

After you've run Art of Illusion from the Configuration setup, you'll be able to run Art of Illusion by clicking the button at the top of the Eclipse window.

The setup for the Debug button is somewhat different than for the External Program. There are many more choices. Figure 1-16 shows how the Debug configuration should be done.

Notice that we're running it as a Java Application, the project is the project we want to debug and the main class is the Art of Illusion main class. When we debug using this configuration, Art of Illusion will run its main class, which will then load the JAR files. When a breakpoint is found in our JAR file, the debugger will stop and we will be able to step through the code as normal.

With the configurations setup, you can use Eclipse to create, compile, debug, and test the plugins you develop.

You can setup the middle button in the same way as the Debug button.

Chapter 2

Controlling the Environment

Tools like Art of Illusion are designed to meet the needs of a broad audience, so it is very likely that you will find things about the way it functions that you wish were different. This chapter demonstrates how you can make changes to the Art of Illusion user interface.

The Hide Score Plugin

Art of Illusion plugins are one way to customize how the tool works. The *private* keyword is used sparingly in the Art of Illusion source code, so there are plenty of opportunities to modify the user interface at runtime. To begin with a simple example, let's look at what it takes to hide the animation score.

A few versions ago, I eagerly installed the new version. While I enjoyed the new features, I immediately saw an element of frustration. Down at the bottom of the screen, the animation score was clearly visible and the four viewports were squashed. This might have been fine if I were doing animations or if my screen had been larger, but I was doing single image ray tracings on a small screen. Every time I would start Art of Illusion, the first thing I would do was to hide the animation score. Anytime you find yourself doing

Figure 2-1: Score at the Bottom

the same thing over and over, it's time to find a way to get the computer to do it for you.

Create the Project

At a high level, this plugin is the same as the Hello World plugin. It has an *extensions.xml* file and a single source file. Use the same techniques you used to create the project for the Hello World plugin to create this project, either creating an Eclipse project or using your preferred development environment. The code

```
<?xml version="1.0" standalone="yes"?>

<extension name="Hide Score" version="0.1" >
  <author>Timothy Fish</author>
  <date>July 2011</date>

  <plugin class="extending.aoi.hide_score.HideScorePlugin" /
>

  <description>This plugin hides the animation score when
Art of Illusion loads.</description>

  <comments>This project is to demonstrate a useful setup
feature of plugins.</comments>

  <history>
    <log version="0.1" date="July 2011" author="Timothy
Fish" >- Initial Version</log>
  </history>

</extension>
```

Example 2-1: extensions.xml

for the *extensions.xml* file shown in Example 2-1 will give you the information you need to create the project.

The name of the project should be "Hide Score". The one package in this project is "extending.aoi.hide_score" and within that package is a class called HideScorePlugin.

HideScorePlugin

As with the Hello World plugin, the heart of this plugin is the processMessage method as is shown in example 2-2. Looking at the code, you can see that where we had a call to MessageDialog before, we now have a call to hideAnimationScore.

This new method is one that we will have to write.

```
public void processMessage(int message, Object[] args) {
  switch (message) {
  case Plugin.SCENE_WINDOW_CREATED:
    layout = (LayoutWindow) args[0];
    hideAnimationScore(layout);
    break;
  }
}
```

Example 2-2: processMessage

As the name implies, the purpose of this method is to hide the animation score, but from what you recall from the Hello World project, you may realize that the timing is a little off. When you ran Art of Illusion with the Hello World plugin installed, the message dialog appeared before the Art of Illusion main window. We can't hide the score before it is made visible. To resolve this problem we need to delay the operation long enough for the window to complete its initialization.

While that may sound difficult, I found it to be sufficient to create a new thread to call the method that will hide the animation score. There is no need for a lengthy delay because the thread that is initializing the window is already scheduled. Because of simple first in-first out ordering, the thread we create will occur after the currently running thread releases control. This is shown in Example 2-3.

```
private void hideAnimationScore(final LayoutWindow layout) {
// Get the object that controls the animation score
// Hide the score
  SwingUtilities.invokeLater(new Runnable() {
// This method will be scheduled to run as a separate
thread.
    public void run() {
      // Hide the Score Window
      layout.setScoreVisible(false);
    }
  });
}
```

Example 2-3: hideAnimationScore

Example 2-3 may need some additional explanation because of the strange code in the method. It's enough to make a C++ programmer cringe, but it is consistent with code you'll find in Java programming language books. The *invokeLater* method schedules the thread to run after what is currently pending. Because showing the score is pending, the score will be drawn, but then our thread will run to hide it. A new class is created within the parameter list that we're passing to the function and we even include the code for the *run* method here. All that code does is tell the layout window to set the visibility of the score to false. If the code were more extensive, it would be better to create a separate class for the thread, but since it is a one line call, this keeps the code concise, though a little hard to read.

Example 2-4 is the complete code listing for *HideScorePlugin.java*. Compile and export the JAR file as you did for Hello World. Run Art of Illusion and

```
package extending.aoi.hide_score;

import javax.swing.SwingUtilities;
import artofillusion.LayoutWindow;
import artofillusion.Plugin;

public class HideScorePlugin implements Plugin {
  private LayoutWindow layout;

  @Override
  public void processMessage(int message, Object[] args) {
    switch (message) {
      case Plugin.SCENE_WINDOW_CREATED:
        layout = (LayoutWindow) args[0];
        hideAnimationScore(layout);
        break;
    }
  }

  private void hideAnimationScore(final LayoutWindow layout)
  {
    // Get the object that controls the animation score
    // Hide the score
    SwingUtilities.invokeLater(new Runnable() {
    // This method will be scheduled to run as a separate
    //thread
    public void run() {
        // Hide the Score Window
        layout.setScoreVisible(false);
      }
    });
  }
}
```

Example 2-4: HideScorePlugin.java

the plugin will cause Art of Illusion to hide the animation score when it loads.

The Preferences Plugin

Suppose you are working on an Art of Illusion project that doesn't require the score, but then you begin an animation project. If the Hide Score plugin is still in place, your problem will be the opposite of what it was. Now you'll want the score to display when Art of Illusion comes up.

The simple solution is to remove the Hide Score plugin from the plugins directory. But suppose you go back to a single frame rendering project and you want to hide the score again. It may be that you've forgotten where you stored the plugin. You can either search for it or you can recreate it using your Java compiler. That might be fine for something as simple as the hide score plugin, but suppose you've made plugins that change other aspects of Art of Illusion as well. A system of adding or removing plugins from the plugins directory could get cumbersome. It would be nice to have a way to choose which features we want to enable and disable. That is the idea behind the Preferences Plugin.

This plugin creates a file named "scoreprefs" in the ".artofillusion" folder. This text file stores a value, "animationScoreVisibility", having a value of *hide* or *show*, as is shown in Example 2-5. Setting the value in this file will determine the initial setting of the score when Art of Illusion loads.

```
#Art of Illusion Animation Score Preferences File
#Sun Jul 17 16:57:30 CDT 2011
animationScoreVisibility=hide
```

Example 2-5: scoreprefs File

Create the Project

The *extensions.xml* file is very similar to what you saw with the previous projects. In fact, if you compare it to the Hide Score Plugin, you will see that it is the same with the exception a change in names, paths and comments.

Because of the similarities, you should have no trouble creating a project with your tool of choice having the project name of "Preferences" and using the "extending.aoi.preferences" as the namespace.

```
<?xml version="1.0" standalone="yes"?>

<extension name="Preferences" version="0.1" >
  <author>Timothy Fish</author>
  <date>July 2011</date>

  <plugin
class="extending.aoi.preferences.PreferencesPlugin" />

  <description>This plugin hides the animation score when
Art of Illusion loads based on the user's preferences.</
description>

  <comments>This project is to demonstrate a useful setup
feature of plugins.</comments>

  <history>
     <log version="0.1" date="July 2011" author="Timothy
Fish" >- Initial Version</log>
  </history>
</extension>
```

Example 2-6: extensions.xml

PreferencesPlugin

The code for the PreferencesPlugin class reveals more interesting aspects. This class serves the same purpose as the HideScorePlugin class, but there are several changes that allow the plugin to read and write to the preferences file.

As before, the entry point for this class is the processMessage method. It is shown in Example 2-7. It builds on what we did in the previous project. There are a few differences.

The first difference you will notice if you compare this version to what we did before is that there is now an if statement that checks the flag variable *firstTimeCalled*. There are times when it is necessary for Art of Illusion to send the SCENE_WINDOW_CREATED message more than once after Art of Illusion comes up. With many plugins, we don't care how many times the message is sent because we want to perform the same action every time. But here, once the plugin comes up for the first time, we want to apply the us-

```
public void processMessage(int message, Object[] args) {
  switch (message) {
    case Plugin.SCENE_WINDOW_CREATED:
      layout = (LayoutWindow) args[0];

      if (firstTimeCalled) {
        preferences = new ScorePreferences();
        HideShow preferenceHide =
          preferences.getPreferenceScoreVisibility();
        setAnimationScoreVisibility(preferenceHide);
        firstTimeCalled = false;
        preferences.savePreferences();
      }
      break;
  }
}
```

Example 2-7: processMessage

er's selection rather than reading the file again and replacing what the user has decided.

Look at the code within the if statement more closely and you'll see that it is retrieving the preferences from the ScorePreferences class and setting the score visibility based on the preferences it returns. Last, the method sends a message to the class to save the preferences. It may seem odd that we would save the preferences when we've just now retrieved them, but this is to store a file to the file system if one does not currently exist, as would be the case if this is the first time this plugin has run or if the user deleted the file.

Setting the visibility has been refactored into a function because in the previous version we needed only to hide the score, since that was the reason the plugin existed. In this version, we may be either hiding or showing the score and that determination is made by the value read from the preferences file.

The Runnable used here is done slightly different from before by not inlining it, but it serves a similar purpose, which is to give the processes doing Art of

Illusion setup time to settle before it attempts to change what they've done.

ScorePreferences

The ScorePreferences class encapsulates the preferences file. Aside from the constructor, ScorePreferences provides only three public functions, *setPreferenceScoreVisibility*, *getPreferenceScoreVisibility*, and *savePreferences*. The assumption is made that there is only a need to load the preferences when the class is created.

The get and set functions are self explanatory. They are shown in Example 2-8.

The *savePreferences* method performs some opera-

```
public HideShow getPreferenceScoreVisibility() {
   return preferenceScoreVisibility;
}
public void setPreferenceScoreVisibility(
      final HideShow preferenceScoreVisibility) {
   this.preferenceScoreVisibility =
                                preferenceScoreVisibility;
}
```

Example 2-8: Get and Set Methods

tions that you may not have seen before, so take a closer look at it. The code is shown in Example 2-9. The first thing it does is copy values into the *properties* variable based on the member variable *preferenceScoreVisibility*. *properties* is of type java.util.Properties, which is an extension of Hashtable. A key/value pair is stored in *properties* with the property name being the key. Here, the key is "animationScoreVisibility" as is the value of *ScoreVisibilityName* and the value is the string "hide" or the string "show", depending on how *preferenceScoreVisibility* is set.

Using this method reduces the effort required to write our preferences to file because Properties will handle much of the work required to output the date

```
/**
 * Save any changed preferences to disk.
 */
public void savePreferences()
{
  // copy visibility setting into properties

  if(this.preferenceScoreVisibility == HideShow.hide){
    properties.put(ScoreVisibilityName, hiddenStr);
  }
  else{
    properties.put(ScoreVisibilityName, visibleStr);
  }

  // Write the preferences to a file.
  File f =
  new File(ApplicationPreferences.getPreferencesDirectory(),
            prefFileName);
  try
  {
    OutputStream out =
      new BufferedOutputStream(new FileOutputStream(f));
    properties.store(
      out,
      "Art of Illusion Animation Score Preferences File");
    out.close();
  }
  catch (IOException ex)
  {
    ex.printStackTrace();
  }
}
```

Example 2-9: savePreferences Method

to a stream. This same method can be used for as many property settings as a plugin needs.

To create a FileOutputStream, it is necessary to instantiate a File. The method uses for the directory name the value returned from *ApplicationPreferences.getPreferencesDirectory()*. ApplicationPreferences is part of Art of Illusion and this call returns the location of the Art of Illusion preferences directory. While the code is not storing preferences to the Art of Illusion preferences file, the file it creates is located in the same location as the Art of Illusion preferences file, ".artofillusion".

An output stream is created based on the file and passed into *properties.store* along with a string of comments.

The work of loading the preferences from the preferences file is accomplished by three methods, as is shown in Example 2-10a and Example 2-10b.

Given an InputStream, which is a file in this case, *loadPreferences* instantiates the properties and calls the

```
/**
 * Load the preferences from an InputStream.
 */
private void loadPreferences(InputStream in)
  throws IOException
{
  properties = new Properties();
  properties.load(in);
  parsePreferences();
}
/**
 * Parse the properties loaded from the preferences file.
 */
private void parsePreferences() {
  // Parse value for animationScoreVisibility.
  this.preferenceScoreVisibility =
    parseHideShowProperty(ScoreVisibilityName,
HideShow.show);
}
```

Example 2-10a: loadPreferences Method

load method to set the value and then calls *parsePreferences*, which then calls *parseHideShowProperty* with the *ScoreVisibilityName* and the default value of *HideShow.show*. Optionally, you could combine these methods into one, but data hiding is better accomplished in the way it is done here.

The last method, *parseHideShowProperty*, does most of the work. the code makes a call to retrieve the property of *ScoreVisibilityName* and sets the return variable to the default value so that it will be returned if the attempt to load the property failed. When the read succeeds, the return value is set accordingly. Upon

```
/**
 * Get a boolean value from the properties read from
 * preference file.
 * @param name Property Name
 * @param defaultVal Value to use if value left blank.
 * @return Value of property as a HideShow enumerated
 * type value.
 */
private HideShow parseHideShowProperty(String name,
                                       HideShow defaultVal)
{
  // Get the property from the pair.
  String prop = properties.getProperty(name);

  // Set the default return value.
  HideShow retVal = defaultVal;

  // If the property has a value, get the boolean
  // representation and return it.
  if (prop != null){
    if(prop.compareToIgnoreCase(hiddenStr) == 0){
      retVal = HideShow.hide;
    }
    else if(prop.compareToIgnoreCase(visibleStr) == 0){
      retVal = HideShow.show;
    }
    else{
      // do nothing, retVal is already defaultVal
    }
  }
  return retVal;
}
```

Example 2-10b: loadPreferences Method

return, the value is stored in *the preferenceScoreVisibility* member variable.

You will find the complete code listing for the Preferences Plugin on the following pages.

```java
package extending.aoi.preferences;

import javax.swing.SwingUtilities;
import extending.aoi.preferences.ScorePreferences.HideShow;
import artofillusion.LayoutWindow;
import artofillusion.Plugin;

/**
 * Plugin to Art of Illusion that will allow the user to set
 * and save his preferences for whether the score should be
 * visible or not when Art of Illusion comes up.
 *
 */
public class PreferencesPlugin implements Plugin {
/**
 * Runnable thread that will set the visibility of the score
 * window after Art of Illusion has had time to initialize.
 *
 * @author Timothy Fish
 *
 */
private class HideScoreRunnable implements Runnable {
  private HideShow visibility;
  /**
   * Constructor
   *
   * @param visibility
   *                 Set whether the score should show or hide.
   *
   */
  public HideScoreRunnable(HideShow visibility) {
    this.visibility = visibility;
  }

  @Override
  /*
   * This function is called by the JVE when it is ready to
   * start the thread.
   */
  public void run() {
    // Show or Hide the Score Window
    switch (visibility) {
      case hide:
        layout.setScoreVisible(false);
        break;
      case show:
        layout.setScoreVisible(true);
        break;
    }
  }
}
```

Example 2-11a: PreferencesPlugin.java

```java
private LayoutWindow layout; // local reference to the main
                             // layout window
/**
 * The firstTimeCalled flag is used to prevent AOI from
 * calling this plugin more than once. Without this check,
 * the animation score will remain hidden, even
 * if the user selects the Show Score menu item.
 */
private boolean firstTimeCalled;

private ScorePreferences preferences;

/**
 * Constructor
 */
public PreferencesPlugin() {
  layout = null;
  firstTimeCalled = true;
  preferences = null;
}

@Override
/*
 * This is the main function of a plugin. Art of Illusion
 * calls this function at various times to pass control to
 * the plugin. In this case, it will read the preferences
 * file and either show or hide the animation score based on
 * the user's preferences.
 *
 * @param message Provides execution state information.
 *
 * @param args Generic variable to pass state dependent
 * information.
 */
public void processMessage(int message, Object[] args) {
  switch (message) {
    case Plugin.SCENE_WINDOW_CREATED:
      layout = (LayoutWindow) args[0];

      if (firstTimeCalled) {
        // It is possible for the scene window to be created
        // more than once after AOI is started.
        // Use score visibility preference first time. After
        // that use normal user input.
        preferences = new ScorePreferences();
        HideShow preferenceHide =
          preferences.getPreferenceScoreVisibility();
        setAnimationScoreVisibility(preferenceHide);
        firstTimeCalled = false;
        preferences.savePreferences();
      }
      break;
  }
}
```

Example 2-11b: PreferencesPlugin.java

56

```
/**
 * Sets the animation score visibility after Art of Illusion
 * has time to initialize.
 *
 * @param visibility
 * Whether the function should show or hide the animation
 * score.
 */
  private void setAnimationScoreVisibility(
    HideShow visibility) {

    // Create a Runnable to set the animation
    //score visibility.
    HideScoreRunnable scoreVisibilitySetter =
      new HideScoreRunnable(visibility);

    // Schedule the Runnable to happen later.
    SwingUtilities.invokeLater(scoreVisibilitySetter);
  }
}
```

Example 2-11c: PreferencesPlugin.java

```
package extending.aoi.preferences;

import java.io.BufferedInputStream;
import java.io.BufferedOutputStream;
import java.io.File;
import java.io.FileInputStream;
import java.io.FileOutputStream;
import java.io.IOException;
import java.io.InputStream;
import java.io.OutputStream;
import java.util.Properties;

import artofillusion.ApplicationPreferences;


/**
 * The ScorePreferences class is modeled after the
 * ApplicationPreferences class.
 * It is the means by which user preferences for the
 * visibility of the animation score can be stored and
 * retrieved when AOI loads.
 * @author Timothy Fish
 *
 */
public class ScorePreferences {

  /**
   * Enumerated type to pass information about whether the
   * score should show or hide when the run() function is
   * called.
```

Example 2-12a: ScorePreferences.java

```
 *
 * @author Timothy Fish
 *
 */
public enum HideShow {
  hide, show
}

private HideShow preferenceScoreVisibility;
private Properties properties;
private final String ScoreVisibilityName =
  "animationScoreVisibility";
private final String visibleStr = "show";
private final String hiddenStr = "hide";
private final String prefFileName = "scoreprefs";

/**
 * Constructor
 */
public ScorePreferences(){
  // Set the hide/show preference to show. (AOI default)
  setPreferenceScoreVisibility(HideShow.show);

  // Open the Score Preferences file in the
  // default location
  File f = new File
   (ApplicationPreferences.getPreferencesDirectory(),
    prefFileName);
  if (!f.exists()) {
    try {
      f.createNewFile();
    } catch (IOException ex) {
      // if exception, print error information
      ex.printStackTrace();
    }
  }

  try {
    // if no problem, load the preferences from the file
    InputStream in =
      new BufferedInputStream(new FileInputStream(f));
    loadPreferences(in);
    in.close();
  }
  catch (IOException ex){
    // if exception, print error information
    ex.printStackTrace();
  }
}
```

Example 2-12b: ScorePreferences.java

58

```java
/**
 * Load the preferences from an InputStream.
 */
private void loadPreferences(InputStream in)
    throws IOException    {
    properties = new Properties();
    properties.load(in);
    parsePreferences();
}

/**
 * Save any changed preferences to disk.
 */
public void savePreferences()    {
    // copy visibility setting into properties

    if(this.preferenceScoreVisibility == HideShow.hide){
        properties.put(ScoreVisibilityName, hiddenStr);
    }
    else{
        properties.put(ScoreVisibilityName, visibleStr);
    }

    // Write the preferences to a file.

    File f = new File
        (ApplicationPreferences.getPreferencesDirectory(),
         prefFileName);
    try{
        OutputStream out =
            new BufferedOutputStream(new FileOutputStream(f));
        properties.store(
            out,
            "Art of Illusion Animation Score Preferences File"
                            );
        out.close();
    }
    catch (IOException ex) {
        ex.printStackTrace();
    }
}

/**
 * Parse the properties loaded from the preferences
 * file.
 */
private void parsePreferences() {
    // Parse value for animationScoreVisibility.
    this.preferenceScoreVisibility =
        parseHideShowProperty(ScoreVisibilityName,
                              HideShow.show);
}
```

Example 2-12c: ScorePreferences.java

```java
/**
 * Get a boolean value from the properties read from
 * preference file.
 * @param name Property Name
 * @param defaultVal Value to use if value left blank.
 * @return Value of property as a HideShow enumerated
 * type value.
 */
private HideShow parseHideShowProperty(
  String name, HideShow defaultVal) {

  // Get the property from the pair.
  String prop = properties.getProperty(name);

  // Set the default return value.
  HideShow retVal = defaultVal;

  // If the property has a value, get the boolean
  // representation and return it.
  if (prop != null){
    if(prop.compareToIgnoreCase(hiddenStr) == 0){
      retVal = HideShow.hide;
    }
    else if(prop.compareToIgnoreCase(visibleStr) == 0){
      retVal = HideShow.show;
    }
    else{
    // do nothing, retVal is already defaultVal
    }
  }
  return retVal;
}

/**
 * Set the user's preference for whether the animation
 * score should be
 * visible or not.
 * @param preferenceScoreVisibility
 */
public void setPreferenceScoreVisibility(
  final HideShow preferenceScoreVisibility) {

  this.preferenceScoreVisibility =
    preferenceScoreVisibility;
}

/**
 * Get the user's preference for whether the animation
 * score should be visible or not.
 * @return
 */
public HideShow getPreferenceScoreVisibility() {
  return preferenceScoreVisibility;
}
}
```

Example 2-12d: ScorePreferences.java

Preferences with Menu Plugin

The next thing to consider is a better way to set the preferences for your plugins. While setting the value in a text file may work fine for something as unutilized as determining whether to show the animation score or not, other features of the plugins you might envision may require the values to be changed more frequently. Also, if you are developing your plugin with other users in mind, it isn't a good idea to set the value in a text file that the user will have difficulty finding and may edit in such a way that the plugin won't respond properly.

A better approach is to allow the user to set the preferences through the Art of Illusion user interface. Art of Illusion has it's own Preferences menu item on the Edit Menu. To maintain consistency, the

Figure 2-2: Animation Menu

plugin preferences should be handled in a similar way, but modifying the Art of Illusion preferences window is not an option for plugins. Since Art of Illusion is open source, it is possible to create a custom compile that includes your preference items in the general preferences window, but that creates more problems than it's worth for most plugin development efforts. To do so, you would have to maintain a separate version of Art of Illusion—a version that most users would not have installed, so they would be unable to use your plugin.

What Art of Illusion will allow is for the plugin to add an item to a menu, as is shown in Figure 2-2. There are two ways this can be accomplished. With plugins that implement the ModellingTool interface, Art of Illusion will automatically add a menu item to the Tools menu. That is demonstrated later in this book with the Room plugin.

Another method is demonstrated in this chapter because the Score Preferences window is not a "tool" in the classic sense of the word. Categorically, it fits better on the Animation menu. The Preferences with Menu plugin adds little functionality that will be of great interest to the typical user of Art of Illusion, but it builds on the previous examples and demonstrates both how to add menu items to any of the menus and how to create a custom window within Art of Illusion.

```
<?xml version="1.0" standalone="yes"?>

<extension name="PreferencesWithMenu" version="0.1" >
  <author>Timothy Fish</author>
  <date>July 2011</date>

  <plugin
class="extending.aoi.preferences.PreferencesDialogPlugin" />

  <description>This plugin hides the animation score when
Art of Illusion loads based on the user's preferences.</
description>

  <comments>This project is to demonstrate a useful setup
feature of plugins.</comments>

  <history>
      <log version="0.1" date="July 2011" author="Timothy
Fish" >- Initial Version</log>
  </history>
</extension>
```

Example 2-13: extensions.xml

Create the Project

There are no significant differences in what you need to do to create this project from what was required for the previous projects. Example 2-13 gives the details of the *extensions.xml* file. From that, you can see that the project name is *PreferencesWithMenu* and the namespace is *extending.aoi.preferences*.

ScorePreferences

You've seen one of the classes for this project in the previous project. The code for ScorePreferences.java is unchanged from what is shown in Example 2-12. Copy that file into your project.

PreferencesDialogPlugin

The PreferencesDialogPlugin class is essentially the same class as the PreferencesPlugin class with a few changes. The relevant changes are in the *processMessage* method. The bold text in Example 2-14 indicates the changes.

```java
public void processMessage(int message, Object[] args) {
  BMenuItem menuItem;
  switch (message) {
    case Plugin.SCENE_WINDOW_CREATED:
      layout = (LayoutWindow) args[0];

      BMenu animationMenu = layout.getAnimationMenu();
      // Add the Animation Score Preferences menu item
      //to the Animation Menu
      animationMenu.addSeparator();
      menuItem = Translate.menuItem("Score Preferences...",
                                    this,
"scoreMenuAction");
      animationMenu.add(menuItem);

      if (firstTimeCalled) {
        preferences = new ScorePreferences();
        HideShow preferenceHide =
          preferences.getPreferenceScoreVisibility();
        setAnimationScoreVisibility(preferenceHide);
        firstTimeCalled = false;
      }
      break;
  }
}
```

Example 2-14: processMessage

The menus are part of the LayoutWindow, so the call to *getAnimationMenu* provides access to the BMenu. The call to addSeparator adds a separator line at the end of the Animation menu. A BMenuItem is created by the call to *Translate.menuItem*.

The purpose of the Translate object is to centralize the text used in Art of Illusion so that it can be translated for the various languages of the users. In this case, it will simply create a BMenuItem with the text shown passed into the first parameter because there isn't a translation defined for other languages. It is, however, a good idea to use the Translate mechanism to ease translation in the future.

The third parameter is a string that defines the callback function that will be called when the user selects the menu item. The *scoreMenuAction* method creates an instance of the workhorse class for this plugin, the ScorePreferencesWindow class.

The full code for PreferencesDialogPlugin.java is shown in Example 2-15.

```
package extending.aoi.preferences;

import javax.swing.SwingUtilities;

import buoy.widget.BMenu;
import buoy.widget.BMenuItem;

import extending.aoi.preferences.ScorePreferences.HideShow;
import artofillusion.LayoutWindow;
import artofillusion.Plugin;
import artofillusion.ui.Translate;

public class PreferencesDialogPlugin implements Plugin {

    /**
     * Runnable thread that will set the visibility of the
     * score window after Art of Illusion has had time to
```

Example 2-15a: PreferencesDialogPlugin.java

```
 * initialize.
 *
 * @author Timothy Fish
 *
 */
private class HideScoreRunnable implements Runnable {

  private HideShow visibility;

    /**
     * Constructor
     *
     * @param visibility
     *        Set whether the score should show or hide.
     *
     */
    public HideScoreRunnable(HideShow visibility) {
      this.visibility = visibility;
    }

    @Override
    /*
     * This function is called by the JVE when it is
     * ready to start the thread.
     */
    public void run() {
      // Show or Hide the Score Window
      switch (visibility) {
        case hide:
          layout.setScoreVisible(false);
          break;
        case show:
          layout.setScoreVisible(true);
          break;
      }
    }
  }

    // local reference to the main layout window
    private LayoutWindow layout;
    /**
     * The firstTimeCalled flag is used to prevent AOI
     * from calling this plugin more than once. Without
     * this check, the animation score will remain
     * hidden, even if the user selects the Show Score
     * menu item.
     */
    private boolean firstTimeCalled;

    private ScorePreferences preferences;
```

Example 2-15b: PreferencesDialogPlugin.java

```
/**
 * Constructor
 */
public PreferencesDialogPlugin() {
layout = null;
firstTimeCalled = true;
preferences = null;
}

@Override
/*
 * This is the main function of a plugin. Art of
 * Illusion calls this function at various times to pass
 * control to the plugin. In this case, it will read the
 * preferences file and either show or hide the
 * animation score based on the user's preferences.
 *
 * @param message Provides execution state information.
 *
 * @param args Generic variable to pass state dependent
 *             information.
 */
public void processMessage(int message, Object[] args) {
  BMenuItem menuItem;
  switch (message) {
  case Plugin.SCENE_WINDOW_CREATED:
    layout = (LayoutWindow) args[0];

    BMenu animationMenu = layout.getAnimationMenu();
    // Add the Animation Score Preferences menu item to
    // the Animation Menu
    animationMenu.addSeparator();
    menuItem = Translate.menuItem(
      "Score Preferences...", this, "scoreMenuAction");
    animationMenu.add(menuItem);

    if (firstTimeCalled) {
      // It is possible for the scene window to be
      // created more than once after AOI is started.
      // Use score visibility preference first time.
      // After that use normal user input.
      preferences = new ScorePreferences();
      HideShow preferenceHide =
        preferences.getPreferenceScoreVisibility();
      setAnimationScoreVisibility(preferenceHide);
      firstTimeCalled = false;
    }
    break;
  }
}
```

Example 2-15c: PreferencesDialogPlugin.java

```
    /**
     * Sets the animation score visibility after
     * Art of Illusion has time to initialize.
     *
     * @param visibility
     * Whether the function should show or hide the
     * animation score.
     */
    private void setAnimationScoreVisibility(
      HideShow visibility) {
    // Create a Runnable to set the animation score
    // visibility.
    HideScoreRunnable scoreVisibilitySetter =
      new HideScoreRunnable(visibility);

    // Schedule the Runnable to happen later.
    SwingUtilities.invokeLater(scoreVisibilitySetter);
    }

@SuppressWarnings("unused")
/**
 * Action code for the Score Preferences menu item.
 */
private void scoreMenuAction(){
  new ScorePreferencesWindow(layout, preferences);
  }

}
```

Example 2-15d: PreferencesDialogPlugin.java

ScorePreferencesWindow

Figure 2-3 shows a simple window to allow the user to set whether the Animation Score should show at startup or not. This window will load when the user selects the menu item. If the user clicks the OK button, the class will store the value selected for the checkbox in the text file that the plugin uses to determine what to do with the Animation Score

The class has two member functions, both of which are called during class initialization. The constructor creates a panel and adds the widgets.

Figure 2-3: Score Preferences Window

Then the constructor waits for the user to select either OK or Cancel.

The code for the class is shown in Example 2-16. In the import section you will notice that several Buoy classes are used. Buoy is a set of classes for developing Java user interfaces. It is used throughout Art of Illusion.

The base window used here is the Art of Illusion class, PanelDialog. The PanelDialog constructor takes as parameters the parent window, a string for the title, and a Buoy Widget. Typically, a dialog needs more than one widget, so a WidgetContainer is passed in. Here, a BTabbedPane is used (more for demonstration purposes than necessity) and the Widget returned from *createScorePanel* is added to it. The *createScorePanel* method adds a BCheckBox to a FormContainer after is has set its state based on the current preference setting.

Once the initialization is done, the dialog waits at dlg.clickedOK() for the user to interact with the panel and click OK or Cancel. Based on that selection, it will then either return without doing anything or it will

```
package extending.aoi.preferences;

import java.awt.Insets;

import extending.aoi.preferences.ScorePreferences.HideShow;
import artofillusion.ui.PanelDialog;
import buoy.widget.BCheckBox;
import buoy.widget.BFrame;
import buoy.widget.BTabbedPane;
import buoy.widget.FormContainer;
import buoy.widget.LayoutInfo;
import buoy.widget.Widget;

/**
 * Animation Score Preferences window used to get
 * preferences for the animation score.
 * @author Timothy Fish
 *
```

Example 2-16a: ScorePreferencesWindow.java

```
*/
public class ScorePreferencesWindow {

  private final String tabName = "Score";
  private final String visibilityCheckBoxName =
      "Show Animation Score at Start Up";
  private final String prefsTitle =
      "Animation Score Preferences";
  private ScorePreferences preferences;
  private BCheckBox scoreBox;
  private static int lastTab;

  public ScorePreferencesWindow(BFrame parent,
                                ScorePreferences prefs) {
    preferences = prefs;
    BTabbedPane tabs = new BTabbedPane();
    tabs.add(createScorePanel(), tabName );

    tabs.setSelectedTab(lastTab);
    PanelDialog dlg = new PanelDialog(parent,
                                      prefsTitle, tabs);
    lastTab = tabs.getSelectedTab();
    if (!dlg.clickedOk()) // Cancel
      return;

    if(scoreBox.getState() == true){ // checked(
      preferences.setPreferenceScoreVisibility(
                                      HideShow.show);
    }
    else{ // not checked
      preferences.setPreferenceScoreVisibility(
                                      HideShow.hide);
    }
    preferences.savePreferences();
  }

  private Widget createScorePanel() {
    boolean scoreChecked =
            preferences.getPreferenceScoreVisibility() ==
                          HideShow.hide ? false : true;
    scoreBox = new BCheckBox(visibilityCheckBoxName,
                          scoreChecked);
    // Layout the panel.

    FormContainer panel = new FormContainer(2, 12);
    panel.setColumnWeight(1, 1.0);
    LayoutInfo centerLayout =
        new LayoutInfo(LayoutInfo.CENTER,
                        LayoutInfo.NONE,
                        new Insets(2, 0, 2, 0), null);

    panel.add(scoreBox, 0, 0, 2, 1, centerLayout);
    return panel;
  }
}
```

Example 2-16b: ScorePreferencesWindow.java

save the preferences using the same method as what the previous plugin used. This time it retrieves the value from the checkbox.

Once the dialog box closes, there is nothing left for the plugin to do until the user selects the menu item again or the layout window is started again.

About Dialog Windows

Plugins often need a way to ask the user for information. In the example, you saw a PanelDialog used for this purpose, to which was added a tabbed panel, a container, and a checkbox. Looking through Art of Illusion, you can see that the windows are quite diverse and there are many more controls than what were demonstrated here. To help you understand what you need to develop the windows that you need for your project, let's look at the basic concepts of how these classes are intended to work together.

The PanelDialog Class

First, there is the PanelDialog class, which is used in our example as the base window. This is part of Art of Illusion and has a structure like that shown in Figure 2-4. The text at the top is the value of the parameter passed into the constructor and it may be null if text is not desired. The OK and Cancel buttons will be drawn automatically. The Panel Area is defined by the widget that is passed into the constructor.

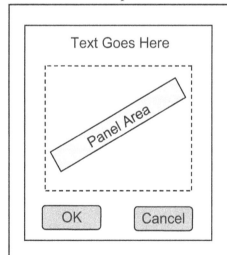

Figure 2-4: PanelDialog

But the PanelDialog is just one of the BDialogs that are defined within Art of Illusion. A similar window is the ComponentsDialog. It is like the PanelDialog, but instead of a single widget, it will accept an array of widgets passed to the constructor.

Another general purpose window is the Floating-Dialog window, which will float above the parent window while allowing the user to continue to interact with the parent window.

Art of Illusion has several other windows that extend BDialog that have more specific purposes. The dialogs are listed below:

⇒ActorEditorWindow
⇒CameraFilterDialog
⇒ColorChooser
⇒ComponentsDialog
⇒CSGDialog
⇒ExternalObjectEditingWindow
⇒FloatingDialog
⇒ImagesDialog
⇒JointEditorDialog
⇒KeystrokeEditor
⇒MaterialMappingDialog
⇒MaterialsDialog
⇒MessageDialog
⇒ObjectMaterialDialog
⇒ObjectTextureDialog
⇒PanelDialog
⇒PathFromCurveDialog
⇒TextureMappingDialog
⇒TexturesDialog
⇒TranformDialog
⇒TransformPointsDialog
⇒UVMappingWindow

Container Objects

The PanelDialog used in the example has room for a single widget. Because we only needed a checkbox, we could have passed the check-box in, but we typically need more than that. To allow for more widgets, the widget passed to the constructor is typically a con-tainer class, as was done in the example. These classes are part of the Buoy API ra-ther than the Art of Illusion API.

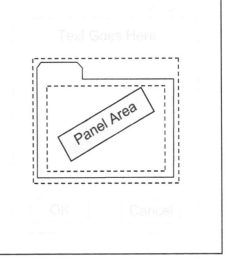

Figure 2-5: Container Objects

The example made use of the BTabbedPane. This would allow us to add more tabs, if needed, but we need another container to hold multiple widgets with-in the tab. For this, we used a FormContainer, which lays out its widgets in a grid. The layout information caused it to center the widget.

There are several available WidgetContainers that you can use for whatever you may need in setting up a window. They are listed below:

⇒BMenu
⇒BMenuBar
⇒BorderContainer
⇒BOutline
⇒BPopupMenu
⇒BScrollPane
⇒BTabbedPane
⇒BToolBar

⇒ColumnContainer
⇒ExplicitContainer
⇒GridContainer
⇒OverlayContainer
⇒RowContainer
⇒WindowWidget
    ⇒BDialog
    ⇒BFrame
    ⇒BWindow

Each serves its purpose and some are better suited for some purposes than others. But each works in a similar fashion, accepting widgets as input and displaying them to the user in accordance to the way the container is designed.

Chapter 3

Drop to Floor

One of the timesavers available in some 3D tools is the ability to place an object near where it is needed and with a key press cause the object to drop to the floor of the simulated room. This is particularly useful when working with animated characters because we

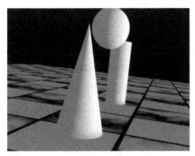

Figure 3-1: Object Dropped to Floor (Before and After)

might move a foot into a position that looks right for the body, but then it looks like the body is levitating. To solve the problem, we drop the whole body so that its lowest point is touching the floor.

The concept is straight forward and it requires very few calculations, but working through the process of developing a plugin that implements this feature will introduce you to how to manipulate Art of Illusion objects through the API.

The Concept

Before we get into the code, let's look at what we hope to accomplish. Figure 3-2 shows a circle that we

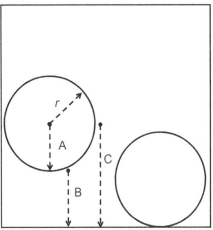

wish to reposition to the "floor" of the box, y=0. To do so we must move the circle the distance B, such that the circle is at the same level as the second circle. Given that length A = B, it is equivalent to moving the center of the circle as indicated by A. This is important because objects in Art of Illusion

Figure 3-2: Reposition From Center

are defined in terms of their origin. That means that the circle is currently located at y=C. C = B + r. Which tells us that B = C - r and we need only to reposition the origin down by a distance equal to its current position minus the distance from the center to the bottom edge of the object.

That is fairly easy for a circle, but consider how you might accomplish the same for a more general shape, Figure 3-3.

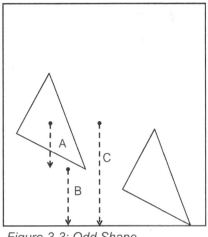

Figure 3-3: Odd Shape

The concept remains the same, but we don't have a radius to work with.

If we think of the objects as a set of connected vertices, then we can say that the lowest point of the object is the lowest vertex of the set. The distance from that point to the floor is the distance that the object must move for it to rest on the floor.

From Concept to Code

What is easily seen in the drawings must be converted into calls made to the Art of Illusion API. We must do so in such a way that the user can select the object to drop through the user interface. We must be able to handle more complex objects than simple triangles. Also, we must also be able to handle compound objects where objects are children of a parent object. Lastly, we must handle the case were more than one object is selected. Then, for good measure, we might as well find a way to deactivate the menu item when no objects are selected.

Once again, there are few changes to the *extensions.xml* file in comparison to what you've seen before. This file is shown in Example 3-1. Create a project for the plugin as you did in the previous examples, taking into account the changes. Figure 3-4 shows

```xml
<?xml version="1.0" standalone="yes"?>
<extension name="Drop to Floor" version="0.1" >
  <author>Timothy Fish</author>
  <date>July 2011</date>
  <plugin
class="extending.aoi.drop_to_floor.DropToFloorPlugin" />
  <description>This plugin adds a menu item that will cause
the selected objects to drop to the "floor" of the scene.
</description>
  <comments>This project is to demonstrate the manipulation
of scene objects.</comments>
  <history>
 <log version="0.1" date="July 2011" author="Timothy Fish" >
- Initial Version</log>
  </history>
</extension>
```

Example 3-1: extensions.xml

what the project should look like in Eclipse. As always the *ArtOfIllusion.jar* file must be included as a Referenced Library. There is a single

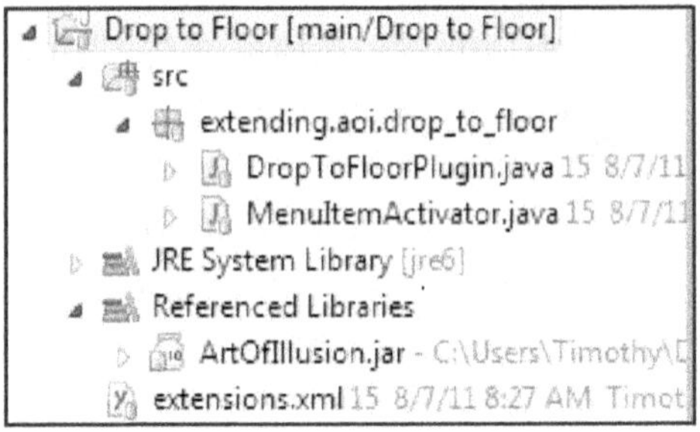

Figure 3-4: Drop to Floor Project

namespace and two classes. The DropToFloorPlugin class is where most of the work takes place. The MenuItemActivator class is a special worker class that deactivates the menu item when no objects are selected.

DropToFloorPlugin

The DropToFloorPlugin class is responsible for two very important things. One, it sets up the user interface so the user can choose to drop an object. Two, it repositions the selected objects.

processMessage

At a high level, this method should be familiar to you by now, but in the specifics shown in Example 3-2 you will notice several changes from the previous projects. To summarize what happens here, this method adds a single menu item to the Object menu and disables the menu item.

The for loop at the top of the method finds the location of the "Convert To Actor…" menu item in the object menu. This allows us to force the new menu item to fall directly after the "Convert To Actor…" menu item and before the selection control menu items at the bottom of the menu. This places our new menu item with other menu items that are similar. The menu items that modify the objects and their positions are located at the top of the menu.

```
public void processMessage(int message, Object[] args) {
  switch (message) {
    case Plugin.SCENE_WINDOW_CREATED:
      layout = (LayoutWindow) args[0];
      BMenu objectMenu = layout.getObjectMenu();
      // Add menu item to the Object menu
      // Locate position after "Convert To Actor..."
      int posConvertToActor = 0;
      for(int i = 0; i < objectMenu.getChildCount(); i++){
        BMenuItem menuIter = null;
        menuIter = (BMenuItem) objectMenu.getChild(i);
        if(menuIter.getText().equalsIgnoreCase(
                               "Convert To Actor...")){
          posConvertToActor = i;
          break;
        }
      }
      posConvertToActor++; // select position after Convert
                           // To Actor or top if not found
      // Create menu item that will call drop to floor code
      Shortcut shortcut =
        new Shortcut('D', Shortcut.SHIFT_MASK |
                          Shortcut.DEFAULT_MASK);
      // Use a shortcut because we'll use this
      // feature frequently.
      // We'll use Ctrl+Shift+D because AOI already uses
      // Ctrl+D for editing keyframes.
      BMenuItem menuItem = Translate.menuItem(
          "Drop to Floor", this, "dropMenuAction", shortcut);
      // Insert menu item
      objectMenu.add(menuItem, posConvertToActor);
      // Disable menu item (until object selected)
      controlEnableDisable(menuItem);
      break;
  }
}
```

Example 3-2: processMessage

Next is a call to create a shortcut. The shortcut is attached to the menu item, so when the user presses the Ctrl+Shift+D on Windows, the callback for the menu item will be called. On the Mac, the DEFAULT_MASK corresponds to the Meta key. There are five possible masks, ALT_MASK, CTRL_MASK, DEFAULT_MASK, META_MASK, and SHIFT_MASK, which can be combined as needed using the bitwise-OR operator. The choice of Ctrl+Shift+D was made for this plugin because Art of Illusion already has a fea-

```
private void controlEnableDisable(BMenuItem menuItem) {
  // Default to disabled, so we can't select it without
  // a selection
  menuItem.setEnabled(false);

  // Schedule thread to set the enabled/disable status
  // of the menuItem
  new MenuItemActivator(menuItem, layout).start();
}
```

Example 3-3: controlEnableDisable

ture that makes use of Ctrl+D and Ctrl+Shift+D was not previously used.

The call to create the menu item is very much like what you saw in Chapter 2, with the exception that it takes the shortcut as a parameter. Then to end the method there is a call to controlEnableDisable, which makes a call to disable the menu item and a call to start the MenuItemActivator. More on that later.

dropMenuAction

Whether the user makes the call via menu or via the shortcut key sequence, when the user asks the plugin to drop the selected object, the entry point is through the dropMenuAction method. The code for this method is shown in Example 3-4.

The first line retrieves all of the objects that have been selected by the user. Because there is nothing to do if no objects are selected, the next line checks to see if there are objects in the collection and exits the method if there are none.

Next is the UndoRecord. We haven't seen this yet in a plugin because the previous projects did nothing to change the scene, but since this plugin changes the location of one or more objects, we will want the option to set everything back the way it was. In Art of Illusion an UndoRecord is used to hold the state of multiple objects, so here it is passed into the methods that will move the selected objects. The state of the ob-

```
private void dropMenuAction(){
  // Get each selected object in turn.
  Collection<ObjectInfo> Objects =
                         layout.getSelectedObjects();

  // if no selected objects, just return;
  if(Objects.isEmpty()){
    return;
  }

  // Create a new UndoRecord. This will be built as we
  // make changes, so we can go back to the previous state
  // of anything we changed.
  UndoRecord undo = new UndoRecord(layout, true);

  for(ObjectInfo obj : Objects){
    // Find the lowest point of the object.
    double newY = 0 - getLowestPointOfObjectGroup(obj).y;

    // Reposition the Object
    repositionObjectAndChildren(obj, newY, undo);
  }

  // Inform the layout window that we're changed something.
  layout.updateImage();

  // Tell the layout window that it can store what we've
  // said is the previous state of the object.
  layout.setUndoRecord(undo);
}
```

Example 3-4: dropMenuAction

ject is stored in the UndoRecord just prior to the object being modified. Whether there is one object, multiple objects, or objects with children, they will be added to the UndoRecord and when execution returns to this level they will all be pushed onto the UndoRecord stack by the last line in this method.

Between the UndoRecord calls the for loop moves through the selected objects and makes calls to get the lowest point and the call to reposition the object. This is done at the group level, so if the user has selected an object group the whole group will drop as expected.

Take a look at Figure 3-5. This is a typical example of a compound object you might want to drop to floor.

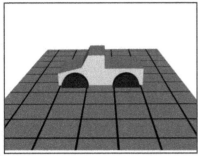
Figure 3-5: Compound Object

The parent object is the truck body. It has two axles that are children. The axles each have two wheels as children. The positioning of the axles was done by sight, to give the drawing a better appearance rather than having a specific location, so once everything as been drawn the body and the wheels ended up slightly below the floor. The result we want is to select the truck body, press Ctrl+Shift+D and achieve the result in Figure 3-6, where both the truck body and its children are all moved the distance required for the wheels to rest on the floor.

Lastly, in the drop-MenuAction method is the call to updateImage. This is to tell the updated window to redraw, since the methods called

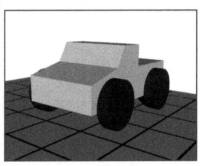
Figure 3-6: After Drop

may have moved some of the objects.

getLowestPointOfObjectGroup

The lowest point of the object group is the lowest point of the lowest object in the group, so the main purpose of the getLowestPointOfObjectGroup method is to make the calls required to get the lowest point of each of the objects and return the lowest one. You should be able to recognize this operation in the for loop of Example 3-5. But you will notice that it deviates from that. It first gets the lowest point of the parent object, but the second line limits the rest of the objects to the children that have **not** been selected.

The assumption here is that if the user were to specifically select some of the children of the object—let's say they selected the truck body and two wheels—they intend to have all of the selected objects drop to the floor. But if the user selects only the truck body then they intend for the wheels to move with the body.

This also avoids a potential problem. Because we are processing all selected items at a higher level,

```
private Vec3 getLowestPointOfObjectGroup(ObjectInfo obj) {

  // Start with object lowest point.
  Vec3 lowestPoint = getObjectLowestPoint(obj);

  ObjectInfo[] notSelectedChildren =
                              getNotSelectedChildren(obj);

  // Check non-selected children for a lower point.
  for(ObjectInfo childObj : notSelectedChildren){
    double distanceChildFromParent =
                              getDistanceY(obj, childObj);
    Vec3 candidateLowestPoint =
                  getLowestPointOfObjectGroup(childObj);
    candidateLowestPoint.y += distanceChildFromParent;
    if(candidateLowestPoint.y < lowestPoint.y){
      lowestPoint = candidateLowestPoint;
    }
  }

  return lowestPoint;
}
```

Example 3-5: getLowestPointOfObjectGroup

some objects could be handled multiple times if they were not excluded here. This could produce unexpected results. If the wheels were to drop to the floor before the truck body, then the lowest point of the children would be different when the body was dropped then what it was when the call was made. That could create a situation in which some objects are moved while others aren't or some objects are moved to the wrong location.

There is a recursive call in this method, which simplifies traversal of the object tree. Because the recursive call is limited to the number of objects in the layout window, this will not create an unbounded loop.

getObjectLowestPoint

Once we get to the level of the objects, it is necessary to get the locations of the individual vertices. We will be looking at this in more detail later in the book, but with the way objects are defined in Art of Illusion, there is no guarantee that an object has vertices. A sphere, for example, can be described in terms of its location and radius. Using vertices for all objects simplifies the algorithm for this plugin, so to get the vertices we first must make a call to the Art of Illusion method convertToTriangleMesh. Using 0.001 as the tolerance ensures that the error between mathematical

```
private Vec3 getObjectLowestPoint(ObjectInfo obj) {
  Vec3 currentLowest = new Vec3(0, obj.getBounds().maxy, 0);
  if(obj.getObject().canConvertToTriangleMesh() !=
                               Object3D.CANT_CONVERT){
    TriangleMesh mesh =
               obj.getObject().convertToTriangleMesh(0.001);
    MeshVertex[] vertices = mesh.getVertices();

    for(int vertexNum = 0;
        vertexNum < mesh.getVertices().length; vertexNum++){
      Vec3 point = new Vec3(vertices[vertexNum].r);
      obj.getCoords().fromLocal().transformDirection(point);

      if(point.y < currentLowest.y){
        currentLowest = point;
      }
    }
  }
  else{
    Vec3 point = new Vec3(0, 0, 0);
    obj.getCoords().fromLocal().transformDirection(point);
    currentLowest = point;
  }
  return currentLowest;
}
```

Example 3-6: getObjectLowestPoint

model of the object and the approximation is visually insignificant.

From the triangle mesh we can get the vertices. We handle each, one at a time. To do so, we must convert them from local object coordinates to scene coordinates. The call to getCoords gets the coordinate system of the object. The call to fromLocal creates a matrix that can be used to transform out of the coordinate system to the scene coordinates, so that when transformDirection is called the vertex, *point*, will be in scene coordinates.

To help understand this, look at Figure 3-7. In object coordinates, the circle represents the lowest point. When the objects are rotated, the object coordinate system also rotates, so that point remains the lowest point. But in scene coordinates it is not the lowest point. Once the object coordinates are converted to scene coordinates the correct

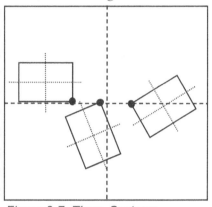

Figure 3-7: Three Systems

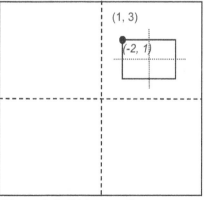

Figure 3-8: Object vs. Scene

lowest point can be found.

Figure 3-8 shows another way to look at it. The point is a (-2, 1) relative to the object, but at (1, 3) in the scene. This is much simplified. In Art of Illusion, we're working with three dimensions instead of two and the object could have a different scale than the scene as well. All of this can be handled through matrix transformations. Fortunately for us, the Art of Illusion API hides much of that and we need only work with the matrixes when we find it beneficial.

In the event that getObjectLowestPoint can't convert the object to a triangle mesh, as the case would be if the object is a light or a camera, it will return the object origin, (0, 0, 0). As with any other point in the object, this must also be converted to scene coordinates before it is returned.

repositionObjectAndChildren

Once the lowest point of the selected object group is known, the next step is to reposition the object group so that the lowest point is at y=0. This is done by the repostionObjectAndChildren method. The reposition methods traverse the object tree, through a recursive call, in much the same way as the methods that found the lowest point.

The children are moved first, so that a distance can be calculated from the parent to the child, along the Y-

```
private void repositionObjectAndChildren(ObjectInfo obj,
                              double newY, UndoRecord undo)
{

  // Get the children that aren't selected.
  // These will move the same amount as the parent object.
  //  The selected children will be placed on floor.
  ObjectInfo[] notSelectedChildren =
                              getNotSelectedChildren(obj);
  for(ObjectInfo childObj : notSelectedChildren){
    double distanceChildFromParent =
                              getDistanceY(obj, childObj);
    double childNewY = newY + distanceChildFromParent;
    repositionObjectAndChildren(childObj, childNewY, undo);
  }

  // Reposition the object itself.
  repositionObject(obj, newY, undo);
}
```

Example 3-7: repositionObjectAndChildren

axis. The method getDistanceY uses the Y component of the origin of two objects and returns the difference. (The origin is in scene coordinates.) That distance is added to the location the object will be in after the move. When there are no more children to reposition the object itself is repositioned to the new position.

repositionObject

The act of repositioning a single object requires little effort. But before we do that, the repositionObject method calls addCommand for the UndoRecord we've been passing around. As the call is made in Example 3-8, we are storing a reference to the coordinate system we're about to modify and a snapshot of what it looks like before the change. Different kinds of changes require us to store different things in the un-

```
private void repositionObject(ObjectInfo obj, double newY,
                                              UndoRecord undo)
{
  // Take a snapshot of the object for the undo record
  // before we mess it up.
  undo.addCommand(UndoRecord.COPY_COORDS, new Object []
            {obj.getCoords(), obj.getCoords().duplicate()});
  // Note that the Origin of a CooridnateSystem is in global
  // coordinates.
  CoordinateSystem coords = obj.getCoords();
  Vec3 orig = coords.getOrigin();
  orig.y = newY;
  coords.setOrigin(orig);
  obj.setCoords(coords);
}
```

Example 3-8: repositionObject

do record. Possible values for the command in the first parameter include, COPY_OBJECT, COPY_COORDS, COPY_OBJECT_INFO, SET_OBJECT, ADD_OBJECT, DELETE_OBJECT, RENAME_OBJECT, ADD_TO_GROUP, REMOVE_FROM_GROUP, SET_GROUP_CONTENTS, SET_TRACK, SET_TRACK_LIST, COPY_TRACK,

COPY_VERTEX_POSITIONS, COPY_SKELETON, SET_MESH_SELECTION, SET_SCENE_SELECTION.

The way to understand these commands is that Art of Illusion will add a record that can undo the action and then it will perform the action. So something like DELETE_OBJECT will add the necessary undo record and then it will delete the object. If the user selects Undo, then the object will be added back into the scene. We are using COPY_COORDS, so a copy of one coordinate system is used to overwrite that of the other after the undo record is stored. We can modify the coordinates and know that if we undo the coordinate system will be returned to what it was before the copy was made.

The modifications that we make in Example 3-8 are that we get the object's coordinates, set the Y component to the new location and then we update the object with the modified coordinate system. Because the origin of the object is now in a new location, all of the points that are calculated relative to the origin are also in a new location.

The complete code for DropToFloorPlugin is shown in example 3-9.

```
package extending.aoi.drop_to_floor;

import java.util.Collection;

import buoy.widget.BMenu;
import buoy.widget.BMenuItem;
import buoy.widget.Shortcut;
import artofillusion.LayoutWindow;
import artofillusion.Plugin;
import artofillusion.UndoRecord;
import artofillusion.math.CoordinateSystem;
import artofillusion.math.Vec3;
import artofillusion.object.MeshVertex;
import artofillusion.object.Object3D;
import artofillusion.object.ObjectInfo;
import artofillusion.object.TriangleMesh;
import artofillusion.ui.Translate;

/**
 * Plugin that can be used to drop the selected objects to
the
 * floor of the scene. The floor is defined as 0 along the
 * Y axis.
 * @author Timothy Fish
 *
 */
public class DropToFloorPlugin implements Plugin {

  private LayoutWindow layout;

  /* (non-Javadoc)
   * @see artofillusion.Plugin#processMessage(int, ja-
va.lang.Object[])
   */
  @Override
  public void processMessage(int message, Object[] args) {
    switch (message) {
    case Plugin.SCENE_WINDOW_CREATED:
      layout = (LayoutWindow) args[0];
      BMenu objectMenu = layout.getObjectMenu();
      // Add menu item to the Object menu
      // Locate position after "Convert To Actor..."
      int posConvertToActor = 0;
      for(int i = 0; i < objectMenu.getChildCount(); i++){
        BMenuItem menuIter = null;
        menuIter = (BMenuItem) objectMenu.getChild(i);
        if(menuIter.getText().equalsIgnoreCase(
                                  "Convert To Actor...")){
          posConvertToActor = i;
          break;
        }
      }
      posConvertToActor++; // select position after Convert
                           // To Actor or top if not found

      // Create menu item that will call drop to floor code
```

Example 3-9a: DropToFloorPlugin.java

```
        Shortcut shortcut =
                new Shortcut('D', Shortcut.SHIFT_MASK |
                        Shortcut.DEFAULT_MASK);
        // Use a shortcut because we'll use this feature
        // frequently. We'll use Ctrl+Shift+D because AOI
        // already uses Ctrl+D for editing keyframes.
        BMenuItem menuItem = Translate.menuItem(
            "Drop to Floor", this, "dropMenuAction", shortcut);

        // Insert menu item
        objectMenu.add(menuItem, posConvertToActor);
        // Disable menu item (until object selected)
        controlEnableDisable(menuItem);
        break;
    }
}

/**
 * Enables/disables the menu item based when conditions
 * change that determine whether the menu item has an
 * object to work on or not.
 * @param menuItem
 */
private void controlEnableDisable(BMenuItem menuItem) {
    // Default to disabled, so we can't select it without a
    // selection
    menuItem.setEnabled(false);

    // Schedule thread to set the enabled/disable status of
    // the menuItem
    new MenuItemActivator(menuItem, layout).start();
}


/**
 * Action code for the Drop to Floor menu item.
 */
@SuppressWarnings("unused")
private void dropMenuAction(){

    // Get each selected object in turn.
    Collection<ObjectInfo> Objects =
                        layout.getSelectedObjects();

    // if no selected objects, just return;
    if(Objects.isEmpty()){
        return;
    }

    // Create a new UndoRecord. This will be built as we
    // make changes, so we can go back to the previous state
    // of anything we changed.
    UndoRecord undo = new UndoRecord(layout, true);

    for(ObjectInfo obj : Objects){
        // Find the lowest point of the object.
```

Example 3-9b: DropToFloorPlugin.java

```
      double newY = 0 - getLowestPointOfObjectGroup(obj).y;

      // Reposition the Object
      repositionObjectAndChildren(obj, newY, undo);

    }

    // Inform the layout window that we're changed
    // something.
    layout.updateImage();

    // Tell the layout window that it can store what we've
    // said is the previous state of the object.
    layout.setUndoRecord(undo);
  }

  /**
   * Reposition the object and non-selected children so that
   * the group is on the floor, where "floor" is defined as
   * the plane where Y = 0. The non-selected children will
   * move with the parent, but the selected children will be
   * repositioned to the floor.
   * @param obj the object to move
   * @param undo
   * @param lowY lowest value of Y for the group
   */
  private void repositionObjectAndChildren(ObjectInfo obj,
                           double newY, UndoRecord undo)
  {

    // Get the children that aren't selected. These will
    // move the same amount as the parent object. The
    // selected children will be placed on floor.
    ObjectInfo[] notSelectedChildren =
                          getNotSelectedChildren(obj);
    for(ObjectInfo childObj : notSelectedChildren){

      double distanceChildFromParent =
                          getDistanceY(obj, childObj);
      double childNewY = newY + distanceChildFromParent;
      repositionObjectAndChildren(childObj, childNewY,
                               undo);
    }

    // Reposition the object itself.
    repositionObject(obj, newY, undo);
  }
```

Example 3-9c: DropToFloorPlugin.java

```java
/**
 * Calculates the distance between the origins of two
 * objects in the Y direction.
 * @param obj
 * @param childObj
 * @return
 */
private double getDistanceY(ObjectInfo obj,
                           ObjectInfo childObj) {
    Vec3 objPoint = obj.getCoords().getOrigin();
    Vec3 childPoint = childObj.getCoords().getOrigin();
    double distanceChildFromParent =
                         (childPoint.y - objPoint.y);
    return distanceChildFromParent;
}

/**
 * Reposition the object so that it is on the floor, where
 * "floor" is defined as the plane where Y = 0.
 * @param obj object to move
 * @param newY lowest value of Y for the object origin
 * @param undo
 */
private void repositionObject(ObjectInfo obj, double newY,
                             UndoRecord undo) {
    // Take a snapshot of the object for the undo record
    // before we mess it up.
    undo.addCommand(UndoRecord.COPY_COORDS, new Object []
            {obj.getCoords(), obj.getCoords().duplicate()});

    // Note that the Origin of a CooridnateSystem is in
    // global coordinates.
    CoordinateSystem coords = obj.getCoords();
    Vec3 orig = coords.getOrigin();
    orig.y = newY;

    coords.setOrigin(orig);
    obj.setCoords(coords);
}


/**
 * Returns the collective lowest point of an object and
 * it's non-selected children.
 * @param obj
 * @return
 */
private Vec3 getLowestPointOfObjectGroup(ObjectInfo obj) {

    // Start with object lowest point.
    Vec3 lowestPoint = getObjectLowestPoint(obj);

    ObjectInfo[] notSelectedChildren =
                            getNotSelectedChildren(obj);

    // Check non-selected children for a lower point.
```

Example 3-9d: DropToFloorPlugin.java

```java
      for(ObjectInfo childObj : notSelectedChildren){
        double distanceChildFromParent =
                                 getDistanceY(obj, childObj);
        Vec3 candidateLowestPoint =
                     getLowestPointOfObjectGroup(childObj);
        candidateLowestPoint.y += distanceChildFromParent;
        if(candidateLowestPoint.y < lowestPoint.y){
          lowestPoint = candidateLowestPoint;
        }
      }

      return lowestPoint;
  }


  /**
   * Returns the lowest point of an object relative to the
   * scene coordinates
   * @param obj the object
   * @return lowest point of the object in the scene
   */
  private Vec3 getObjectLowestPoint(ObjectInfo obj) {
    Vec3 currentLowest = new Vec3(0, obj.getBounds().maxy,
0);
    if(obj.getObject().canConvertToTriangleMesh() !=
                                Object3D.CANT_CONVERT){
      TriangleMesh mesh =
              obj.getObject().convertToTriangleMesh(0.001);
      MeshVertex[] vertices = mesh.getVertices();

      for(int vertexNum = 0;
          vertexNum < mesh.getVertices().length;
          vertexNum++){
        Vec3 point = new Vec3(vertices[vertexNum].r);
        obj.getCoords().fromLocal().transformDirection
(point);

        if(point.y < currentLowest.y){
          currentLowest = point;
        }
      }
    }
    else{
      Vec3 point = new Vec3(0, 0, 0);
      obj.getCoords().fromLocal().transformDirection(point);
      currentLowest = point;
    }
    return currentLowest;
  }




  /**
```

Example 3-9e: DropToFloorPlugin.java

```
 * Return the number of non-selected children the object
 * has.
 * @param obj
 * @return
 */
 private ObjectInfo[] getNotSelectedChildren(ObjectInfo
obj){
    // Get the children.
    ObjectInfo[] children = obj.getChildren();

    // Determine the number of selected children.
    int selectedCount = 0;
    for(ObjectInfo childObj : children){
      if(!childObj.selected){
        selectedCount++;
      }
    }

    // Allocate an array to hold the non-selected children.
    ObjectInfo[] notSelectedChildren =
                            new ObjectInfo[selectedCount];

    // Put the non-selected children in the array.
    int i=0;
    for(ObjectInfo childObj : children){
      if(!childObj.selected){
        notSelectedChildren[i] = childObj;
        i++;
      }
    }

    // Return the array.
    return notSelectedChildren;
  }

}
```

Example 3-9f: DropToFloorPlugin.java

MenuItemActivator

Good user interface design requires that menu items that cannot be used be hidden or deactivated. In Art of Illusion, we see an example of this on the edit menu and the Make Live Duplicate menu item. When an object is selected, the menu item is selectable, but when no object is selected it is grayed out. Part of our goal in developing plugins is to give the user of our plugin an experience that is consistent with the parent tool. Within the limitations that exist, a user should never have to think about the plugin as being an add on once the plugin is installed. For us, that means that we need a way for our plugin to deactivate the menu item when the conditions for its use are not met and reactivate it when they are. For that we need the MenuItemActivator class.

This class was instantiated when the menu item was added and it works by running as a separate thread that repeatedly checks the number of selected items. If none are selected then it will deactivate the menu item. If at least one is selected then it will activate the menu item. To keep the thread from hogging too much of the processing power, there is a ¼ second delay between times it does the check. This delay will go unnoticed by the users because it will take the user longer than that to select an object and then locate the menu item on the objects menu.

This approach can be used anywhere you need something to wait for a specific condition to be met. Here it is waiting for the right number of items to be selected, but another place where it would be useful is if a plugin needs to wait on another program. For example, we might have a another software package that will generate an object we would like to use in Art of Illusion. We might develop a plugin that can pass that software the information it needs from our scene, but the software doesn't have the ability to tell Art of Illusion when it is finished. Our plugin could have a thread that checks for the existence of a file that the software generates. When that file is found, the plugin could trigger the next stage of processing.

As you can see in Example 3-10, the class doesn't require much code. The menu item and the layout window are passed in as references to the constructor so that the class will be able to check for the number of selected items and to activate the menu item. The check is done by the objectsAreSelected method. The run method has what amounts to an infinite loop that enables or disables the menu item and then sleeps for a while.

```
package extending.aoi.drop_to_floor;

import artofillusion.LayoutWindow;
import buoy.widget.BMenuItem;

/**
 * Thread to check for object selection after Drop To Floor
 * menu item created
 * @author Timothy Fish
 *
 */
public class MenuItemActivator extends Thread {
  private BMenuItem theMenuItem;
  private LayoutWindow theLayout;

  // refresh menuItem every quarter-second
  private static final long inverseRefreshRate = 250;

  /**
   * Constructor
   * @param menuItem Non-null menu item
   * @param layout non-null layout window
   */
  public MenuItemActivator(BMenuItem menuItem,
                                LayoutWindow layout) {
    // Assumption: theMenuItem && theLayout are not null
    theMenuItem = menuItem;
    theLayout = layout;
  }
```

Example 3-10a: MenuItemActivator.java

```
/**
 * Method that does checks the selection status.
 */
@Override
public void run() {
  // do while menu item exists
  while(theMenuItem != null && theLayout != null){
    // Check for object selection
    if(objectsAreSelected()){
      theMenuItem.setEnabled(true);
    }
    else{
      theMenuItem.setEnabled(false);
    }
    try {
      // Sleep most of the time so processor can do other
      // things. Updating every quarter-second is more
      // than sufficient since the user can't select the
      // menu item that quickly after object selection.
      Thread.sleep(inverseRefreshRate );
    } catch (InterruptedException e) {
      // This should never happen.
      e.printStackTrace();
    }
  }
}

/**
 * Function to determine if there is at least one object
 * selected.
 * @return true if there are objects selected, false if
 * not
 */
private boolean objectsAreSelected() {
  return !theLayout.getSelectedObjects().isEmpty();
}
}
```

Example 3-10b: MenuItemActivator.java

You will be seeing variations on this class again in this book as several of the examples require menu items and some require the ability to update objects as the user is making changes.

Chapter 4

PointAt Plugin

Sometimes, when we are creating a 3D scene, we want one object to point at a specific location or object. It might be a case where we need objects like those

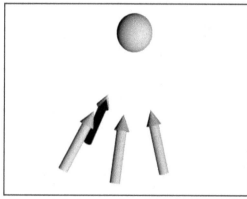

Figure 4-1: Arrows Pointing

shown in Figure 4-1 to point at another object, but more commonly, we might want a light or a camera to point at a location. If we were to do that by manual manipulation, it could require several minutes of moving and rotating and adjusting until it just right. And it still might not be right because our hand might not be steady enough on the mouse to get the objects pointed at the exact location. On the other hand, if we can let the computer do it, those several minutes turn into a few seconds. With it saving so much time, it is worth taking the time to understand what is required to implement this feature as a plugin or as part of a script.

From the standpoint of what we need from the Art of Illusion API, the Point At Plugin is similar to the Drop To Floor plugin. But instead of moving the objects, we need to rotate the objects.

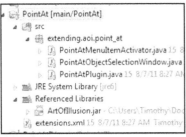

Figure 4-2: PointAt Project

Also, there is more math involved because it is necessary to determine the direction from one object to the other and point an object in that direction.

Figure 4-2 shows that the this project has a similar set of files, with a window object added. The user will call this plugin by selecting two objects and then selecting the menu item from the objects menu. The additional class is a window that will request the user specify which object points at the other. This window is shown in Figure 4-3. We'll look at

Figure 4-3: PointAt Window

Point At Options

◉ Cube 1 points at Sphere 1

○ Sphere 1 points at Cube 1

OK   Cancel

```xml
<?xml version="1.0" standalone="yes"?>
<extension name="Point At" version="0.1" >
  <author>Timothy Fish</author>
  <date>July 2011</date>
  <plugin class="extending.aoi.point_at.PointAtPlugin" />
  <description>This plugin adds the capability to point the
selected object at.</description>
  <comments>This project is to demonstrate the manipulation
of scene objects and the use of windows in the user inter-
face.
</comments>
  <history>
    <log version="0.1" date="July 2011" author="Timothy
Fish" >- Initial Version</log>
  </history>
</extension>
```

Example 4-1: extensions.xml

how we can improve on this window later, but it will work for now.

Create the Project

The changes to *extensions.xml* are minimal. The code is shown in Example 4-1.If you create the project in Eclipse, it should look something like Figure 4-2. When you export to a jar file, export to *PointAt.jar.*

Because so much of the code in this project is similar to things you've seen in previous chapters, much of the code will be provided in the code listing without comment. We will focus primarily on what we are trying to accomplish and how to use the Art of Illusion API to make it happen.

The Concept

Look at Figure 4-4. We have here a compound object made up of to cylinders and a null object, and a target object that is a sphere. Before we look at pointing at the sphere with code, lets look at what we would do if we did it by hand.

We would first select the Pointer parent object. Then in the top left view port we would drag the top center handle until the pointer in the top right view

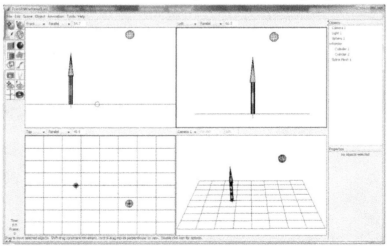

Figure 4-4: Object to Point at Another

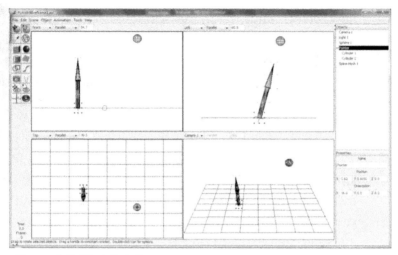

Figure 4-5: First Rotation

port appeared to point at the sphere. The result would be what you see in Figure 4-5. Because the object still isn't pointing at the sphere, we would drag the top center handle in the top right viewport and we would end up with something like what is in Figure 4-6.

We might have to go back to the other viewport and make some adjustments, but as you can see, it is quite close to where we want it. There is no reason to

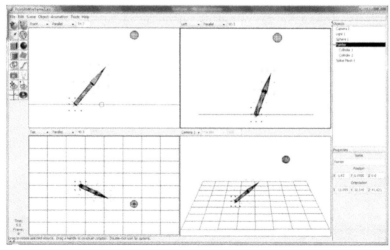

Figure 4-6: Second Rotation

use the user interface to do it, but the PointAt plugin makes use of the same concept. It first calculates the amount to rotate the object in one direction and then it is able to correctly find the amount of rotation in the second direction.

First, we must find the direction we want the ob-

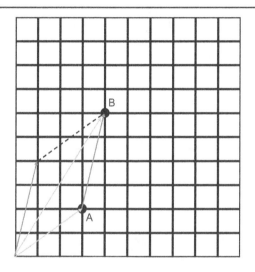

Figure 4-7: If A is the vector from (0, 0) to (3, 2) and B is the vector from (0, 0) to (4, 6), then B-A is the vector from (0, 0) to (1, 4). B-A has the same direction as the vector from A to B, (3, 2) to (4, 6).

ject to point. One of the properties of vectors is that when we subtract them it gives us a direction vector that is equivalent to the direction from one to the other. This is demonstrated in Figure 4-7. This is shown in 2D to make it easier to see, but the property holds for three dimensional vectors as well.

To get the angle, we find the vectors from the scene origin to each of the object origins and we subtract the one for the pointer from the pointee. This gives us the direction. But once we get the direction, we must rotate the pointer so that it points in the same direction. Figure 4-8 shows a situation in which the direction from point A to point B is known but the object has not yet been rotated to match. The location is correct, but the angle is wrong.

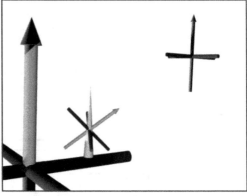

Figure 4-8: Rotate to Match Angle

The plugin handles this by making calls to calculate the amount of rotation. First the rotation around the X-axis is calculated. Figure 4-9 shows the initial state of the pointer relative to the direction it needs to point. To achieve this rotation, we will first rotate around X, as is shown in Figure 4-10. If the Y-axis is pointing in the direction of the pointee, then this rotation rotates the pointer so that its own Y-axis falls into the XY plane. The amount of rotation

Figure 4-9: Initial Relative to New

Figure 4-10: Rotate Around X

required to get it there is given by the equation below, where y and z are the y and z components of vector B minus vector A:

The case where y is zero is a special case that the

PointAt

$$\theta = \tan^{-1} \frac{-z}{y}$$

code must handle, but we will ignore that for now. You recall that $z/y = \tan\theta$, for a right triangle.

What may not be as obvious is how this applies to

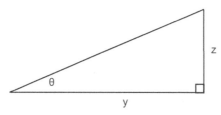

Figure 4-11: Right Triangle

an object that we are trying to rotate by an amount that causes it to point in the chosen direction. If you can imagine that the X-axis is coming straight out of the page in Figure 4-11, then you can see that $-\theta$ is the amount we must rotate the X-axis to cause the hypotenuse to fall on the XY plane, Figure 4-12.

Next, we must calculate the angle to rotate along the Z-axis. That is the angle between the dashed line in

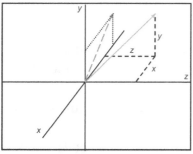

Figure 4-12: Rotate to XY

Figure 4-12 and the Y-axis. Consider what we know about the right triangle. z_1 is 0. y_1 is not equal y_0. $x_1 = x_0$. We know that y_1 is equal to the original line projected onto the ZY plane. Applying the Pythagorean Theorem, we find that y_1 is given by the following equation:

$$y_1 = \sqrt{y^2 + z^2}$$

With the new y value, we can apply the same identity as before and calculate the second angle we need to rotate about the Z-axis:

$$\phi = \tan^{-1} \frac{x}{\sqrt{y^2 + z^2}}$$

Once that rotation takes place, the object will align with the Y-axis is as is shown in Figure 4-13.

Figure 4-13: Rotate Around Z

Special Objects

From a conceptual level, the choice of which axis we should point at a another object is arbitrary. At the practical level, we want to choose the axis that seems the most natural. In Art of Illusion, when we draw a cone (a cylinder with one end with a radius of zero), the point is on the Y-axis. So it makes sense for us to say that to point at something we will rotate the object's coordinate system so that the Y-axis is pointing in the direction of the object. But this is not true for all objects. In most cases, through the use of Null objects, the user can pick what part of the object he actually wants to point at another object. But when it comes to objects like cameras and lights, we don't want to have to create a Null object, align it with the camera, make the camera a child of the Null object and then only move the camera by moving the Null object. This would make the user interface more difficult than it needs to be. The alternative is to handle cameras and lights in a different way than we handle a cone.

When you look at the line drawing for a newly created camera in Art of Illusion, Figure 4-14, you see that the top of the camera is up, but the lens is pointing out along the Z-axis. Since the direction of the lens determines what the camera

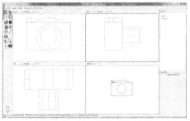

Figure 4-14: Camera

sees, when we point the camera at something we intend the Z-axis to point in that direction. It turns out that lights in Art of Illusion work the same way. So in the plugin code it is necessary to make special accommodations. The calculations are the same, no matter which axis we choose to point with, we just need to switch the variables.

PointAt Code

On the next few pages you will find the code for the PointAt plugin. With the description provided above, and what you learned from previous plugins, you will be able to read the code and see how it is doing what it does.

```
/**
 *
 */
package extending.aoi.point_at;

import java.util.Collection;

import buoy.widget.BMenu;
import buoy.widget.BMenuItem;
import artofillusion.LayoutWindow;
import artofillusion.Plugin;
import artofillusion.UndoRecord;
import artofillusion.math.CoordinateSystem;
import artofillusion.math.Vec3;
import artofillusion.object.Light;
import artofillusion.object.ObjectInfo;
import artofillusion.object.SceneCamera;
import artofillusion.ui.Translate;
import java.lang.Math;

/**
 * @author Timothy Fish
 *
 */
public class PointAtPlugin implements Plugin {

    private LayoutWindow layout;
    private ObjectInfo pointer;
    private ObjectInfo pointee;
    public static final int numObjectsRequired = 2;

    /* (non-Javadoc)
     * @see artofillusion.Plugin#processMessage(int, ja-
va.lang.Object[])
     */
    @Override
    public void processMessage(int message, Object[] args) {
      switch (message) {
      case Plugin.SCENE_WINDOW_CREATED:
        layout = (LayoutWindow) args[0];

        BMenu objectMenu = layout.getObjectMenu();
        // Add menu item to the Object menu
        // Locate position after "Convert To Actor..."
        int posConvertToActor = 0;
        for(int i = 0; i < objectMenu.getChildCount(); i++){
          BMenuItem menuIter = null;
          menuIter = (BMenuItem) objectMenu.getChild(i);
          if(menuIter.getText().equalsIgnoreCase(
                                  "Convert To Actor...")){
            posConvertToActor = i;
            break;
          }
        }
        posConvertToActor++;//select position after Convert To
                            // Actor or top if not found
```

Example 4-2a: PointAtPlugin.java

```
            // Create menu item that will call drop to floor code
            BMenuItem menuItem = Translate.menuItem(
                    "Point At...", this, "pointAtMenuAction");

            // Insert menu item
            objectMenu.add(menuItem, posConvertToActor);

            // Disable menu item (until object selected)
            controlEnableDisable(menuItem);
            break;
        }

    }

    /**
     * Enables/disables the menu item based when conditions
     * change that determine whether the menu item has an
     * object to work on or not.
     * @param menuItem
     */
    private void controlEnableDisable(BMenuItem menuItem) {

        // Default to disabled, so we can't select it without a
        // selection
        menuItem.setEnabled(false);

        // Schedule thread to set the enabled/disable status of
        // the menuItem
        new PointAtMenuItemActivator(menuItem, layout).start();
    }

    /**
     * Action code for the Point At menu item.
     */
    @SuppressWarnings("unused")
    private void pointAtMenuAction(){

        Collection<ObjectInfo> objects =
                                layout.getSelectedObjects();
        if(objects.size() == numObjectsRequired ) {
            // Create a new UndoRecord. This will be built as we
            // make changes, so we can go back to the previous
            // state of anything we changed.
            UndoRecord undo = new UndoRecord(layout, true);

            // We need to know which object points at which, so
            // bring up a window for the user to tell us.
            ObjectInfo objA = (ObjectInfo) objects.toArray()[0];
            ObjectInfo objB = (ObjectInfo) objects.toArray()[1];

            setPointeeFromUserInput(objA, objB);

            for(ObjectInfo obj : objects){
                if(obj != this.pointee){ // don't point something at
                                         // itself
```

Example 4-2b: PointAtPlugin.java

```java
          pointPointerAtPointee(this.pointer, undo);
        }
      }

      layout.updateImage();

      // Tell the layout window that it can store what we've
      // said is the previous state of the object.
      layout.setUndoRecord(undo);
    }
    else{
      // We should never get here because the menu item is
      // disabled.
      System.err.println("ERROR: PointAtPlugin - number of
selected objects not equal "+numObjectsRequired);
    }

  }

  /**
   * Rotates the pointer to point at the pointee.
   * @param pointer
   * @param undo
   */
  private void pointPointerAtPointee(ObjectInfo pointer,
                          UndoRecord undo) {

    // Take a snapshot of the object for the undo record
    // before we mess it up.
    undo.addCommand(UndoRecord.COPY_COORDS,
          new Object [] {pointer.getCoords(),
                    pointer.getCoords().duplicate()});


    Vec3 locA = pointer.getCoords().getOrigin();
    CoordinateSystem orgA = pointer.getCoords().duplicate();

    Vec3 locB = pointee.getCoords().getOrigin();
    Vec3 BminusA = locB.minus(locA);

    double x = BminusA.x;
    double y = BminusA.y;
    double z = BminusA.z;

    double xRot = 0;
    double yRot = 0;
    double zRot = 0;

    if(!specialPointerObject()){
      // Normal Setup
      xRot = calculateXRotate(y, z);
      yRot = calculateYRotate();
      zRot = calculateZRotate(x, y, z);
    }
    else if(specialPointerObject()){
      // Handle special objects, like cameras.
```

Example 4-2c: PointAtPlugin.java

```
      // note that a SceneCamera is not the same thing as a
      // Camera

      // Set Object to known state.
      pointer.getCoords().setOrientation(0,0,0);

      xRot = calculateXRotateSpecial(x, y, z);
      yRot = calculateYRotateSpecial(x, y, z);
      zRot = calculateZRotateSpecial()*0.0;
    }

  pointer.getCoords().setOrientation(xRot, yRot, zRot);
  rotateChildren(pointer, pointer, orgA, undo);
}

/**
 * @param parent
 * @param undo
 * @param orgA Original coordinate systems of pointer
 */
private void rotateChildren(ObjectInfo parent,
                           ObjectInfo pointer,
                 CoordinateSystem orgA, UndoRecord undo) {
  for(ObjectInfo child : parent.getChildren()){
    undo.addCommand(UndoRecord.COPY_COORDS, new Object []
      {child.getCoords(), child.getCoords().duplicate()});
    CoordinateSystem coords = child.getCoords();

    // set rotation center at pointer origin
    coords.transformCoordinates(orgA.toLocal());
    // move everything back, but to the new location
    coords.transformCoordinates(
                      pointer.getCoords().fromLocal());

    rotateChildren(child, pointer, orgA, undo);
  }
}

/**
 * Returns true iff the object is a SceneCamera or a Light
 * and false otherwise.
 * @return
 */
private boolean specialPointerObject() {
  boolean ret = false;

  if((pointer.getObject() instanceof SceneCamera)){
    ret = true;
  }
  else if((pointer.getObject() instanceof Light)){
    ret = true;
  }
  else{
    ret = false;
  }
```

Example 4-2d: PointAtPlugin.java

111

```java
    return ret;
}

/**
 * Calculates the second rotation.
 * @param x
 * @param y
 * @param z
 * @return
 */
private double calculateZRotate(double x,
                                double y, double z) {
  double sqrtYYZZ = Math.sqrt(y*y + z*z);
  double ret = 0; // return value;
  if(sqrtYYZZ != 0){

    ret = Math.toDegrees(Math.atan(x/sqrtYYZZ));

    if(sqrtYYZZ < 0){
      // angle is on the other size
      ret += 180.0;
    }
  }
  // Handle differently because the angle gives two
  // possible directions.
  else if(x > 0){
    ret = 90.0;
  }
  else if(x < 0){
    ret = -90.0;
  }
  return ret;
}

/**
 * Returns a valid angle for Y.
 * @return
 */
private double calculateYRotate() {
  // Zero is as good as any value.
  return 0.0;
}

/**
 * Calculates rotation that will put direction vector in
 * the XY plane.
 * @param y
 * @param z
 * @return
 */
private double calculateXRotate(double y, double z) {
  double ret = 0;

  if(y != 0){
    ret = Math.toDegrees(Math.atan(-z/y));
```

Example 4-2e: PointAtPlugin.java

```
    if(y < 0){
      ret += 180.0;
    }
  }
  // Handle differently because the angle gives two
  // possible directions.
  else if(z > 0){
    ret = -90.0;
  }
  else if(z < 0){
    ret = 90.0;
  }
  return ret;
}

/**
 * Calculates the first rotation.
 * This function is for special object like cameras and
 * lights.
 * @param x
 * @param y
 * @param z
 * @return
 */
private double calculateYRotateSpecial(double x,
                                double y, double z) {
  double ret = 0;

  if(z != 0){
    ret = Math.toDegrees(Math.atan(-x/z));

    if(z < 0){
      ret += 180.0;
    }
  }
  // Handle differently because the angle gives two
  // possible directions.
  else if(x > 0){
    ret = -90.0;
  }
  else if(x < 0){
    ret = 90.0;
  }
  return ret;
}

/**
 * Returns the Special Z rotation.
 * This function is for special object like cameras and
 * lights.
 * @return
 */
private double calculateZRotateSpecial() {
  // We can set it to 0.0 because any value of Z can be
  // used.
  return 0.0;
```

Example 4-2f: PointAtPlugin.java

```java
    }

    /**
     * Calculates rotation that will put direction vector in
     * the XZ plane. This function is for special object like
     * camer as and lights.
     * @param y
     * @param z
     * @return
     */
    private double calculateXRotateSpecial(double x,
                                    double y, double z) {
        double sqrtXXZZ = Math.sqrt(x*x + z*z);
        double ret = 0; // return value;
        if(sqrtXXZZ != 0){

            ret = Math.toDegrees(Math.atan(y/sqrtXXZZ));

            if(sqrtXXZZ < 0){
                // angle is on the other size
                ret += 180.0;
            }
        }
        // Handle differently because the angle gives two
        // possible directions.
        else if(y > 0){
            ret = 90.0;
        }
        else if(y < 0){
            ret = -90.0;
        }
        return ret;
    }


    /**
     * Displays a window for the user to select whether he
     * wants objA to point at objB or objB to point at objA.
     * @param objA
     * @param objB
     */
    private void setPointeeFromUserInput(ObjectInfo objA,
            ObjectInfo objB) {

        PointAtObjectSelectionWindow window =
                new PointAtObjectSelectionWindow(layout, objA,
objB);

        pointer = window.getPointer();
        pointee = window.getPointee();

    }
}
```

Example 4-2g: PointAtPlugin.java

```
/**
 *
 */
package extending.aoi.point_at;

import artofillusion.object.ObjectInfo;
import artofillusion.ui.PanelDialog;
import buoy.widget.BFrame;
import buoy.widget.BRadioButton;
import buoy.widget.ColumnContainer;
import buoy.widget.RadioButtonGroup;

/**
 * @author Timothy Fish
 *
 */
public class PointAtObjectSelectionWindow {
  /**
   * Class to setup the layout of the
   * PointAtObjectSelectionWindow.
   */
  private class PointAtDialogPanel extends ColumnContainer {
    private RadioButtonGroup theRadioButtonGroup;
    private String objAPointerText;
    private String objBPointerText;
    private BRadioButton objAPointerRadioButton;
    private BRadioButton objBPointerRadioButton;

    /**
     * Constructor - handles widget placement
     */
    PointAtDialogPanel(ObjectInfo objA, ObjectInfo objB){
      super(); // Call the ColumnContainer constructor

      // Set the display text. Note that getName() and
      // getString() are very different.
      objAPointerText = objA.getName() + " points at " +
                        objB.getName();
      objBPointerText = objB.getName() + " points at " +
                        objA.getName();

      theRadioButtonGroup = new RadioButtonGroup();

      objAPointerRadioButton = new BRadioButton
              (objAPointerText, true, theRadioButtonGroup);
      objBPointerRadioButton = new BRadioButton
              (objBPointerText, false, theRadioButtonGroup);

      add(objAPointerRadioButton);
      add(objBPointerRadioButton);

    }
```

Example 4-3a: PointAtObjectSelectionWindow.java

```java
    /**
     * Returns true if objA is the pointer and false if objB
     * is the pointer.
     * @return
     */
    public boolean getObjAPointer() {
        return objAPointerRadioButton.getState();
    }

}

private ObjectInfo pointer;
private ObjectInfo pointee;
private final String windowTitle = "Point At Options";
private PointAtDialogPanel thePanel;

/**
 * Displays window for the user to select the object that
 * points at the pointee.
 * @param parent
 * @param objA
 * @param objB
 */
public PointAtObjectSelectionWindow(BFrame parent,
                    ObjectInfo objA, ObjectInfo objB){
    pointer = objA;
    pointee = objB;

    thePanel = new PointAtDialogPanel(objA, objB);

    PanelDialog dlg = new PanelDialog(parent, windowTitle ,
                            thePanel);

    if (dlg.clickedOk()){
        // code for what to do after user accepts
        if(thePanel.getObjAPointer()){
            pointer = objA;
            pointee = objB;
        }
        else{
            pointer = objB;
            pointee = objA;
        }
    }
    else{
        // User clicked cancel, so everything should remain
        // unchanged.
        ;
    }
}
```

Example 4-3b: PointAtObjectSelectionWindow.java

```java
/**
 * Returns the object that points.
 * @return
 */
public ObjectInfo getPointer() {
  return pointer;
}

/**
 * Returns the object we're to point at.
 * @return
 */
public ObjectInfo getPointee() {
  return pointee;
}
}
```

Example 4-3c: PointAtObjectSelectionWindow.java

```java
package extending.aoi.point_at;

import artofillusion.LayoutWindow;
import buoy.widget.BMenuItem;

/**
 * Thread to check for object selection after PointAt menu
item created
 * @author Timothy Fish
 *
 */
public class PointAtMenuItemActivator extends Thread {
  private BMenuItem theMenuItem;
  private LayoutWindow theLayout;
  // refresh menuItem every quarter-second
  private static final long inverseRefreshRate = 250;

  /**
   * Constructor
   * @param menuItem Non-null menu item
   * @param layout non-null layout window
   */
  public PointAtMenuItemActivator(BMenuItem menuItem,
                                  LayoutWindow layout) {
    // Assumption: theMenuItem && theLayout are not null
    theMenuItem = menuItem;
    theLayout = layout;
  }
```

Example 4-4a: PointAtMenuItemActivator.java

```java
/**
 * Method that does checks the selection status.
 */
@Override
public void run() {
    // do while menu item exists
    while(theMenuItem != null && theLayout != null){
        // Check for object selection
        if(twoObjectsAreSelected()){
            theMenuItem.setEnabled(true);
        }
        else{
            theMenuItem.setEnabled(false);
        }
        try {
            // Sleep most of the time so processor can do other
            // things. Updating every quarter-second is more
            // than sufficient since the user can't select the
            // menu item that quickly after object selection.
            Thread.sleep(inverseRefreshRate );
        } catch (InterruptedException e) {
            // This should never happen.
            e.printStackTrace();
        }
    }
}

/**
 * Function to determine if two and only two objects are
 * selected.
 * @return true if there are objects selected, false if
 * not
 */
private boolean twoObjectsAreSelected() {
    int numSelected = theLayout.getSelectedObjects().size();
    final int properSize = 2;
    return (numSelected == properSize);
}
```

Example 4-4b: PointAtMenuItemActivator.java

PointAt Plugin Take Two

The Point At plugin in the first part of this chapter gets the job done, but it has a few problems. The primary problem is the user interface. If you installed the plugin and selected an item, you might have noticed that the menu item was still grayed out. So maybe you selected several items and saw that it was still grayed out. You might have gotten the impression at this point that you had done something wrong. But if you read the documentation you might have realized that it will only work when two objects and only two objects are selected.

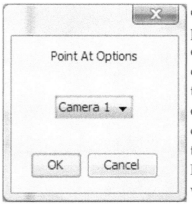

Figure 4-15: PointAtII Window

To correct this problem, we can make some changes to the plugin so that the user need only select one item and if he does happen to select more than one item then all of those objects will end up pointing at one object rather than causing the menu item to be disabled. Figure 4-15 is a window that will allow the user to select the object to point at from among the available objects. The Widget for this window is the BComboBox, which must have a list of names. To build the list, the code retrieves the object list and adds the value returned by getName. Note that getName returns a very different value than getString. The value by getName is the same value as is listed in the object list in the layout window.

There are few other changes, so the code for this project will be listed without further comment.

```
/**
 *
 */
package extending.aoi.point_at_ii;

import java.util.Collection;

import buoy.widget.BMenu;
import buoy.widget.BMenuItem;
import artofillusion.LayoutWindow;
import artofillusion.Plugin;
import artofillusion.UndoRecord;
import artofillusion.math.CoordinateSystem;
import artofillusion.math.Vec3;
import artofillusion.object.Light;
import artofillusion.object.ObjectInfo;
import artofillusion.object.SceneCamera;
import artofillusion.ui.Translate;
import java.lang.Math;

import extending.aoi.point_at_ii.PointAtIIMenuItemActivator;
import extending.aoi.point_at_ii.
                        PointAtIIObjectSelectionWindow;

/**
 * @author Timothy Fish
 *
 */
public class PointAtIIPlugin implements Plugin {

    private LayoutWindow layout;
    private ObjectInfo pointee;
    public static final int numObjectsRequired = 1;

    /* (non-Javadoc)
     * @see artofillusion.Plugin#processMessage(int, ja-
va.lang.Object[])
     */
    @Override
    public void processMessage(int message, Object[] args) {
      switch (message) {
      case Plugin.SCENE_WINDOW_CREATED:
        layout = (LayoutWindow) args[0];

        BMenu objectMenu = layout.getObjectMenu();
        // Add menu item to the Object menu
        // Locate position after "Convert To Actor..."
        int posConvertToActor = 0;
        for(int i = 0; i < objectMenu.getChildCount(); i++){
          BMenuItem menuIter = null;
          menuIter = (BMenuItem) objectMenu.getChild(i);
          if(menuIter.getText().equalsIgnoreCase(
                              "Convert To Actor...")){
            posConvertToActor = i;
            break;
          }
```

Example 4-5a: PointAtIIPlugin.java

```
        }
        posConvertToActor++; // select position after Convert
To Actor or top if not found

        // Create menu item that will call drop to floor code
        BMenuItem menuItem = Translate.menuItem(
                "Point At II...", this,
"pointAtMenuAction");

        // Insert menu item
        objectMenu.add(menuItem, posConvertToActor);

        // Disable menu item (until object selected)
        controlEnableDisable(menuItem);
        break;
    }

}

/**
 * Enables/disables the menu item based when conditions
 * change that determine whether the menu item has an
 * object to work on or not.
 * @param menuItem
 */
private void controlEnableDisable(BMenuItem menuItem) {

    // Default to disabled, so we can't select it without a
    // selection
    menuItem.setEnabled(false);

    // Schedule thread to set the enabled/disable status of
    // the menuItem
    new PointAtIIMenuItemActivator(menuItem, layout).
                                                    start();
}

/**
 * Action code for the Point At menu item.
 */
@SuppressWarnings("unused")
private void pointAtMenuAction(){

    Collection<ObjectInfo> objects =
                                layout.getSelectedObjects();
    if(!objects.isEmpty()){
        // Create a new UndoRecord. This will be built as we
        // make changes, so we can go back to the previous
        // state of anything we changed.
        UndoRecord undo = new UndoRecord(layout, true);

        if(setPointeeFromUserInput()){

            for(ObjectInfo obj : objects){
                // don't point something at itself
                if(obj != this.pointee){
```

Example 4-5b: PointAtIIPlugin.java

```
                  pointPointerAtPointee(obj, undo);
            }
        }

        layout.updateImage();

        // Tell the layout window that it can store what
        // we've said is the previous state of the object.
        layout.setUndoRecord(undo);
    }
    else{
        // We should never get here because the menu item is
        // disabled.
        System.err.println("ERROR: PointAtIIPlugin - number
of selected objects not equal "+numObjectsRequired);
    }
  }
}

/**
 * Rotates the pointer to point at the pointee.
 * @param pointer
 * @param undo
 */
private void pointPointerAtPointee(ObjectInfo pointer,
                                   UndoRecord undo) {

    // Take a snapshot of the object for the undo record
    // before we mess it up.
    undo.addCommand(UndoRecord.COPY_COORDS,
            new Object [] {pointer.getCoords(),
                          pointer.getCoords().duplicate()});

    Vec3 locA = pointer.getCoords().getOrigin();
    CoordinateSystem orgA = pointer.getCoords().duplicate();

    Vec3 locB = pointee.getCoords().getOrigin();
    Vec3 BminusA = locB.minus(locA);

    double x = BminusA.x;
    double y = BminusA.y;
    double z = BminusA.z;

    double xRot = 0;
    double yRot = 0;
    double zRot = 0;

    if(!specialPointerObject(pointer)){
      // Normal Setup
      xRot = calculateXRotate(y, z);
      yRot = calculateYRotate();
      zRot = calculateZRotate(x, y, z);
    }
    else if(specialPointerObject(pointer)){
      // Handle special objects, like cameras.
```

Example 4-5c: PointAtIIPlugin.java

```
      // note that a SceneCamera is not the same thing as a
      // Camera
      // Set Object to known state.
      pointer.getCoords().setOrientation(0,0,0);

      xRot = calculateXRotateSpecial(x, y, z);
      yRot = calculateYRotateSpecial(x, y, z);
      zRot = calculateZRotateSpecial()*0.0;
    }

    pointer.getCoords().setOrientation(xRot, yRot, zRot);
    rotateChildren(pointer, pointer, orgA, undo);
  }

  /**
   * @param parent
   * @param undo
   * @param orgA Original coordinate systems of pointer
   */
  private void rotateChildren(ObjectInfo parent,
                              ObjectInfo pointer,
                              CoordinateSystem orgA,
                              UndoRecord undo) {
    for(ObjectInfo child : parent.getChildren()){
      undo.addCommand(UndoRecord.COPY_COORDS, new Object []
        {child.getCoords(), child.getCoords().duplicate()});
      CoordinateSystem coords = child.getCoords();

      // set rotation center at pointer origin
      coords.transformCoordinates(orgA.toLocal());

      // move everything back, but to the new location
      coords.transformCoordinates(
                        pointer.getCoords().fromLocal());
      rotateChildren(child, pointer, orgA, undo);
    }
  }

  /**
   * Returns true iff the object is a SceneCamera or a Light
   * and false otherwise.
   * @return
   */
  private boolean specialPointerObject(ObjectInfo pointer) {
    boolean ret = false;

    if((pointer.getObject() instanceof SceneCamera)){
      ret = true;
    }
    else if((pointer.getObject() instanceof Light)){
      ret = true;
    }
    else{
      ret = false;
    }
```

Example 4-5d: PointAtIIPlugin.java

123

```java
        return ret;
    }

    /**
     * Calculates the second rotation.
     * @param x
     * @param y
     * @param z
     * @return
     */
    private double calculateZRotate(double x,
                                    double y, double z) {
        double sqrtYYZZ = Math.sqrt(y*y + z*z);
        double ret = 0; // return value;
        if(sqrtYYZZ != 0){

            ret = Math.toDegrees(Math.atan(x/sqrtYYZZ));

            if(sqrtYYZZ < 0){
                // angle is on the other size
                ret += 180.0;
            }
        }
        // Handle differently because the angle gives two
        // possible directions.
        else if(x > 0){
            ret = 90.0;
        }
        else if(x < 0){
            ret = -90.0;
        }
        return ret;
    }

    /**
     * Returns a valid angle for Y.
     * @return
     */
    private double calculateYRotate() {
        // Zero is as good as any value.
        return 0.0;
    }

    /**
     * Calculates rotation that will put direction vector in
     * the XY plane.
     * @param y
     * @param z
     * @return
     */
    private double calculateXRotate(double y, double z) {
        double ret = 0;

        if(y != 0){
            ret = Math.toDegrees(Math.atan(-z/y));
```

Example 4-5e: PointAtIIPlugin.java

```
      if(y < 0){
        ret += 180.0;
      }
    }
    // Handle differently because the angle gives two
    // possible directions.
    else if(z > 0){
      ret = -90.0;
    }
    else if(z < 0){
      ret = 90.0;
    }
    return  ret;
  }

/**
  * Calculates the first rotation.
  * This function is for special object like cameras and
  * lights.
  * @param x
  * @param y
  * @param z
  * @return
  */
private double calculateYRotateSpecial(double x,
                                      double y, double z) {
    double ret = 0;

    if(z != 0){
      ret = Math.toDegrees(Math.atan(-x/z));

      if(z < 0){
        ret += 180.0;
      }
    }
    // Handle differently because the angle gives two
    // possible directions.
    else if(x > 0){
      ret = -90.0;
    }
    else if(x < 0){
      ret = 90.0;
    }
    return  ret;
  }

/**
  * Returns the Special Z rotation.
  * This function is for special object like cameras and
  * lights.
  * @return
  */
private double calculateZRotateSpecial() {
    // We can set it to 0.0 because any value of Z can be
    // used.
    return 0.0;
```

Example 4-5e: PointAtIIPlugin.java

```java
    }

/**
 * Calculates rotation that will put direction vector in
 * the XZ plane. This function is for special object like
 * cameras and lights.
 * @param y
 * @param z
 * @return
 */
private double calculateXRotateSpecial(double x,
                                       double y, double z) {
    double sqrtXXZZ = Math.sqrt(x*x + z*z);
    double ret = 0; // return value;
    if(sqrtXXZZ != 0){

        ret = Math.toDegrees(Math.atan(y/sqrtXXZZ));

        if(sqrtXXZZ < 0){
            // angle is on the other size
            ret += 180.0;
        }
    }
    // Handle differently because the angle gives two
    // possible directions.
    else if(y > 0){
        ret = 90.0;
    }
    else if(y < 0){
        ret = -90.0;
    }
    return ret;
}


/**
 * Displays a window for the user to select whether he
 * wants objA to point at objB or objB to point at objA.
 */
private boolean setPointeeFromUserInput() {

    PointAtIIObjectSelectionWindow window =
                new PointAtIIObjectSelectionWindow(layout);

    pointee = window.getPointee();

    return (pointee != null);

}
}
```

Example 4-5f: PointAtIIPlugin.java

```
/**
 *
 */
package extending.aoi.point_at_ii;

import java.util.Collection;

import artofillusion.LayoutWindow;
import artofillusion.Scene;
import artofillusion.object.ObjectInfo;
import artofillusion.ui.PanelDialog;
import buoy.widget.BComboBox;
import buoy.widget.ColumnContainer;

/**
 * @author Timothy Fish
 *
 */
public class PointAtIIObjectSelectionWindow {
  /**
   * Class to setup the layout of the PointAtObjectSelection
   * Window.
   */
  private class PointAtDialogPanel extends ColumnContainer {
    private BComboBox theObjectsList;
    Collection<ObjectInfo> theObjects;

    /**
     * Constructor - handles widget placement
     */
    PointAtDialogPanel(Collection<ObjectInfo> objects){
      super(); // Call the ColumnContainer constructor

      theObjects = objects;

      theObjectsList = new BComboBox();
      // Set the display text. Note that getName() and
      // getString() are very different.
      for(ObjectInfo object : objects ){
              theObjectsList.add(object.getName());
      }

      add(theObjectsList);

    }

    public ObjectInfo getPointee() {
      int selectedIndex = theObjectsList.getSelectedIndex();
      if(selectedIndex >= 0){
        return (ObjectInfo)theObjects.toArray()
[selectedIndex];
      }
      else{
        return null;
      }
    }
```

Example 4-6a: PointAtIIObjectSelectionWindow.java

```java
        }

    private ObjectInfo pointee;
    private final String windowTitle = "Point At Options";
    private PointAtDialogPanel thePanel;

    /**
     * Displays window for the user to select the pointee.
     * @param parent
     */
    public PointAtIIObjectSelectionWindow(LayoutWindow
parent){
        Scene scene = parent.getScene();

        pointee = null;

        Collection<ObjectInfo> selectableObjects =
                                    scene.getAllObjects();
        thePanel = new PointAtDialogPanel(selectableObjects);

        PanelDialog dlg = new PanelDialog(parent,
                                    windowTitle, thePanel);

        if (dlg.clickedOk()){
            // code for what to do after user accepts
            pointee = thePanel.getPointee();
        }
        else{
            // User clicked cancel, so everything should remain
            // unchanged.
            ;
        }
    }

    /**
     * Returns the object we're to point at. Returns null if
     * none selected.
     * @return
     */
    public ObjectInfo getPointee() {
        return pointee;
    }
}
```

Example 4-6b: PointAtIIObjectSelectionWindow.java

```
package extending.aoi.point_at_ii;

import artofillusion.LayoutWindow;
import buoy.widget.BMenuItem;

/**
 * Thread to check for object selection after PointAt menu
 * item created
 * @author Timothy Fish
 *
 */
public class PointAtIIMenuItemActivator extends Thread {
  private BMenuItem theMenuItem;
  private LayoutWindow theLayout;
  // refresh menuItem every quarter-second
  private static final long inverseRefreshRate = 250;
  /**
   * Constructor
   * @param menuItem Non-null menu item
   * @param layout non-null layout window
   */
  public PointAtIIMenuItemActivator(BMenuItem menuItem,
                                    LayoutWindow layout) {
    // Assumption: theMenuItem && theLayout are not null
    theMenuItem = menuItem;
    theLayout = layout;
  }

  /**
   * Method that does checks the selection status.
   */
  @Override
  public void run() {
    // do while menu item exists
    while(theMenuItem != null && theLayout != null){
      // Check for object selection
      if(anObjectIsSelected()){
        theMenuItem.setEnabled(true);
      }
      else{
        theMenuItem.setEnabled(false);
      }
      try {
        // Sleep most of the time so processor can do other
        // things Updating every quarter-second is more
        // than sufficient since the user can't select the
        // menu item that quickly after object selection.
        Thread.sleep(inverseRefreshRate );
      } catch (InterruptedException e) {
        // This should never happen.
        e.printStackTrace();
      }
    }
  }

  /**
```

Example 4-7a: PointAtIIMenuItemActivator.java

```
 * Function to determine if at least one object is
 * selected.
 * @return true if there are objects selected, false if
 * not
 */
private boolean anObjectIsSelected() {
    int numSelected = theLayout.getSelectedObjects().size();
    final int properSize = 1;
    return (numSelected >= properSize);
}

}
```

Example 4-7b: PointAtIIMenuItemActivator.java

```
<?xml version="1.0" standalone="yes"?>

<extension name="Point At II" version="0.1" >
  <author>Timothy Fish</author>
  <date>July 2011</date>

  <plugin
class="extending.aoi.point_at_ii.PointAtIIPlugin" />

  <description>This plugin adds the capability to point mul-
tiple object at a single object.</description>

  <comments>This project is to demonstrate the manipulation
of scene objects and the use of windows in the user inter-
face.</comments>

  <history>
      <log version="0.1" date="July 2011" author="Timothy
Fish" >- Initial Version</log>
  </history>

</extension>
```

Example 4-8: extensions.xml

Chapter 5

Resting One Object on Another

In Chapter 3 we looked at dropping an object to the floor. In Chapter 4 we looked at rotating an object based on where another is located. What if we could build on both of those and create a plugin that will allow us to rest one object on another. The application is obvious. Suppose you have a scene in which there is a table. The table itself

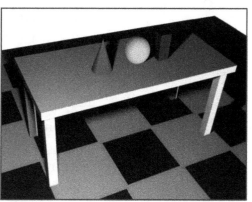

Figure 5-1: Objects on a Table

is resting on the floor, but you have other objects that you want to place on the table. Or perhaps you have several objects and you want an object to rest on top of them without any of them pushing through the surface. Using the mouse and the cursor keys, you could align it to the proper spot, but what we would like is for the computer to do that for us, so we can move on to the more interesting things.

While the tedious work of positioning an object on a table with a mouse isn't very enjoyable, it is an interesting problem when we attempt to do the same thing programmatically. In fact, it is so much of an interesting problem that it is nearly outside the scope of this book. When we created the plugin to drop an object to the floor, the problem was that shown in Figure 5-2. We found the lowest point on the object, and then we moved the object the distance that point was from the plane y=0. Our greatest difficulty with that problem was in finding the lowest point of the object, which we did by comparing each vertex and

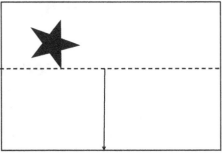

Figure 5-2: Find lowest point and drop to the known floor location of y=0.

keeping the one with the lowest y-value in scene coordinates.

Here the problem is finding the first point that will collide with another object when the object travels along a path in the –y direction. As Figure 5-3 shows, that point may not be the lowest point of the object and it may not collide with the highest point of the other object. In fact, it may not collide with some objects or with any object at all.

One possibility in handling this situation is to measure from each vertex in the object down

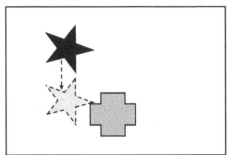

Figure 5-3: Find point that will collide with another object first, when the object moves down.

to the objects be-low it. The short-est distance is the amount the ob-ject must be moved. This is represented in Figure 5-4. This approach seems simple enough,

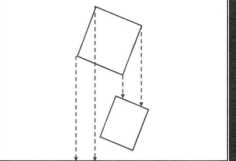

Figure 5-4: From Each Vertex

but how do we determine when a vertex collides with another object?

In our previous work, it was sufficient to use the vertices because we knew that every vertex was on a line that was perpendicular to the y=0 plane and we needed only to calculate the distance. In our current situation, we have one object defined by vertices that we expect to collide with another object defined by vertices. Even in Figure 5-4, you can see that none of the vertices will collide with the vertices of the other object. The collision takes place on a line that connects the vertices. If we were to rely solely on the vertex collisions, the upper rectangle would pass through the lower rectangle with no collisions detected.

Any 3D object can be approximated by a triangle mesh. We used that concept before, but rather than using only the vertices, this time we need to detect the collision of the triangles of two objects. If the triangles in the triangle mesh are small enough, the error between where the triangles collide and where the objects would collide based on the mathematical model is indiscernible to the eye. That will be sufficient for most users.

That being said, one of the things that Art of Illusion plugins are ideally suited for is to provide a means to model mathematical and scientific data, and provide a display of the results. If that is what you hope to accomplish, you may require more accurate collision detection, but for those of us who just want to draw pretty pictures, a bunch of tiny triangles is sufficient.

When using triangles, greater accuracy is achieved with more triangles. That could require us to measure the distance between every triangle on the object we are placing and the triangles in every other object in the scene. Given the number of triangles some scenes have, that could be a significant operation. To reduce that effort, we should first use the bounding boxes of the objects to eliminate as many as we can. If the bounding boxes would not collide by moving the object down, then we know that no triangles will collide.

Next comes the more difficult part, we must find where the triangles will collide.

Finding Triangle Collisions

Figure 5-5 shows some examples of how triangles intersect. There are two possible collisions. One is a collision in which a vertex will strike the interior of the lower triangle. The other is one in which an edge will strike the edge of the other triangle. Then there are also cases in which no collision occurs.

Vertex Collisions

The first three examples in Figure 5.5 are examples in which a vertex collision may occur. In the two on

Figure 5-5: Intersections

the left, it is dependent on how close each of the verti-ces are to the plane of the other triangle. In the exam-ple on the right, at least one vertex will collide with the triangle on its downward trajectory.

Figure 5-6 is one case where a vertex will collide with the lower triangle. To handle this case, we first find the intersection of a line passing through the ver-

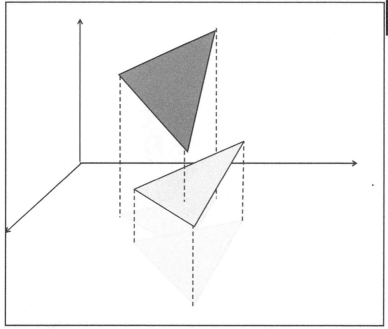

Figure 5-6: Vertex Collision

tex perpendicular to the y=0 plane, with the plane in-dicated by the vertices of the lower triangle. Once that intersection is found, we check to see if the point lies within the lower triangle. If it does, we compare the distance to that point with any other distances we've calculated, keeping the smallest distance. In Figure 5-6, that point will have the smallest distance and the upper triangle will need to move down by that amount.

Edge Collisions

If we modify Figure 5-6 slightly and bring the upper triangle forward to where the front vertex is out of the way of the lower triangle, we have the other kind of collision, as is shown in Figure 5-7.

Here, the collision will occur on the two edges. The problem here is that we have to find the point at

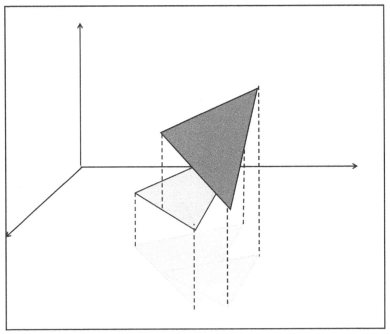

Figure 5-7: Edge Collision

which the collision will occur. We no longer have a point that we can drop to the triangle plane. What we do instead is to map the two triangle to the y=0 plane and then find the line intersections using the parametric equations of a line. For our purposes, y is replaced by z when looking for the intersection. Once the value

$$x_1(t) = a_x + (b_x - a_x)t$$

$$y_1(t) = a_y + (b_y - a_y)t$$

of t is known, we can substitute it back in for the line segment of the triangle. If t < 0 or 1 < t, then the intersection does not occur. Otherwise, we find the distance between the two points we found. If that distance is the lowest distance then it will be used as the distance to move the upper triangle.

If you enjoy working math problems, you may enjoy working through it yourself. I'll leave that to you. The rest of this chapter is a listing of the code for this plugin.

The interesting stuff is in *PlaceOnPlugin.java*. *Triangle.java* is just a structure for defining triangles. You have seen versions of the other files before.

Figure 5-8: PlaceOn Project

```xml
<?xml version="1.0" standalone="yes"?>

<extension name="Place On" version="0.1" >
  <author>Timothy Fish</author>
  <date>July 2011</date>

  <plugin class="extending.aoi.place_on.PlaceOnPlugin" />

  <description>This plugin will drop the selected object(s)
to the first visible non-special object below it.</
description>

  <comments>This project is to demonstrate the manipulation
of scene objects and the use of windows in the user inter-
face.</comments>

  <history>
    <log version="0.1" date="July 2011" author="Timothy
Fish" >- Initial Version</log>
  </history>
</extension>
```

Example 5-1: extensions.xml

```java
/**
 * Plugin that will drop an object to the first visible,
 * non-special object it encounters below it. A collision is
 * deemed to be when a vertex of the object falls within a
 * triangle of an object below it.
 */
package extending.aoi.place_on;

import java.util.ArrayList;
import java.util.Collection;

import buoy.widget.BMenu;
import buoy.widget.BMenuItem;
import artofillusion.LayoutWindow;
import artofillusion.Plugin;
import artofillusion.UndoRecord;
import artofillusion.math.BoundingBox;
import artofillusion.math.Mat4;
import artofillusion.math.Vec2;
import artofillusion.math.Vec3;
import artofillusion.object.Light;
import artofillusion.object.NullObject;
import artofillusion.object.Object3D;
import artofillusion.object.ObjectInfo;
import artofillusion.object.ReferenceImage;
import artofillusion.object.SceneCamera;
import artofillusion.object.TriangleMesh;
import artofillusion.object.TriangleMesh.Face;
import artofillusion.ui.Translate;

/**
 * @author Timothy Fish
 *
 */
public class PlaceOnPlugin implements Plugin {

    private LayoutWindow layout;
    private static final int numObjectsRequired = 1;
    private static final double meshToleranceObject = 0.010;
    private static final double meshToleranceNominee = 0.100;

    /* (non-Javadoc)
     * @see artofillusion.Plugin#processMessage(int, ja-
va.lang.Object[])
     */
    @Override
    public void processMessage(int message, Object[] args) {
        switch (message) {
        case Plugin.SCENE_WINDOW_CREATED:
            layout = (LayoutWindow) args[0];

            BMenu objectMenu = layout.getObjectMenu();
            // Add menu item to the Object menu
            // Locate position after "Convert To Actor..."
            int posConvertToActor = 0;
            for(int i = 0; i < objectMenu.getChildCount(); i++){
```

Example 5-2a: PlaceOnPlugin.java

```java
      BMenuItem menuIter = null;
      menuIter = (BMenuItem) objectMenu.getChild(i);
      if(menuIter.getText().equalsIgnoreCase(
                               "Convert To Actor...")){
        posConvertToActor = i;
        break;
      }
    }
    posConvertToActor++;//select position after Convert To
                       // Actor or top if not found

    // Create menu item that will call drop to floor code
    BMenuItem menuItem = Translate.menuItem("Place On",
                              this, "placeOnMenuAction");

    // Insert menu item
    objectMenu.add(menuItem, posConvertToActor);

    // Disable menu item (until object selected)
    controlEnableDisable(menuItem);
    break;
  }

}

/**
 * Enables/disables the menu item based when conditions
 * change that determine whether the menu item has an
 * object to work on or not.
 * @param menuItem
 */
private void controlEnableDisable(BMenuItem menuItem) {

  // Default to disabled, so we can't select it without a
  // selection
  menuItem.setEnabled(false);

  // Schedule thread to set the enabled/disable status of
  // the menuItem
  new PlaceOnMenuItemActivator(menuItem, layout).start();
}

/**
 * Action code for the Place On menu item.
 */
@SuppressWarnings("unused")
private void placeOnMenuAction(){

  Collection<ObjectInfo> objects =
                        layout.getSelectedObjects();
  if(objects.toArray().length == numObjectsRequired){
    // Create a new UndoRecord. This will be built as we
    // make changes, so we can go back to the previous
    // state of anything we changed.
    UndoRecord undo = new UndoRecord(layout, true);
```

Example 5-2b: PlaceOnPlugin.java

```java
    for(ObjectInfo obj : objects){
        placeObjectOnNextObject(obj, undo);
    }

    layout.updateImage();

    // Tell the layout window that it can store what we've
    // said is the previous state of the object.
    layout.setUndoRecord(undo);
    }
}

/**
 * Places the object on the nearest object below it.
 * @param obj
 * @param undo
 */
private void placeObjectOnNextObject(ObjectInfo obj,
                                     UndoRecord undo) {
    if(obj == null) { return; } //quick exit for null object

    // Search bounding boxes for objects that are
    // candidates.
    Collection<ObjectInfo> candidates = findCandidateObjects
(obj);

    // For each candidate, find the shortest upward ray that
    // intersects the object.
    double shortestYDistance = Double.MAX_VALUE;

    for(ObjectInfo nominee : candidates){
        // Given two objects, find the collision point if one
        // were to be dropped on top of the other. Return the
        // y distance at that point.

        // define a direction vector
        Vec3 direction = new Vec3(0, -1, 0);
        // Get point on objA, relative to objA origin where
        // collision will occur.
        double collisionDistance =
            findDistanceToCollisionPoint(obj, nominee,
direction);

        if(collisionDistance < shortestYDistance){
            shortestYDistance = collisionDistance;
        }
    }

    // Take a snapshot of the object for the undo record
    // before we mess it up.
    undo.addCommand(UndoRecord.COPY_COORDS, new Object []
            {obj.getCoords(), obj.getCoords().duplicate()});

    // Reposition the object so that it rests on the point
    // given by the shortest shortest ray.
    if(shortestYDistance < Double.MAX_VALUE){
```

Example 5-2c: PlaceOnPlugin.java

```
        Vec3 origin = obj.getCoords().getOrigin();
        origin.y -= shortestYDistance;
        obj.getCoords().setOrigin(origin);
      }
  }


  /**
   * Returns distance objA must travel in direction given
   * before it will have its first collision with objB.
   * Returns Double.MAX_VALUE
   * if no collision is possible.
   * @param objA
   * @param objB
   * @param direction
   * @return
   */
  private double findDistanceToCollisionPoint(
                                      ObjectInfo objA,
                                      ObjectInfo objB,
                                      Vec3 direction) {

      double ret = Double.MAX_VALUE;

      // if we can't do anything, just quit
      if(objA.getObject().canConvertToTriangleMesh() ==
                      Object3D.CANT_CONVERT){ return ret; }
      if(objB.getObject().canConvertToTriangleMesh() ==
                      Object3D.CANT_CONVERT){ return ret; }

      TriangleMesh meshA = objA.getObject
().convertToTriangleMesh(meshToleranceObject);
      TriangleMesh meshB = objB.getObject
().convertToTriangleMesh(meshToleranceNominee);

      // for each face in A, check for collision with each
      // face in B
      for(Face faceA : meshA.getFaces()){
        Mat4 fromA = objA.getCoords().fromLocal();
        // get a triangle from objA, with points in scene
        // coordinates
        Triangle triangleA = convertFaceToTriangle(meshA,
                                              faceA,
                                              fromA);

        for(Face faceB : meshB.getFaces()){
          Mat4 fromB = objB.getCoords().fromLocal();
          Triangle triangleB = convertFaceToTriangle(meshB,
                                              faceB,
                                              fromB);

          double currentCollisionDistance =
                  findTriangleCollisionDistance(triangleA,
                                      triangleB, direction);
          if(currentCollisionDistance < ret){
            // check to see if this is the first collision
            ret = currentCollisionDistance;
```

Example 5-2d: PlaceOnPlugin.java

```
        }
      }
    }

    return ret;
}
/**
 * Given a face defined in a Triangle Mesh, creates a
 * triangle with point values transformed from local to
 * by the matrix.
 * @param mesh
 * @param face
 * @param matrix
 * @return
 */
private Triangle convertFaceToTriangle(TriangleMesh mesh,
                              Face face, Mat4 matrix) {
    Vec3 p0 = new Vec3(mesh.getVertexPositions()[face.v1]);
    matrix.transform(p0);
    Vec3 p1 = new Vec3(mesh.getVertexPositions()[face.v2]);
    matrix.transform(p1);
    Vec3 p2 = new Vec3(mesh.getVertexPositions()[face.v3]);
    matrix.transform(p2);

    Triangle triangle = new Triangle(p0, p1, p2);
    return triangle;
}

/**
 * Given two triangles in the same coordinate system,
 * finds the distance between them along the direction
 * vector. If triangle will not collide with triangleB in
 * that direction, this method
 * will return Double.MAX_VALUE.
 * @param triangleA
 * @param triangleB
 * @param direction
 * @return
 */
private double findTriangleCollisionDistance(
    Triangle triangleA,
    Triangle triangleB, Vec3 direction) {

    Vec3 b = triangleB.getP0();
    Vec3 normalB = triangleB.getNormal();
    Vec3 normal = normalB;
    double dist0 = 0;
    double dist1 = 0;
    double dist2 = 0;
    double denominator = direction.dot(normal);
    double numerator = 0;

    // exit now, direction parallel to plane
    if(denominator == 0) { return Double.MAX_VALUE; }

    // point A0
```

Example 5-2e: PlaceOnPlugin.java

142

```
    Vec3 a0 = triangleA.getP0();
    numerator = a0.minus(b).dot(normal);
    dist0 = Math.abs(numerator/denominator);

    Vec3 P0 = a0.plus(direction.times(dist0));

    if(!pointInTriangle(triangleB, P0, direction)){
      dist0 = Double.MAX_VALUE;
    }

    // point A1
    Vec3 a1 = triangleA.getP1();
    numerator = a1.minus(b).dot(normal);
    dist1 = Math.abs(numerator/denominator);
    Vec3 P1 = a1.plus(direction.times(dist1));

    if(!pointInTriangle(triangleB, P1, direction)){
      dist1 = Double.MAX_VALUE;
    }

    // point A2
    Vec3 a2 = triangleA.getP2();
    numerator = a2.minus(b).dot(normal);
    dist2 = Math.abs(numerator/denominator);
    Vec3 P2 = a2.plus(direction.times(dist2));

    if(!pointInTriangle(triangleB, P2, direction)){
      dist2 = Double.MAX_VALUE;
    }


    double dist = Math.min(dist0, Math.min(dist1, dist2));

    // Find intersections between line segments.
    // Intersection will occur directly in line with the
    // intersection where the lines are mapped to the
    // y=0 plane. Check each line of triangleA against
    // each line of triangleB.
    Vec3 b0 = triangleB.getP0();
    Vec3 b1 = triangleB.getP1();
    Vec3 b2 = triangleB.getP2();

    dist = Math.min(dist,findLineCollision(a0, a1, b0, b1));
    dist = Math.min(dist,findLineCollision(a0, a1, b1, b2));
    dist = Math.min(dist,findLineCollision(a0, a1, b2, b0));

    dist = Math.min(dist,findLineCollision(a1, a2, b0, b1));
    dist = Math.min(dist,findLineCollision(a1, a2, b1, b2));
    dist = Math.min(dist,findLineCollision(a1, a2, b2, b0));

    dist = Math.min(dist,findLineCollision(a2, a0, b0, b1));
    dist = Math.min(dist,findLineCollision(a2, a0, b1, b2));
    dist = Math.min(dist,findLineCollision(a2, a0, b2, b0));

    return dist;
}
```

Example 5-2f: PlaceOnPlugin.java

```java
/**
 * Finds the distance from segment [a0, a1] to [b0, b1].
 * @param a0
 * @param a1
 * @param b0
 * @param b1
 * @return distance to collision
 */
private double findLineCollision(Vec3 a0, Vec3 a1,
                                 Vec3 b0, Vec3 b1) {
    Vec2 a = a0.dropAxis(1);
    Vec2 b = a1.dropAxis(1);
    Vec2 c = b0.dropAxis(1);
    Vec2 d = b1.dropAxis(1);
    double dist = Double.MAX_VALUE;

    double D = (b.x-a.x)*(d.y-c.y)-(b.y-a.y)*(d.x-c.x);
    double t0 = 0;
    double u0 = 0;
    if (D != 0){
        t0 = ((c.x-a.x)*(d.y-c.y)-(c.y-a.y)*(d.x-c.x)) / D;
        u0 = (a.x + (b.x-a.x)*t0-c.x)/(d.x-c.x);
        if(0<=t0 && t0<=1 && 0<=u0 && u0<=1){
            // intersection exists
            Vec3 pA = new Vec3();

            pA.x = a0.x + (a1.x-a0.x)*t0;
            pA.y = a0.y + (a1.y-a0.y)*t0;
            pA.z = a0.z + (a1.z-a0.z)*t0;

            Vec3 pB = new Vec3();
            pB.x = b0.x + (b1.x-b0.x)*u0;
            pB.y = b0.y + (b1.y-b0.y)*u0;
            pB.z = b0.z + (b1.z-b0.z)*u0;

            dist = Math.abs(pA.distance(pB));
        }
    }

    return dist;
}

private boolean pointInTriangle(Triangle triangleB,
Vec3 P, Vec3 direction) {
    // Transpose triangleB onto the plane perpendicular to
    // direction.
    Mat4 xRotMatrix = Mat4.xrotation(
                          calculateXRotate(direction));
    Mat4 yRotMatrix = Mat4.yrotation(
                          calculateYRotate(direction));
    Mat4 zRotMatrix = Mat4.zrotation(
                          calculateZRotate(direction));
    Mat4 rotationMatrix =
            xRotMatrix.times(yRotMatrix).times(zRotMatrix);
```

Example 5-2g: PlaceOnPlugin.java

```java
    Triangle projB = new Triangle(
        rotationMatrix.times(triangleB.getP0()),
        rotationMatrix.times(triangleB.getP1()),
        rotationMatrix.times(triangleB.getP2()));

    //Transpose P onto the plane perpendicular to direction.
    Vec3 projP = rotationMatrix.times(P);

    // Determine if P is on the same side of each edge as
    // the opposite point.
    if(SameSide(projP, projB.getP0(), projB.getP1(),
                                        projB.getP2())
    && SameSide(projP, projB.getP1(), projB.getP2(),
                                        projB.getP0())
    && SameSide(projP, projB.getP2(), projB.getP0(),
                                        projB.getP1())){
        return true;
    }
    // else
    return false;
}

/**
 * Returns true if the two points are on the same side of
 * the line given by linePoint1 and linePoint2.
 * @param point1
 * @param point2
 * @param linePoint1
 * @param linePoint2
 * @return
 */
private boolean SameSide(Vec3 point1, Vec3 point2,
                        Vec3 linePoint1, Vec3 linePoint2)
{
    // Two points are on the same side of a line if the dot
    // product of the cross product of each point minus a
    // point on the line and a second point on the line
    // minus the first point is >= 0.
    Vec3 crossPoint1 = (linePoint2.minus(linePoint1)).cross
(point1.minus(linePoint1));
    Vec3 crossPoint2 = (linePoint2.minus(linePoint1)).cross
(point2.minus(linePoint1));
    if(crossPoint1.dot(crossPoint2) >= 0){
        return true;
    }
    //else

    return false;
}

/**
 * Calculates the second rotation, which will align the
 * direction
 * vector with the y-axis.
 * @param x
```

Example 5-2h: PlaceOnPlugin.java

```java
 * @param y
 * @param z
 * @return
 */
private double calculateZRotate(Vec3 direction) {
  // Note that this is essentially the same code as we
  // used for the Point At Plugin
  double x = direction.x;
  double y = direction.y;
  double z = direction.z;
  double sqrtYYZZ = Math.sqrt(y*y + z*z);
  double ret = 0; // return value;
  if(sqrtYYZZ != 0){

    ret = Math.toDegrees(Math.atan(x/sqrtYYZZ));

    if(sqrtYYZZ < 0){
      // angle is on the other size
      ret += 180.0;
    }
  }
  // Handle differently because the angle gives two
  // possible directions.
  else if(x > 0){
    ret = 90.0;
  }
  else if(x < 0){
    ret = -90.0;
  }
  return ret;
}

/**
 * Returns a valid angle for Y.
 * @return
 */
private double calculateYRotate(Vec3 direction) {
  // Note that this is essentially the same code as we
  // used for the Point At Plugin

  // Zero is as good as any value.
  return 0.0;
}

/**
 * Calculates rotation that will put direction vector in
 * the XY plane.
 * @param y
 * @param z
 * @return
 */
private double calculateXRotate(Vec3 direction) {
  // Note that this is essentially the same code as we
  // used for the Point At Plugin
  double y = direction.y;
  double z = direction.z;
```

Example 5-2:i PlaceOnPlugin.java

```
   double ret = 0;

   if(y != 0){
     ret = Math.toDegrees(Math.atan(-z/y));

     if(y < 0){
       ret += 180.0;
     }
   }
   // Handle differently because the angle gives two
   // possible directions.
   else if(z > 0){
     ret = -90.0;
   }
   else if(z < 0){
     ret = 90.0;
   }
   return  ret;
 }

 private Collection<ObjectInfo> findCandidateObjects
(ObjectInfo obj) {
   // Determine is the boundary boxes are close enough to
   // what we're looking for.

   ArrayList<ObjectInfo> objects =
                             new ArrayList<ObjectInfo>();

   BoundingBox OB = obj.getBounds();
   Vec3 oMax = new Vec3(OB.maxx, OB.maxy, OB.maxz);
   Vec3 oMin = new Vec3(OB.minx, OB.miny, OB.minz);
   obj.getCoords().fromLocal().transform(oMax);
   obj.getCoords().fromLocal().transform(oMin);

   for(ObjectInfo candidate : layout.getScene
().getAllObjects()){

     if(!candidate.isVisible() || isSpecial(candidate)) {
     } // skip this object
     else if(candidate == obj) {
     } // no self collisions
     else{
       objects.add(candidate);
     }

   }
   return objects;
 }

 /**
  * returns true if the object is a special object, like a
  * camera, a light, or a null object.
  */
 private boolean isSpecial(ObjectInfo obj) {
     boolean ret = false;
```

Example 5-2j: PlaceOnPlugin.java

```
      if((obj.getObject() instanceof SceneCamera)){
        ret = true;
      }
      else if(obj.getObject() instanceof Light){
        ret = true;
      }
      else if(obj.getObject() instanceof NullObject){
        ret = true;
      }
      else if(obj.getObject() instanceof ReferenceImage){
        ret = true;
      }
      else{
        ret = false;
      }

      return ret;
  }
}
```

Example 5-2k: PlaceOnPlugin.java

```
/**
 * A simple class to hold the points of a triangle and to
 * compute their normal.
 */
package extending.aoi.place_on;

import artofillusion.math.Vec3;

/**
 * @author Timothy Fish
 *
 */
public class Triangle {
  private Vec3 p0;
  private Vec3 p1;
  private Vec3 p2;
  private Vec3 normal;

  public Triangle(final Vec3 p0, final Vec3 p1, final Vec3
p2){
    this.p0 = p0;
    this.p1 = p1;
    this.p2 = p2;
    this.setNormal();
  }

  private void setNormal() {
    Vec3 n = p1.minus(p0).cross(p2.minus(p0));
    this.normal = n.times(1/Math.sqrt(n.dot(n)));
  }

  public Vec3 getNormal(){
    return normal;
  }
```

Example 5-3a: Triangle.java

```java
public void setP0(Vec3 p0) {
   this.p0 = p0;
   this.setNormal();
}

public Vec3 getP0() {
   return p0;
}

public void setP1(Vec3 p1) {
   this.p1 = p1;
   this.setNormal();
}

public Vec3 getP1() {
   return p1;
}

public void setP2(Vec3 p2) {
   this.p2 = p2;
   this.setNormal();
}

public Vec3 getP2() {
   return p2;
}
}
```

Example 5-3b: Triangle.java

```java
/**
 * Thread to control the active status of the Place on menu
 * item.
 */
package extending.aoi.place_on;

import artofillusion.LayoutWindow;
import buoy.widget.BMenuItem;

/**
 * @author Timothy Fish
 *
 */
public class PlaceOnMenuItemActivator extends Thread {
   private BMenuItem theMenuItem;
   private LayoutWindow theLayout;
   // refresh menuItem every quarter-second
   private static final long inverseRefreshRate = 250;
   /**
    * Constructor
    * @param menuItem Non-null menu item
    * @param layout non-null layout window
```

Example 5-4: PlaceOnMenuItemActivator.java

```java
    */
    public PlaceOnMenuItemActivator(BMenuItem menuItem,
                                    LayoutWindow layout) {
        // Assumption: theMenuItem && theLayout are not null
        theMenuItem = menuItem;
        theLayout = layout;
    }

    /**
     * Method that does checks the selection status.
     */
    @Override
    public void run() {
        while(theMenuItem != null && theLayout != null){
            // do while menu item exists
            // Check for object selection
            if(anObjectIsSelected()){
                theMenuItem.setEnabled(true);
            }
            else{
                theMenuItem.setEnabled(false);
            }
            try {
                // Sleep most of the time so processor can do other
                // things. Updating every quarter-second is more
                // than sufficient since the user can't select the
                // menu item that quickly after object selection.
                Thread.sleep(inverseRefreshRate );
            } catch (InterruptedException e) {
                // This should never happen.
                e.printStackTrace();
            }
        }
    }

    /**
     * Function to determine if one and only one object is
     * selected.
     * @return true if there are objects selected, false if
     * not
     */
    private boolean anObjectIsSelected() {
        int numSelected = theLayout.getSelectedObjects().size();
        final int properSize = 1;
        return (numSelected == properSize);
    }
}
```

Example 5-4: PlaceOnMenuItemActivator.java

Chapter 6

New Objects

Open up Art of Illusion and on the tool palette you will see a few objects that you can add to your scene. There is a sphere, a cube, and a cylinder, from which it is easy to create a cone. There are polygon shapes. There is a camera and some lights. There is a curve and a mesh. Look in the menus and you'll find a few more. And through the tools available, you can create nearly anything you might want, so even though some other software packages have hundreds of objects to choose from, Art of Illusion doesn't feel like it is missing anything critical. All of the basic building blocks are there, but sometimes you might wish an object you use frequently was easier to create. Instead of having to find it in a file or having to recreate it, it would be nice if you could just click a button and draw it on the screen. That's exactly what we're going to do.

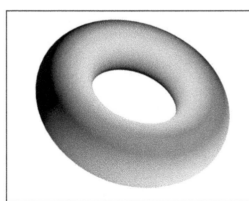

Figure 6-1: A Torus

One of the basic objects that Art of Illusion doesn't handle easily is the *torus*. To create one, you can either use the torus option in the mesh tool or you can use the lathe tool which can also create a torus. But in this chapter we're going to look at what it takes to create one for the tool palette. Our purpose in doing so is twofold. One thing it will do is demonstrate how to add buttons to the tool palette. The other thing it will do is demonstrate how to create Art of Illusion objects. The torus isn't very complex, but if you understand what it takes to draw a torus then you will be able to create other objects as well.

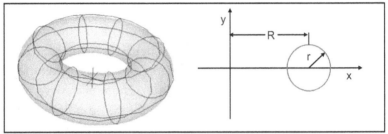

Figure 6-2: A Torus

The Structure of a Torus

Let's look at what a torus is. As Figure 6-2 shows, a torus is an object that is defined by a major radius, R, and a minor radius, r. It is a surface of rotation, formed by rotating the circle with radius r about the y-axis. This is why it is possible to create one with Art of Illusion out of the box with the lathe tool. The torus is represented by:

$$x = (R + r\cos\phi)\cos\theta$$
$$y = r\sin\phi$$
$$z = (R + r\cos\phi)\sin\theta$$

The angle θ represents the angle of rotation and φ represents the angle within the smaller circle.

Building an Object in Art of Illusion

Objects in Art of Illusion extend the Object3D class. The Object3D class is an abstract class that defines an object as having all the things you would expect including textures, materials, and properties. Two very important things that it defines are that an Object3D has a RenderingMesh and a WireframeMesh. These define the shape of the object that is displayed. The RenderingMesh defines the shape that is displayed when the scene is rendered. The WireframeMesh defines the shape that is displayed in viewports in wireframe mode. The WireframeMesh is also used in other modes when a RenderingMesh isn't available.

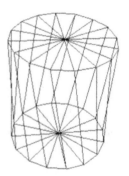 

Figure 6-3: WireframeMesh and RenderingMesh

With some objects, a RenderingMesh doesn't make sense, such as with the cameras and the lights, which must be visible for us to position them in the scene, but we don't want them in the final scene. We will look at an object that has only a WireframeMesh later, but for the torus we need both the WireframeMesh and the RendingMesh.

One of the differences between a WireframeMesh and a RenderingMesh is that the WireframeMesh is usually a simplified version of the object. When you look at Figure 6-3, you can see that while there are triangles forming the top of the wireframe, the sides are angled with no perpendicular lines. A WireframeMesh is literally a line drawing. A RenderingMesh is a collection of triangles.

Drawing a Square

Before we look at the details of creating the meshes for the torus, let's look at one of the most simple objects, the square. For the purposes of this example, the square will lie on the y=0 plane. It is also centered on the origin, which is where we typically want to draw the objects we create.

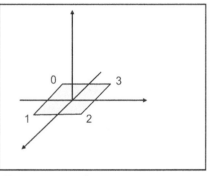

Figure 6-4: A Square

WireframeMesh

The WireframeMesh takes as inputs to its constructor three arrays. The first, *vert*, is a Vec3 array that holds the set of vertices. The second is the *from* array, which holds an int that represents the starting vertex of a line. The last is the *to* array. It holds an int that represents the ending vertex of a line.

For the square in Figure 6-4, the *vert* array would be the following:

```
vert[0] = new Vec3(-0.5, 0.0, -0.5);
vert[1] = new Vec3(-0.5, 0.0, 0.5);
vert[2] = new Vec3(0.5, 0.0, 0.5);
vert[3] = new Vec3(0.5, 0.0, -0.5);
```

This code defines the locations of each of the three vertices, but nothing will be drawn without the values of the other arrays defined. You may find it easier to think of the to/from arrays as being together.

```
from[0] = 0;  to[0] = 1;
from[1] = 1;  to[1] = 2;
from[2] = 2;  to[2] = 3;
from[3] = 3;  to[3] = 0;
```

Figure 6-5: Wireframe Drawing

This code defines a wireframe that draws in the order shown in Figure 6-5. It touches each vertex in turn and then returns to the beginning. But order is not required, as long as the lines you need are drawn.

RenderingMesh

The RenderingMesh is more involved than the WireframeMesh, but it is a similar concept. The RenderingMesh is made up of triangles. For the torus, we're able to take a shortcut because of this and use the function that creates the TriangleMesh for both the TriangleMesh and the RenderingMesh, but you can also create the RenderingMesh separately from the TriangleMesh, which will give you more flexibility in how you render the object.

The constructor of the RenderingMesh takes three arrays, a TextureMapping, and a MaterialMapping. The last two are classes with interfaces that are used to define how the texture and the material map to the RenderingMesh triangles. Given a set of vertices and normal the TextureMapping will return a RenderingTriangle to be rendered to the scene. Given a point inside an object, the MaterialMapping will return the material properties. Nether of these have anything to do with defining the shape of the object and unless we need to handle the texture or material in a special way, the parent class default handling is sufficient.

The arrays have more importance at this point. The third array, *triangle*, is an array of RenderingTriangles. Each RenderingTriangle is made up of three vertices and three normals. The three vertices are three numbers referring to indexes of the first array, *vert*, having type Vec3. The normals are three numbers referring to indexes of the second array, norm, having type Vec3.

Figure 6-6 shows the square as it is formed by two triangles. The vert array can be the same values as before because the location of the four vertices are the same here as for the WireframeMesh.

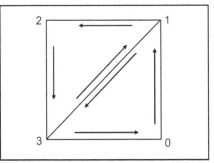

Figure 6-6: RenderingMesh

```
vert[0] = new Vec3(-0.5, 0.0, -0.5);
vert[1] = new Vec3(-0.5, 0.0, 0.5);
vert[2] = new Vec3(0.5, 0.0, 0.5);
vert[3] = new Vec3(0.5, 0.0, -0.5);
```

A normal is a vector that is perpendicular to the surface being modeled. In Figure 6-7, there are four normals pointing straight up from each of the corners of the square, one normal per vertex. Each normal having the value (0.0, 1.0, 0.0) would be sufficient. Some vertices may require multiple normals. If you are wondering why there are so many when they all have the same value, the normals are used in the shading algo-

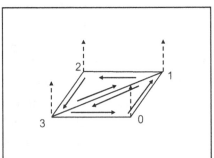

Figure 6-7: Normals

rithms. For this simple square, the whole thing will be shaded as a flat surface, but if these triangles represented the surface of a curved object, such as a sphere or a torus, they would not be perpendicular to the triangle but to the curve that the triangle approximates. Using a weighted average based on the three normals of a RenderingTriangle and the location, the normal at any location on the triangle can be calculated and the object can be shaded accordingly. The result is that the object looks smooth, rather than being a bunch of triangles.

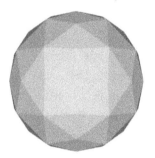 

Figure 6-8: The Effect of Normals

This is demonstrated in Figure 6-8. The first image is how TriangleMesh looks when only one normal is used per triangle. The image on the right is the same TriangleMesh but with the normals at each vertex being perpendicular to the sphere rather than the triangle.

For our square, we really can get by with one normal:

```
norm[0] = new Vec3(0.0, 1.0, 0.0);
```

But for an object like the torus, or even a simple cube, we would need more than that.

The array of triangles is then defined as the following, moving counter clockwise around the triangle:

```
Triangle[0] =
    new RenderingTriangle(0,1,3,0,0,0);
Triangle[1] =
    new RenderingTriangle(3,1,2,0,0,0);
```

Drawing a Torus

Many of the same principles apply to drawing a torus that apply in drawing a square, but there is much more to calculate. As with the square, the calculation used to determine the location of the vertices can be the same, though we may need fewer vertices for the wireframe than for the RenderingMesh.

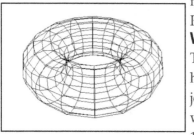

Figure 6-9: Torus Wireframe

WireframeMesh

The wireframe in Figure 6-9 has the appearance of an object made up of 16 wedges, with each wedge formed by 16 rectangles. In the code, the number 16 is represented by the constant SEGMENTS. There are an equal number of vertices to the number of rectangle sections, so the size of the *verts* array is SEGMENTS*SEGMENTS or 256. We must connect four lines to each vertex. To do that, we draw a line from a vertex to a neighboring vertex to the side and the vertex ahead. So the size of both the *from* array and the *to* array is 2*SEGMENTS*SEGMENTS.

RenderingMesh

To get the RenderingMesh for the torus, we first create a TriangleMesh then call getRenderingMesh. This reduces our work because we need the TriangleMesh anyway and the normals produced for the TriangleMesh are sufficient for the rendering mesh.

The TriangleMesh is similar to the WireframeMesh, but it is made up of vertices and faces. A face is a triangle that is drawn in counterclockwise order. The drawing order is important because that determines which side of the face it the front and which is the back. Both triangles in Figure 6-6 have their front toward the reader.

Each face uses three ints to specify which three vertices are the corners of the triangle. The numbers are indexes in the *vert* array. There are 2*segments*segments faces in a torus, but we can't assume that is 512 faces. When creating a TriangleMesh we must use a tolerance. No portion of a triangle can be more than the tolerance away from the real object the mesh approximates.

Figure 6-10 illustrates this. Suppose the arc is the ideal shape we wish to model. We place vertices along the curve and we connect them with straight lines. At the midpoint of the line, the distance from the object we are modeling could be significant. The tolerance defined in Art of Illusion specifies how far that midpoint can be off. With a lower tolerance, the numbers of ver-

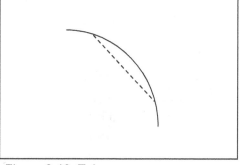

Figure 6-10: Tolerance

tices must increase so that distance is smaller. With a larger tolerance, we can place the vertices farther apart. It is up to the user to decide how much error he is willing to accept. For the torus, we use a very low tolerance for the RenderingMesh, so the torus has a nice smooth surface.

Drawing an Object with the Mouse

When you've used Art of Illusion, you may not have given it much thought how the tool translates a click and drag into an object. You may have selected a cube, clicked the screen, dragged the handles to the right size and there was the cube. A user of a tool like Art of Illusion shouldn't have to worry about what magic goes on behind the scenes. For that matter, it shouldn't seem like magic at all. It should seem so natural that the user can't think what else might happen when he drags the mouse across the screen.

But since we're creating a custom object, we don't have the luxury of naiveté. When the user drags the mouse across the screen, Art of Illusion will give us the 2D coordinates, but it is up to us to write the code that translates that action into a 3D object. On the mouseDragged event, Art of Illusion will give us the xSize and the ySize. These we pass into the Object3D defined setSize method along with some value for the zSize. Depending on the object, this may be the same value as xSize, ySize, or a combination of the two. From those inputs, we must set the internal member variables to create an object of the correct size.

Let's look at a bad example first. The size of the torus is defined by the size of the majorRadius and the minorRadius. Suppose we used the xSize, which is the distance the user dragged the mouse from left to right to set the majorRadius and the ySize to set the minorRadius. That would give us an object twice the thickness that we wanted.

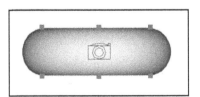 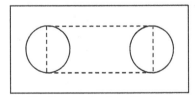

Figure 6-11: xSize and ySize set majorRadius and minorRadius

Knowing that we need the radius instead of the diameter, we might decide to divide by two. That would give us the object in Figure 6-11. The handles look partly correct, but the object is still wider than the handles. Given our understanding of what a torus is, this makes sense, but it doesn't make sense from a user interface standpoint. When dragging the handles of an object, we always want the handles to be at the edge of the object, not somewhere in the middle. When they are on the edge, we can drag them to where we want the object to end up.

For the torus, that means a little extra work. The ySize handling is fine with the minorRadius being set to ySize/2.0, because the height of the object is always minorRadius*2.0. To get the majorRadius correct, we need it to be (xSize+ySize)/2.0, because the majorRadius goes to the center of the ring. This will give us what we see in Figure 6-12.

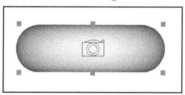 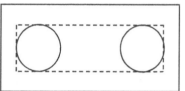

Figure 6-12: xSize and ySize set majorRadius and minorRadius

Create the Project

For the past several chapters, when we looked at what we needed to do to create the project, there were very few changes from the previous projects. In this chapter, that is not the case.

Just looking at the project in Figure 6-13, you can see that there are more files than we've seen before. *TorusPluging.java* and *extensions.xml* look familiar, but the others are different. There are even a couple of graphics files in there and strangely enough, they have the same name, though they are in separate packages.

Extensions.xml

The *extensions.xml* file is still a good place to start because it provides us with a quick view of the project. This time there is something new. I have highlighted it in bold so you won't miss

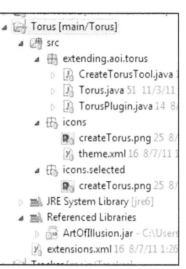

Figure 6-13: Torus Project

it. The resource tag is used to specify where to find the information Art of Illusion needs when it draws the icon on the tool palette. The name is given as "icons/theme.xml" which you can see is one of the files in the project.

```xml
<?xml version="1.0" standalone="yes"?>

<extension name="Torus" version="0.1" >
  <author>Timothy Fish</author>
  <date>July 2011</date>

  <plugin class="extending.aoi.torus.TorusPlugin" />

  <description>This plugin will allow the user to create a
torus from the Tool Palette.</description>
  <resource name="icons/theme.xml" id="Torus"
type="UITheme"/>
  <comments>This project is to demonstrate adding items to
the tool palette, as well as saving object to the the .AOL
file.</comments>

  <history>
    <log version="0.1" date="July 2011" author="Timothy
Fish" >- Initial Version</log>
  </history>
</extension>
```

Example 6-1: extensions.xml

Theme.xml

This file defines a theme named Torus. By saying that it isn't selectable, it won't show up in the Art of Illusion preferences window, but we will still be able to use it. The name is passed into initButton in the Cre-

```
<?xml version="1.0" standalone="yes"?>
<theme>
  <name>Torus</name>
  <selectable>false</selectable>
</theme>
```

Example 6-2: theme.xml

ateTorusTool class, along with the name of the image file.

createTorus.png

There are two image files in the project, both with the name "createTorus.png." One is located in icons along with *theme.xml* and the other is located in icons.selected. Essentially, both are part of the Torus theme because of the *theme.xml* defining that theme is within the icons area. The png file in the icons area is the default icon for the torus button. The image file in icons.selected is also in the theme and in the icons area, but within a specialized area. That image file will only be used if the button is in the selected state. In the workspace directory structure, that is how they appear.

Figure 6-13: createTorus.png files

The easiest way to create these icons is to render the object you are creating, size it to fit the 32 pixel square icon and overlay the rendered image on the blank. If you are creating an object, you should use blue. For changing the shape of an object, you should use green. Lights are yellow. Cameras and camera movement are brown, with the camera movement icons also having an eye in the background.

If you download the source code for Art of Illusion, the blanks are located in ArtofIllusion.Icons and ArtofIllusion.Icons.Selected. They have the name

```java
/**
 * Torus Plugin
 */
package extending.aoi.torus;

import artofillusion.LayoutWindow;
import artofillusion.Plugin;
import artofillusion.ui.ToolPalette;

/**
 * @author Timothy Fish
 *
 */
public class TorusPlugin implements Plugin {

    private LayoutWindow layout;
    private ToolPalette toolPalette;
    private CreateTorusTool theTorusTool;

    public TorusPlugin(){
        layout = null;
        toolPalette = null;
        theTorusTool = null;
    }
    /**
     * Entry point for the plugin.
     */
    @Override
    public void processMessage(int message, Object[] args) {
        switch (message) {
        case Plugin.SCENE_WINDOW_CREATED:
            // Do initialization first.
            layout = (LayoutWindow) args[0];
            toolPalette = layout.getToolPalette();
            theTorusTool = new CreateTorusTool(layout);

            // Add the Torus button to the Tool Palette
            toolPalette.addTool(theTorusTool);

            break;
        }
    }
}
```

Example 6-3: TorusPlugin.java

buttonBackground.png. As the name implies, these are the same backgrounds that are used with the standard buttons, with no images overlaid. If you use these, then your buttons will look the same as the standard buttons.

TorusPlugin Class

For this plugin all the processMessage method needs to do is to instantiate the tool and add it to the tool palette. To do this we call getToolPalette to get the palette from the layout window. The constructor for the CreateTorusTool class is called to create an instance of the tool. It is then passed into addTool, a member method of ToolPalette. ToolPalette does what is needed to retrieve the necessary data from the tool to place a button on the palette. If it is unable to find the icon, it will place a default button on the palette. The ToolPalette also handles the call to Create-TorusTool when the user clicks the button.

CreateTorusTool Class

CreateTorusTool extends the EditingTool class. When the user clicks the button on the tool palette, the activate method is called. This method is the place to set the help text that appears at the bottom of the layout window. The whichClicks method returns which clicks the tool should handle. For the torus, we want to handle ALL_CLICKS. Other possible values are OBJECT_CLICKS and HANDLE_CLICKS. We also want a tool tip, so we have getToolTipText return a string when it is called.

The other methods are for mouse handling. The longest of these is the mouseDragged method, which implements what was explained previously. If the object is null, it will create one. Otherwise, dragging the mouse will resize the object.

When we create an object we must also setup things like the PositionTrack and the RotationTrack for animation. We call addTrack for the ObjectInfo, a class that holds the object and provides information that the object does not have internally.

The location of the mouse on the screen is very different than the indicated point in the scene. Differences in the amount we have zoomed in on an object can cause differences between the value retrieved from the mouse and the value in the world. To resolve this problem, we must map the mouse coordinates to the world of the scene. This is done with the method convertScreenToWorld. This is a member of the camera used for the viewport. Once this conversion is done, the sizes can be passed into setSize and the object will increase or decrease in size to match.

```java
/**
 *
 */
package extending.aoi.torus;

import java.awt.Point;

import artofillusion.Camera;
import artofillusion.LayoutWindow;
import artofillusion.Scene;
import artofillusion.UndoRecord;
import artofillusion.ViewerCanvas;
import artofillusion.animation.PositionTrack;
import artofillusion.animation.RotationTrack;
import artofillusion.math.CoordinateSystem;
import artofillusion.math.Vec3;
import artofillusion.object.ObjectInfo;
import artofillusion.ui.EditingTool;
import artofillusion.ui.EditingWindow;
import artofillusion.ui.Translate;
import buoy.event.WidgetMouseEvent;

/**
 * @author Timothy Fish
 *
 */
public class CreateTorusTool extends EditingTool {
  private static final double majorRadius = 2;
```

Example 6-4a: CreateTorusTool.java

```
  private static final double minorRadius = 0.5;
  static int counter = 1;
  private Point clickPoint;
  private ObjectInfo objInfo;

  /**
   * @param win
   */
  public CreateTorusTool(EditingWindow win) {
    super(win);

    // Name is the icon name without an extension.
    // extensions.xml defines the theme.xml file and the
    // theme.xml file defines the Torus theme
    // which contains the createTorus button.
    initButton("Torus:createTorus");

  }

  public void activate()
  {
    super.activate();
    theWindow.setHelpText(Translate.text("Create Torus:
Width controls radius and height controls thickness."));
  }

  public int whichClicks()
  {
    return ALL_CLICKS;
  }

  public String getToolTipText()
  {
    return Translate.text("Create Torus");
  }

  public void mousePressed(WidgetMouseEvent e,
                           ViewerCanvas view)
  {
    clickPoint = e.getPoint();
  }

  public void mouseDragged(WidgetMouseEvent e,
                           ViewerCanvas view)
  {
    if (objInfo == null)
    {
      // Create the torus.

      Scene theScene = ((LayoutWindow)theWindow).getScene();
      objInfo = new ObjectInfo(new Torus(majorRadius,
                                         minorRadius),
                               new CoordinateSystem(),
                               "Torus "+counter);
      counter++;
      objInfo.addTrack(new PositionTrack(objInfo), 0);
```

Example 6-4b: CreateTorusTool.java

```
        objInfo.addTrack(new RotationTrack(objInfo), 1);
        UndoRecord undo = new UndoRecord(theWindow, false);
        int sel[] = ((LayoutWindow)
                        theWindow).getSelectedIndices();
        ((LayoutWindow) theWindow).addObject(objInfo, undo);
        undo.addCommand(UndoRecord.SET_SCENE_SELECTION,
                        new Object [] {sel});
        theWindow.setUndoRecord(undo);
        ((LayoutWindow) theWindow).setSelection
                            (theScene.getNumObjects()-1);
}

// Determine the size and position for the torus.

Camera cam = view.getCamera();
Point dragPoint = e.getPoint();
Vec3 v1;
Vec3 v2;
Vec3 v3;
Vec3 orig;
Vec3 xdir;
Vec3 ydir;
Vec3 zdir;
double xsize;
double ysize;
double zsize;

v1 = cam.convertScreenToWorld(clickPoint,
                    Camera.DEFAULT_DISTANCE_TO_SCREEN);
v2 = cam.convertScreenToWorld(new Point(dragPoint.x,
        clickPoint.y), Camera.DEFAULT_DISTANCE_TO_SCREEN);
v3 = cam.convertScreenToWorld(dragPoint,
                    Camera.DEFAULT_DISTANCE_TO_SCREEN);
orig = v1.plus(v3).times(0.5);
if (dragPoint.x < clickPoint.x)
   xdir = v1.minus(v2);
else
   xdir = v2.minus(v1);
if (dragPoint.y < clickPoint.y)
   ydir = v3.minus(v2);
else
   ydir = v2.minus(v3);
xsize = xdir.length();
ysize = ydir.length();
xdir = xdir.times(1.0/xsize);
ydir = ydir.times(1.0/ysize);
zdir = xdir.cross(ydir);
zsize = Math.min(xsize, ysize);

// Update the size and position, and redraw the display.

((Torus) objInfo.getObject()).setSize(xsize,
                            ysize, zsize);
objInfo.getCoords().setOrigin(orig);
objInfo.getCoords().setOrientation(zdir, ydir);
objInfo.clearCachedMeshes();
```

Example 6-4c: CreateTorusTool.java

```
      theWindow.updateImage();
   }

   public void mouseReleased(WidgetMouseEvent e, ViewerCanvas
view)
   {
      objInfo = null;
      theWindow.setModified();
   }
}
```

Example 6-4d: CreateTorusTool.java

```
/**
 * Torus Object
 */
package extending.aoi.torus;

import java.io.DataInputStream;
import java.io.DataOutputStream;
import java.io.IOException;
import java.io.InvalidObjectException;

import artofillusion.Property;
import artofillusion.RenderingMesh;
import artofillusion.Scene;
import artofillusion.WireframeMesh;
import artofillusion.animation.Keyframe;
import artofillusion.animation.PoseTrack;
import artofillusion.math.BoundingBox;
import artofillusion.math.Vec2;
import artofillusion.math.Vec3;
import artofillusion.object.Object3D;
import artofillusion.object.ObjectInfo;
import artofillusion.object.TriangleMesh;
import artofillusion.texture.Texture;
import artofillusion.texture.TextureMapping;
import artofillusion.ui.ComponentsDialog;
import artofillusion.ui.EditingWindow;
import artofillusion.ui.Translate;
import artofillusion.ui.ValueField;
import buoy.widget.Widget;

/**
 * @author Timothy Fish
 *
```

Example 6-5a: Torus.java

```
*/
public class Torus extends Object3D {
    private static final double HALF = 0.5;
    private double majorRadius;
    private double minorRadius;

    private BoundingBox bounds;
    private RenderingMesh cachedMesh;
    private WireframeMesh cachedWire;

    private static final int SEGMENTS = 16;
    private static double sine[], cosine[];

    private static final String majorRadiusTitle = "Radius";
    private static final String minorRadiusTitle =
                                           "Thickness";
    private static final String editWindowTitle =
                                           "Edit Torus";
    // Version number of the torus object.
    static final short CURRENT_VERSION = 1;

    // Constants used instead of enum here because AOI uses
    // integer values as the index were these are used.
    private static final int enumMajorRadius = 0;
    private static final int enumMinorRadius = 1;
    private static final Property PROPERTIES[] =
                                         new Property [] {
        new Property(Translate.text(majorRadiusTitle), 0.0,
                     Double.MAX_VALUE, 1.0),
        new Property(Translate.text(minorRadiusTitle), 0.0,
                     Double.MAX_VALUE, 1.0)
    };

    /**
     * Fast sine and cosine handling for the wireframe mesh.
     */
    static
    {
        sine = new double [SEGMENTS];
        cosine = new double [SEGMENTS];
        for (int i = 0; i < SEGMENTS; i++)
        {
            sine[i] = Math.sin(i*2.0*Math.PI/SEGMENTS);
            cosine[i] = Math.cos(i*2.0*Math.PI/SEGMENTS);
        }
    }

    /**
     * Constructor
     */
    public Torus(double majorRadius, double minorRadius) {
        this.majorRadius = majorRadius;
        this.minorRadius = minorRadius;

        bounds = new BoundingBox(
                -majorRadius-minorRadius,
```

Example 6-5b: Torus.java

```
                majorRadius+minorRadius,
                -minorRadius, minorRadius,
                -majorRadius-minorRadius,
                majorRadius+minorRadius
        );
    }


    /**
     * Sets the values in this object to match those in the
     * object passed through the parameter.
     */
    @Override
    public void copyObject(Object3D obj) {
        Torus t = (Torus) obj;

        setSize(2.0*(t.majorRadius+t.minorRadius),
                2.0*t.minorRadius,
                2.0*(t.majorRadius+t.minorRadius));

        copyTextureAndMaterial(obj);
        cachedMesh = null;
        cachedWire = null;
    }

    /**
     * Returns a new object that is a duplicate of this one.
     */
    @Override
    public Object3D duplicate() {
        Torus obj = new Torus(majorRadius, minorRadius);
        obj.copyTextureAndMaterial(this);
        return obj;
    }

    /**
     * Returns the outer bounds of the object.
     */
    @Override
    public BoundingBox getBounds() {
        return bounds;
    }

    /**
     * Returns a mesh for viewing in wireframe mode or for
     * when the object won't be rendered in the scene.
     * Cameras and lights, for example, have only a
     * wireframe mesh. A Torus needs both a wireframe mesh
     * and a rendering mesh.
     */
    @Override
    public WireframeMesh getWireframeMesh() {
        final int segments = SEGMENTS;
        Vec3 vert[];
        int from[], to[];
        // if we've already created a wireframe mesh,
```

Example 6-5c: Torus.java

```
            // us that one
            if (cachedWire != null) {  return cachedWire; }

            // Wireframe meshes are made up of a set of vertices
            // with lines drawn between them. The vert array
            // stores each vertex and the from and to arrays
            // define lines to draw. The most simple being
            // the one line wireframe mesh, which would have two
            // vertices vert[0], vert[1] and from[0] == 0,
            // to[0] == 1. A triangle would have vert[0],
            // vert[1], and vert[2], with from[0] == 0, to[0] ==
            // 1, from[1] == 1, to[1] == 2, from[2] == 2, to[2]
            // == 0. They are used for wireframe displays and
            // normal displays of  hidden objects, like cameras
            // and lights.
            vert = new Vec3 [segments*segments];
            from = new int [2*segments*segments];
            to = new int [2*segments*segments];
            // create large circle
            double x;
            double y;
            double z;
            for(int majorIndex = 0; majorIndex < segments;
                                             majorIndex++){
                // create small circle
                for(int minorIndex = 0; minorIndex < segments;
                                             minorIndex++){
                    // create new vertex
                    x = (majorRadius+(minorRadius*cosine
                            [minorIndex]))*(cosine[majorIndex]);
                    y = (minorRadius*sine[minorIndex]);
                    z = (majorRadius+(minorRadius*cosine
                            [minorIndex]))*(sine[majorIndex]);

                    vert[majorIndex*segments+minorIndex] =
                                        new Vec3(x, y, z);

                    // draw small circles
                    from[majorIndex*segments+minorIndex] =
                                majorIndex*segments+minorIndex;
                    to[majorIndex*segments+minorIndex] =
                                majorIndex*segments+minorIndex+1;

                    // connect the circles
                    From[segments*segments+
                            minorIndex+segments*majorIndex] =
                            0+minorIndex+segments*majorIndex;
                    if(majorIndex < segments-1){
                        to[segments*segments+
                        minorIndex+segments*majorIndex] =
                            segments+minorIndex+
                            segments*majorIndex;
                    }
                    else{
                        to[segments*segments+
                        minorIndex+segments*majorIndex] =
```

Example 6-5d: Torus.java

```
                                        minorIndex;
            }
        }
        // link back to the first one
        to[majorIndex*segments+segments-1] =
                            majorIndex*segments+0;
    }

    return (cachedWire = new WireframeMesh(vert,
                                    from, to));
}

/**
 * Sets the size of the object such that the bounding
 * box matches the sizes when this function returns.
 */
@Override
public void setSize(double xsize, double ysize,
                    double zsize) {
    minorRadius = ysize/2.0;
    majorRadius = xsize/2.0 - minorRadius;

    bounds = new BoundingBox(
            -majorRadius-minorRadius,
            majorRadius+minorRadius,
            -minorRadius, minorRadius,
            -majorRadius-minorRadius,
            majorRadius+minorRadius
    );

    cachedMesh = null;
    cachedWire = null;
}

/**
 * Returns the ability for the object to convert the
 * internal representation of the object to a triangle
 * mesh. In this case it is APPROXIMATELY because the
 * internal representation is the radius of two circles.
 */
public int canConvertToTriangleMesh()
{
    return APPROXIMATELY;
}

/**
 * Return a TriangleMesh which reproduces the shape of
 * this object. This method returns a TriangleMesh which
 * reproduces the object to within the specified
 * tolerance. That is, no point on the mesh is further
 * than tol from the corresponding point on the original
 * surface.
 */
public TriangleMesh convertToTriangleMesh(double tol)
{
    Vec3 vertices[];
```

Example 6-5e: Torus.java

```
TriangleMesh mesh;
int faces[][];

final int segments = findSegmentCount(tol);
final int numberOfVertices = segments*segments;

// Find the list of faces.
vertices = new Vec3[numberOfVertices];
faces = new int [2 * numberOfVertices][];

// Each face is an array of 3 vertex numbers in
// counter-clockwise order when viewed from the
// outside.

double x;
double y;
double z;
int faceCount = 0;
// large circle
for(int majorIndex = 0; majorIndex < segments;
                                    majorIndex++){
    double majorTheta =
                (2*Math.PI*majorIndex)/segments;
    // small circle
    for(int minorIndex = 0; minorIndex < segments;
                                    minorIndex++){

        double minorTheta =
                (2*Math.PI*minorIndex)/segments;
        // create new vertex
        x = (majorRadius+
            (minorRadius*Math.cos(minorTheta)))*
            (Math.cos(majorTheta));
        y = (minorRadius*Math.sin(minorTheta));
        z = (majorRadius+
            (minorRadius*Math.cos(minorTheta)))*
            (Math.sin(majorTheta));

        int v0 = majorIndex*segments+minorIndex;
        vertices[v0] = new Vec3(x, y, z);
        int v1;
        int v2;

        // for each vertex define two faces

        // first face
        if(minorIndex+1 < segments){
            v1 = v0 + 1;
        }
        else{
            v1 = v0 - (segments-1);
        }
        v2 = v0 + segments;
        if(v2 >= numberOfVertices){
            v2 -= numberOfVertices;
```

Example 6-5f: Torus.java

```
            }

            faces[faceCount] = new int[3];
            faces[faceCount][0] = v0;
            faces[faceCount][1] = v1;
            faces[faceCount][2] = v2;
            faceCount++;

            // second face
            v2 = v1;
            v1 = v2 - segments;
            if(v1 < 0){
                v1 += numberOfVertices;
            }

            faces[faceCount] = new int[3];
            faces[faceCount][0] = v0;
            faces[faceCount][1] = v1;
            faces[faceCount][2] = v2;
            faceCount++;

        }
    }

    mesh = new TriangleMesh(vertices, faces);
    mesh.copyTextureAndMaterial(this);
    return mesh;
}

/**
 * Finds a number of segments that will give us a
 * TriangleMesh that has no vertex that is greater than
 * tol away from the ideal point location.
 * @param tol
 * @return
 */
private int findSegmentCount(double tol) {
    // Note that the greatest deviations from the
    // tolerance will be at the mid-point of a line
    // between two points drawn on the largest circle in
    // the torus, so we need only to find a number of
    // segments that will keep the points on the outside
    // close enough that their mid-point will be within
    // the tolerance.

    double radius = majorRadius+minorRadius;
    // The first point is on the x axis, at the farthest
    // point.
    Vec2 p0 = new Vec2(radius, 0);
    Vec2 p1 = new Vec2();
    Vec2 pM = new Vec2(); // mid-point of p0 and p1
    Vec2 pC = new Vec2(); // point on circle nearest pM
    int segs = 3 - 1; // number of segments, 3 so that
                      // torus never flat
    double distanceFromCircle;
```

Example 6-5g: Torus.java

175

```
        // Calculate new p1 and segs until
        // distanceFromCircle <= tol
        do{
            segs++;
            double theta = 2*Math.PI/segs;
            double halfTheta = theta/2;

            p1.set(Math.cos(theta)*radius,
                    Math.sin(theta)*radius);
            pM = p1.plus(p0).times(HALF);
            pC.set(Math.cos(halfTheta)*radius,
                    Math.sin(halfTheta)*radius);
            distanceFromCircle = pM.distance(pC);
        }while(distanceFromCircle > tol);

        return segs*3; // multiply by 3 because default tol
                        // doesn't give us a smooth curve
    }

    /**
     * Creates and returns the mesh that is displayed during
     * normal editing or when the scene is rendered.
     */
    public RenderingMesh getRenderingMesh(double tol,
                    boolean interactive, ObjectInfo info)
    {

        if (interactive && cachedMesh != null)
            return cachedMesh;

        RenderingMesh mesh = convertToTriangleMesh
            (tol).getRenderingMesh(tol, interactive, info);
        if (interactive)
            cachedMesh = mesh;

        return mesh;
    }

    /**
     * Sets the texture for the object.
     */
    public void setTexture(Texture tex,
                    TextureMapping mapping)
    {
        super.setTexture(tex, mapping);
        cachedMesh = null;
        cachedWire = null;
    }

    /**
     * Tells the system if the object can be edited or not.
     */
    public boolean isEditable()
    {
        return true;
    }
```

Example 6-5h: Torus.java

```
/**
 * Defines the edit window for editing the object.
 */
public void edit(EditingWindow parent, ObjectInfo info,
                 Runnable callback)
{

    ValueField xField =
     new ValueField(majorRadius,ValueField.POSITIVE, 5);
    ValueField yField =
     new ValueField(minorRadius,ValueField.POSITIVE, 5);

    ComponentsDialog dlg =
      new ComponentsDialog(parent.getFrame(),
        Translate.text(editWindowTitle),
        new Widget [] {xField, yField},
        new String [] {Translate.text(majorRadiusTitle),
                    Translate.text(minorRadiusTitle)});
    if (!dlg.clickedOk())
        return;

    setSize(2.0*xField.getValue()+2.0*yField.getValue(),
            2.0*yField.getValue(),
            2.0*xField.getValue()+2.0*yField.getValue());
    callback.run();
}


/**
 * The following two methods are used for reading and
 * writing files.  The first is a constructor which
 * reads the necessary data from an input stream. The
 * other writes the object's representation to an output
 * stream.
 */

public Torus(DataInputStream in, Scene theScene)
             throws IOException, InvalidObjectException
{
    super(in, theScene);

    short version = in.readShort();
    if (version != CURRENT_VERSION){
        throw new InvalidObjectException(
                  "Torus data is version "+version+
                  " not "+CURRENT_VERSION+".");
    }
    majorRadius = in.readDouble();
    minorRadius = in.readDouble();
    bounds = new BoundingBox(
            -(majorRadius+minorRadius),
            (majorRadius+minorRadius),
            -minorRadius, minorRadius,
            -(majorRadius+minorRadius),
            (majorRadius+minorRadius));
}
```

Example 6-5i: Torus.java

```java
/**
 * Writes the Torus data to the file.
 */
public void writeToFile(DataOutputStream out,
                        Scene theScene) throws IOException
{
    super.writeToFile(out, theScene);

    out.writeShort(CURRENT_VERSION);
    out.writeDouble(majorRadius);
    out.writeDouble(minorRadius);
}

/**
 * Returns the properties of this object.
 */
public Property[] getProperties()
{
    return (Property []) PROPERTIES.clone();
}

/**
 * Upon request from the user interface, returns the
 * property specified by the index value.
 */
public Object getPropertyValue(int index)
{
    switch (index)
    {
    case enumMajorRadius:
        return new Double(majorRadius);
    case enumMinorRadius:
        return new Double(minorRadius);
    }
    return null;
}

/**
 * Sets the property value that the used has entered
 * into the property window on the lower right-hand side
 * (default) of the screen.
 */
public void setPropertyValue(int index, Object value)
{
    double val = ((Double) value).doubleValue();
    if (index == enumMajorRadius){
        setSize(2.0*(val+minorRadius), 2.0*minorRadius,
                2.0*(val+minorRadius));
    }
    else if (index == enumMinorRadius){
        setSize(2.0*(majorRadius+val), 2.0*val,
                2.0*(majorRadius+val));
    }
}
```

Example 6-5h: Torus.java

```
/** Return a Keyframe which describes the current pose
 * of this object.
 */

public Keyframe getPoseKeyframe()
{
    return new TorusKeyframe(majorRadius, minorRadius);
}

/** Modify this object based on a pose keyframe. */

public void applyPoseKeyframe(Keyframe k)
{
    TorusKeyframe key = (TorusKeyframe) k;

    setSize(2.0*(key.majorRadius+key.minorRadius),
            2.0*key.minorRadius,
            2.0*(key.majorRadius+key.minorRadius));
}

/** This will be called whenever a new pose track is
 * created for this object.  It allows the object to
 * configure the track by setting its graphable values,
 * subtracks, etc.
 */

public void configurePoseTrack(PoseTrack track)
{
    track.setGraphableValues(new String []
                {majorRadiusTitle, minorRadiusTitle},
            new double [] {2.0*majorRadius,
                           2.0*minorRadius},
            new double [][] {{0.0, Double.MAX_VALUE},
                             {0.0, Double.MAX_VALUE}});
}

/** Return an array containing the names of the
 * graphable values for the keyframes returned by
 * getPoseKeyframe().
 */

public String [] getPoseValueNames()
{
    return new String [] {majorRadiusTitle,
                          minorRadiusTitle};
}

/** Get the default list of graphable values for a
 * keyframe returned by getPoseKeyframe().
 */

public double [] getDefaultPoseValues()
{
    return new double [] {2.0*majorRadius,
                          2.0*minorRadius};
}
```

Example 6-5i: Torus.java

```
/** Get the allowed range for graphable values for
 * keyframes returned by getPoseKeyframe().
 * This returns a 2D array, where elements [n][0] and
 * [n][1] are the minimum and maximum allowed values,
 * respectively, for the nth graphable value.
 */

public double[][] getPoseValueRange()
{
    return new double [][] {{0.0, Double.MAX_VALUE},
                            {0.0, Double.MAX_VALUE}};
}

/** Allow the user to edit a keyframe returned by
 * getPoseKeyframe(). */

public void editKeyframe(EditingWindow parent,
                         Keyframe k,
                         ObjectInfo info)
{
    TorusKeyframe key = (TorusKeyframe) k;
    ValueField xField = new ValueField
            (2.0*key.majorRadius, ValueField.POSITIVE, 5);
    ValueField yField = new ValueField
            (2.0*key.minorRadius, ValueField.POSITIVE, 5);

    ComponentsDialog dlg = new ComponentsDialog(
            parent.getFrame(),
            Translate.text(editWindowTitle),
            new Widget [] {xField, yField},
            new String [] {Translate.text
                                    (majorRadiusTitle),
            Translate.text(minorRadiusTitle)});
    if (!dlg.clickedOk())
        return;
    key.majorRadius = 0.5*xField.getValue();
    key.minorRadius = 0.5*yField.getValue();
}

/** Inner class representing a pose for a torus. */

public static class TorusKeyframe implements Keyframe
{
    public double majorRadius;
    public double minorRadius;

    public TorusKeyframe(double majorRadius,
                         double minorRadius)
    {
        this.majorRadius = majorRadius;
        this.minorRadius = minorRadius;
    }

    /** Create a duplicate of this keyframe. */
    public Keyframe duplicate()
```

Example 6-5j: Torus.java

```
    {
        return new TorusKeyframe(majorRadius,
                                 minorRadius);
    }

    /** Create a duplicate of this keyframe for a
     * (possibly different) object.
     */

    public Keyframe duplicate(Object owner)
    {
        return new TorusKeyframe(majorRadius,
                                 minorRadius);
    }

    /** Get the list of graphable values for this
     * keyframe.
     */

    public double [] getGraphValues()
    {
        return new double [] {majorRadius, minorRadius};
    }

    /** Set the list of graphable values for this
     * keyframe.
     */

    public void setGraphValues(double values[])
    {
        majorRadius = values[enumMajorRadius];
        minorRadius = values[enumMinorRadius];
    }

    /** These methods return a new Keyframe which is a
     *   weighted average of this one and one,
     *   two, or three others.
     */
    public Keyframe blend(Keyframe o2, double weight1,
                                      double weight2)
    {
        TorusKeyframe k2 = (TorusKeyframe) o2;

        return new TorusKeyframe(
            weight1*majorRadius+weight2*k2.majorRadius,
            weight1*minorRadius+weight2*k2.minorRadius);
    }

    /** These methods return a new Keyframe which is a
     * weighted average of this one and one, two, or
     * three others.
     */
    public Keyframe blend(Keyframe o2, Keyframe o3,
        double weight1, double weight2, double weight3)
    {
        TorusKeyframe k2 = (TorusKeyframe) o2;
```

Example 6-5k: Torus.java

181

```java
        TorusKeyframe k3 = (TorusKeyframe) o3;

        return new TorusKeyframe(
            weight1*majorRadius+weight2*k2.majorRadius+
            weight3*k3.majorRadius,
            weight1*minorRadius+weight2*k2.minorRadius+
            weight3*k3.minorRadius);
    }

    /** These methods return a new Keyframe which is a
     * weighted average of this one and one, two, or
     * three others.
     */
    public Keyframe blend(Keyframe o2, Keyframe o3,
                          Keyframe o4, double weight1,
                          double weight2, double weight3,
                          double weight4)
    {
        TorusKeyframe k2 = (TorusKeyframe) o2;
        TorusKeyframe k3 = (TorusKeyframe) o3;
        TorusKeyframe k4 = (TorusKeyframe) o4;

        return new TorusKeyframe(
           weight1*majorRadius+weight2*k2.majorRadius+
           weight3*k3.majorRadius+weight4*k4.majorRadius,
           weight1*minorRadius+weight2*k2.minorRadius+
           weight3*k3.minorRadius+weight4*k4.minorRadius
        );
    }

    /** Determine whether this keyframe is identical to
     * another one.
     */
    public boolean equals(Keyframe k)
    {
        if (!(k instanceof TorusKeyframe))
            return false;
        TorusKeyframe key = (TorusKeyframe) k;
        return (key.majorRadius == majorRadius &&
                key.minorRadius == minorRadius);
    }

    /** Write out a representation of this keyframe to a
     * stream.
     */
    public void writeToStream(DataOutputStream out)
                                    throws IOException
    {
        out.writeDouble(majorRadius);
        out.writeDouble(minorRadius);
        out.writeShort(CURRENT_VERSION);
    }

    /** Reconstructs the keyframe from its serialized
     * representation.
     */
```

Example 6-5l: Torus.java

```
public TorusKeyframe(DataInputStream in,
                Object parent) throws IOException
{
    this(in.readDouble(), in.readDouble());

    short version = in.readShort();
    if (version != CURRENT_VERSION){
        throw new InvalidObjectException(
                "Torus keyframe data is version "
                +version+" not "
                +CURRENT_VERSION+".");
    }
    }
    }
}
```

Example 6-5m: Torus.java

Chapter 7

Tracking Movement

Suppose you create a scene in Art of Illusion and in that scene there is a character whose eyes you want to always look at one thing. It might be the camera. You want it to always appear he is making eye contact with the person looking at the image. Or maybe it is a cat watching a ball. You want the cat's eyes on the ball, no matter where the ball might go.

Straight out of the box with Art of Illusion the way you would do that is to rotate the object at various keyframes so that they are tracking the object. With the PointAt plugin we saw earlier, your work is reduced, but you still have to use several keyframes. In this chapter, we're going combine the concept of the PointAt plugin with what we learned in the last chapter and in order to create an object that will track the movement of another object.

Figure 7-1 is a sequence of images that were generated after changing only the location of the white

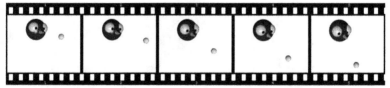

Figure 7-1: A head and eyes tracking a sphere's movement

sphere. It may be difficult to fully appreciate, since it is shown to you on the pages of a book, but because both the head and the eyes are tracking the target, only one change is needed and everything else points where it should. You may have seen similar features in other 3D products.

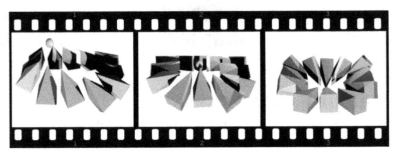

Figure 7-2: Several pointers all tracking one object.

You may be able to tell more from Figure 7-2. As we move the sphere through the scene, The objects that are tracking it update in real-time. Here, there are several pointers and a light that are tracking the object.

The Tracker object is a variation on Art of Illusion's Null object. The primary purpose of the Null object is to provide the means to set an arbitrary origin for an object or a group of objects. One reason we might want something like that is for a hinged box, as shown in Figure 7-3, or perhaps a door or window that swings on one side. By placing the Null

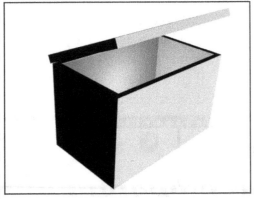

Figure 7-3: A Hinged Box

object where the hinge should be and rotating the Null object, the lid of the box stays were we want it, even as the lid swings open.

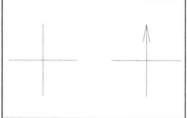

Figure 7-4: Null and Tracker

The Tracker object builds on that concept, but rather than our needing to drag the handles of the tracker to get it to rotate, the object will rotate in response to the movement of the object it is tracking. Using the same concept as is described in this chapter, there is a potential to create a whole family of objects that respond to each other. For example, instead of just tracking an object by pointing, a Gear object could be implemented that rotates at some ratio of the rotation of another gear. It would then be easy to animate a set of gears so that all turn at the correct speed when we rotate the drive gear, instead of having to rotate each gear independently.

I'll leave that to you to implement. For now, let's turn our attention back to the Tracker object. Like the Null object, the Tracker object is invisible, but it has a wireframe drawing to show us where it is in the scene. Figure 7-4 shows the Null object next to the Tracker object. When the tracker has a target defined, the arrow will always point in the direction of the target.

Most of the files (Figure 7-5) are familiar to you in terms of what they do because they are built on concepts that were introduced in previous chapters. You should have

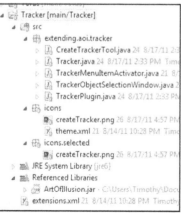

Figure 7-5: Tracker Project

no trouble gleaning the details from the source code listing. The one area that needs special attention is that of the object tracking the other object.

You are already familiar with what is required to rotate the object to point at another object. This was covered with the PointAt plugin, but that was done only when the user selects the menu item. In this plugin, the rotation takes place when the user moves the target object.

The thing you've seen before that is the most similar to what is done to accomplish this is the menu item activators that have been used for several of the plugins in this book. The Tracker object has a member class that extends the Thread class. When the command comes in to track an object, the Tracker creates an instance of the TrackerThread and tells it to run. After that, the TrackerThread attempts to update the direction of the Tracker at a rate of 60 Hertz. This is the refresh rate of many computer screens, so you will not notice any delay between when you move the object and when the tracker updates.

The icons for this plugin are shown in Figure 7-6. The image is a representation of the axes, since that is also how the wireframe looks for the object.

The next several pages show the source code for the plugin.

Figure 7-6: createTracker.png files

```
<?xml version="1.0" standalone="yes"?>

<extension name="Tracker" version="0.1" >
  <author>Timothy Fish</author>
  <date>August 2011</date>

  <plugin class="extending.aoi.tracker.TrackerPlugin" />

  <description>This plugin creates a special null object
that will track the movements of another object.</
description>
  <resource name="icons/theme.xml" id="Tracker"
type="UITheme"/>
  <comments>This project is to demonstrate adding items to
the tool palette, as well as saving object to the the .AOL
file.</comments>

  <history>
     <log version="0.1" date="August 2011" author="Timothy
Fish" >- Initial Version</log>
  </history>
</extension>
```

Example 7-1: Extensions.xml

```
package extending.aoi.tracker;

import java.util.Collection;

import artofillusion.LayoutWindow;
import artofillusion.Plugin;
import artofillusion.UndoRecord;
import artofillusion.object.ObjectInfo;
import artofillusion.ui.ToolPalette;
import artofillusion.ui.Translate;
import buoy.widget.BMenu;
import buoy.widget.BMenuItem;

/**
 * @author Timothy Fish
 *
 */
public class TrackerPlugin implements Plugin {

  private LayoutWindow layout;
  private ToolPalette toolPalette;
  private CreateTrackerTool theTrackerTool;
  private ObjectInfo pointee;
  private boolean xLock;
  private boolean yLock;
  private boolean zLock;

  public TrackerPlugin(){
    layout = null;
    toolPalette = null;
```

Example 7-2a: TrackerPlugin.java

189

```java
        theTrackerTool = null;

    }
    /**
     * Entry point for the plugin.
     */
    @Override
    public void processMessage(int message, Object[] args) {
        switch (message) {
        case Plugin.SCENE_WINDOW_CREATED:
            // Do initialization first.
            layout = (LayoutWindow) args[0];
            toolPalette = layout.getToolPalette();
            theTrackerTool = new CreateTrackerTool(layout);

            // Add the Tracker button to the Tool Palette
            toolPalette.addTool(theTrackerTool);

            BMenu objectMenu = layout.getObjectMenu();
            // Add menu item to the Object menu
            // Locate position after "Convert To Actor..."
            int posConvertToActor = 0;
            for(int i = 0; i < objectMenu.getChildCount(); i++){
                BMenuItem menuIter = null;
                menuIter = (BMenuItem) objectMenu.getChild(i);
                if(menuIter.getText().equalsIgnoreCase(
                                    "Convert To Actor...")){
                    posConvertToActor = i;
                    break;
                }
            }
            // select position after Convert To Actor or top if
            // not found
            posConvertToActor++;
            // Create menu item that will call drop to floor code
            BMenuItem menuItem = Translate.menuItem(
                    "Track Object...", this, "trackMenuAction");

            // Insert menu item
            objectMenu.add(menuItem, posConvertToActor);

            // Disable menu item (until object selected)
            controlEnableDisable(menuItem);


            break;
        }

    }

    /**
     * Enables/disables the menu item based when conditions
     * change that determine whether the menu item has an
     * object to work on or not.
     * @param menuItem
     */
```

Example 7-2b: TrackerPlugin.java

```java
private void controlEnableDisable(BMenuItem menuItem) {

    // Default to disabled, so we can't select it without
    // a selection
    menuItem.setEnabled(false);

    // Schedule thread to set the enabled/disable status
    // of the menuItem
    new TrackerMenuItemActivator(menuItem, layout).start();
}

/**
 * Action code for the Tracker menu item.
 */
@SuppressWarnings("unused")
private void trackMenuAction(){

    Collection<ObjectInfo> objects =
layout.getSelectedObjects();
    if(!objects.isEmpty()){
        // Create a new UndoRecord. This will be built as we
        // make changes, so we can go back to the previous
        // state of anything we changed.
        UndoRecord undo = new UndoRecord(layout, true);

        if(setPointeeAndLocksFromUserInput()){
            for(ObjectInfo obj : objects){
                // Only works for Trackers
                if(obj.getObject() instanceof Tracker){
                    Tracker t = (Tracker)obj.getObject();
                    // don't point something at itself
                    if(obj != this.pointee){
                        Tracker.pointAt(obj, pointee);
                        t.lockXAxis = this.xLock;
                        t.lockYAxis = this.yLock;
                        t.lockZAxis = this.zLock;
                    }
                }
            }


        }
        else{
            // Stop tracking an object.
            for(ObjectInfo obj : objects){
                // Only works for Trackers
                if(obj.getObject() instanceof Tracker){
                    Tracker.pointAt(obj, null);
                }
            }
        }
        layout.updateImage();

        // Tell the layout window that it can store what we've
        // said is the previous state of the object.
        layout.setUndoRecord(undo);
```

Example 7-2c: TrackerPlugin.java

```java
    }
  }
  /**
   * Displays a window for the user to select whether he
   * wants objA to point at objB or objB to point at objA.
   */
  private boolean setPointeeAndLocksFromUserInput() {
    Collection<ObjectInfo> objects =
                          layout.getSelectedObjects();
    Tracker theFirstTracker = null;
    for(ObjectInfo obj : objects){
      // Find first selected tracker
      if(obj.getObject() instanceof Tracker){
        theFirstTracker = (Tracker) obj.getObject();
        break;
      }
    }
    TrackerObjectSelectionWindow window =
      new TrackerObjectSelectionWindow(layout,
          theFirstTracker.getTargetId(),
          theFirstTracker.lockXAxis,
          theFirstTracker.lockYAxis,
          theFirstTracker.lockZAxis);

    pointee = window.getPointee();
    xLock = window.getXLocked();
    yLock = window.getYLocked();
    zLock = window.getZLocked();

    return (pointee != null);
  }
}
```

Example 7-2d: TrackerPlugin.java

```java
package extending.aoi.tracker;

import artofillusion.LayoutWindow;
import artofillusion.object.ObjectInfo;
import buoy.widget.BMenuItem;

public class TrackerMenuItemActivator extends Thread {
  private BMenuItem theMenuItem;
  private LayoutWindow theLayout;
  // refresh menuItem every quarter-second
  private static final long inverseRefreshRate = 250;

  /**
   * Constructor
   * @param menuItem Non-null menu item
   * @param layout non-null layout window
   */
  public TrackerMenuItemActivator(BMenuItem menuItem,
                            LayoutWindow layout) {
    // Assumption: theMenuItem && theLayout are not null
```

Example 7-3a: TrackerMenuItemActivator.java

```
      theMenuItem = menuItem;
      theLayout = layout;
   }
   /**
    * Method that does checks the selection status.
    */
   @Override
   public void run() {
      // do while menu item exists
      while(theMenuItem != null && theLayout != null){
         // Check for object selection
         if(onlyTrackersAreSelected()){
            theMenuItem.setEnabled(true);
         }
         else{
            theMenuItem.setEnabled(false);
         }
         try {
            // Sleep most of the time so processor can do other
            // things. Updating every quarter-second is more
            // than sufficient since the user can't select the
            // menu item that quickly after object selection.
            Thread.sleep(inverseRefreshRate );
         } catch (InterruptedException e) {
            // This should never happen.
            e.printStackTrace();
         }
      }
   }

   /**
    * Function to determine if at least one object is
    * selected.
    * @return true if there are objects selected, false if
    * not
    */
   private boolean onlyTrackersAreSelected() {
      int numSelected = theLayout.getSelectedObjects().size();
      final int properSize = 1;
      boolean ret = false;
      if(numSelected >= properSize){
         for(ObjectInfo obj : theLayout.getSelectedObjects()){
            if(obj.getObject() instanceof Tracker){
               // must have a tracker to return true
               ret = true;
            }
            else{
               // return false if any are not Trackers
               ret = false;
               break;
            }
         }
      }
      return ret;
   }
}
```

Example 7-3b: TrackerMenuItemActivator.java

```
/**
 *
 */
package extending.aoi.tracker;

import java.awt.Point;

import buoy.event.WidgetMouseEvent;
import artofillusion.Camera;
import artofillusion.LayoutWindow;
import artofillusion.Scene;
import artofillusion.UndoRecord;
import artofillusion.ViewerCanvas;
import artofillusion.animation.PositionTrack;
import artofillusion.animation.RotationTrack;
import artofillusion.math.CoordinateSystem;
import artofillusion.math.Vec3;
import artofillusion.object.ObjectInfo;
import artofillusion.ui.EditingTool;
import artofillusion.ui.EditingWindow;
import artofillusion.ui.Translate;

/**
 * Class to create a tracker, which is a special null object
 * that can be set to track the movement of another object in
 * the scene.
 * @author Timothy Fish
 *
 */
public class CreateTrackerTool extends EditingTool {
  static int counter = 1;
  private Point clickPoint;
  private ObjectInfo objInfo;


  /**
   * constructor
   * @param win
   */
  public CreateTrackerTool(EditingWindow win) {
    super(win);

    // Name is the icon name without an extension.
    // extensions.xml defines the theme.xml file and the
    // theme.xml file defines the Torus theme which contains
    // the createTorus button.
    initButton("Tracker:createTracker");
  }

  public void activate()
  {
    super.activate();
    theWindow.setHelpText(Translate.text(
            "Create Tracker: Click to place tracker."));
  }
```

Example 7-4a: CreateTrackerTool.java

194

```java
public int whichClicks()
{
  return ALL_CLICKS;
}

public String getToolTipText()
{
  return Translate.text("Create Tracker");
}

/**
 * Adds the Tracker object to the scene where the user
 * clicks.
 */
public void mousePressed(WidgetMouseEvent e,
                         ViewerCanvas view)
{
  clickPoint = e.getPoint();

  UndoRecord undo = new UndoRecord(theWindow, false);
  // Create the Tracker
  Scene theScene = ((LayoutWindow) theWindow).getScene();
  objInfo = new ObjectInfo(new Tracker(theScene),
                           new CoordinateSystem(),
                           "Tracker "+counter);
  ((Tracker)objInfo.getObject()).initialize();
  counter++;
  objInfo.addTrack(new PositionTrack(objInfo), 0);
  objInfo.addTrack(new RotationTrack(objInfo), 1);

  int sel[] =
           (LayoutWindow) theWindow).getSelectedIndices();
  ((LayoutWindow) theWindow).addObject(objInfo, undo);
  undo.addCommand(UndoRecord.SET_SCENE_SELECTION,
                  new Object [] {sel});
  theWindow.setUndoRecord(undo);
  ((LayoutWindow) theWindow).setSelection
                             (theScene.getNumObjects()-1);

  // Determine position of the Tracker.
  Camera cam = view.getCamera();
  Vec3 orig;

  orig = cam.convertScreenToWorld(clickPoint,
                    Camera.DEFAULT_DISTANCE_TO_SCREEN);

  // Update the position, and redraw the display.
  objInfo.getCoords().setOrigin(orig);
  objInfo.clearCachedMeshes();
  theWindow.updateImage();

}
```

Example 7-4b: CreateTrackerTool.java

```
   public void mouseReleased(WidgetMouseEvent e,
                             ViewerCanvas view)
   {
     objInfo = null;
     theWindow.setModified();
   }

}
```

Example 7-4c: CreateTrackerTool.java

```
/**
 *
 */
package extending.aoi.tracker;

import java.io.DataInputStream;
import java.io.DataOutputStream;
import java.io.IOException;
import java.io.InvalidObjectException;
import java.util.List;
import java.util.concurrent.Semaphore;

import artofillusion.Scene;
import artofillusion.WireframeMesh;
import artofillusion.math.BoundingBox;
import artofillusion.math.CoordinateSystem;
import artofillusion.math.Vec3;
import artofillusion.object.NullObject;
import artofillusion.object.Object3D;
import artofillusion.object.ObjectInfo;

/**
 * Special null object that tracks the movement of another
 * object.
 * @author Timothy Fish
 *
 */
public class Tracker extends NullObject {
  private static Semaphore pointSemaphore =
                              new Semaphore(1, true);
  private static WireframeMesh mesh;
  private static final int PLUG_IN_VERSION = 1;
  private static final int NO_TARGET = -1;
  private static final long
              INVERSE_FREQUENCY = 1000/60; // millis/hertz

  private ObjectInfo target = null;
  private ObjectInfo trackerInfo = null;
  private int targetId = NO_TARGET;
  private Scene theScene = null;
  private TrackingThread theThread = null;

  public boolean lockXAxis = false;
  public boolean lockYAxis = false;
```

Example 7-5a: Tracker.java

```
public boolean lockZAxis = false;

// Create a wire frame that looks like that of a
// NullObject, but it has a pointer along the Y axis to
// indicate the direction the Tracker is pointing.
static
{
  Vec3 vert[];
  double r = 0.25;
  int from[];
  int to[];

  new BoundingBox(-0.25, 0.25, -0.25, 0.25, -0.25, 0.25);
  vert = new Vec3 [10];
  from = new int [7];
  to = new int [7];
  vert[0] = new Vec3(r, 0.0, 0.0);
  vert[1] = new Vec3(-r, 0.0, 0.0);
  vert[2] = new Vec3(0.0, r, 0.0);
  vert[3] = new Vec3(0.0, -r, 0.0);
  vert[4] = new Vec3(0.0, 0.0, r);
  vert[5] = new Vec3(0.0, 0.0, -r);
  vert[6] = new Vec3(r*0.1, r*0.5, 0.0);
  vert[7] = new Vec3(-r*0.1, r*0.5, 0.0);
  vert[8] = new Vec3(0.0, r*0.5, r*0.1);
  vert[9] = new Vec3(0.0, r*0.5, -r*0.1);
  from[0] = 0;
  to[0] = 1;
  from[1] = 2;
  to[1] = 3;
  from[2] = 4;
  to[2] = 5;

  from[3] = 2;
  to[3] = 6;
  from[4] = 2;
  to[4] = 7;
  from[5] = 2;
  to[5] = 8;
  from[6] = 2;
  to[6] = 9;
  mesh = new WireframeMesh(vert, from, to);
}

/**
 * Thread that rotates the object when other objects
 * update.
 * @author Timothy
 */
protected class TrackingThread extends Thread {
  /**
   * constructor
   */
  public TrackingThread() {
  }
```

Example 7-5b: Tracker.java

```
/**
 * Operating function of the thread.Points the tracker
 * in the right direction when an object moves.
 */
public void run(){
  // Track target while there is a target to track.
  while(true){

    // delay for a little while between each frame
    try {
      sleep(INVERSE_FREQUENCY);
    } catch (InterruptedException e) {
      // Should never happen, so print an error.
      e.printStackTrace();
    }

    obtainSemaphore();

    // Note that we won't track the object until one
    // frame after we have a valid target.

    if(target != null && target.getId() == targetId &&
       trackerInfo != null){
      pointAtTarget(trackerInfo, target);
    }
    // Find object indicated by targetId
    else if(target == null || target.getId() !=
targetId)
    {
      if(targetId != NO_TARGET){
        target = findObject(targetId);
      }
    }
    else{
      // trackerInfo isn't set, so do setup
      initialize();
    }

    releaseSemaphore();
  }
}

/**
 * Release Semaphore so another Tracker can manipulate
 * objects.
 */
private void releaseSemaphore() {
  Tracker.pointSemaphore.release();
}

/**
 * Block until the Semaphore is available so that
 * Trackers aren't all trying to manipulate objects at
 * the same time.
 */
private void obtainSemaphore() {
```

Example 7-5c: Tracker.java

```java
    // Block while other trackers are working.
    try {
      Tracker.pointSemaphore.acquire();
    } catch (InterruptedException e) {
      e.printStackTrace();
    }
  }

  /**
   * Finds the object that matches the id
   * @param id
   */
  private ObjectInfo findObject(int id) {
    List<ObjectInfo> theObjects =
                              theScene.getAllObjects();

    // find id in the list of objects and point at the
    // object
    for(ObjectInfo object : theObjects){
      if(object.getId() == id){
        return object; // found it, so exit loop early
      }
    }
    return null; // not found
  }

  /**
   * Calculates the second rotation.
   * @param x
   * @param y
   * @param z
   * @return
   */
  private double calculateZRotate(double x, double y,
                                  double z) {
    double sqrtYYZZ = Math.sqrt(y*y + z*z);
    double ret = 0; // return value;
    if(sqrtYYZZ != 0){

      ret = Math.toDegrees(Math.atan(x/sqrtYYZZ));

      if(sqrtYYZZ < 0){
        // angle is on the other size
        ret += 180.0;
      }
    }
    // Handle differently because the angle gives two
    // possible directions.
    else if(x > 0){
      ret = 90.0;
    }
    else if(x < 0){
      ret = -90.0;
    }
    return ret;
  }
```

Example 7-5d: Tracker.java

```java
/**
 * @param parent
 * @param orgA Original coordinate systems of pointer
 */
private void rotateChildren(ObjectInfo parent,
                            ObjectInfo pointer,
                            CoordinateSystem orgA) {
  for(ObjectInfo child : parent.getChildren()){
    CoordinateSystem coords = child.getCoords();

    // set rotation center at pointer origin
    coords.transformCoordinates(orgA.toLocal());
    // move everything back, but to the new location
    coords.transformCoordinates(pointer.getCoords().
                                        fromLocal());
    rotateChildren(child, pointer, orgA);
  }
}

/**
 * Returns a valid angle for Y.
 * @return
 */
private double calculateYRotate() {
  // Zero is as good as any value.
  return 0.0;
}

/**
 * Calculates rotation that will put direction vector in
 * the XY plane.
 * @param y
 * @param z
 * @return
 */
private double calculateXRotate(double y, double z) {
  double ret = 0;

  if(y != 0){
    ret = Math.toDegrees(Math.atan(-z/y));

    if(y < 0){
      ret += 180.0;
    }
  }
  // Handle differently because the angle gives two
  // possible directions.
  else if(z > 0){
    ret = -90.0;
  }
  else if(z < 0){
    ret = 90.0;
  }
  return  ret;
}
```

Example 7-5e: Tracker.java

```java
/**
 * Rotates the pointer to point at the target.
 * @param pointer
 */
private void pointAtTarget(ObjectInfo pointer,
                          ObjectInfo target) {

  if(pointer == null || target == null) { return; }

  Vec3 locA = pointer.getCoords().getOrigin();
  CoordinateSystem orgA =
                    pointer.getCoords().duplicate();

  Vec3 locB = target.getCoords().getOrigin();
  Vec3 BminusA = locB.minus(locA);

  double x = BminusA.x;
  double y = BminusA.y;
  double z = BminusA.z;

  // default to current rotation for each axis
  double xRot =
            pointer.getCoords().getRotationAngles()[0];
  double yRot =
            pointer.getCoords().getRotationAngles()[1];
  double zRot =
            pointer.getCoords().getRotationAngles()[2];

  if(!lockXAxis){
    xRot = calculateXRotate(y, z);
  }

  if(!lockYAxis){
    yRot = calculateYRotate();
  }

  if(!lockZAxis){
    zRot = calculateZRotate(x, y, z);
  }
                          :
  pointer.getCoords().setOrientation(xRot, yRot, zRot);
  rotateChildren(pointer, pointer, orgA);
  }

}

/**
 * constructor
 * @param theScene
 * @param undo
 *
 */
public Tracker(Scene theScene) {
  this.theScene  = theScene;
}
```

Example 7-5f: Tracker.java

```java
/**
 * Returns a duplicate of the existing object. Sets
 * the targetId to the same as this object, so the new
 * Tracker will track the same object as the first.
 * @return
 */
public Object3D duplicate()
{
  Tracker t = new Tracker(this.theScene);

  t.lockXAxis = this.lockXAxis;
  t.lockYAxis = this.lockYAxis;
  t.lockZAxis = this.lockZAxis;

  if(this.targetId != NO_TARGET){
    t.pointAt(theScene, this.targetId);
  }
  return t;
}

/**
 * Makes this object like the one passed in. Changes the
 * targetId so that this object will now track the same
 * object as the first.
 * @param obj
 */
public void copyObject(Object3D obj)
{
  if(obj instanceof Tracker){
    Tracker t = (Tracker)obj;

    this.lockXAxis = t.lockXAxis;
    this.lockYAxis = t.lockYAxis;
    this.lockZAxis = t.lockZAxis;

    if(t.targetId != NO_TARGET){
      pointAt(theScene, t.targetId);
    }

  }
}

/**
 * Constructor for reading data from the file.
 * @param in
 * @param theScene
 * @throws IOException
 * @throws InvalidObjectException
 */
public Tracker(DataInputStream in, Scene theScene)
                throws IOException, InvalidObjectException
{
    super(in, theScene);

    this.theScene = theScene;
```

Example 7-5g: Tracker.java

```
      short version = in.readShort();
      if (version != PLUG_IN_VERSION){
        throw new InvalidObjectException("");
      }

      int id = in.readInt();
      if(id != NO_TARGET){
        pointAt(theScene, id);
      }

      this.lockXAxis = in.readBoolean();
      this.lockYAxis = in.readBoolean();
      this.lockZAxis = in.readBoolean();
    }

    /**
     * Points the tracker at the object.
     * @param theScene Scene that contains the objects.
     * @param id Id of the object to point at.
     */
    private void pointAt(Scene theScene, int id) {
      this.theScene = theScene;
      // set the point at id
      targetId = id;

      // if theThread isn't started yet, do it now
      if(theThread == null){
        theThread = new TrackingThread();
        theThread.start();
      }
    }

    /**
     * Does the things that the constructor can't do yet.
     * This method should be called after the tracker is
     * assigned to an ObjectInfo object.
     */
    public void initialize() {
      if(theScene == null){ return; }

      List<ObjectInfo> theObjects = theScene.getAllObjects();

      // find object in the list of objects and set
      // trackerInfo
      for(ObjectInfo object : theObjects){
        if(object.getObject() == this){
          trackerInfo = object; // found it, exit loop early
        }
      }
    }

    /**
     * Writes the Tracker to the file.
     * @param out
     * @param theScene
     * @throws IOException
```

Example 7-5h: Tracker.java

```java
    */
    public void writeToFile(DataOutputStream out,
                        Scene theScene) throws IOException{
      super.writeToFile(out, theScene);

      // Write Version Info
      out.writeShort(PLUG_IN_VERSION);

      // Write identifying information for object we're
      // pointing at.
      out.writeInt(targetId);

      // Write the axis locks
      out.writeBoolean(lockXAxis);
      out.writeBoolean(lockYAxis);
      out.writeBoolean(lockZAxis);
    }
    /**
     * Points the tracker at the specified target.
     * @param tracker
     * @param target
     * @param undo
     */
    public static void pointAt(ObjectInfo tracker,
                           ObjectInfo target){
      if(!(tracker.getObject() instanceof Tracker)) return;

      Tracker t = (Tracker)tracker.getObject();

      if(target != null){
        // begin the tracking thread
        t.pointAt(t.theScene, target.getId());
      }
      else{
        t.clearTarget();
      }
    }

    /**
     * Sets the Tracker to track nothing.
     */
    private void clearTarget() {
      this.theThread = null;
      targetId = NO_TARGET;
      target = null;
    }

    public int getTargetId() {
      return this.targetId;
    }

    public WireframeMesh getWireframeMesh()
    {
      return mesh;
    }
}
```

Example 7-5i: Tracker.java

```
package extending.aoi.tracker;

import java.util.Collection;

import artofillusion.LayoutWindow;
import artofillusion.Scene;
import artofillusion.object.ObjectInfo;
import artofillusion.ui.PanelDialog;
import buoy.widget.BCheckBox;
import buoy.widget.BComboBox;
import buoy.widget.BLabel;
import buoy.widget.ColumnContainer;

/**
 * Window that the user sees when he chooses to have the
 * tracker point at an object.
 * @author Timothy Fish
 *
 */
public class TrackerObjectSelectionWindow {
  /**
   * Class to setup the layout of the
   * TrackerObjectSelectionWindow.
   */
  private class TrackDialogPanel extends ColumnContainer {
    private BComboBox theObjectsList;
    Collection<ObjectInfo> theObjects;
    private BCheckBox theXCheckBox;
    private BCheckBox theYCheckBox;
    private BCheckBox theZCheckBox;
    private BLabel theObjectsListLabel;

    /**
     * Constructor - handles widget placement
     */
    TrackDialogPanel(Collection<ObjectInfo> objects,
                     int targetId, boolean xChecked,
                     boolean yChecked, boolean zChecked){
      super(); // Call the ColumnContainer constructor

      theObjects = objects;

      theObjectsListLabel = new BLabel();
      theObjectsListLabel.setText("Target");
      add(theObjectsListLabel);

      theObjectsList = new BComboBox();
      theObjectsList.add("No Object");
      int targetIndex = 0;
      int index = 0;
      // Set the display text. Note that getName() and
      // getString() are very different.
      for(ObjectInfo object : objects ){
        index++;
        theObjectsList.add(object.getName());
        if(object.getId() == targetId){
```

Example 7-6a: TrackerObjectSelectionWindow.java

205

```java
        targetIndex = index;
      }
    }
    theObjectsList.setSelectedIndex(targetIndex);
    add(theObjectsList);

    theXCheckBox = new BCheckBox();
    theXCheckBox.setText("Lock X Axis");
    theXCheckBox.setState(xChecked);
    add(theXCheckBox);

    theYCheckBox = new BCheckBox();
    theYCheckBox.setText("Lock Y Axis");
    theYCheckBox.setState(yChecked);
    add(theYCheckBox);

    theZCheckBox = new BCheckBox();
    theZCheckBox.setText("Lock Z Axis");
    theZCheckBox.setState(zChecked);
    add(theZCheckBox);
  }

  /**
   * Return the ObjectInfo for the object the user
   * selected.
   * @return
   */
  public ObjectInfo getPointee() {
    // The "No Object" choice places one more item in the
    // list than the Array has. So remove it and either
    // return the object in the array or null if No Object
    // selected.
    int selectedIndex =
                    theObjectsList.getSelectedIndex()-1;
    if(selectedIndex >= 0){
      return (ObjectInfo)theObjects.toArray()
                                    [selectedIndex];
    }
    else{
      return null;
    }
  }
}

private ObjectInfo pointee;
private final String windowTitle = "Tracker Options";
private TrackDialogPanel thePanel;

/**
 * Displays window for the user to select the pointee.
 * @param parent
 */
public TrackerObjectSelectionWindow(LayoutWindow parent,
          int targetId, boolean xLocked, boolean yLocked,
          boolean zLocked){
  Scene scene = parent.getScene();
```

Example 7-6b: TrackerObjectSelectionWindow.java

```java
      pointee = null;

      Collection<ObjectInfo> selectableObjects =
                           scene.getAllObjects();
      thePanel = new TrackDialogPanel(selectableObjects,
                   targetId, xLocked, yLocked, zLocked);

      PanelDialog dlg = new PanelDialog(parent, windowTitle,
                                          thePanel);

      if (dlg.clickedOk()){
        // code for what to do after user accepts
        pointee = thePanel.getPointee();
      }
      else{
        // User clicked cancel, so everything should remain
        // unchanged.
        ;
      }
   }

   /**
    * Returns the object we're to point at. Returns null if
    * none selected.
    * @return
    */
   public ObjectInfo getPointee() {
      return pointee;
   }

   public boolean getXLocked() {
      return thePanel.theXCheckBox.getState();
   }

   public boolean getYLocked() {
      return thePanel.theYCheckBox.getState();
   }

   public boolean getZLocked() {
      return thePanel.theZCheckBox.getState();
   }
}
```

Example 7-6c: TrackerObjectSelectionWindow.java

Chapter 8

Procedural Modules

Nothing is more important in a 3D modeling tool than the ability to apply textures to an object. A sphere is just a sphere, until we apply a texture and it becomes a globe, or it becomes beach ball, or it becomes an eye. Textures can be the difference between something ordinary and a truly remarkable scene. So it stands to reason that you would like to have as much control over the textures as you possibly can.

Art of Illusion already has a powerful mechanism

Figure 8-1: Spheres on a Tile Floor

for handling textures. A texture can be a Uniform texture, an Image Mapped texture, a Procedural 2D texture, or a Procedural 3D texture. The first is a convenient way to handle the most simple textures that have one color across the entire surface of the object. The second, is a simplified means to map an image from an external source to the surface of the object. The last two provide the same capability as the first two, but they add the ability for the user to have Art of Illusion generate a texture using a procedure.

Procedural textures have several advantages over an image map. They are easy to create and no matter how large you make your output image, they don't suffer from pixelation. That means you don't have to have super large image files floating around your work environment. That's not to say that you can eliminate image maps completely, but there are advantages to reducing their use.

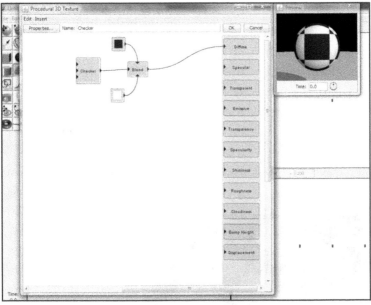

Figure 8-2: Creating a Checkerboard Pattern

In light of that goal, Art of Illusion comes with all of the basic stuff you would expect to find in the procedural textures area, but you're sure to find something that you wish it had but doesn't. For me, that was a Tile pattern. Art of Illusion has the standard checker pattern (Figure 8-2), but it doesn't have a tile pattern with grout between the tiles. But there are plenty of things it could be. Maybe you want a different marble pattern. Maybe you want Art of Illusion to texture an object based on some form of external data that Art of Illusion doesn't currently support[1].

Whatever it is, the way to create a new capability for textures and materials is by creating a plugin that extends the Module class. The Module class is a special type of plugin that defines the modules like those in Figure 8-2. It is also different from the other plugins we've looked at because modules in plugins are automatically added to the texture window menu in a submenu called Plugins. This is as good of a place for it as any, so we can focus on the module itself, rather than spending time considering the user interface.

A Module Defined

In Art of Illusion, a module looks something like what is shown in Figure 8-3. Each module has at least one output and zero or more inputs.

Figure 8-3: Simple Module, can take numbers or colors as inputs and output numbers or colors.

The inputs and outputs have a type of either a number or a color. Outputs of the number type can be connected to inputs of the number type and outputs of the color type can be connected to inputs of the color type. Much like a mathematical function, the module makes a calculation based on the inputs to determine the output values. A set of inputs you will often see for Art of

---

1. Consult with legal experts before developing code for Open Source software, such Art of Illusion, to access data files with formats that you wish to prevent other people from accessing.

Illusion are the coordinates X, Y, Z. You may also see time passed in. But you could see something like the Blend module that takes a fractional value and two colors as inputs so that it can output a color that is that ratio of the two colors.

Coding a Module

In some ways, this plugin in simpler than the others because it resides in one class, but in others it is more difficult because it has several concepts we don't deal with regularly, all in a small space. We have to deal with the inputs and outputs of the module, as well as a conceptual representation of the texture it creates.

Input/Output Ports

The first thing we need is a way to represent the ports in a way that we recognize them in code. The methods that handle the ports refer to them using an integer value. These values are sequential because they are stored in arrays internally. The input ports are stored in one array and the output ports are stored in another. Instead of referring to the ports by number, it is better to refer to them by name.

In some languages, we would create an enumerated type. Java is quirky when it comes to enumerated types, so a better choice is to create several named constants. The following is the list of inputs for the Tile-Module:

```
private static final int X_PORT = 0;
private static final int Y_PORT = 1;
private static final int Z_PORT = 2;
private static final int COLOR_1_PORT = 3;
private static final int COLOR_2_PORT = 4;
private static final int MORTAR_WIDTH_PORT = 5;
private static final int MORTAR_COLOR_PORT = 6;
```

The names give us a clear indication of what the ports are for. The output port is similar:

```
private static final int COLOR_PORT = 0;
```

But there is only one. If there were more, these too would be numbered sequentially.

We also need some default values. We want to be able to drop the module onto the screen and have it work in an expected way without providing inputs. The X, Y, and Z ports are expected to have the X, Y, or Z location of the point Art of Illusion is drawing, unless we provide it with inputs that specify differently, so they don't have a default value. For the others, we'll set the default values as Blue, White, Yellow, and 0.05, respectively. The 0.05 represents 5% of the tile width. The following is the code for the constants:

```
private static final RGBColor COLOR1DEFAULT =
                        new RGBColor(0.0, 0.0, 1.0);
private static final RGBColor COLOR2DEFAULT =
                        new RGBColor(0.0, 1.0, 1.0);
private static final RGBColor MORTARCOLORDEFAULT =
                        new RGBColor(1.0, 1.0, 0.0);
private static final double MORTARWIDTHDEFAULT = 0.05;
```

The RGBColor specifices color in terms of Red, Green, and Blue with values from 0.0 to 1.0.

Now, take a look at Example 8-1. In this constructor, each of the ports are created in order. Ordering is important here because we refer to them by their index. The first value passed into the IOPort constructor is the type, which can be either IOPort.NUMBER or IOPort.COLOR. The second specifies whether it is an input or an output. In the first array, they will all be inputs and in the second, they will all be outputs.

The third input specifies the location of the port. If you want it on the left of the rectangle, then use IOPort.LEFT. On the Top, IOPort.TOP. Bottom, IOPort.BOTTOM. Right, IOPort.RIGHT. When there is more than one on a side, as is the case with the input

```
public TileModule(Point position)
{
   super(Translate.text("Tile"),
   new IOPort [] {
      new IOPort(IOPort.NUMBER, IOPort.INPUT, IOPort.LEFT,
                 new String [] {"X", "(X)"}),
      new IOPort(IOPort.NUMBER, IOPort.INPUT, IOPort.LEFT,
                 new String [] {"Y", "(Y)"}),
      new IOPort(IOPort.NUMBER, IOPort.INPUT, IOPort.LEFT,
                 new String [] {"Z", "(Z)"}),
      new IOPort(IOPort.COLOR, IOPort.INPUT, IOPort.TOP,
                 new String [] {"Color 1", "(Blue)"}),
      new IOPort(IOPort.COLOR, IOPort.INPUT, IOPort.TOP,
                 new String [] {"Color 2", "(White)"}),
      new IOPort(IOPort.NUMBER, IOPort.INPUT, IOPort.BOTTOM,
                 new String [] {"Mortar Width", "(0.05)"}),
      new IOPort(IOPort.COLOR, IOPort.INPUT, IOPort.BOTTOM,
                 new String [] {"Mortar Color", "(Yellow)"})
   },
   new IOPort [] {
      new IOPort(IOPort.COLOR, IOPort.OUTPUT, IOPort.RIGHT,
                 new String [] {"Color"})
   },
   position);
   color = new RGBColor(0.0,0.0, 0.0);
}
```

Example 8-1: TileModule Constructor

array, the ports will appear in order from top to bottom or left to right along that side.

Lastly, there is a array of String with two values that are the display string and the help string for the port. The resulting module from these values is shown in Figure 8-4. The X, Y, and Z inputs are on the left side. The two colors for the tiles are at the top. The grout color and width are at the bottom. These all combine to return the color of the current point when getColor is called. (The current point is set when init() is

Figure 8-4: Tile Module

called.) The getColor method is approximately half the size of the class.

The Color of a Point

The TileModule will return one of three colors when getColor is called, but the value is dependent on where the point is located. First, getColor verifies that it needs to return a different color. If it doesn't, it returns the previous color and processing is over for that iteration.

Next, getColor determines which values it should use. For the colors, the variable is first set to the default value and then, if there is a module connected to the input, the value is retrieved. This is shown by the following:

```
RGBColor color1 = COLOR1DEFAULT.duplicate();
if(linkFrom[COLOR_1_PORT] != null){
  linkFrom[COLOR_1_PORT].getColor(linkFromIndex
[COLOR_1_PORT],
                               color1, blur);
}
```

Next, there must be values for xsize, ysize, zsize, x, y, and z. These are handled in a similar way, based on whether the ports have connected inputs or not. For the sizes, we default to half the point size plus the blur. Otherwise, we use the value error from the connected port. If the size is more than 0.5, we blend the colors together and return that as a value.

Getting x, y, and z is similar. We either use the point location or we use the value from getAverageValue. The value returned from getAverageValue is the value returned from the connected port. The term average is used here because the value may be formed from several different values. This is because the points in space do not have a one-to-on match with the pixels in the texture. The size, location, etc. can make a difference in how they line up.

Figure 8-5 may give you an idea of what is happening. If we think of the texture as a simple bitmap, a point in the scene may correspond to one of the three areas circled

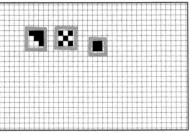

Figure 8-5: Possible Pixels

with gray. So the color of the pixel drawn on the screen would be gray for the first two, and black for the third, but the pixels in the texture would only ever be black and white.

But for the TileModule, we will stick to one of three colors, rather than blending them. This will give us sharp breaks between the colors. But in other situations, you may want to blend the colors more.

Next, we map our location to a value between -0.5 and 0.5 by removing the integer part and subtracting from 0.5. The purpose of this is to have a repeating pattern set on a size of 1.0 and the grout being in the middle.

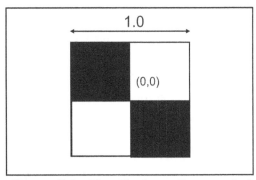

Figure 8-6: The Texture. Represented here in 2D, but depending on which quadrant the point falls into a color is returned. If it is within the mortar area, the mortar color is returned. Otherwise, one of the two tile colors is returned. The points are mapped to −0.5 to 0.5.

The color of the point is determined by which area the point falls into, as Figure 8-6 explains.

The Eclipse project is as is shown in Figure 8-7. There are only two files to create. After exporting to the JAR file, place the JAR file in the plugins directory and there will be a new module in the procedural textures screens that you can use.

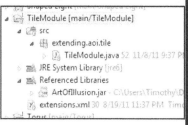

Figure 8-7: TileModule Project

```xml
<?xml version="1.0" standalone="yes"?>

<extension name="TileModule" version="0.1" >
  <author>Timothy Fish</author>
  <date>August 2011</date>

  <plugin class="extending.aoi.tile.TileModule" />

  <description>This plugin creates a procedural module that
will produce textures that look like tiles separated by
grout.</description>
  <resource name="icons/theme.xml" id="TileModule"
type="UITheme"/>
  <comments>This project is to demonstrate adding procedural
modules.</comments>

  <history>
    <log version="0.1" date="August 2011" author="Timothy
Fish" >- Initial Version</log>
  </history>

</extension>
```

Example 8-2: Extensions.xml

```java
/**
 *
 */
package extending.aoi.tile;

import java.awt.Point;

import artofillusion.math.RGBColor;
import artofillusion.procedural.IOPort;
import artofillusion.procedural.Module;
import artofillusion.procedural.PointInfo;
import artofillusion.ui.Translate;

/**
 * Procedural Module for a texture that is made up of tiles
 * with grout.
 * @author Timothy Fish
 *
 */
public class TileModule extends Module {
  private  boolean colorOk;
  private  double lastBlur;
  private  PointInfo point;
  private RGBColor color;

  // The following constants serve as array indexes and are
  // in the order that each port was created in the
  // constructor.
  // Input Ports
  private static final int X_PORT = 0;
  private static final int Y_PORT = 1;
  private static final int Z_PORT = 2;
  private static final int COLOR_1_PORT = 3;
  private static final int COLOR_2_PORT = 4;
  private static final int MORTAR_WIDTH_PORT = 5;
  private static final int MORTAR_COLOR_PORT = 6;
  // Output Ports
  private static final int COLOR_PORT = 0;

  // Default colors
  // Blue
  private static final RGBColor COLOR1DEFAULT =
                    new RGBColor(0.0, 0.0, 1.0);
  // White
  private static final RGBColor COLOR2DEFAULT =
                    new RGBColor(1.0, 1.0, 1.0);
  // Yellow
  private static final RGBColor MORTARCOLORDEFAULT =
                    new RGBColor(1.0, 1.0, 0.0);
  // mortar width that is 5% of tile width
  private static final double MORTARWIDTHDEFAULT = 0.05;

  public TileModule(){
    this(new Point(0,0));
  }
```

Example 8-3a: TileModule.java

218

```java
public TileModule(Point position)
{
  super(Translate.text("Tile"),
    new IOPort [] {
      new IOPort(IOPort.NUMBER, IOPort.INPUT, IOPort.LEFT,
                 new String [] {"X", "(X)"}),
      new IOPort(IOPort.NUMBER, IOPort.INPUT, IOPort.LEFT,
                 new String [] {"Y", "(Y)"}),
      new IOPort(IOPort.NUMBER, IOPort.INPUT, IOPort.LEFT,
                 new String [] {"Z", "(Z)"}),
      new IOPort(IOPort.COLOR, IOPort.INPUT, IOPort.TOP,
                 new String [] {"Color 1", "(Blue)"}),
      new IOPort(IOPort.COLOR, IOPort.INPUT, IOPort.TOP,
                 new String [] {"Color 2", "(White)"}),
      new IOPort(IOPort.NUMBER, IOPort.INPUT, IOPort.BOTTOM,
                 new String [] {"Mortar Width", "(0.05)"}),
      new IOPort(IOPort.COLOR, IOPort.INPUT, IOPort.BOTTOM,
                 new String [] {"Mortar Color", "(Yellow)"})
    },
    new IOPort [] {
      new IOPort(IOPort.COLOR, IOPort.OUTPUT, IOPort.RIGHT,
                 new String [] {"Color"})
    },
    position);
  color = new RGBColor(0.0,0.0, 0.0);
}

/* New point, so the color will need to be recalculated.
*/

public void init(PointInfo p)
{
  colorOk = false;
  point = p;
}

public void getColor(int which, RGBColor c, double blur)
{
  // If change needed, return last color.
  if (colorOk && blur == lastBlur)
  {
    c.copy(color);
    return;
  }
  colorOk = true;
  lastBlur = blur;

  RGBColor color1 = COLOR1DEFAULT.duplicate();
  if(linkFrom[COLOR_1_PORT] != null){
    linkFrom[COLOR_1_PORT].getColor(
              linkFromIndex[COLOR_1_PORT], color1, blur);
  }

  RGBColor color2 = COLOR2DEFAULT.duplicate();
  if(linkFrom[COLOR_2_PORT] != null){
    linkFrom[COLOR_2_PORT].getColor(
```

Example 8-3b: TileModule.java

```
                   linkFromIndex[COLOR_2_PORT], color2, blur);
    }

    RGBColor mortarColor = MORTARCOLORDEFAULT.duplicate();
    if(linkFrom[MORTAR_COLOR_PORT] != null){
      linkFrom[MORTAR_COLOR_PORT].getColor(
      linkFromIndex[MORTAR_COLOR_PORT], mortarColor, blur);
    }

    double mortarWidth = MORTARWIDTHDEFAULT;
    if(linkFrom[MORTAR_WIDTH_PORT] != null){
      mortarWidth =
        linkFrom[MORTAR_WIDTH_PORT].getAverageValue(
                   linkFromIndex[MORTAR_WIDTH_PORT], blur);
    }

    // Retrieve the point information

    // size of point relative to texture, with room for blur
    double xsize = (linkFrom[X_PORT] == null) ?
0.5*point.xsize+blur : linkFrom[X_PORT].getValueError
(linkFromIndex[X_PORT], blur);
    double ysize = (linkFrom[Y_PORT] == null) ?
0.5*point.ysize+blur : linkFrom[Y_PORT].getValueError
(linkFromIndex[Y_PORT], blur);
    double zsize = (linkFrom[Z_PORT] == null) ?
0.5*point.zsize+blur : linkFrom[Z_PORT].getValueError
(linkFromIndex[Z_PORT], blur);
    if (xsize >= 0.5 || ysize >= 0.5 || zsize >= 0.5)
    {
      c.setRGB((color1.red+color2.red)/2.0,
(color1.green+color2.green)/2.0,
(color1.blue+color2.blue)/2.0);
      return;
    }

    // location of point
    double x = (linkFrom[X_PORT] == null) ? point.x :
linkFrom[X_PORT].getAverageValue(linkFromIndex[X_PORT],
blur);
    double y = (linkFrom[Y_PORT] == null) ? point.y :
linkFrom[Y_PORT].getAverageValue(linkFromIndex[Y_PORT],
blur);
    double z = (linkFrom[Z_PORT] == null) ? point.z :
linkFrom[Z_PORT].getAverageValue(linkFromIndex[Z_PORT],
blur);

    double xIntPart = Math.rint(x);
    double yIntPart = Math.rint(y);
    double zIntPart = Math.rint(z);
    double xFloatPart = 0.5-Math.abs(x-xIntPart);
    double yFloatPart = 0.5-Math.abs(y-yIntPart);
    double zFloatPart = 0.5-Math.abs(z-zIntPart);
    int i = (int) xIntPart;
    int j = (int) yIntPart;
    int k = (int) zIntPart;
```

Example 8-3c: TileModule.java

```java
      double value = ((i+j+k)&1) == 0 ? 1.0 : 0.0;
      double error;

      if (xFloatPart > xsize && yFloatPart > ysize &&
          zFloatPart > zsize)
      {
        if(mortarWidth>0.0){
          if(xFloatPart < xsize+mortarWidth/2.0
             || yFloatPart < ysize+mortarWidth/2.0
             || zFloatPart < zsize+mortarWidth/2.0){
            c.copy(mortarColor);
            colorOk = true;
            return;
          }
        }

        error = 0.0;
        //c.copy(mortarColor);
        c.setRGB(color2.red*value+(1.0-value)*color1.red,
            color2.green*value +(1.0-value)*color1.green,
            color2.blue*value + (1.0-value)*color1.blue);
        colorOk = true;
        return;
      }
      else{
        double e1 = xFloatPart/xsize;
        double e2 = yFloatPart/ysize;
        double e3 = zFloatPart/zsize;
        if (e1 < e2 && e1 < e3)
        {
          error = 0.5-0.5*e1;
        }
        else if (e2 < e1 && e2 < e3)
        {
          error = 0.5-0.5*e2;
        }
        else
        {
          error = 0.5-0.5*e3;
        }
        value = error*(1.0-value) + (1.0-error)*value;
      }
      if(which == COLOR_PORT){
        if(mortarWidth > 0.0){
          c.copy(mortarColor);
        }
        else{
          c.copy(color1);
        }
        colorOk = true;
      }
}
```

Example 8-3d: TileModule.java

```
public Module duplicate()
{
    TileModule mod = new TileModule(new Point(bounds.x,
                                              bounds.y));

    mod.color.copy(color);
    return mod;
}
}
```

Example 8-3e: TileModule.java

Chapter 9

Four Walls and a Roof

Up to this point, most of our attention has been on molding the Art of Illusion user interface to our will and creating new things within Art of Illusion. This next plugin looks at what it takes to place predefined objects in the scene. Manipulating objects within a scene falls into a category that is generally handled by items on the Tools menu in Art of Illusion. The out of the box Array tool makes a number of copies of the selected object and places them in the scene. The Boolean tool forms a new object that is either the combination of or the difference between two objects. The Lathe tool creates an object that is the rotation of one of the curves in the scene. A tool is something that aids you in manipulating the objects in the scene, often working with objects that Art of Illusion includes out of the box.

This plugin will demonstrate how to create a tool that resides on the Tools menu and that will manipulate the placement of objects within the scene. The tool itself creates a room with four walls, a roof and a floor. It's not a particularly special object, but it is something we do frequently, if we want light from the scene to reflect back into the scene, rather than shooting off into the blackness of the void.

Examine the images in Figure 9-1. The images on the right use the same render settings as the images on the left, with one modification. The images on the left have no walls while the images on the right have walls and a ceiling surrounding the scene. There is no change in the lighting between one and the other, but the lighting appears very different. The big difference is that the images with the walls visible have noticeably softer lighting than the images on the left.

This same result is possible if we just draw a cube around our scene. There isn't much point in creating a special tool to draw something so simple. Instead, our tool will create a room, with the floor at (0, 0, 0), four independent walls, and a ceiling. They will be children of a null object, so they can be moved as a unit, but more importantly, each wall can be made visible or invisible at will. This will make it easier to position objects in the scene, using the walls as a guide, with-

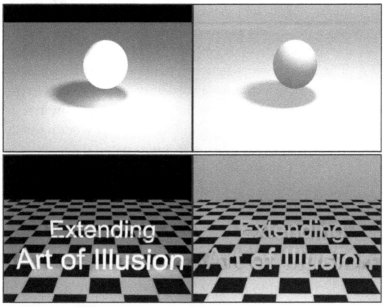

Figure 9-1: With Walls and Without Walls

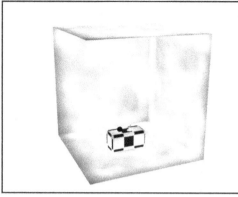

Figure 9-2: Room with Two Walls Hidden

out the need for the camera to be close enough to be inside the room.

As is shown in Figure 9-3, the room setup allows the user to select the size of the room, and the initial visibility of each of the sides. Depending on your needs, you could build on this concept and create a tool that will create a room with a door or window in the wall. You could create a tool that creates more than one room, so that from the scene in one room you would be able to see through a door into another room. But here, we'll keep it to the one room.

Adding Objects to the Scene

The new stuff for this plugin is how objects are added to the scene. We see that in the buildRoom method. The first line is:

Figure 9-3: Setup

```
ObjectInfo roomInfo = new ObjectInfo(new NullObject(),
                        new CoordinateSystem(),
                        "Room "+nextRoomCount() );
```

The last line is:

```
layout.addObject(roomInfo, undo);
```

Between these lines, the method creates walls and adds them to room-Info. They first create vectors, from which curves are created and then the curves are turned into Triangle-Meshes. But notice what is happening. The line shown above creates a

Figure 9-4: Null Menu

NullObject(). In so doing, it is creating the same object that is created when you select Null from the Create Primitive Menu.

When you look at the source code for the buildRoom method and the createSide method, you will see that it is doing the same thing as what is happening behind the scenes when you select one of the curve drawing tools (Figure 9-5) and draw it on the screen.

Figure 9-5: Curve Tools

Notice that createSide adds the side object to both the room object and to the layout window. This is done in the last two lines of the method.

```
roomInfo.addChild(sideInfo, roomInfo.getChildren().length);
layout.getScene().addObject(sideInfo, undo);
```

The order in which these things are done is important here. You should first add the children to an object. Add the children to the scene and then add the object to the scene. If you were to add the room to the scene first, then the walls would be created, but they would not be selectable in the layout window and you would not be able to hide/show the walls. It would just be a giant box in the scene.

Another difference between this plugin and most of the other plugins we've looked at is the entry point of the plugin. For plugins of type ModellingTool, the entry point is the commandSelected method. This is because Art of Illusion takes care of adding it to a menu for us. The class has to give it a name to place on the menu, which is done through the method get-Name, but no other processing is done until the user selects the menu item and Art of Illusion calls commandSelected for the plugin.

For this tool, commandSelected displays a window for the user to select the various options. For other tools you develop, you may not need a window at all.

Create the Project

There are only two files in the Room plugin project. *Extensions.xml* is as simple as always and *Room.java* has been added. Unlike some of the projects, this project includes the class for the dialog window in the main class. In some ways, this helps to simplify things. In others, it may make it more difficult because more is going on in one file. Use the method that seems to make the most sense for you and your project.

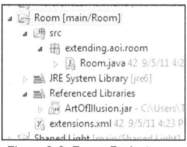

Figure 9-6: Room Project

```xml
<?xml version="1.0" standalone="yes"?>

<extension name="Room" version="0.1" >
  <author>Timothy Fish</author>
  <date>August 2011</date>

  <plugin class="extending.aoi.room.Room" />

  <description>This plugin creates a room with four walls a
floor and a ceiling.</description>

  <comments>This project is to demonstrate the development
of a ModelingTool.</comments>

  <history>
     <log version="0.1" date="September 2011" au-
thor="Timothy Fish" >- Initial Version</log>
  </history>

</extension>
```

Example 9-1: Extensions.xml

```java
/**
 *
 */
package extending.aoi.room;

import artofillusion.LayoutWindow;
import artofillusion.ModellingTool;
import artofillusion.UndoRecord;
import artofillusion.math.CoordinateSystem;
import artofillusion.math.Vec3;
import artofillusion.object.Curve;
import artofillusion.object.NullObject;
import artofillusion.object.ObjectInfo;
import artofillusion.object.TriangleMesh;
import artofillusion.ui.PanelDialog;
import artofillusion.ui.ValueSelector;
import buoy.widget.BCheckBox;
import buoy.widget.BLabel;
import buoy.widget.ColumnContainer;

/**
 * @author Timothy Fish
 *
 */
public class Room implements ModellingTool {

    /**
     * @author Timothy Fish
     *
     */
```

Example 9-2a: Room.java

```
private class RoomDialogPanel extends ColumnContainer {

  ValueSelector widthSelector;
  ValueSelector depthSelector;
  ValueSelector heightSelector;
  BCheckBox ceilingCheckBox;
  BCheckBox floorCheckBox;
  BCheckBox frontCheckBox;
  BCheckBox backCheckBox;
  BCheckBox leftCheckBox;
  BCheckBox rightCheckBox;
  private static final double defaultValue = 25.0;
  private static final double minSize = 0.0;
  private static final double maxSize = 1000.0;
  private static final double increment = 0.1;
  private static final boolean defaultVisibility = true;

  public RoomDialogPanel(){
    add(new BLabel("Width"));
    widthSelector = new ValueSelector(defaultValue,
                           minSize, maxSize, increment);
    add(widthSelector);

    add(new BLabel("Depth"));
    depthSelector = new ValueSelector(defaultValue,
                           minSize, maxSize, increment);
    add(depthSelector);

    add(new BLabel("Height"));
    heightSelector = new ValueSelector(defaultValue,
                           minSize, maxSize, increment);
    add(heightSelector);

    ceilingCheckBox = new BCheckBox("Ceiling Visible",
                                    defaultVisibility);
    add(ceilingCheckBox);

    floorCheckBox = new BCheckBox("Floor Visible",
                                    defaultVisibility);
    add(floorCheckBox);

    frontCheckBox = new BCheckBox("Front Visible",
                                    defaultVisibility);
    add(frontCheckBox);


    backCheckBox = new BCheckBox("Back Visible",
                                    defaultVisibility);
    add(backCheckBox);

    leftCheckBox = new BCheckBox("Left Visible",
                                    defaultVisibility);
    add(leftCheckBox);

    rightCheckBox = new BCheckBox("Right Visible",
                                    defaultVisibility);
```

Example 9-2b: Room.java

```java
        add(rightCheckBox);
    }

    public double getWidth() {
        return widthSelector.getValue();
    }

    public double getDepth() {
        return depthSelector.getValue();
    }

    public double getHeight() {
        return heightSelector.getValue();
    }

    public boolean getCeilingVisible() {
        return ceilingCheckBox.getState();
    }

    public boolean getFloorVisible() {
        return floorCheckBox.getState();
    }

    public boolean getFrontVisible() {
        return frontCheckBox.getState();
    }

    public boolean getBackVisible() {
        return backCheckBox.getState();
    }

    public boolean getLeftVisible() {
        return leftCheckBox.getState();
    }

    public boolean getRightVisible() {
        return rightCheckBox.getState();
    }

}

private LayoutWindow layout;
private final String windowTitle = "Room Setup";
private double width;
private double depth;
private double height;
private boolean ceilingVisible;
private boolean floorVisible;
private boolean frontVisible;
private boolean backVisible;
private boolean leftVisible;
private boolean rightVisible;
private int roomCount = 0;

/**
 * Call-back for when menu item is selected.
```

Example 9-2c: Room.java

```
    */
    @Override
    public void commandSelected(LayoutWindow window) {
        // Create a new UndoRecord. This will be built as we
        // make changes, so we can go back to the previous state
        // of anything we changed.
        UndoRecord undo = new UndoRecord(window, true);

        layout = window;
        if(setRoomSizeAndOptions()){

            buildRoom(undo);
            window.updateImage();

            // Tell the layout window that it can store what we've
            // said is the previous state of the object.
            window.setUndoRecord(undo);
        }
    }

    /**
     * Create the walls of the room based on the class
     * variables.
     * @param undo
     */
    private void buildRoom(UndoRecord undo) {
        // Add a null object to the scene
        ObjectInfo roomInfo = new ObjectInfo(new NullObject(),
            new CoordinateSystem(),
            "Room "+nextRoomCount() );

        float roomSmoothness[] = {0.0f, 0.0f, 0.0f, 0.0f};
        // Add ceiling
        Vec3[] ceilingVertices = new Vec3[4];
        ceilingVertices[0] = new Vec3(-(width/2.0), height,
                                        -(depth/2.0));
        ceilingVertices[1] = new Vec3((width/2.0), height,
                                        -(depth/2.0));
        ceilingVertices[2] = new Vec3((width/2.0), height,
                                        (depth/2.0));
        ceilingVertices[3] = new Vec3(-(width/2.0), height,
                                        (depth/2.0));
        createSide(undo, roomInfo, roomSmoothness, "Ceiling",
                    ceilingVertices, ceilingVisible);


        // Add floor
        Vec3[] floorVertices = new Vec3[4];
        floorVertices[0] = new Vec3(-(width/2.0), 0.0,
                                    -(depth/2.0));
        floorVertices[1] = new Vec3((width/2.0), 0.0,
                                    -(depth/2.0));
        floorVertices[2] = new Vec3((width/2.0), 0.0,
                                    (depth/2.0));
        floorVertices[3] = new Vec3(-(width/2.0), 0.0,
                                    (depth/2.0));
```

Example 9-2d: Room.java

```
          createSide(undo, roomInfo, roomSmoothness, "Floor",
                  floorVertices, floorVisible);

          // Add front
          Vec3[] frontVertices = new Vec3[4];
          frontVertices[0] = new Vec3(-(width/2.0), 0.0,
                                    (depth/2.0));
          frontVertices[1] = new Vec3((width/2.0), 0.0,
                                    (depth/2.0));
          frontVertices[2] = new Vec3((width/2.0), height,
                                    (depth/2.0));
          frontVertices[3] = new Vec3(-(width/2.0), height,
                                    (depth/2.0));
          createSide(undo, roomInfo, roomSmoothness, "Front",
                  frontVertices, frontVisible);

          // Add back
          Vec3[] backVertices = new Vec3[4];
          backVertices[0] = new Vec3(-(width/2.0), 0.0,
                                    -(depth/2.0));
          backVertices[1] = new Vec3((width/2.0), 0.0,
                                    -(depth/2.0));
          backVertices[2] = new Vec3((width/2.0), height,
                                    -(depth/2.0));
          backVertices[3] = new Vec3(-(width/2.0), height,
                                    -(depth/2.0));
          createSide(undo, roomInfo, roomSmoothness, "Back",
                  backVertices, backVisible);

          // Add left
          Vec3[] leftVertices = new Vec3[4];
          leftVertices[0] = new Vec3(-(width/2.0), 0.0,
                                    (depth/2.0));
          leftVertices[1] = new Vec3(-(width/2.0), 0.0,
                                    -(depth/2.0));
          leftVertices[2] = new Vec3(-(width/2.0), height,
                                    -(depth/2.0));
          leftVertices[3] = new Vec3(-(width/2.0), height,
                                    (depth/2.0));
          createSide(undo, roomInfo, roomSmoothness, "Left",
                  leftVertices, leftVisible);

          // Add right
          Vec3[] rightVertices = new Vec3[4];
          rightVertices[0] = new Vec3((width/2.0), 0.0,
                                    (depth/2.0));
          rightVertices[1] = new Vec3((width/2.0), 0.0,
                                    -(depth/2.0));
          rightVertices[2] = new Vec3((width/2.0), height,
                                    -(depth/2.0));
          rightVertices[3] = new Vec3((width/2.0), height,
                                    (depth/2.0));
          createSide(undo, roomInfo, roomSmoothness, "Right",
                  rightVertices, rightVisible);

          layout.addObject(roomInfo, undo);
```

Example 9-2e: Room.java

```
}

/**
 * Creates a side of the room and adds it to the scene.
 * @param undo
 * @param roomInfo
 * @param roomSmoothness
 * @param sideName
 * @param sideVertices
 */
private void createSide(UndoRecord undo,
    ObjectInfo roomInfo,
    float[] roomSmoothness, String sideName,
    Vec3[] sideVertices,
    boolean visible) {
  Curve side = new Curve(sideVertices, roomSmoothness,
                        Curve.NO_SMOOTHING, true);
  TriangleMesh sideMesh = side.convertToTriangleMesh(1.0);
  ObjectInfo sideInfo = new ObjectInfo(
      sideMesh,
      new CoordinateSystem(new Vec3(0,0,0), 0.0, 0.0,0.0),
                        sideName);
  sideInfo.setVisible(visible);
  roomInfo.addChild(sideInfo,
                    roomInfo.getChildren().length);
  layout.getScene().addObject(sideInfo, undo);
}

/**
 * Returns next number for the room.
 * @return
 */
private int nextRoomCount() {
  roomCount++;
  return roomCount;
}

/**
 * Displays dialog for user to select room options.
 * @return true if ok select, false if canceled
 */
private boolean setRoomSizeAndOptions() {
  RoomDialogPanel thePanel = new RoomDialogPanel();


  PanelDialog dlg = new PanelDialog(layout, windowTitle,
thePanel);

  if (dlg.clickedOk()){
    // User clicked ok, so store the selected value.
    width = thePanel.getWidth();
    depth = thePanel.getDepth();
    height = thePanel.getHeight();
    ceilingVisible = thePanel.getCeilingVisible();
    floorVisible = thePanel.getFloorVisible();
```

Example 9-2f: Room.java

```java
        frontVisible = thePanel.getFrontVisible();
        backVisible = thePanel.getBackVisible();
        leftVisible = thePanel.getLeftVisible();
        rightVisible = thePanel.getRightVisible();

        return true;
      }
      else{
        // User clicked cancel, so everything should remain
        // unchanged.
        return false;
      }
  }

  /**
   * Return the menu item name.
   */
  @Override
  public String getName() {
    return "Create Room...";
  }

}
```

Example 9-2g: Room.java

Chapter 10

Simulating Cloth

My interest in writing plugins for Art of Illusion began out of a desire to have cloth simulation capability within Art of Illusion. At the time there was talk on discussion boards along the lines of "someone should go do that" and I really expected and hoped that someone more motivated than me would take on the task. From what I have seen on the Art of Illusion discussion board, this does not appear to be the case.

I'm pleased to say that my own efforts have proved fruitful, though I would describe the plugin that I have developed as still being in Beta development. The framework is certainly there and I have been able to generate a few cloth animations that I've been happy with. My reasons for saying it is still a Beta version is that the way it handles collisions with other objects is not what I would like and collisions with moving objects are

Figure 10-1: US Flag Simulated with Art of Illusion

still a mess. I suspect that the speed could be improved. The plugin is a huge memory hog. And during collision detection it appears to find collisions in places where there are no objects. Even with its shortcomings, I believe you will find value in understanding how the features are implemented.

Most cloth simulators work on the concept of a number of masses that are connected by a series of springs. The books on the subject usually show an image similar to the one shown in Figure 10-2. Each ball in the image represents a mass and the lines between them represent springs that constrain them. Each mass has various forces that pull on them. One of these forces is gravity. There may be other external forces, such as wind or other objects pushing against the cloth. Each of these forces are calculated for each mass and added to the velocity of the mass to determine the new velocity of the mass. But because these masses are connected via springs when one of the masses is moved it will change the tension on its springs. The forces from the springs are also added to the velocity of the mass. This propagates through the springs to the other masses resulting in one part of the cloth responding to changes in another part of the cloth.

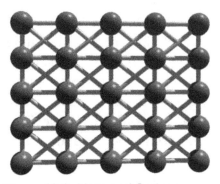

Figure 10-2: Mass and Springs

This concept of cloth simulation is helpful in explaining how it works but it gets more complicated when we start to put it into practice. First, some cloth simulations have produced better results when it isn't just the neighboring masses that are connected by springs but the neighbors of the neighbors are connected. Second, when our goal is to render objects in a scene we may want our cloth to be some other shape than rectangular. We might not want it to be one of the primitive shapes at all. We might want it to be the shape of a man's shirt or a woman's dress. For that we need an algorithm that will define masses and springs for any odd shaped object.

The Cloth Maker Plugin

Before we get into the details of how the cloth simulation is implemented let me explain how it is used. A cloth can be any shape, so we must first begin with a scene object that is the shape we desire and then convert it into a cloth. To do this we select the object and then select "Convert to Cloth..." from the Object menu. This brings up a dialog that requests information concerning how accurately we want to represent the object as a triangle mesh. The smaller the numbers the more triangles there will be. More triangles give us better looking results but with the tradeoff that it requires more computational resources. Calculations for cloth simulations can take a significant amount of time.

When you click okay the original object will be replaced by a cloth. The appearance will not change but now when you select the cloth you can choose "Generate Cloth Simulation..." from the Object menu. This brings up another window that will allow you to specify which vertices to simulate and which to freeze in place. It also has various settings for the simulation. After confirming this window the tool will spend several minutes generating the simulation. The end result is that a number of animation frames will be added to the object. This allows you to either render a movie of the cloth simulation or to render a particular frame by selecting that time in the timeline.

While other objects in the scene change how the cloth behaves as it drapes over them, the plugin also includes a Fan object that can be used to apply a wind force to the cloth. If the fan is animated then the cloth will respond to the changing forces produced by the fan.

```xml
<?xml version="1.0" standalone="yes"?>

<extension name="Cloth Maker" version="0.1" >
  <author>Timothy Fish</author>
  <date>September 2018</date>

  <plugin
class="extending.aoi.clothmaker.ClothMakerPlugin" />

  <description>This plugin adds cloth simulation to Art of
Illusion. This plugin provides the capability for an object
in the scene to be converted into a cloth object and for a
cloth simulation to be calculated for that object. This
simulation will be used during animation to calculate the
distortion of the cloth object. This plugin also provides
the capability to convert the distorted cloth to a rigid
object that can be manipulated as a non-cloth object. This
plugin also adds a Fan scene object which extends the
WindSource class. A WindSource produces a force on a cloth
object that is both time and position dependent.
</description>
  <resource name="icons/theme.xml" id="ClothMaker"
type="UITheme"/>
  <comments>This plugin takes the work from the
HangingCloth cloth simulator and turns
    it into a refined tool that can be used within Art of
Illusion. </comments>

  <history>
    <log version="0.1" date="September 2018"
author="Timothy Fish" >- Initial Version</log>
  </history>

</extension>
```

Example 10-1: Extensions.xml

The Design

Because of the amount of code involved I will not provide all of the code in the book but will provide an overview of what the code does, leaving it to the reader to download the code from the website. The *extensions.xml* file is simple. It defines the plugin class as "extending.aoi.clothmaker.ClothMakerPlugin" and it defines the resource file as "icons/theme.xml".

ClothMakerPlugin

The ClothMakerPlugin class implements Plugin. The ClothMakerPlugin class defines several default values that are used by the cloth simulator. They are included here so that they are all in one place.

In terms of what this file does there is nothing that hasn't been demonstrated in one of the previous plugins. The message handler handles only the SCENE_WINDOW_CREATED message. It adds a Fan tool to the tool palette. It also creates three menu items for the Object Menu. As has been done with other menu items, it instantiates a menu item activator that controls whether these menu items are enabled or disabled based on the state of the scene.

The most interesting code in this file is at the end of the callback function for the "Convert to Cloth..." menu item:

```
Cloth cloth = new Cloth(info, meshTolerance, massDistance,
        springConstant, dampingConstant, collisionDistance);
ObjectInfo C = new ObjectInfo(cloth, new CoordinateSystem(),
                info.getName()+" (Cloth "+counter+")");
C.coords.setOrigin(info.coords.getOrigin());
C.coords.setOrientation(info.coords.getZDirection(),
                info.coords.getUpDirection());
counter++;
layout.setUndoRecord(new UndoRecord(layout, false,
        UndoRecord.COPY_OBJECT_INFO, new Object [] {info,
                                info.duplicate()}));
layout.addObject(C, new UndoRecord(layout, false));
layout.removeObject(layout.getScene().indexOf(info),
                new UndoRecord(layout, false));
```

In this section a Cloth is instantiated using the selected scene object as the first input to the constructor. You will see more about how this works when you look at the Cloth class, but the goal is to create a cloth object that looks as much as possible like the object from which it was created. If the object is a flat sheet of some kind then the cloth should look like a flat sheet. If the object is a cube or a sphere then the cloth should look like a cube or a sphere. The appearance will change when the simulation is run but the conversion should not change how the scene looks.

This section also removes the original object from the scene. You should see similarity between how the Convert to Cloth feature works and how the Convert to Triangle Mesh feature works.

The next section adds a track to the score. We've added tracks to the score before. What makes this case interesting is that the track we are adding is of type ClothTrack, which is a class written specifically for this plugin.

```
layout.setSelection(layout.getScene().indexOf(C));
Score theScore = layout.getScore();
theScore.addTrack(layout.getSelectedObjects().toArray(),
ClothTrack.class, new Object [] {layout.getScene()}, true);
layout.updateImage();
layout.updateMenus();
```

ClothMenuItemActivator

ClothMenuItemActivator enables the "Convert to Cloth..." menu item if one and only one non-cloth is selected. It enables "Generate Cloth Simulation..." if one and only one cloth is selected.

Cloth

A Cloth is an Object3D and implements Mesh. When the "Convert to Cloth..." menu item is used a Cloth is instantiated with the selected object passed into the constructor. Cloth creates a TriangleMesh from the object and uses the connected vertices to define a set of Masses and Springs. It is common to use a mass and spring simulation to simulate cloth but most documentation on such simulations begin with a convenient set of masses and springs laid out in an array. Because we cannot assume every cloth is a flat sheet and for simplicity, the Cloth uses the vertices wherever they are placed in the triangle mesh. Springs are added between connected vertices and the initial state of the spring is assumed to be at rest. A cloth with no external forces on it and no self collision detection should naturally return to the initial state.

You can think of the Cloth object as being the state data for a cloth. This is where the masses and the springs are stored. The cloth contains masses and springs. The Cloth is a sort of snapshot in time that specifies these things. The Cloth doesn't have to know at the beginning of the animation it was hanging straight or that after a few seconds it will be lying crumpled on the floor of the scene. It just needs to know its state right now, whatever "now" means.

ClothDistortion

In a cloth simulation the position of the vertices in the cloth object change over time. Consider the two images in Figure 10-3. They are both the same scene object, but time and gravity has produced the second during a cloth simulation. Everything about

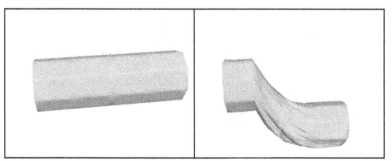

Figure 10-3: Distorted Cloth

these two images is the same, right down to the number of vertices that each have, but the location of those vertices is different. To define how the vertices change between these two we use a Distortion.

In Art of Illusion a Distortion is a special object that defines how the vertices of another object change. Built into Art of Illusion are some distortions that do things like break an object into its triangles and make them appear to fly off into space like an explosion or to warp the shape of the object. Given a specified time and the state of the scene, the ClothDistortion calculates what the cloth should look like. In particular, the transform function returns a Cloth object for each frame. The heart of the cloth simulation is in this class. It uses the previous frame as a starting point and returns the Cloth for the current frame.

For the images in Figure 10-3 there are a few hundred frames that lie between the first image and the second. Each is a step in the cloth simulation. Each is calculated using a call to the transform() function of the ClothDistortion class. There are two transform functions. The smaller tranform() function is used to play back the cloth simulation once the calculations are done, but the second tranform () function takes a Cloth as the first parameter and the frame number we want to calculate as the second parameter. It returns a Cloth that is like the Cloth we passed in but it has been modified as it should be for the frame we asked the ClothDistortion to calculate. This means that the resulting Cloth will have the vertices in different locations, the masses will have different velocities, and the springs will have different tensions.

In general, a Distortion takes an object as input and outputs an object that is distorted in some way. For the ClothDistortion the way the object is modified is that the calculations for a cloth simulation have been applied to it. This is where you will find the bulk of the cloth simulation algorithm.

Retrieve the Previous State

You should think of these transformations in terms of animation frames. Little by little as we move frame by frame through an animation the cloth is changed by the state of the scene in that timeframe. To calculate the current state we must first determine the state of the cloth in the previous frame. Frame 0 is always the initial state that exists when we select the "Generate Cloth Simulation..." menu item.

After initializing the positions array to the vertex locations of the cloth that is passed in, tranform makes the following call:

```
SimFrame prevSF = load_prev_mesh(frame);
if(prevSF == null) {
  prevSF = new SimFrame(frame, retObj);
}
```

This call looks for the immediately previous frame in memory. If there isn't one prevSF is initialized to the initial frame. The values from prevSF are used to initialize arrays P, W, and V which we will populate with Position, Weight, and Velocity information for each vertex in the cloth object.

Calculate the Forces

The for loop loops through each mass/vertex in the cloth. The following variables are used:

g : gravity

t : time

m : mass

u : velocity of the mass

F : force on the mass

k : spring constant

c : damping constant

a : acceleration vector

s : displacement vector

v : velocity vector

We first calculate the force that is on each mass due to gravity and it's own velocity. This is given by the following:

$$F = g \cdot m - (u \cdot c)$$

If the velocity is zero then this is simply the force vector due to gravity, so we should expect that with no other forces applied we would see the cloth move downward.

The u variable is the velocity vector that carries over from the previous step. The damping constant, c, is used to control how important the existing velocity is to the force calculation. This is one of the values the user is able to change. A large value for the damping constant causes the existing velocity to impact the simulation more.

Next we add the other external forces. For now, the only external forces are those produced by a Fan object. The object itself is discussed later, but the Fan object is intended to be the base class object for a variety of wind producing objects that can be added to the scene. Each Fan is animated using an animation track, so we apply the animation to the Fan at the time of the frame we are calculating for the cloth simulation and call getForce() to get the amount of force the Fan has on the vertex. We add the forces from each Fan to the force from above.

Lastly, we add the forces that are coming from each of the Springs that are connected to the mass. The force from each Spring is given by the following:

$$F = \hat{d}(-k(L_{rest} - L_{current}))$$

The variable $\hat{d}$ is the directional vector of the force. We multiply this by the spring constant, k, times the length of the spring at rest minus the current length of the spring. You will notice that when two connected masses are at the resting length from each other the force is zero. If these are pulled apart from each other then the force will increase, pulling them back toward each other. If they are pushed together the force will increase, pushing them apart from each other.

There are some masses that we give a zero force vector. In the cloth editor we have the option of selecting some vertexes and freezing them in place. Giving these vertexes a force of zero results in them staying where they are.

Calculate New Positions

Once the force vector for each mass is determined we can determine how that changes the position of each mass. We first calculate the acceleration vector:

$$a = \frac{F}{m}$$

The displacement vector is given by

The new velocity is given by

$$v = u + at$$

The new position is the current position plus the displacement vector, s, but we constrain how much the mass can move at each step using the clamp() function. This prevents the vertices from jumping around too much, causing points to show up in our animations.

Detect Collisions

After the new positions are calculated we compare each vertex location to the other objects in the scene. If they fall within the bounding box of one of those objects we take a closer look to see if the line between the vertex and its previous location intersects an object in the scene. If it does, we calculate the point a which the intersection occurred and we reposition the vertex there with a velocity of zero.

This works fairly well with stationary objects. Things get more complicated with objects that are moving. The details of how a collision is detected are in the CollisionDetector class. Within the ClothDistortion class we check the return values from CollisionDetector and determine vertex positioning based on those value. We first check to see if a self-collision has occurred. The situation where the new vertex location is colliding with another part of the cloth is handled by reverting to the previous vertex location. The assumption is that no self-collision occurred in the previous frame so there won't be one if we leave the vertex were it was.

Figure 10-4: Flag Colliding with Sphere

Next, we check for collisions with the other objects in the scene without respect to whether the objects have moved or not. We ignore objects that are outside a small bounding box around the vertex. If there is a collision within that bounding box then the CollisionDetector will tell us the location of that collision and we set the vertex to that position. We set the velocity of the vertex to zero.

Lastly, we pass the CollisionDetector the objects that have moved between the two time frames. These are passed one at a time to allow for the differences in movement of the various objects.

CollisionDetector

The CollisionDetector class is a helper class that provides the functionality to determine when the Cloth collides with other objects in the scene. When collisions are detected the forces on the cloth are adjusted to prevent the cloth from going through the other objects.

isSpecial

The isSpecial() function returns true if an object that is passed to it is of a type that cloth shouldn't collide with. The special objects are lights, cameras, null objects, and reference images.

findCandidateObjects

The findCandidateObjects() function takes a bounding box as input and searches through the objects in the scene to find those that intersect the bounding box. By limiting our candidate objects to only those that may be close enough to the cloth to impact it we greatly reduce the number of comparisons that must take place when searching for collisions.

findDistanceToCollisionPoint

When repositioning a vertex that is going to collide with something we need to know how far from its current position the collision occurs. This function is used to provide us with that information.

We also have a couple of special case functions that provide us with this information for when colliding with a Cylinder or with an Ellipsoid. By having a special case we don't have to convert them into triangle meshes. Triangle meshes work well for the general case but require a large number of triangles to produce smooth objects and to avoid odd looking artifacts.

getLastDistanceToCollision

When the class detects a collision it stores information about where it occurred so that objects outside of the class can request that information without making another costly collision search.

ClothTrack

A Cloth Track is an animation track that stores various aspects of the simulation. It also creates the ClothDistortion. At this time the only thing it does is allow the user to disable the cloth simulation distortion, but the ability to keyframe various attributes of the cloth could be added if someone desired to do so. One wouldn't normally expect to see cloth constants change mid-simulation , but the possibility is there.

ClothSimEditorWindow

This window displays the Cloth and allows vertices to be selected and various simulation settings to be changed. This window also kicks off the calculation of the simulation.

In Figure 10-5 you can see that this is where you set most of the values related to simulating cloth. You can specify some of the vertices to lock in place by selecting them and choosing "Lock in Place" from the Mesh menu. Most of the input fields need no explanation, but some might.

Drape Frames is the number of frames simulated before time zero of the animation. The advantage over just starting the animation later is that drape frames are not stored, so you can create a longer simulation without taking up as much memory. Sim Frames is how many visible frames there are. Drape

Frames is the number of frames that are calculated between visible frames. Collision Distance is how close to an object a vertex has to be to hit it. A larger collision distance will help keep the cloth from appearing to be inside the object. Spring Constant is how stiff the cloth is. Damping Constant is how much impact the existing velocity of a vertex has on the simulation.

ClothMeshViewer

The ClothMeshViewer is a MeshViewer that displays the Cloth object. This special viewer is need-

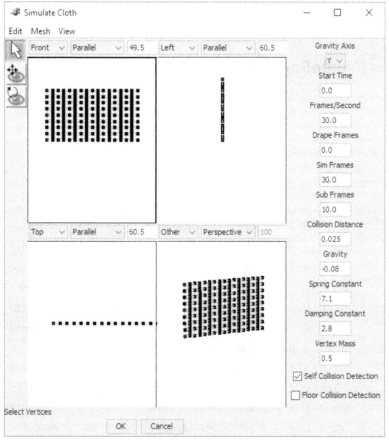

Figure 10-5: ClothSimEditorWindow with ClothMeshViewer and SelectTool in use.

ed because when generating the simulation we have the capability to freeze specific vertices so that they remain in place. These vertices are displayed in blue.

SelectTool

This tool is added to the tool menu of the ClothSimEditorWindow to allow the user to select vertices. By default the editor window is already in selection mode, but if one of the other two tools are used it is necessary to have a means by which to tell it to change back into selection mode. The SelectTool button does this.

The code for this is very similar to other tools that are used for plugins in this book, it just appears on an editor window instead of on the main button bar.

CreateFanTool

This class provides a button that can be used to add a Fan to the scene. As with the SelectTool, the code is just the same type of thing as is described in more detail by other plugins that appear earlier in this book.

Fan

A Fan is a scene object that applies a directional wind force to Cloth objects that are in the scene. A Fan is only visible as a wireframe object when editing and does not appear in the rendered scene. The base Fan class specifies the magnitude and falloff (distance from fan the force exists). The Fan is a steady-state force with some randomness built into it. If you need a wind force that responds in some way other than that then you should write a class that extends Fan. However, even with just a steady force it is possible to get the appearance of changing wind by keyframing the rotation track of the fan. You can also remove the impact of the fan entirely by using keyframes that po-

sition the fan outside the falloff
range when the wind force is
undesirable and positioning it
closer when the wind is desira-
ble. Also, the wind from the fan
is not included in the simulation
at all when the Fan object is invisible.

Figure 10-6: Fan

Processing the Simulation

As mentioned above, the bulk of the processing for the simulation occurs in the ClothDistortion class. This is done in the Update function. As with
most particle simulations the general algorithm for a
cloth simulation is as follows:

1. Calculate forces on each particle

2. Adjust the velocity of each particle

3. Reposition the particle based on velocity and
   time

4. Detect collisions and reposition particle to avoid
   collision

5. Recalculate the spring tension

6. Repeat

In the Update function we are doing these calculations as a delta from the previous frame. Or if we
use subframes then we are doing it as a delta from the
previous subframe. If we have 30 frames per second
then we reposition each vertex by the amount it
moves within 1/30 second. There are a number of
different forces on each mass. Gravity applies to each
mass. Wind applies to each mass. These forces have a
magnitude and a direction. These forces are added to
the directional velocity of the mass. But in the cloth

simulation there are also springs that connect the masses together. The springs define how the masses interact with each other, but they are also just another force that must me added to the velocity of a mass.

From the algorithm above, numbers 1 through 5 are done within the update function of the ClothDistortion class. Number 6 is accomplished via a loop that appears in the doSim function of the ClothSimEditorWindow. When the user clicks the Ok button the values are read from the data entry boxes by the doSim function. It then goes into a loop. Drape frames are treated as negative time values so that they will not appear in the animation. Both drape frames and simulation frames are multiplied by the sub-Frames value to determine the number of times the body of the loop must be executed. Inside the loop the simulateCloth function of the ClothTrack class is called. Each time it is called a new ClothDistortion is instantiated and transform is called and a new frame containing the Cloth returned from the transform is returned. These frames are stored so that we will not need to recalculate them when the animation is running. During the actual animation and rendering the distortion just returns the stored values.

This process can be described as the following:

1. Set cloth simulation inputs via the ClothSimEditor-Window

2. For the track associated with the Cloth object generate a frame

3. For the new frame use the distortion class to calculate vertex locations for the time of the frame.

4. Repeat 2 and 3 until all frames are generated

We use a Track in this situation because in an animation it is the Track that has frames. The Distortion will tell us how one frame differs from another.

Problems and Improvements

As I come to the close of this chapter I find myself asking myself whether the Cloth Maker Plugin is ready to be released into the world. There always seems to be "one more thing" for me to fix. Even when it comes to possible improvements that could be made I no sooner think of one than I find myself deciding to try to put it into the code before I publish the book. I have seen a number of cloth simulators and this one still has a ways to go, though I believe it is good enough for people to start playing with and maybe even create some scenes in Art of Illusion that they couldn't otherwise create.

Here are some of the problems that I've noticed:

Sharp edges—Corners of objects tend to poke through the cloth. This is less noticeable for cloths with a larger number of vertices, but it frequently occurs.

Long jumps—with some objects I've seen some of the vertices jump to the opposite side of the object, creating a stretched or bunched up look. One workaround is to hide that object while generating the cloth simulation and use a dummy object of a similar shape for the cloth simulation. Then hide the dummy and use the original during rendering.

Motion—when objects are moving in the scene the cloth doesn't always respond well. Often the object will push through the cloth and the cloth will fall away.

Behavior based on vertex count—Increasing the number of vertexes changes the length of simulation time a cloth object takes.

Cloth isn't centered in the edit window—when the cloth edit window comes up it shows the scene without drawing the cloth in the center. This works for most cases but it will be difficult to find the cloth if the cloth is off in some corner of a large scene.

Here are some of the improvements I believe the plugin would benefit from:

Choosing collision objects—It would be nice to be able to select the objects the cloth collides with rather than having to hide those we want to exclude.

A preview window—Currently, the plugin goes off and generates the cloth simulation and the user doesn't see any result until it is done. It would be better if they could watch as it is built and be able to stop it if it isn't doing what they hoped.

Convert distorted object to solid—For scenes where we are just rending one image we may use the cloth simulator to generate a particular image, such as that of a tablecloth falling from a table. Once it is created we don't want to keep the steps it took to get there since that requires a significant amount of memory. It would be nice to be able to convert the cloth to a mesh that is the same distorted shape as the one we see on the screen.

The Ongoing Effort

Because a project like this is never complete, I created a repository on GitHub:

https//github.com/TimothyFish/AOI-cloth-maker

Any fixes or improvements that are made to the plugin will be stored there. My hope is that the plugin will eventually advance well beyond the state that is described in this book. My own efforts related to that will depend greatly on how much I use the tool and my tolerance for the weaknesses of the tool as they currently exist. If others would to make improvements to the ClothMaker plugin I would welcome their input.

Quick Reference

The next section of this book is a quick reference of the classes contained in the Art of Illusion API and the Buoy API, which Art of Illusion uses for windowing capability. This reference also includes a listing of math equations that you may find useful when working with 3D graphics.

The classes included in this reference are listed first by package and then they are listed in alphabetical order by class name. For each class, the public and protected member elements are listed, along with function parameters. When writing code for Art of Illusion scripts and plugins, it is through these interfaces that you will be able to access the class information, either by calling functions directly or by overriding the functions in the child classes you create. You can think of this information as the "header file" information. It does not include the body of the source code or descriptions of the functions. You should consult the Art of Illusion and Buoy source file documentation if you need more information, but use this reference to jog your memory or to provide an overview of what is available.

Chapter 11

The artofillusion Package

The artofillusion package defines interfaces to the outside world. It defines the tools that the user selects when creating a scene. This includes such classes as CreateCubeTool, CreateSphereTool, and Create-LightTool. It defines the windows that the user sees with classes like CurveEditorWindow, LayoutWindow, and ObjectEditorWindow. It defines some of the plugin interfaces, for use with plugin development. Other plugin interface are scattered through the other packages.

artofillusion.ApplicationPreferences

This class handles the application wide preferences. It loads the preferences from the file, saves the preferences to file, initiates the PreferencesWindow, and provides a location from which to retrieve the preferences through code.

```
public class ApplicationPreferences{
  public ApplicationPreferences();
  public ApplicationPreferences(InputStream in);
  public void savePreferences();
  public static File getPreferencesDirectory();
  public final Renderer getDefaultRenderer();
  public final void setDefaultRenderer(Renderer rend);
  public final Renderer getObjectPreviewRenderer()
  public final void setObjectPreviewRenderer(Renderer rend);
  public final Renderer getTexturePreviewRenderer();
```

259

```
    public final void setTexturePreviewRenderer(Renderer rend);
    public final int getDefaultDisplayMode();
    public final void setDefaultDisplayMode(int mode);
    public final double getInteractiveSurfaceError();
    public final void setInteractiveSurfaceError(double tol);
    public final Locale getLocale();
    public final void setLocale(Locale locale);
    public final int getUndoLevels();
    public final void setUndoLevels(int levels);
    public final boolean getUseOpenGL();
    public final void setUseOpenGL(boolean use);
    public final boolean getKeepBackupFiles();
    public final void setKeepBackupFiles(boolean keep);
    public final boolean getUseCompoundMeshTool();
    public final void setUseCompoundMeshTool(boolean use);
    public final boolean getReverseZooming();
    public final void setReverseZooming(boolean reverse);
}
```

artofillusion.ArtOfIllusion

This class is the class that starts up Art of Illusion. It also holds the application's global variables. The members of this class are static, so no instance of the class is required to access its data.

```
public class ArtOfIllusion{
    public static final String APP_DIRECTORY,
                               PLUGIN_DIRECTORY;
    public static final String TOOL_SCRIPT_DIRECTORY,
                               OBJECT_SCRIPT_DIRECTORY,
                               STARTUP_SCRIPT_DIRECTORY;
    public static final ImageIcon APP_ICON;
    public static Font defaultFont;
    public static int standardDialogInsets;

    public static void main(String args[]);
    public static String getVersion();
    public static String getMajorVersion();
    public static ApplicationPreferences getPreferences();
    public static void newWindow();
    public static void newWindow(final Scene theScene);
    public static void addWindow(EditingWindow win);
    public static void closeWindow(EditingWindow win);
    public static EditingWindow[] getWindows();
    public static void quit();
    public static Class getClass(String name)
                            throws ClassNotFoundException;
    public static String loadFile(File f) throws IOException;
    public static boolean saveScene(Scene sc, LayoutWindow fr);
    public static void openScene(BFrame fr);
```

```
public static void openScene(File f, BFrame fr);
public static void copyToClipboard(ObjectInfo obj[],
                                   Scene scene);
public static void pasteClipboard(LayoutWindow win);
public static int getClipboardSize();
public static String getCurrentDirectory();
public static void setCurrentDirectory(String currentDirectory);
}
```

artofillusion.BevelExtrudeTool

This class is the tool that handles the bevels and extrudes of TriangleMeshes. In the user interface, this tool is found in the Object Edit window for a triangle mesh.

```
public class BevelExtrudeTool extends MeshEditingTool{
  public BevelExtrudeTool(EditingWindow fr,
                          MeshEditController controller);
  public int whichClicks();
  public boolean allowSelectionChanges();
  public String getToolTipText();
  public void drawOverlay(ViewerCanvas view);
  public void mousePressed(WidgetMouseEvent e,
                           ViewerCanvas view);
  public void mouseDragged(WidgetMouseEvent e,
                           ViewerCanvas view);
  public void mouseReleased(WidgetMouseEvent e,
                            ViewerCanvas view);
  protected void handlePressed(HandlePressedEvent ev);
  protected void handleDragged(HandleDraggedEvent ev);
  protected void handleReleased(HandleReleasedEvent ev);
  public void iconDoubleClicked();
}
```

artofillusion.Camera

The Camera is a conceptual representation that is used to keep track of transformations within a scene. This is not the same thing as the camera object that users are able to place in the scene and control. That type of camera is defined by artofillusion.object.SceneCamera. Camera also draws some simple shapes.

```
public class Camera implements Cloneable{
  public static final double
DEFAULT_DISTANCE_TO_SCREEN;
```

```
public Camera();
public void setDistToScreen(double dist);
public double getDistToScreen();
public double getClipDistance();
public void setClipDistance(double distance);
public boolean isPerspective();
public Camera duplicate();
public void setScreenTransform(Mat4 screenTransform,
                               int width, int height);
public void setScreenParams(double newViewDist,
                            double newScale,
                            int newHres, int newVres);
public void setScreenParamsParallel(double newScale,
                                    int newHres, int newVres);
public void setSize(int newHres, int newVres);
public Dimension getSize();
public void setGrid(double spacing);
public void setCameraCoordinates(CoordinateSystem coords);
public void setViewTransform(Mat4 worldToView,
                             Mat4 viewToWorld);
public CoordinateSystem getCameraCoordinates();
public void setObjectTransform(Mat4 m);
public final Mat4 getObjectToWorld();
public final Mat4 getObjectToView();
public final Mat4 getObjectToScreen();
public final Mat4 getWorldToView();
public final Mat4 getWorldToScreen();
public final Mat4 getViewToScreen();
public final Mat4 getViewToWorld();
public Vec3 convertScreenToWorld(Point p, double depth);
public Vec3 convertScreenToWorld(Point p, double depth,
boolean snapToGrid);
public Vec3 convertScreenToWorld(Vec2 p, double depth,
boolean snapToGrid);
public Vec3 findDragVector(Vec3 p, int dx, int dy);
public Vec3 findDragVector(Vec3 p, double dx, double dy);
public Rectangle findScreenBounds(BoundingBox bb);

public static final int NOT_VISIBLE;
public static final int NEEDS_CLIPPING;
public static final int VISIBLE;

public int visibility(BoundingBox bb);
public void drawLine(Graphics g, Vec3 from, Vec3 to);
public void drawClippedLine(Graphics g, Vec3 from, Vec3 to);
public void drawLineTo(Graphics g, Vec3 to);
public void drawClippedLineTo(Graphics g, Vec3 to);
public void drawBox(Graphics g, BoundingBox bb);
public void drawClippedBox(Graphics g, BoundingBox bb);
public void drawBezier(Graphics g, Vec3 v1, Vec3 v2, Vec3 v3,
Vec3 v4);
public void drawClippedBezier(Graphics g, Vec3 v1, Vec3 v2,
Vec3 v3, Vec3 v4);
```

```
public void drawBezier2(Graphics g, Vec3 v1, Vec3 v2, Vec3 v3,
Vec3 v4);
void divideAndDraw(Graphics g, int x1, int x2, int x3, int x4, int y1,
int y2, int y3, int y4, int w1, int w2, int w3, int w4, int count);
}
```

artofillusion.CameraFilterDialog

This class defines the window that the user uses to select the various filters that can be used for post processing a rendered image.

```
public class CameraFilterDialog extends BDialog implements Ren-
derListener{
public CameraFilterDialog(EditingWindow parent,
SceneCamera camera, CoordinateSystem cameraCoords);
public void imageUpdated(Image image);
public void statusChanged(String status);
public void imageComplete(ComplexImage image);
public void renderingCanceled();
public static class FiltersPanel extends FormContainer
{
  public FiltersPanel(SceneCamera camera,
                  Runnable filterChangedCallback);
  public ArrayList<ImageFilter> getFilters();
}
}
```

artofillusion.CompoundImplicitEditor Window

This class represents the window for editing CompoundImplicitObjects.

```
public class CompoundImplicitEditorWindow extends ObjectEditor-
Window{
public CompoundImplicitEditorWindow(EditingWindow parent,
String title, CompoundImplicitObject obj, Runnable onClose);
protected ViewerCanvas createViewerCanvas(int index, RowCon-
tainer controls);
protected void createViewMenu();
public void updateMenus();
public Scene getScene();
protected void doOk();
protected void doCancel();
public void renderPreviewCommand();
}
```

artofillusion.CreateCameraTool

This is the EditingTool for creating SceneCameras.

```
public class CreateCameraTool extends EditingTool{
  public CreateCameraTool(LayoutWindow fr);
  public void activate();
  public int whichClicks();
  public String getToolTipText();
  public void mousePressed(WidgetMouseEvent e,
                    ViewerCanvas view);
  public void mouseReleased(WidgetMouseEvent e,
                    ViewerCanvas view);
}
```

artofillusion.CreateCubeTool

This is the tool for creating a cube.

```
public class CreateCubeTool extends EditingTool{
  public CreateCubeTool(LayoutWindow fr);
  public void activate();
  public int whichClicks();
  public String getToolTipText();
  public void mousePressed(WidgetMouseEvent e,
                    ViewerCanvas view);
  public void mouseDragged(WidgetMouseEvent e,
                    ViewerCanvas view);
  public void mouseReleased(WidgetMouseEvent e,
                    ViewerCanvas view);
}
```

artofillusion.CreateCurveTool

This is the tool for creating curves.

```
public class CreateCurveTool extends EditingTool{
  public static final int HANDLE_SIZE;
  public CreateCurveTool(EditingWindow fr);
  public void activate();
  public void deactivate();
  public int whichClicks();
  public String getToolTipText();
  public boolean hilightSelection();
  public void drawOverlay(ViewerCanvas view);
  public void mousePressed(WidgetMouseEvent e,
                    ViewerCanvas view);
  public void mouseDragged(WidgetMouseEvent e,
                    ViewerCanvas view);
  public void mouseReleased(WidgetMouseEvent e,
```

```
                        ViewerCanvas view);
    public void keyPressed(KeyPressedEvent e,
                        ViewerCanvas view);
    public void iconDoubleClicked();
}
```

artofillusion.CreateCylinderTool

This is the tool for drawing cylinders.

```
public class CreateCylinderTool extends EditingTool{
    public CreateCylinderTool(LayoutWindow fr);
    public void activate();
    public int whichClicks();
    public String getToolTipText();
    public void mousePressed(WidgetMouseEvent e,
                        ViewerCanvas view);
    public void mouseDragged(WidgetMouseEvent e,
                        ViewerCanvas view);
    public void mouseReleased(WidgetMouseEvent e,
                        ViewerCanvas view);
    public void iconDoubleClicked();
}
```

artofillusion.CreateLightTool

This is the tool for adding lights to the scene.

```
public class CreateLightTool extends EditingTool{
    public CreateLightTool(LayoutWindow fr);
    public void activate();
    public int whichClicks();
    public String getToolTipText();
    public void mousePressed(WidgetMouseEvent e,
                        ViewerCanvas view);
    public void mouseDragged(WidgetMouseEvent e,
                        ViewerCanvas view);
    public void mouseReleased(WidgetMouseEvent e,
                        ViewerCanvas view);
}
```

artofillusion.CreatePolygonTool

This is the tool for creating polygons.

```
public class CreatePolygonTool extends EditingTool{
    public CreatePolygonTool(LayoutWindow fr);
    public void activate();
    public int whichClicks();
    public String getToolTipText();
    public void mousePressed(WidgetMouseEvent e,
                        ViewerCanvas view);
```

```
public void mouseDragged(WidgetMouseEvent e,
                         ViewerCanvas view);
public void mouseReleased(WidgetMouseEvent e,
                          ViewerCanvas view);
public void iconDoubleClicked();
}
```

artofillusion.CreateSphereTool

This is the tool for drawing spheres.

```
public class CreateSphereTool extends EditingTool{
public CreateSphereTool(LayoutWindow fr);
public void activate();
public int whichClicks();
public String getToolTipText();
public void mousePressed(WidgetMouseEvent e,
                         ViewerCanvas view);
public void mouseDragged(WidgetMouseEvent e,
                         ViewerCanvas view);
public void mouseReleased(WidgetMouseEvent e,
                          ViewerCanvas view);
}
```

artofillusion.CreateSplineMeshTool

This is the tool for creating a spline mesh.

```
public class CreateSplineMeshTool extends EditingTool{
public CreateSplineMeshTool(LayoutWindow fr);
public void activate();
public int whichClicks()
public String getToolTipText()
public void mousePressed(WidgetMouseEvent e,
                         ViewerCanvas view);
public void mouseReleased(WidgetMouseEvent e,
                          ViewerCanvas view);
public void iconDoubleClicked();
}
```

artofillusion.CreateVertexTool

In the Triangle Mesh Editing window, this is the
tool that will create a vertex.

```
public class CreateVertexTool extends MeshEditingTool{
public CreateVertexTool(EditingWindow fr,
                        MeshEditController controller);
public void activate();
public int whichClicks();
public String getToolTipText();
```

```
    public void mousePressed(WidgetMouseEvent e,
                          ViewerCanvas view);
    public void mouseDragged(WidgetMouseEvent e,
                          ViewerCanvas view);
    public void mouseReleased(WidgetMouseEvent e,
                          ViewerCanvas view);
}
```

artofillusion.CSGDialog

This is the dialog window that will allow the user to specify options for Boolean modeling of objects.

```
public class CSGDialog extends BDialog{
  public CSGDialog(EditingWindow window, CSGObject obj);
  public boolean clickedOk();
}
```

artofillusion.CSGEditorWindow

This window is for editing the Boolean modeled objects.

```
public class CSGEditorWindow extends ObjectEditorWindow{
  public CSGEditorWindow(EditingWindow parent, String title,
CSGObject obj, Runnable onClose);
  protected ViewerCanvas createViewerCanvas(int index,
RowContainer controls);
  protected void createViewMenu();
  public void updateMenus();
  public Scene getScene();
  protected void doOk();
  protected void doCancel();
  public void renderPreviewCommand();
}
```

artofillusion.CurveEditorWindow

This is the window for editing curves.

```
public class CurveEditorWindow extends MeshEditorWindow
implements EditingWindow{
  protected BMenu editMenu, meshMenu, smoothMenu;
  protected BMenuItem editMenuItem[], meshMenuItem[];
  protected BCheckBoxMenuItem smoothItem[];
  protected Runnable onClose;

  public CurveEditorWindow(EditingWindow parent, String title,
ObjectInfo obj, Runnable onClose, boolean allowTopology);
```

```
    protected CurveEditorWindow(EditingWindow parent, String title,
ObjectInfo obj);
    protected BMenu createShowMenu();
    public ObjectInfo getObject();
    public void setObject(Object3D obj);
    public void setMesh(Mesh mesh);
    public boolean[] getSelection();
    public void setSelection(boolean sel[]);
    public int[] getSelectionDistance();
    public int getSelectionMode();
    public void setSelectionMode(int mode);
    public void updateMenus();
    protected void doOk();
    protected void doCancel();
    protected void freehandModeChanged();
    public void selectAllCommand();
    public void extendSelectionCommand();
    public void invertSelectionCommand();
    public void deleteCommand();
    public void subdivideCommand();
    public void setSmoothnessCommand();
    public void toggleClosedCommand();
    public void adjustDeltas(Vec3 delta[]);
}
```

artofillusion.CurveViewer

This is the class that will display a curve so the user can edit it.

```
public class CurveViewer extends MeshViewer{
    public CurveViewer(MeshEditController window,
                    RowContainer p);
    protected void drawObject();
    protected void mousePressed(WidgetMouseEvent e);
    protected void mouseDragged(WidgetMouseEvent e);
    protected void mouseReleased(WidgetMouseEvent e);
}
```

artofillusion. ExternalObjectEditingWindow

This class defines a window that is used for editing external objects.

```
public class ExternalObjectEditingWindow extends BDialog{
    public ExternalObjectEditingWindow(EditingWindow parent, Ex-
ternalObject obj, ObjectInfo info, Runnable onClose);
}
```

artofillusion.LayoutWindow

The LayoutWindow is the main window for Art of Illusion.

```
public class LayoutWindow extends BFrame implements
EditingWindow, PopupMenuManager{
  protected Preferences preferences;

  public LayoutWindow(Scene s);
  protected void loadPreferences();
  protected void savePreferences();
  public void rebuildItemList();
  public void rebuildScriptsMenu();
  public void showPopupMenu(Widget w, int x, int y);
  public BMenu getFileMenu();
  public BMenu getEditMenu();
  public BMenu getSceneMenu();
  public BMenu getObjectMenu();
  public BMenu getAnimationMenu();
  public BMenu getToolsMenu();
  public BMenu getViewMenu();
  public BPopupMenu getPopupMenu();
  public DockingContainer getDockingContainer
(BTabbedPane.TabPosition position);
  public void setWaitCursor();
  public void clearWaitCursor();
  public Dimension getMinimumSize();
  public boolean confirmClose();
  public void setTool(EditingTool tool);
  public void setHelpText(String text);
  public BFrame getFrame();
  public void updateImage();
  public void updateMenus();
  public void setUndoRecord(UndoRecord command);
  public void setModified();
  public boolean isModified();
  public void addObject(Object3D obj, CoordinateSystem coords,
String name, UndoRecord undo);
  public void addObject(ObjectInfo info, UndoRecord undo);
  public void addObject(ObjectInfo info, int index, UndoRecord
undo);
  public void removeObject(int which, UndoRecord undo);
  public void setObjectName(int which, String name);
  public void setTime(double time);
  public Scene getScene();
  public ViewerCanvas getView();
  public ViewerCanvas[] getAllViews();
  public void setCurrentView(ViewerCanvas view);
  public Score getScore();
  public ToolPalette getToolPalette();
  public void setObjectListVisible(boolean visible);
  public void setScoreVisible(boolean visible);
```

```
public void setSplitView(boolean split);
public boolean getSplitView();
public int[] getSelectedIndices();
public Collection<ObjectInfo> getSelectedObjects();
public boolean isObjectSelected(ObjectInfo info);
public boolean isObjectSelected(int index);
public int[] getSelectionWithChildren();
public void setSelection(int which);
public void setSelection(int which[]);
public void addToSelection(int which);
public void clearSelection();
public void removeFromSelection(int which);
public void linkExternalCommand();
public void saveCommand();
public void saveAsCommand();
public void undoCommand();
public void redoCommand();
public void cutCommand();
public void copyCommand();
public void pasteCommand();
public void clearCommand();
public void selectAllCommand();
public void duplicateCommand();
public void severCommand();
public void editObjectCommand();
public void objectLayoutCommand();
public void transformObjectCommand();
public void alignObjectsCommand();
public void setTextureCommand();
public void setMaterialCommand();
public void renameObjectCommand();
public void convertToTriangleCommand();
public void convertToActorCommand();
public void createScriptObjectCommand();
public void jumpToTimeCommand();
public void bindToParentCommand();
public void renderCommand();
public void toggleViewsCommand();
public void setTemplateCommand();
public void setGridCommand();
public void frameWithCameraCommand(boolean selectionOnly);
public void texturesCommand();
public void showTexturesDialog(Scene target);
public void materialsCommand();
public void environmentCommand();
}
```

artofillusion.ListChangeListener

This defines an interface for an object that will listen for when a list changes.

```
public interface ListChangeListener{
```

```
    public void itemAdded(int index, Object obj);
    public void itemRemoved(int index, Object obj);
    public void itemChanged(int index, Object obj);
}
```

artofillusion.MaterialMappingDialog

This is the dialog used to choose material mappings.

```
public class MaterialMappingDialog extends BDialog{
    public MaterialMappingDialog(BFrame parent, Object3D obj);
}
```

artofillusion.MaterialPreviewer

This class is a component that will display a preview of the material.

```
public class MaterialPreviewer extends CustomWidget
implements RenderListener{
    public static final int HANDLE_SIZE;
    public MaterialPreviewer(Texture tex, Material mat, int width,
int height);
    public MaterialPreviewer(Texture tex, Material mat, Object3D obj,
int width, int height);
    public MaterialPreviewer(ObjectInfo obj, int width, int height);
    public ObjectInfo getObject();
    public Scene getScene();
    public void setTexture(Texture tex, TextureMapping map);
    public void setMaterial(Material mat, MaterialMapping map);
    public synchronized void render();
    public synchronized void cancelRendering();
    public void imageUpdated(Image image);
    public void statusChanged(String status);
    public void imageComplete(ComplexImage image);
    public void renderingCanceled();
}
```

artofillusion.MaterialsDialog

This dialog is for editing the list of materials available in the scene.

```
public class MaterialsDialog extends BDialog implements
ListChangeListener{
    public MaterialsDialog(BFrame fr, Scene sc);
    public void dispose();
    public void itemAdded(int index, Object obj);
    public void itemRemoved(int index, Object obj);
```

```
public void itemChanged(int index, Object obj);
public static Material showNewMaterialWindow(WindowWidget
parent, Scene theScene);
}
```

artofillusion.MeshEditorWindow

This is the class for the window to edit mesh objects.

```
public abstract class MeshEditorWindow extends
ObjectEditorWindow implements MeshEditController,
EditingWindow{
    protected Mesh oldMesh;
    protected BMenu viewMenu, colorSurfaceMenu;
    protected BMenuItem undoItem, redoItem, templateItem,
axesItem, splitViewItem;
    protected BCheckBoxMenuItem displayItem[], coordsItem[],
showItem[], colorSurfaceItem[];
    protected int meshTension, tensionDistance;
    protected static int lastMeshTension;
    protected static int lastTensionDistance;
    protected static final double[] tensionArray;
    protected static byte lastRenderMode[];
    protected static boolean lastShowMesh[];
    protected static boolean lastShowSurface[];
    protected static boolean lastShowSkeleton[];
    protected static boolean lastShowScene[];
    protected static boolean lastFreehand, lastUseWorldCoords;

    public MeshEditorWindow(EditingWindow parent, String title,
ObjectInfo obj);
    public void dispose();
    protected ViewerCanvas createViewerCanvas(int index,
RowContainer controls);
    protected void createViewMenu();
    protected BMenu createShowMenu();
    protected BMenu createColorSurfaceMenu();
    protected void loadPreferences();
    protected void savePreferences();
    public abstract void setMesh(Mesh mesh);
    public abstract boolean[] getSelection();
    public abstract void setSelection(boolean selected[]);
    public abstract int[] getSelectionDistance();
    public void objectChanged();
    public Scene getScene();
    public void undoCommand();
    public void redoCommand();
    public void updateMenus();
    public boolean isFreehand();
    public void setFreehand(boolean freehand);
    public void setPointsCommand();
    public void transformPointsCommand();
```

```
public void randomizeCommand();
public void centerCommand();
public void setTensionCommand();
public double getMeshTension();
public int getTensionDistance();
public TextureParameter getFaceIndexParameter();
public TextureParameter getJointWeightParam();
public boolean isExtraParameter(TextureParameter param);
public void setParametersCommand();
protected void setVertexParametersCommand();
protected void setFaceParametersCommand();
public abstract void deleteCommand();;
public void deleteJointCommand();
public void setJointParentCommand();
public void editJointCommand();
public void bindSkeletonCommand();
public void unbindSkeletonCommand();
protected void importSkeletonCommand();
public void renderPreviewCommand();
public abstract void adjustDeltas(Vec3 delta[]);
}
```

artofillusion.MeshViewer

This is an abstract class that defines the common things for viewing a mesh.

```
public abstract class MeshViewer extends ObjectViewer{
public static final int HANDLE_SIZE;
protected boolean showMesh, showSurface, showSkeleton;
protected TextureParameter surfaceColoringParameter;
public MeshViewer(MeshEditController controller, RowContainer
p);
public int getSelectedJoint();
public void setSelectedJoint(int id);
public boolean [] getLockedJoints();
public boolean isJointLocked(int id);
public void lockJoint(int id);
public void unlockJoint(int id);
public boolean getMeshVisible();
public void setMeshVisible(boolean visible);
public boolean getSurfaceVisible();
public void setSurfaceVisible(boolean visible);
public boolean getSkeletonVisible();
public void setSkeletonVisible(boolean visible);
public boolean getSkeletonDetached();
public void setSkeletonDetached(boolean detached);
public TextureParameter getSurfaceTextureParameter();
public void setSurfaceTextureParameter(TextureParameter
param);
public double[] estimateDepthRange();
}
```

artofillusion.ModellingTool

This is the interface of objects that go on the Tools menu. When used for a plugin, Art of Illusion will automatically add ModellingTools to the menu.

```
public interface ModellingTool{
  public String getName();
  public void commandSelected(LayoutWindow window);
}
```

artofillusion.MoveObjectTool

This is the tool from the tool palette that moves objects in the scene.

```
public class MoveObjectTool extends EditingTool{
  public MoveObjectTool(EditingWindow fr);
  public void activate();
  public int whichClicks();
  public boolean allowSelectionChanges();
  public String getToolTipText();
  public void mousePressedOnObject(WidgetMouseEvent e,
ViewerCanvas view, int obj);
  public void mouseDragged(final WidgetMouseEvent e, final
ViewerCanvas view);
  public void mouseReleased(WidgetMouseEvent e,
ViewerCanvas view);
  public void keyPressed(KeyPressedEvent e, ViewerCanvas
view);
  public void iconDoubleClicked();
}
```

artofillusion. MoveScaleRotateMeshTool

This is a tool that will move, scale, and rotate a mesh.

```
public class MoveScaleRotateMeshTool extends MeshEditingTool
{
  public MoveScaleRotateMeshTool(EditingWindow fr,
MeshEditController controller);
  public int whichClicks();
  public boolean allowSelectionChanges();
  public String getToolTipText();
  public void drawOverlay(ViewerCanvas view);
  public void mousePressed(WidgetMouseEvent e,
ViewerCanvas view);
```

```
    public void mousePressedOnHandle(WidgetMouseEvent e,
ViewerCanvas view, int obj, int handle);
    public void mouseDragged(WidgetMouseEvent e,
ViewerCanvas view);
    public void mouseReleased(WidgetMouseEvent e,
ViewerCanvas view);
    protected void handlePressed(HandlePressedEvent ev);
    protected void handleDragged(HandleDraggedEvent ev);
    protected void handleReleased(HandleReleasedEvent ev);
    public void keyPressed(KeyPressedEvent e,
ViewerCanvas view);
}
```

artofillusion. MoveScaleRotateObjectTool

This is a tool that will move, scale, and rotate an object.

```
public class MoveScaleRotateObjectTool extends EditingTool{
    public MoveScaleRotateObjectTool(LayoutWindow fr);
    public int whichClicks();
    public boolean allowSelectionChanges();
    public String getToolTipText();
    public LayoutWindow getWindow();
    public void drawOverlay(ViewerCanvas view);
    public void mousePressed(WidgetMouseEvent e, ViewerCanvas
view);
    public void mousePressedOnObject(WidgetMouseEvent e,
ViewerCanvas view, int obj);
    public void mouseDragged(WidgetMouseEvent e, ViewerCanvas
view);
    public void mouseReleased(WidgetMouseEvent e,
ViewerCanvas view);
    protected void handlePressed(HandlePressedEvent ev);
    protected void handleDragged(HandleDraggedEvent ev);
    protected void handleReleased(HandleReleasedEvent ev);
    public void keyPressed(KeyPressedEvent e, ViewerCanvas
view);
    protected BoundingBox findSelectionBounds(Camera cam);
    public void iconDoubleClicked();
}
```

artofillusion.MoveViewTool

This is the tool that moves the viewport.

```
public class MoveViewTool extends EditingTool{
    public MoveViewTool(EditingWindow fr);
    public void activate();
    public int whichClicks();
```

```
public boolean hilightSelection();
public String getToolTipText();
public void mousePressed(WidgetMouseEvent e, ViewerCanvas
view);
public void mouseDragged(WidgetMouseEvent e, ViewerCanvas
view);
public void mouseReleased(WidgetMouseEvent e,
ViewerCanvas view);
}
```

artofillusion.ObjectEditorWindow

This is an abstract class that defines a window that can be used to edit an object.

```
public abstract class ObjectEditorWindow extends BFrame
implements EditingWindow{
  protected EditingWindow parentWindow;
  protected ObjectInfo objInfo;
  protected ViewerCanvas theView[];
  protected BorderContainer viewPanel[];
  protected FormContainer viewsContainer;
  protected int numViewsShown, currentView;
  protected ToolPalette tools;
  protected EditingTool defaultTool, currentTool;
  protected BLabel helpText;
  protected BMenuBar menubar;
  protected UndoStack undoStack;
  protected Preferences preferences;
  protected static boolean lastShowAxes, lastShowGrid,
lastSnapToGrid;
  protected static int lastNumViews, lastGridSubdivisions;
  protected static double lastGridSpacing;

  public ObjectEditorWindow(EditingWindow parent, String title,
ObjectInfo obj);
  protected void initialize();
  protected abstract ViewerCanvas createViewerCanvas(int index,
RowContainer controls);
  protected void recursivelyAddListeners(Widget w);
  protected void loadPreferences();
  protected void savePreferences();
  protected boolean [] loadBooleanArrayPreference(String key,
boolean def[]);
  protected void saveBooleanArrayPreference(String key, boolean
value[]);
  public void setTool(EditingTool tool);
  public boolean confirmClose();
  public void setHelpText(String text);
  public BFrame getFrame();
  public void updateImage();
  public void setUndoRecord(UndoRecord command);
  public void setModified();
```

```
protected void keyPressed(KeyPressedEvent e);
public ViewerCanvas getView();
public void setCurrentView(ViewerCanvas view);
public ToolPalette getToolPalette();
public ViewerCanvas[] getAllViews();
public void showAxesCommand();
public void showTemplateCommand();
public void toggleViewsCommand();
public void setTemplateCommand();
public void setGridCommand();
public void undoCommand();
public void redoCommand();
protected abstract void doOk();
protected abstract void doCancel();
public void setVisible(boolean visible);
public void dispose();
}
```

artofillusion.ObjectMaterialDialog

This is the class for the dialog that lets the user choose the material for an object.

```
public class ObjectMaterialDialog extends BDialog implements
ListChangeListener{
public ObjectMaterialDialog(LayoutWindow parent, ObjectInfo
objects[]);
public void dispose();
public void itemAdded(int index, Object obj);
public void itemRemoved(int index, Object obj);
public void itemChanged(int index, Object obj);
}
```

artofillusion.ObjectPreviewCanvas

This is object is a preview that the user can move and rotate, but not edit.

```
public class ObjectPreviewCanvas extends ViewerCanvas{
public ObjectPreviewCanvas(ObjectInfo obj);
public ObjectPreviewCanvas(ObjectInfo obj, RowContainer p);
public void objectChanged();
public ObjectInfo getObject();
public void setObject(Object3D obj);
public double[] estimateDepthRange();
public synchronized void updateImage();
protected void renderObject();
protected void mousePressed(WidgetMouseEvent e);
protected void mouseDragged(WidgetMouseEvent e);
protected void mouseReleased(WidgetMouseEvent e);
}
```

artofillusion.ObjectPropertiesPanel

This is the panel that displays the properties of the selected objects.

```
public class ObjectPropertiesPanel extends ColumnContainer{
    public ObjectPropertiesPanel(LayoutWindow window);
    protected void rebuildContents();
    public Dimension getPreferredSize();
    public Dimension getMinimumSize();
}
```

artofillusion.ObjectSet

This is for a named list of objects in the scene.

```
public class ObjectSet{
    public ObjectSet(String name, int objectIDs[]);
    public ObjectSet(String name, ObjectInfo objects[]);
    public String getName();
    public void setName(String name);
    public int[] getObjectIDs();
    public List<ObjectInfo> getObjects(Scene scene);
}
```

artofillusion.ObjectTextureDialog

This dialog is for selecting the textures of objects.

```
public class ObjectTextureDialog extends BDialog implements
ListChangeListener{
    public ObjectTextureDialog(LayoutWindow parent, ObjectInfo
objects[]);
    public void dispose();
    public void setCallback(Runnable cb);
    public void itemRemoved(int index, Object obj);
    public void itemChanged(int index, Object obj);
}
```

artofillusion.ObjectViewer

This is an abstract class for classes that display a single object and allow users to edit it.

```
public abstract class ObjectViewer extends ViewerCanvas{
    protected MeshEditController controller;
    protected boolean showScene, useWorldCoords,
freehandSelection, draggingBox, squareBox, sentClick;
    protected Point clickPoint, dragPoint;
```

```
    protected Vector<Point> selectBoundsPoints;
    protected Shape selectBounds;
    protected ObjectInfo thisObjectInScene;
    protected Scene theScene;

    public ObjectViewer(MeshEditController controller,
RowContainer p);
    public MeshEditController getController();
    public double[] estimateDepthRange();
    public synchronized void updateImage();
    protected abstract void drawObject();
    public CoordinateSystem getDisplayCoordinates();
    public boolean getFreehandSelection();
    public void setFreehandSelection(boolean freehand);
    public Scene getScene();
    public void setScene(Scene sc, ObjectInfo thisObject);
    public boolean getSceneVisible();
    public void setSceneVisible(boolean visible);
    public boolean getUseWorldCoords();
    public void setUseWorldCoords(boolean use);
    public void beginDraggingSelection(Point p, boolean square);
    public void endDraggingSelection();
    public boolean selectionRegionContains(Point p);
    public boolean selectionRegionIntersects(Point p1, Point p2);
    protected void mouseDragged(WidgetMouseEvent e);
    public void previewObject();
}
```

artofillusion.Plugin

Plugins add features to Art of Illusion. This interface defines what a general purpose plugin must have in order for Art of Illusion to use it. The processMessage method works as a callback that Art of Illusion calls when various events happen. The specific event that triggered the callback is identified by the *message* parameter. The static final member variables are the messages that Art of Illusion may identify as having called the method. When you implement processMessage in you class, use a switch statement to handle each message you need to handle.

```
public interface Plugin{
    public static final int APPLICATION_STARTING;
    public static final int APPLICATION_STOPPING;
    public static final int SCENE_WINDOW_CREATED;
    public static final int SCENE_WINDOW_CLOSING;
```

```
public static final int SCENE_SAVED;
public static final int OBJECT_WINDOW_CREATED;
public static final int OBJECT_WINDOW_CLOSING;

public void processMessage(int message, Object args[]);
}
```

artofillusion.PluginRegistry

Art of Illusion uses this class to find and load the plugins that are in the plugins directory during startup.

```
public class PluginRegistry{
  public static void scanPlugins();
  public static void scanPlugins(List<ClassLoader> loaders);
  public static List<ClassLoader> getPluginClassLoaders();
  public static void addCategory(Class category);
  public static List<Class> getCategories();
  public static void registerPlugin(Object plugin);
  public static <T> List<T> getPlugins(Class<T> category);
  public static Object getPluginObject(String classname);
  public static void registerResource(String type, String id,
ClassLoader loader, String name, Locale locale)
throws IllegalArgumentException;
  public static List<String> getResourceTypes();
  public static List<PluginResource> getResources(String type);
  public static PluginResource getResource(String type, String id);
  public static void registerExportedMethod(Object plugin, String
method, String id) throws IllegalArgumentException;
  public static List<String> getExportedMethodIds();
  public static Object invokeExportedMethod(String id,
Object... args) throws NoSuchMethodException,
InvocationTargetException;
  public static class PluginResource;
  {
    public String getType();
    public String getId();
    public InputStream getInputStream();
    public URL getURL();
    public String getName();
    public ClassLoader getClassLoader();
  }
}
```

artofillusion.PreferencesWindow

This is the class for the window that is used to edit Art of Illusion preferences.

```
public class PreferencesWindow{
```

```
    public PreferencesWindow(BFrame parent);
}
```

artofillusion.Property

This class defines an arbitrary property of an object. A property has a name and a type. The type of property is one of the values given by the static final member variables of type PropertyType.

```
public class Property{
    public static final PropertyType DOUBLE;
    public static final PropertyType INTEGER;
    public static final PropertyType BOOLEAN;
    public static final PropertyType STRING;
    public static final PropertyType COLOR;
    public static final PropertyType ENUMERATION;

    public Property(String name, double min, double max, double
defaultValue);
    public Property(String name, int min, int max, int value);
    public Property(String name, boolean value);
    public Property(String name, String defaultValue);
    public Property(String name, RGBColor defaultValue);
    public Property(String name, Object allowedValues[], Object
defaultValue);
    public String getName();
    public PropertyType getType();
    public Object getDefaultValue();
    public double getMinimum();
    public double getMaximum();
    public Object[] getAllowedValues();
    public boolean isLegalValue(Object value);
    public boolean equals(Object obj);
    public int hashCode();
    public static class PropertyType
    {
      private PropertyType();
    }
}
```

artofillusion.RecentFiles

This is the class that maintains the list of recently accessed scene files.

```
public class RecentFiles{
    public static void createMenu(BMenu menu);
    public static void addRecentFile(File file);
}
```

artofillusion.Renderer

This interface defines the methods the classes that will render a scene must have to be used by Art of Illusion. Classes that implement the Renderer interface are loaded as Renderer plugins by Art of Illusion.

```
public interface Renderer{
  public String getName();
  public void renderScene(Scene theScene, Camera theCamera,
RenderListener listener, SceneCamera sceneCamera);
  public void cancelRendering(Scene theScene);
  public Widget getConfigPanel();
  public boolean recordConfiguration();
  public void configurePreview();
  public Map<String, Object> getConfiguration();
  public void setConfiguration(String property, Object value);
}
```

artofillusion.RenderingDialog

This is the class that allows the user to watch as a scene is being rendered.

```
public class RenderingDialog extends BDialog
implements RenderListener{
  public RenderingDialog(BFrame parent, Renderer rend, Scene
sc, Camera cam, ObjectInfo sceneCamera);
  public RenderingDialog(BFrame parent, Renderer rend, Scene
sc, Camera cam, ObjectInfo sceneCamera,
double start, double end, int fps, int subimages, ImageSaver
imgsaver);
  public void imageUpdated(Image image);
  public void statusChanged(String status);
  public void imageComplete(ComplexImage image);
  public void renderingCanceled();
}
```

artofillusion.RenderingMesh

A RenderingMesh is an object that describes the object that is to be rendered to the screen. It is made up of triangles that approximate the object that is being modeled. Every object that is visible in the scene must provide a RenderingMesh to Art of Illusion, but the object may maintain a different internal representation of the object.

```
public class RenderingMesh{
    public Vec3 vert[], norm[], faceNorm[];
    public ParameterValue param[];
    public RenderingTriangle triangle[];
    public TextureMapping mapping;
    public MaterialMapping matMapping;

    public RenderingMesh(Vec3 vert[], Vec3 norm[],
RenderingTriangle triangle[], TextureMapping mapping,
MaterialMapping matMapping);
    public void setParameters(ParameterValue param[]);
    public void transformMesh(Mat4 trans);
    public int [] getVertexIndices();
}
```

artofillusion.RenderingTriangle

A RenderingTriangle is a triangle within a RenderingMesh that is to be rendered to the screen.

```
public abstract class RenderingTriangle{
    public int index, v1, v2, v3, n1, n2, n3;
    public RenderingMesh theMesh;
    protected static ThreadLocal tempParamValues;

    public RenderingTriangle(int v1, int v2, int v3, int n1, int n2, int
n3);
    public TextureMapping getTextureMapping();
    public abstract void getTextureSpec(TextureSpec spec, double
angle, double u, double v, double w, double size, double t);
    public abstract void getTransparency(RGBColor trans, double
angle, double u, double v, double w, double size, double t);
    public abstract double getDisplacement(double u, double v,
double w, double size, double t);
    public void setMesh(RenderingMesh mesh, TextureMapping
map, int index);
    public double [] getParameters(double u, double v, double w);
}
```

artofillusion.RendererListener

This is the interface for an object that will call a renderer and then listen for the renderer to complete its task.

```
public interface RenderListener{
```

```
    public void imageUpdated(Image image);
    public void statusChanged(String status);
    public void imageComplete(ComplexImage image);
    public void renderingCanceled();
}
```

artofillusion.RenderSetupDialog

This is the dialog the user uses to setup rendering within Art of Illusion.

```
public class RenderSetupDialog{
    public RenderSetupDialog(BFrame parent, Scene theScene);
    public static void renderImmediately(BFrame parent, Scene
theScene);
}
```

artofillusion.ReshapeMeshTool

This is the tool that is used for moving the vertices of a mesh in the mesh edit window.

```
public class ReshapeMeshTool extends MeshEditingTool{
    public ReshapeMeshTool(EditingWindow fr, MeshEditController
controller);
    public void activate();
    public int whichClicks();
    public boolean allowSelectionChanges();
    public String getToolTipText();
    public void mousePressedOnHandle(WidgetMouseEvent e,
ViewerCanvas view, int obj, int handle);
    public void mouseDragged(WidgetMouseEvent e, ViewerCanvas
view);
    public void mouseReleased(WidgetMouseEvent e,
ViewerCanvas view);
    public void keyPressed(KeyPressedEvent e, ViewerCanvas
view);
}
```

artofillusion.RotateMeshTool

This is the tool that is use for rotating the vertices of a mesh in the mesh edit window.

```
public class RotateMeshTool extends MeshEditingTool{
    public static final int HANDLE_SIZE;
    public RotateMeshTool(EditingWindow fr, MeshEditController
controller, boolean only2D);
    public void activate();
    public int whichClicks();
```

```
public boolean allowSelectionChanges();
public String getToolTipText();
public void drawOverlay(ViewerCanvas view);
public void mousePressed(WidgetMouseEvent e, ViewerCanvas
view);
public void mouseDragged(WidgetMouseEvent e, ViewerCanvas
view);
public void mouseReleased(WidgetMouseEvent e,
ViewerCanvas view);
protected void handlePressed(HandlePressedEvent ev);
protected void handleDragged(HandleDraggedEvent ev);
protected void handleReleased(HandleReleasedEvent ev);
}
```

artofillusion.RotateObjectTool

This is the tool for rotating objects in a scene.

```
public class RotateObjectTool extends EditingTool{
public RotateObjectTool(EditingWindow fr);
public void activate();
public int whichClicks();
public boolean allowSelectionChanges();
public String getToolTipText();
public void mousePressedOnObject(WidgetMouseEvent e,
ViewerCanvas view, int obj);
public void mousePressedOnHandle(WidgetMouseEvent e,
ViewerCanvas view, int obj, int handle);
public void mouseDragged(final WidgetMouseEvent e, final
ViewerCanvas view);
public void mouseReleased(WidgetMouseEvent e,
ViewerCanvas view);
public void keyPressed(KeyPressedEvent e, ViewerCanvas
view);
public void iconDoubleClicked();
}
```

artofillusion.RotateViewTool

This is the tool for rotating the viewport.

```
public class RotateViewTool extends EditingTool{
public RotateViewTool(EditingWindow fr);
public void activate();
public int whichClicks();
public boolean hilightSelection();
public String getToolTipText();
public void mousePressed(WidgetMouseEvent e, ViewerCanvas
view);
public void mouseDragged(WidgetMouseEvent e, ViewerCanvas
view);
public void mouseReleased(WidgetMouseEvent e,
```

ViewerCanvas view);
}

artofillusion.SafeFileOutputStream

This class writes to a file in such a way that if the operation is interrupted prematurely, the original file will not have been corrupted.

```
public class SafeFileOutputStream extends FilterOutputStream{
    public static final int OVERWRITE;
    public static final int CREATE;
    public static final int APPEND;
    public static final int KEEP_BACKUP;

    public SafeFileOutputStream(String path, int mode)
        throws IOException;
    public SafeFileOutputStream(File file, int mode)
        throws IOException;
    public void open(String path, int mode)
        throws IOException;
    public void open(File file, int mode)
        throws IOException;
    public void abort()
        throws IOException;
    public void close()
        throws IOException;
    public void write(byte[] array)
        throws IOException;
    public void write(int value)
        throws IOException;
}
```

artofillusion.ScaleMeshTool

This is the tool for scaling the vertices of a mesh in the mesh edit window.

```
public class ScaleMeshTool extends MeshEditingTool{
    public static final int HANDLE_SIZE;

    public ScaleMeshTool(EditingWindow fr, MeshEditController controller);
    public int whichClicks();
    public boolean allowSelectionChanges();
    public String getToolTipText();
    public void drawOverlay(ViewerCanvas view);
    public void mousePressed(WidgetMouseEvent e, ViewerCanvas view);
    public void mouseDragged(WidgetMouseEvent e, ViewerCanvas view);
```

```
   public void mouseReleased(WidgetMouseEvent e,
ViewerCanvas view);
   protected void handlePressed(HandlePressedEvent ev);
   protected void handleDragged(HandleDraggedEvent ev);
   protected void handleReleased(HandleReleasedEvent ev);
}
```

artofillusion.ScaleObjectTool

This is the tool for scaling an object.

```
public class ScaleObjectTool extends EditingTool{
   public ScaleObjectTool(EditingWindow fr);
   public void activate();
   public int whichClicks();
   public boolean allowSelectionChanges();
   public String getToolTipText();
   public void mousePressedOnHandle(WidgetMouseEvent e,
ViewerCanvas view, int obj, int handle);
   public void mousePressedOnObject(WidgetMouseEvent e,
ViewerCanvas view, int obj);
   public void mouseDraggedMoveOp(final WidgetMouseEvent e,
final ViewerCanvas view);
   public void mouseDraggedScaleOp(WidgetMouseEvent e,
ViewerCanvas view);
   public void mouseDragged(WidgetMouseEvent e, ViewerCanvas
view);
   public void mouseReleased(WidgetMouseEvent e,
ViewerCanvas view);
   public void iconDoubleClicked();
}
```

artofillusion.Scene

A Scene is the collection of objects in a scene, as
well as the materials and textures required to render
them. This is also where environment settings, such as
the ambient color and the fog, are set and stored.

```
public class Scene{
   public Scene();
   public String getName();
   public void setName(String newName);
   public String getDirectory();
   public void setDirectory(String newDir);
   public double getTime();
   public void setTime(double t);
   public void applyTracksToObject(ObjectInfo info);
   public void applyTracksAfterModification(Collection<ObjectInfo>
changedObjects);
   public int getFramesPerSecond();
```

```java
public void setFramesPerSecond(int n);
public RGBColor getAmbientColor();
public void setAmbientColor(RGBColor color);
public int getEnvironmentMode();
public void setEnvironmentMode(int mode);
public Texture getEnvironmentTexture();
public void setEnvironmentTexture(Texture tex);
public TextureMapping getEnvironmentMapping();
public void setEnvironmentMapping(TextureMapping map);
public ParameterValue [] getEnvironmentParameterValues();
public void setEnvironmentParameterValues(ParameterValue
value[]);
public RGBColor getEnvironmentColor();
public void setEnvironmentColor(RGBColor color);
public RGBColor getFogColor();
public void setFogColor(RGBColor color);
public boolean getFogState();
public double getFogDistance();
public void setFog(boolean state, double dist);
public boolean getShowGrid();
public void setShowGrid(boolean show);
public boolean getSnapToGrid();
public void setSnapToGrid(boolean snap);
public double getGridSpacing();
public void setGridSpacing(double spacing);
public int getGridSubdivisions();
public void setGridSubdivisions(int subdivisions);
public void addObject(Object3D obj, CoordinateSystem coords,
String name, UndoRecord undo);
public void addObject(ObjectInfo info, UndoRecord undo);
public void addObject(ObjectInfo info, int index, UndoRecord
undo);
public void removeObject(int which, UndoRecord undo);
public void addMaterial(Material mat);
public void addMaterial(Material mat, int index);
public void removeMaterial(int which);
public void reorderMaterial(int oldIndex, int newIndex);
public void addTexture(Texture tex);
public void addTexture(Texture tex, int index);
public void removeTexture(int which);
public void reorderTexture(int oldIndex, int newIndex);
public void changeMaterial(int which);
public void changeTexture(int which);
public void addMaterialListener(ListChangeListener ls);
public void removeMaterialListener(ListChangeListener ls);
public void addTextureListener(ListChangeListener ls);
public void removeTextureListener(ListChangeListener ls);
public Object getMetadata(String name);
public void setMetadata(String name, Object value);
public Set<String> getAllMetadataNames();
public void showTexturesDialog(BFrame parent);
public void showMaterialsDialog(BFrame parent);
public void addImage(ImageMap im);
public boolean removeImage(int which);
```

```
   public void replaceObject(Object3D original, Object3D
replaceWith, UndoRecord undo);
   public void objectModified(Object3D obj);
   public void setSelection(int which);
   public void setSelection(int which[]);
   public void addToSelection(int which);
   public void clearSelection();
   public void removeFromSelection(int which);
   public int getNumObjects();
   public ObjectInfo getObject(int i);
   public ObjectInfo getObject(String name);
   public ObjectInfo getObjectById(int id);
   public List<ObjectInfo> getAllObjects();
   public int indexOf(ObjectInfo info);
   public int getNumTextures();
   public List<ObjectInfo> getCameras();
   public int indexOf(Texture tex);
   public Texture getTexture(int i);
   public Texture getTexture(String name);
   public int getNumMaterials();
   public Material getMaterial(int i);
   public Material getMaterial(String name);
   public int indexOf(Material mat);
   public int getNumImages();
   public ImageMap getImage(int i);
   public int indexOf(ImageMap im);
   public Texture getDefaultTexture();
   public int [] getSelection();
   public int [] getSelectionWithChildren();
   public boolean errorsOccurredInLoading();
   public String getLoadingErrors();
   public Scene(File f, boolean fullScene) throws IOException,
InvalidObjectException;
   public Scene(DataInputStream in, boolean fullScene) throws
IOException, InvalidObjectException;
   public void writeToFile(File f) throws IOException;
   public void writeToStream(DataOutputStream out) throws
IOException;
}
```

artofillusion.SceneChangedEvent

An editing window sends this event to indicate
that it has changed something in the scene.

```
public class SceneChangedEvent{
   public SceneChangedEvent(EditingWindow window);
   public EditingWindow getWindow();
}
```

artofillusion.SceneViewer

This is a component for displaying a view of the scene.

```
public class SceneViewer extends ViewerCanvas{
    public SceneViewer(Scene s, RowContainer p, EditingWindow
fr);
    public SceneViewer(Scene s, RowContainer p, EditingWindow fr,
boolean forceSoftwareRendering);
    public EditingWindow getEditingWindow();
    public Scene getScene();
    public void rebuildCameraList();
    public ObjectInfo[] getCameras();
    public void setOrientation(int which);
    public double[] estimateDepthRange();
    public Vec3 getDefaultRotationCenter();
    public void updateImage();
    public void beginDraggingBox(Point p, boolean square);
    protected void mousePressed(WidgetMouseEvent e);
    protected void mouseReleased(WidgetMouseEvent e);
    protected void processMouseScrolled(MouseScrolledEvent ev);
}
```

artofillusion.SkewMeshTool

This is the tool for skewing the vertices of a mesh in the mesh editing window.

```
public class SkewMeshTool extends MeshEditingTool{
    public static final int HANDLE_SIZE;

    public SkewMeshTool(EditingWindow fr, MeshEditController
controller);
    public int whichClicks();
    public boolean allowSelectionChanges();
    public String getToolTipText();
    public void drawOverlay(ViewerCanvas view);
    public void mousePressed(WidgetMouseEvent e, ViewerCanvas
view);
    public void mouseDragged(WidgetMouseEvent e, ViewerCanvas
view);
    public void mouseReleased(WidgetMouseEvent e,
ViewerCanvas view);
    protected void handlePressed(HandlePressedEvent ev);
    protected void handleDragged(HandleDraggedEvent ev);
    protected void handleReleased(HandleReleasedEvent ev);
}
```

artofillusion.SplineMeshEditorWindow

This is the edit window for SplineMesh objects.

```
public class SplineMeshEditorWindow extends
MeshEditorWindow implements EditingWindow{
  public SplineMeshEditorWindow(EditingWindow parent, String
title, ObjectInfo obj, Runnable onClose, boolean allowTopology);
  public ObjectInfo getObject();
  public void setObject(Object3D obj);
  public void setSelectionMode(int mode);
  public int getSelectionMode();
  public boolean[] getSelection();
  public void setSelection(boolean sel[]);
  public int[] getSelectionDistance();
  public void setMesh(Mesh mesh);
  public void setTool(EditingTool tool);
  public void updateImage();
  public void updateMenus();
  public void removeExtraParameters();
  public TextureParameter getJointWeightParam();
  protected void doOk();
  protected void doCancel();
  public void bindSkeletonCommand();
  public void unbindSkeletonCommand();
  public void setPointsCommand();
  public void selectAllCommand();
  public void extendSelectionCommand();
  public void invertSelectionCommand();
  public void deleteCommand();
  public void adjustDeltas(Vec3 delta[]);
}
```

artofillusion.SplineMeshViewer

This is a component for displaying a SplineMesh.

```
public class SplineMeshViewer extends MeshViewer{
  public SplineMeshViewer(MeshEditController window,
RowContainer p);
  protected void drawObject();
  protected void mousePressed(WidgetMouseEvent e);
  protected void mouseDragged(WidgetMouseEvent e);
  protected void mouseReleased(WidgetMouseEvent e);
}
```

artofillusion.TaperMeshTool

This is the tool for tapering the vertices of a mesh
in the mesh edit window.

```
public class TaperMeshTool extends MeshEditingTool{
  public static final int HANDLE_SIZE;

  public TaperMeshTool(EditingWindow fr, MeshEditController
controller);
  public int whichClicks();
  public boolean allowSelectionChanges();
  public String getToolTipText();
  public void drawOverlay(ViewerCanvas view);
  public void mousePressed(WidgetMouseEvent e, ViewerCanvas
view);
  public void mouseDragged(WidgetMouseEvent e, ViewerCanvas
view);
  public void mouseReleased(WidgetMouseEvent e,
ViewerCanvas view);
  protected void handlePressed(HandlePressedEvent ev);
  protected void handleDragged(HandleDraggedEvent ev);
  protected void handleReleased(HandleReleasedEvent ev);
}
```

artofillusion.TextureMappingDialog

This is the dialog for choosing the texture mapping
for an object.

```
public class TextureMappingDialog extends BDialog{
  public TextureMappingDialog(BFrame parent, Object3D obj, int
layer);
  public void setPreviewMapping(TextureMapping newmap);
}
```

artofillusion.TextureParameter

A TextureParameter is a parameter that effects the
appearance of the object.

```
public class TextureParameter{
  public final Object owner;
  public final String name;
  public final double minVal, maxVal, defaultVal;
  public int identifier, type;

  public static final int NORMAL_PARAMETER;
  public static final int X_COORDINATE;
  public static final int Y_COORDINATE;
  public static final int Z_COORDINATE;

  public TextureParameter(Object owner, String name, double
minVal, double maxVal, double defaultVal);
  public TextureParameter duplicate();
  public TextureParameter duplicate(Object owner);
```

```
public boolean equals(Object o);
public int hashCode();
public void assignNewID();
public static synchronized int getUniqueID();
public void setID(int newid);
public Widget getEditingWidget(double currentValue);
}
```

artofillusion.TexturesDialog

This is the dialog the user uses to edit the list of textures in the scene.

```
public class TexturesDialog extends BDialog implements
ListChangeListener{
    public TexturesDialog(BFrame fr, Scene sc);
    public void dispose();
    public void itemAdded(int index, Object obj);
    public void itemRemoved(int index, Object obj);
    public void itemChanged(int index, Object obj);
    public static Texture showNewTextureWindow(WindowWidget
parent, Scene theScene);
}
```

artofillusion.ThickenMeshTool

This is the tool for adjusting the thickness of meshes in the mesh edit window.

```
public class ThickenMeshTool extends MeshEditingTool{
    public ThickenMeshTool(EditingWindow fr, MeshEditController
controller);
    public boolean allowSelectionChanges();
    public String getToolTipText();
    public void drawOverlay(ViewerCanvas view);
    public void mousePressed(WidgetMouseEvent e, ViewerCanvas
view);
    public void mouseDragged(WidgetMouseEvent e, ViewerCanvas
view);
    public void mouseReleased(WidgetMouseEvent e,
ViewerCanvas view);
    protected void handlePressed(HandlePressedEvent ev);
    protected void handleDragged(HandleDraggedEvent ev);
    protected void handleReleased(HandleReleasedEvent ev);
}
```

artofillusion.TitleWindow

This is the window that displays the title and credits for Art of Illusion.

```
public class TitleWindow extends BWindow{
  public TitleWindow();
  public void dispose();
}
```

artofillusion.TransformDialog

This is the dialog that allows a user to enter values to transform an object.

```
public class TransformDialog extends BDialog{
  public TransformDialog(BFrame parent, String title, double
values[], boolean transformLabels, boolean extraOptions);
  public TransformDialog(BFrame parent, String title, boolean
transformLabels, boolean extraOptions);
  public double [] getValues();
  public boolean clickedOk();
  public boolean applyToChildren();
  public boolean useSelectionCenter();
}
```

artofillusion.TransformPointsDialog

This is the dialog that allows the user to enter values to transform the points of an object in the object edit window.

```
public class TransformPointsDialog extends BDialog{
  public TransformPointsDialog(BFrame parent);
  public double [] getValues();
  public boolean useSelectionCenter();
}
```

artofillusion.Translator

This is an interface for importing and exporting scenes in different file formats. Classes that implement the Translator interface are loaded by Art of Illusion as Translator plugins.

```
public interface Translator{
  public String getName();
  public boolean canImport();
  public boolean canExport();
  public void importFile(BFrame parent);
  public void exportFile(BFrame parent, Scene theScene);
}
```

artofillusion.TriMeshBeveler

This class is for beveling a triangle mesh.

```
public class TriMeshBeveler{
  public static final int BEVEL_FACES;
  public static final int BEVEL_FACE_GROUPS;
  public static final int BEVEL_EDGES;
  public static final int BEVEL_VERTICES;

  public TriMeshBeveler(TriangleMesh theMesh, boolean
selection[], int bevelMode);
  public TriangleMesh bevelMesh(double height, double width);
  public boolean [] getNewSelection();
}
```

artofillusion.TriMeshEditorWindow

This is the window for editing a TriangleMesh.

```
public class TriMeshEditorWindow extends MeshEditorWindow
implements EditingWindow{
  protected static boolean lastProjectOntoSurface, lastTolerant,
lastShowQuads;

  public TriMeshEditorWindow(EditingWindow parent, String title,
ObjectInfo obj, Runnable onClose, boolean allowTopology);
  protected void loadPreferences();
  protected void savePreferences();
  public ObjectInfo getObject();
  public void setObject(Object3D obj);
  public void setMesh(Mesh mesh);
  public void objectChanged();
  public void setTool(EditingTool tool);
  public void updateImage();
  public void updateMenus();
  public boolean [] getHiddenFaces();
  public void setHiddenFaces(boolean hidden[]);
  public void removeExtraParameters();
  public TextureParameter getFaceIndexParameter();
  public TextureParameter getJointWeightParam();
  public boolean getProjectOntoSurface();
  public void setProjectOntoSurface(boolean project);
  protected void doOk();
  public boolean isTolerant();
  public void setTolerant(boolean tol);
  public boolean isQuadMode();
  public void setQuadMode(boolean quads);
  public boolean isEdgeHidden(int which);
  public void setSelectionMode(int mode);
  public int getSelectionMode();
```

```
public void setSelection(boolean sel[]);
public boolean[] getSelection();
public int[] getSelectionDistance();
protected void doCancel();
public void bindSkeletonCommand();
public void setPointsCommand();
public void selectAllCommand();
public void hideSelectionCommand();
public void showAllCommand();
public void selectObjectBoundaryCommand();
public void selectSelectionBoundaryCommand();
public void invertSelectionCommand();
public void selectEdgeLoopCommand();
public void selectEdgeStripCommand();
public void extendSelectionCommand();
public void deleteCommand();
public void subdivideCommand();
public void simplifyCommand();
public void optimizeCommand();
public void bevelCommand();
public void closeBoundaryCommand();
public void joinBoundariesCommand();
public void extractFacesCommand();
public void extractCurveCommand();
public void setSmoothnessCommand();
public void reverseNormalsCommand();
public void adjustDeltas(Vec3 delta[]);
}
```

artofillusion.TriMeshSelectionUtilities

This class is a set of static methods for selecting parts of a TriangleMesh.

```
public class TriMeshSelectionUtilities{
  public static boolean[] convertSelection(TriangleMesh mesh, int
oldMode, boolean selection[], int newMode);
  public static boolean[] findSelectionBoundary(TriangleMesh
mesh, int oldMode, boolean selection[]);
  public static boolean[] findEdgeLoops(TriangleMesh mesh,
boolean selection[]);
  public static boolean[] findEdgeStrips(TriangleMesh mesh,
boolean selection[]);
}
```

artofillusion.TriMeshSimplifier

This is the class that is used to simplify a Triangle-Mesh.

```
public class TriMeshSimplifier implements Runnable{
```

```
public TriMeshSimplifier(TriangleMesh theMesh, boolean
selection[], double tolerance, BFrame fr);
    public void run();
}
```

artofillusion.TriMeshViewer

This is a component that will display and allow editing of a TriangleMesh.

```
public class TriMeshViewer extends MeshViewer{
    public TriMeshViewer(MeshEditController window,
RowContainer p);
    protected void drawObject();
    protected void mousePressed(WidgetMouseEvent e);
    protected void mouseDragged(WidgetMouseEvent e);
    protected void mouseReleased(WidgetMouseEvent e);
    public int findClickTarget(Point pos, Vec3 uvw);
}
```

artofillusion.TubeEditorWindow

This is the window the user uses to edit tube objects.

```
public class TubeEditorWindow extends CurveEditorWindow{
    public TubeEditorWindow(EditingWindow parent, String title,
ObjectInfo obj, Runnable onClose, boolean allowTopology);
    protected BMenu createShowMenu();
    public void updateMenus();
    protected void doOk();
    protected void doCancel();
    public void deleteCommand();
    public void subdivideCommand();
    public void setThicknessCommand();
}
```

artofillusion.TubeViewer

This is a component for displaying a Tube that is being edited.

```
public class TubeViewer extends CurveViewer{
    public TubeViewer(MeshEditController window,
RowContainer p);
    protected void drawObject();
}
```

artofillusion.UndoRecord

Art of Illusion uses UndoRecords as the means by which to undo the last action. The record itself is a set of commands. When the user asks Art of Illusion to undo an action. It will perform the commands needed to take it back to the last state stored on the stack. When working with plugins, you must create UndoRecords for any action your code performs or undo will not be possible. Each UndoRecord can have multiple commands added to is. All commands will be process when the UndoRecord is removed from the stack and processed.

```
public class UndoRecord{
  // commands
  public static final int COPY_OBJECT;
  public static final int COPY_COORDS;
  public static final int COPY_OBJECT_INFO;
  public static final int SET_OBJECT;
  public static final int ADD_OBJECT;
  public static final int DELETE_OBJECT;
  public static final int RENAME_OBJECT;
  public static final int ADD_TO_GROUP;
  public static final int REMOVE_FROM_GROUP;
  public static final int SET_GROUP_CONTENTS;
  public static final int SET_TRACK;
  public static final int SET_TRACK_LIST;
  public static final int COPY_TRACK;
  public static final int COPY_VERTEX_POSITIONS;
  public static final int COPY_SKELETON;
  public static final int SET_MESH_SELECTION;
  public static final int SET_SCENE_SELECTION;

  public UndoRecord(EditingWindow win, boolean isRedo);
  public UndoRecord(EditingWindow win, boolean isRedo, int
theCommand, Object commandData[]);
  public boolean isRedo();
  public List<Integer> getCommands();
  public void addCommand(int theCommand, Object
commandData[]);
  public void addCommandAtBeginning(int theCommand, Object
commandData[]);
  public UndoRecord execute();
  protected void cacheToDisk();
}
```

artofillusion.UndoStack

This is the stack that stores UndoRecords. Records are removed in the reverse order to which they are placed on the stack and processed.

```
public class UndoStack{
  public UndoStack();
  public boolean canUndo();
  public boolean canRedo();
  public void addRecord(UndoRecord record);
  public void executeUndo();
  public void executeRedo();
}
```

artofillusion.ViewerCanvas

This is the superclass of components that display objects in Art of Illusion.

```
public abstract class ViewerCanvas extends CustomWidget{
  protected Camera theCamera;
  protected ObjectInfo boundCamera;
  protected EditingTool currentTool, activeTool, metaTool, altTool;
  protected PopupMenuManager popupManager;
  protected int renderMode, gridSubdivisions, orientation;
  protected double gridSpacing, scale;
  protected boolean perspective, hideBackfaces, showGrid,
snapToGrid, drawFocus, showTemplate, showAxes;
  protected ActionProcessor mouseProcessor;
  protected Image templateImage;
  protected CanvasDrawer drawer;
  protected Dimension prefSize;
  protected Map<ViewerControl,Widget> controlMap;
  protected Vec3 rotationCenter;

  protected final ViewChangedEvent viewChangedEvent;

  public static Color backgroundColor;
  public static Color lineColor;
  public static Color handleColor;
  public static Color highlightColor;
  public static Color specialHighlightColor;
  public static Color disabledColor;
  public static Color surfaceColor;
  public static RGBColor surfaceRGBColor;
  public static RGBColor transparentColor;
  public static RGBColor lowValueColor;
  public static RGBColor highValueColor;

  public static final int RENDER_WIREFRAME;
```

```
public static final int RENDER_FLAT;
public static final int RENDER_SMOOTH;
public static final int RENDER_TEXTURED;
public static final int RENDER_TRANSPARENT;

public static final int VIEW_FRONT;
public static final int VIEW_BACK;
public static final int VIEW_LEFT;
public static final int VIEW_RIGHT;
public static final int VIEW_TOP ;
public static final int VIEW_BOTTOM;
public static final int VIEW_OTHER;

public ViewerCanvas();
public ViewerCanvas(boolean useOpenGL);
public CanvasDrawer getCanvasDrawer();
protected void buildChoices(RowContainer row);
protected void processMouseScrolled(MouseScrolledEvent ev);
protected void mousePressed(WidgetMouseEvent ev);
protected void mouseDragged(WidgetMouseEvent ev);
protected void mouseReleased(WidgetMouseEvent ev);
public void setPreferredSize(Dimension size);
public Dimension getPreferredSize();
public Dimension getMinimumSize();
public ActionProcessor getActionProcessor();
public Camera getCamera();
public Scene getScene();
public void setTool(EditingTool tool);
public EditingTool getCurrentTool();
public void setMetaTool(EditingTool tool);
public void setAltTool(EditingTool tool);
public void setPerspective(boolean perspective);
public boolean isPerspective();
public double getScale();
public void setScale(double scale);
public boolean getDrawFocus();
public void setDrawFocus(boolean draw);
public boolean getShowAxes();
public void setShowAxes(boolean show);
public boolean getTemplateShown();
public void setShowTemplate(boolean show);
public Image getTemplateImage();
public void setTemplateImage(Image im);
public void setTemplateImage(File f) throws
InterruptedException;
public Vec3 getRotationCenter();
public void setRotationCenter(Vec3 rotationCenter);
public Vec3 getDefaultRotationCenter();
public void setPopupMenuManager(PopupMenuManager
manager);
protected void showPopupIfNeeded(WidgetMouseEvent ev);
public void adjustCamera(boolean perspective);
public ObjectInfo getBoundCamera();
public void setBoundCamera(ObjectInfo boundCamera);
```

```
    public void setGrid(double spacing, int subdivisions, boolean
show, boolean snap);
    public boolean getShowGrid();
    public boolean getSnapToGrid();
    public double getGridSpacing();
    public int getSnapToSubdivisions();
    public void frameBox(BoundingBox bb);
    public void prepareCameraForRendering();
    public abstract double[] estimateDepthRange();
    public synchronized void updateImage();
    protected void drawCoordinateAxes();
    public int getRenderMode();
    public void setRenderMode(int mode);
    public int getOrientation();
    public void setOrientation(int which);
    public void copyOrientationFromCamera();
    public void drawDraggedShape(Shape shape);
    public void drawBorder();
    public void drawHRule(int y, Color color);
    public void drawVRule(int x, Color color);
    public void drawBox(int x, int y, int width, int height, Color color);
    public void drawBoxes(java.util.List<Rectangle> box, Color
color);
    public void renderBox(int x, int y, int width, int height, double
depth, Color color);
    public void renderBoxes(java.util.List<Rectangle> box,
java.util.List<Double>depth, Color color);
    public void drawLine(Point p1, Point p2, Color color);
    public void renderLine(Vec3 p1, Vec3 p2, Camera cam, Color
color);
    public void renderLine(Vec2 p1, double zf1, Vec2 p2, double zf2,
Camera cam, Color color);
    public void renderWireframe(WireframeMesh mesh, Camera
cam, Color color);
    public void renderMeshTransparent(RenderingMesh mesh,
VertexShader shader, Camera cam, Vec3 viewDir, boolean
hideFace[]);
    public void renderMesh(RenderingMesh mesh, VertexShader
shader, Camera cam, boolean closed, boolean hideFace[]);
    public void drawString(String text, int x, int y, Color color);
    public void drawImage(Image image, int x, int y);
    public void renderImage(Image image, Vec3 p1, Vec3 p2, Vec3
p3, Vec3 p4);
    public void drawShape(Shape shape, Color color);
    public void fillShape(Shape shape, Color color);
    public static boolean isOpenGLAvailable();
    public static List getViewerControls();
    public static void addViewerControl(ViewerControl control);
    public static void addViewerControl(int index, ViewerControl
control);
    public static void removeViewerControl(ViewerControl control);
    public Map getViewerControlWidgets();
}
```

artofillusion.WireframeMesh

The WireframeMesh of an object is used for displaying in wireframe mode and for when the object is of a type that will not be visible in the final rendering. The WireframeMesh is made up of a list of vertices and lines. Each vertex has an index in the array. A line is defined by specifying the index of a vertex in the *from* array and another in the *to* array. The *from* and *to* arrays must be the same size and they must not specify an index that is not in the *vert* array.

```
public class WireframeMesh{
  public Vec3 vert[];
  public int from[], to[];

  public WireframeMesh(Vec3 vert[], int from[], int to[]);
}
```

Chapter 12

The artofillusion.animation Package

The artofillusion.animation package contains the classes that are required for animation within Art of Illusion. It includes definitions of actors, skeletons, keyframes, and the score where the animation is edited.

artofillusion.animation.Actor

An Actor is an object that can have gestures that combine to form poses. The Actor object wraps an Object3D, in order to give that object more functionality.

```
public class Actor extends ObjectWrapper{
  public Actor(Object3D obj);
  public void addGesture(Gesture p, String name);
  public void deleteGestureWithID(int id);
  public int getNumGestures();
  public Gesture getGesture(int i);
  public Gesture getGestureWithID(int id);
  public String getGestureName(int i);
  public void setGestureName(int i, String name);
  public int getGestureID(int i);
  public int getGestureIndex(int id);
  public Object3D duplicate();
  public Object3D copyObject(Object3D obj);
  public void setSize(double xsize, double ysize, double zsize);
  public boolean isEditable();
  public void edit(EditingWindow parent, ObjectInfo info, Runnable
cb);
  public boolean canSetTexture();
  public boolean canSetMaterial();
  public void setTexture(Texture tex, TextureMapping map);
```

303

```
public void setMaterial(Material mat, MaterialMapping map);
public void setParameterValues(ParameterValue val[]);
public void setParameterValue(TextureParameter param,
ParameterValue value);
public void shapeMeshFromGestures(Object3D obj);
public void writeToFile(DataOutputStream out, Scene theScene)
throws IOException;
public Actor(DataInputStream in, Scene theScene) throws
IOException, InvalidObjectException;
public Property[] getProperties();
public Object getPropertyValue(int index);
public void setPropertyValue(int index, Object value);
public Keyframe getPoseKeyframe();
public void applyPoseKeyframe(Keyframe k);
public void configurePoseTrack(PoseTrack track);
public void editKeyframe(EditingWindow parent, Keyframe k,
ObjectInfo info);
public static Actor getActor(Object3D obj);
public static class ActorKeyframe implements Keyframe;
{
public ActorKeyframe();
public ActorKeyframe(int id[], double weight[]);
public int getNumGestures();
public int getGestureID(int index);
public double getGestureWeight(int index);
public void addGesture(int addID, double addWeight);
public void deleteGesture(int which);
public Keyframe duplicate(Object owner);
public Keyframe duplicate();
public void copy(ActorKeyframe key);
public double [] getGraphValues();
public void setGraphValues(double values[]);
public Keyframe blend(Keyframe o2, double weight1, double
weight2);
public Keyframe blend(Keyframe o2, Keyframe o3, double
weight1, double weight2, double weight3);
public Keyframe blend(Keyframe o2, Keyframe o3, Keyframe
o4, double weight1, double weight2, double weight3, double
weight4);
public boolean equals(Keyframe k);
public Keyframe createObjectKeyframe(Actor actor);
public void writeToStream(DataOutputStream out) throws
IOException;
public ActorKeyframe(DataInputStream in, Object parent)
throws IOException;
}
}
```

artofillusion.animation.
ActorEditorWindow

This is the edit window for Actors.

```
public class ActorEditorWindow extends BDialog{
  public ActorEditorWindow(EditingWindow parent, ObjectInfo info,
Actor obj, ActorKeyframe key, Runnable cb);
}
```

artofillusion.animation. AnimationPreviewer

This class displays a wireframe preview of the animation.

```
public class AnimationPreviewer implements Runnable{
  public AnimationPreviewer(LayoutWindow parent);
  public void run();
}
```

artofillusion.animation.ArrayKeyframe

This is a keyframe that holds an array of doubles. A keyframe represents a state at a single location in animation time, so all of the values in the array are for that one time.

```
public class ArrayKeyframe implements Keyframe{
  public double val[];

  public ArrayKeyframe(double values[]);
  public Keyframe duplicate();
  public Keyframe duplicate(Object owner);
  public double [] getGraphValues();
  public void setGraphValues(double values[]);
  public Keyframe blend(Keyframe o2, double weight1, double
weight2);
  public Keyframe blend(Keyframe o2, Keyframe o3, double
weight1, double weight2, double weight3);
  public Keyframe blend(Keyframe o2, Keyframe o3, Keyframe o4,
double weight1, double weight2, double weight3, double weight4);
  public boolean equals(Keyframe k);
  public void writeToStream(DataOutputStream out)
throws IOException;
  public ArrayKeyframe(DataInputStream in, Object parent)
throws IOException;
}
```

artofillusion.animation. BooleanKeyframe

This class stores a boolean in a keyframe.

```
public class BooleanKeyframe implements Keyframe{
  public boolean val;

  public BooleanKeyframe(boolean b);
  public Keyframe duplicate();
  public Keyframe duplicate(Object owner);
  public double [] getGraphValues();
  public void setGraphValues(double values[]);
  public Keyframe blend(Keyframe o2, double weight1, double
weight2);
  public Keyframe blend(Keyframe o2, Keyframe o3, double
weight1, double weight2, double weight3);
  public Keyframe blend(Keyframe o2, Keyframe o3, Keyframe o4,
double weight1, double weight2, double weight3, double weight4);
  public boolean equals(Keyframe k);
  public void writeToStream(DataOutputStream out)
throws IOException;
  public BooleanKeyframe(DataInputStream in, Object parent)
throws IOException;
}
```

artofillusion.animation. ConstraintTrack

This object is a track that limits the values for position and orientation.

```
public class ConstraintTrack extends Track{
  public ConstraintTrack(ObjectInfo info);
  public void edit(LayoutWindow win);
  public void apply(double time);
  public Track duplicate(Object obj);
  public void copy(Track tr);
  public double [] getKeyTimes();
  public int moveKeyframe(int which, double time);
  public void deleteKeyframe(int which);
  public boolean isNullTrack();
  public Track [] getSubtracks();
  public boolean canAcceptAsParent(Object obj);
  public Object getParent();
  public void setParent(Object obj);
  public ObjectInfo [] getDependencies();
  public void deleteDependencies(ObjectInfo obj);
  public void updateObjectReferences(Map<ObjectInfo, ObjectInfo> objectMap);
```

```
public void writeToStream(DataOutputStream out, Scene scene)
throws IOException;
    public void initFromStream(DataInputStream in, Scene scene)
throws IOException, InvalidObjectException;
}
```

artofillusion.animation. EditKeyframesDialog

This is a dialog for doing bulk editing of keyframes. The possible operations are MOVE, COPY, RESCALE, LOOP, and DELETE.

```
public class EditKeyframesDialog{
    public static final int MOVE;
    public static final int COPY;
    public static final int RESCALE;
    public static final int LOOP;
    public static final int DELETE;

    public EditKeyframesDialog(LayoutWindow win, int operation);
}
```

artofillusion.animation. FilterParameterTrack

This track makes it possible to keyframe ImageFilter parameters.

```
public class FilterParameterTrack extends Track{
    public FilterParameterTrack(Object parent, ImageFilter filter);
    public ImageFilter getFilter();
    public void apply(double time);
    public Track duplicate(Object obj);
    public void copy(Track tr);
    public double [] getKeyTimes();
    public Timecourse getTimecourse();
    public void setKeyframe(double time, Keyframe k,
Smoothness s);
    public Keyframe setKeyframe(double time, Scene sc);
    public Keyframe setKeyframeIfModified(double time, Scene sc);
    public int moveKeyframe(int which, double time);
    public void deleteKeyframe(int which);
    public boolean isNullTrack();
    public Track [] getSubtracks();
    public boolean canAcceptAsParent(Object obj);
    public Object getParent();
    public void setParent(Object obj);
    public int getSmoothingMethod();
```

```
    public void setSmoothingMethod(int method);
    public String [] getValueNames();
    public double [] getDefaultGraphValues();
    public double[][] getValueRange();
    public void writeToStream(DataOutputStream out, Scene sc)
throws IOException;
    public void initFromStream(DataInputStream in, Scene scene)
throws IOException, InvalidObjectException;
    public void editKeyframe(LayoutWindow win, int which);
    public void edit(LayoutWindow win);
}
```

artofillusion.animation.Gesture

A Gesture is how the bones of a skeleton are bent. Gestures can be blended into poses. One Gesture might be defined with the fingers of a hand closed and another with them open. The hand could then move between those two Gestures during animation. The Gesture class is an interface that other classes use.

```
public interface Gesture extends Keyframe{
    public Gesture blend(Gesture p[], double weight[]);
    public Skeleton getSkeleton();
    public void setSkeleton(Skeleton s);
    public void textureChanged(TextureParameter oldParams[],
TextureParameter newParams[]);
    public ParameterValue getTextureParameter(TextureParameter
param);
    public void setTextureParameter(TextureParameter param,
ParameterValue value);
}
```

artofillusion.animation.IKSolver

This is the class that does inverse kinematics calculations (motions necessary to achieve a desired position) for skeletons.

```
public class IKSolver{
    public IKSolver(Skeleton s, boolean locked[], boolean moving[]);
    public boolean solve(Vec3 target[], int maxSteps);
}
```

artofillusion.animation.IKTrack

This Track modifies the shape of an object using inverse kinematics (motions necessary to achieve a desired position).

```
public class IKTrack extends Track{
  public IKTrack(ObjectInfo info);
  public boolean getUseGestures();
  public void setUseGestures(boolean use);
  public void edit(LayoutWindow win);
  public void apply(double time);
  public Track duplicate(Object obj);
  public void copy(Track tr);
  public double [] getKeyTimes();
  public int moveKeyframe(int which, double time);
  public void deleteKeyframe(int which);
  public boolean isNullTrack();
  public Track [] getSubtracks();
  public boolean canAcceptAsParent(Object obj);
  public Object getParent();
  public void setParent(Object obj);
  public ObjectInfo [] getDependencies();
  public void deleteDependencies(ObjectInfo obj);
  public void updateObjectReferences(Map<ObjectInfo, ObjectInfo> objectMap);
  public void writeToStream(DataOutputStream out, Scene scene)
throws IOException;
  public void initFromStream(DataInputStream in, Scene scene)
throws IOException, InvalidObjectException;
}
```

artofillusion.animation.Joint

A Joint is a unit in a skeleton that is able to bend, but its position is constrained by a parent Joint that is also in the skeleton.

```
public class Joint{
  public CoordinateSystem coords;
  public String name;
  public DOF angle1, angle2, twist, length;
  public Joint parent, children[];
  public int id;

  public Joint(CoordinateSystem coords, Joint parentJoint, String name);
  public Joint duplicate();
  public void copy(Joint j);
  public boolean equals(Joint j);
```

```
public void recalcCoords(boolean recursive);
public Mat4 getTransform();
public Mat4 getInverseTransform();
public void calcAnglesFromCoords(boolean recursive);
public class DOF
{
   public double min, max, minComfort, maxComfort, stiffness,
pos;
   public boolean fixed, comfort, loop;

   public DOF(double min, double max, double pos);
   public DOF duplicate();
   public void copy(DOF d);
   public boolean equals(DOF t);
   public void set(double val);
   public double getScaledForce(double f);
   public double getForceScale(double f);
   public double getClippedForce(double f);
   public void writeToStream(DataOutputStream out)
throws IOException;
   public DOF(DataInputStream in) throws IOException;
}
}
```

artofillusion.animation. JointEditorDialog

This is the dialog for editing joints.

```
public class JointEditorDialog extends BDialog{
   public JointEditorDialog(MeshEditorWindow win, int jointID);
}
```

artofillusion.animation.Keyframe

A Keyframe is use to represent a state that exists at a particular frame of the animation. Objects go through transformation from one Keyframe to the next to achieve the state defined in the Keyframe. This is the interface for objects that define more specific Keyframes.

```
public interface Keyframe{
   public Keyframe duplicate();
   public Keyframe duplicate(Object owner);
   public double [] getGraphValues();
   public void setGraphValues(double values[]);
   public Keyframe blend(Keyframe o2, double weight1, double
weight2);
```

```
    public Keyframe blend(Keyframe o2, Keyframe o3, double
weight1, double weight2, double weight3);
    public Keyframe blend(Keyframe o2, Keyframe o3, Keyframe o4,
double weight1, double weight2, double weight3, double weight4);
    public boolean equals(Keyframe k);
    public void writeToStream(DataOutputStream out)
throws IOException;
}
```

artofillusion.animation.Marker

The Marker class holds information about the graphical element that is drawn on the time axis.

```
public class Marker{
    public double position;
    public String name;
    public Color color;

    public Marker(double position, String name, Color color);
}
```

artofillusion.animation.MeshGesture

This is a Gesture that shapes a Mesh.

```
public abstract class MeshGesture implements Gesture{
    protected abstract Mesh getMesh();
    protected abstract Vec3 [] getVertexPositions();
    protected abstract void setVertexPositions(Vec3 pos[]);
    public Gesture blend(Gesture p[], double weight[]);
    public void blendSkeleton(MeshGesture average, MeshGesture
p[], double weight[]);
    public void blendSurface(MeshGesture average, MeshGesture
p[], double weight[]);
}
```

artofillusion.animation.NullKeyframe

This is a Keyframe that contains no information and does nothing. It may be useful as a placeholder.

```
public class NullKeyframe implements Keyframe{
    public NullKeyframe();
    public Keyframe duplicate();
    public Keyframe duplicate(Object owner);
    public double [] getGraphValues();
    public void setGraphValues(double values[]);
    public Keyframe blend(Keyframe o2, double weight1, double
weight2);
    public Keyframe blend(Keyframe o2, Keyframe o3, double
```

```
       weight1, double weight2, double weight3);
         public Keyframe blend(Keyframe o2, Keyframe o3, Keyframe o4,
       double weight1, double weight2, double weight3, double weight4);
         public boolean equals(Keyframe k);
         public void writeToStream(DataOutputStream out) throws
       IOException;
          public NullKeyframe(DataInputStream in, Object parent) throws
       IOException;
       }
```

artofillusion.animation.ObjectRef

This is a reference to another object or a joint within in a skeleton.

```
       public class ObjectRef{
         public ObjectRef();
         public ObjectRef(ObjectInfo info);
         public ObjectRef(ObjectInfo info, Joint j);
         public ObjectRef(int objectID, int jointID, Scene sc);
         public boolean equals(Object obj);
         public ObjectInfo getObject();
         public Joint getJoint();
         public CoordinateSystem getCoords();
         public ObjectRef duplicate();
         public void copy(ObjectRef ref);
         public void writeToStream(DataOutputStream out) throws
       IOException;
         public ObjectRef(DataInputStream in, Scene theScene) throws
       IOException
         public String toString();
       }
```

artofillusion.animation. ObjectRefSelector

This object is a component that is used for selecting an object or joint.

```
       public class ObjectRefSelector extends RowContainer{
         public ObjectRefSelector(ObjectRef obj, LayoutWindow win,
       String prompt, ObjectInfo exclude);
         public ObjectRef getSelection();
         public void setEnabled(boolean enable);
       }
```

artofillusion.animation. ObjectRefTreeElement

This class allows an ObjectRef to be used in in a TreeList.

```
public class ObjectRefTreeElement extends TreeElement{
  public ObjectRefTreeElement(ObjectRef obj, TreeElement
parent, TreeList tree, ObjectInfo exclude);
  public String getLabel();
  public boolean canAcceptAsParent(TreeElement el);
  public void addChild(TreeElement el, int position);
  public void removeChild(Object object);
  public Object getObject();
  public void setEnabled(boolean enable);
  public boolean isGray();
}
```

artofillusion.animation. PathFromCurveDialog

This is the dialog that allows a path to be created from a curve.

```
public class PathFromCurveDialog extends BDialog{
  public PathFromCurveDialog(LayoutWindow win, Object sel[]);
}
```

artofillusion.animation.PoseTrack

This is the animation track for controlling the pose of an object.

```
public class PoseTrack extends Track{
  public PoseTrack(ObjectInfo info);
  public void apply(double time);
  public Track duplicate(Object obj);
  public void copy(Track tr);
  public double [] getKeyTimes();
  public Timecourse getTimecourse();
  public void setKeyframe(double time, Keyframe k,
Smoothness s);
  public Keyframe setKeyframe(double time, Scene sc);
  public Keyframe setKeyframeIfModified(double time, Scene sc);
  public int moveKeyframe(int which, double time);
  public void deleteKeyframe(int which);
  public boolean isNullTrack();
  public Track [] getSubtracks();
  public boolean canAcceptAsParent(Object obj);
```

```
    public Object getParent();
    public void setParent(Object obj);
    public int getSmoothingMethod();
    public void setSmoothingMethod(int method);
    public boolean isRelative();
    public void setRelative(boolean rel);
    public String [] getValueNames();
    public double [] getDefaultGraphValues();
    public double[][] getValueRange();
    public void setGraphableValues(String names[], double
defaults[], double ranges[][]);
    public void setSubtracks(Track extraSubtracks[]);
    public void writeToStream(DataOutputStream out, Scene sc)
throws IOException;
    public void initFromStream(DataInputStream in, Scene scene)
throws IOException, InvalidObjectException;
    public void editKeyframe(LayoutWindow win, int which);
    public void edit(LayoutWindow win);
}
```

artofillusion.animation.PositionTrack

This is the animation track for controlling the position of an object.

```
public class PositionTrack extends Track{
    public static final int ABSOLUTE;
    public static final int RELATIVE;

    public static final int WORLD;
    public static final int PARENT;
    public static final int OBJECT;
    public static final int LOCAL;

    public PositionTrack(ObjectInfo info);
    public PositionTrack(ObjectInfo info, String name, boolean
affectX, boolean affectY, boolean affectZ);
    public void apply(double time);
    public Track duplicate(Object obj);
    public void copy(Track tr);
    public double [] getKeyTimes();
    public Timecourse getTimecourse();
    public void setKeyframe(double time, Keyframe k,
Smoothness s);
    public Keyframe setKeyframe(double time, Scene sc);
    public Keyframe setKeyframeIfModified(double time, Scene sc);
    public int moveKeyframe(int which, double time);
    public void deleteKeyframe(int which);
    public boolean isNullTrack();
    public boolean affectsX();
    public boolean affectsY();
    public boolean affectsZ();
    public Track [] getSubtracks();
```

```
    public boolean canAcceptAsParent(Object obj);
    public Object getParent();
    public void setParent(Object obj);
    public int getSmoothingMethod();
    public void setSmoothingMethod(int method);
    public boolean isRelative();
    public void setRelative(boolean rel);
    public int getCoordinateSystem();
    public void setCoordinateSystem(int system);
    public ObjectRef getCoordsObject();
    public void setCoordsObject(ObjectRef obj);
    public int getApplyToJoint();
    public void setApplyToJoint(int jointID);
    public String [] getValueNames();
    public double [] getDefaultGraphValues();
    public double[][] getValueRange();
    public ObjectInfo [] getDependencies();
    public void deleteDependencies(ObjectInfo obj);
    public void updateObjectReferences(Map<ObjectInfo, ObjectIn-
fo> objectMap);
    public void writeToStream(DataOutputStream out, Scene scene)
throws IOException;
    public void initFromStream(DataInputStream in, Scene scene)
throws IOException, InvalidObjectException;
    public void editKeyframe(LayoutWindow win, int which);
    public void edit(LayoutWindow win);
}
```

artofillusion.animation. ProceduralPositionTrack

This track uses a procedure to position the object.

```
public class ProceduralPositionTrack extends Track implements
ProcedureOwner{
    public static final int ABSOLUTE;
    public static final int RELATIVE;

    public static final int WORLD;
    public static final int PARENT;
    public static final int OBJECT;
    public static final int LOCAL;

    public ProceduralPositionTrack(ObjectInfo info);
    public void apply(double time);
    public Track duplicate(Object obj);
    public void copy(Track tr);
    public double [] getKeyTimes();
    public Timecourse getTimecourse();
    public void setKeyframe(double time, Keyframe k,
Smoothness s);
    public Keyframe setKeyframe(double time, Scene sc);
```

```
    public int moveKeyframe(int which, double time);
    public void deleteKeyframe(int which);
    public boolean isNullTrack();
    public Track [] getSubtracks();
    public boolean canAcceptAsParent(Object obj);
    public Object getParent();
    public void setParent(Object obj);
    public int getSmoothingMethod();
    public void setSmoothingMethod(int method);
    public boolean isRelative();
    public void setRelative(boolean rel);
    public int getCoordinateSystem();
    public void setCoordinateSystem(int system);
    public ObjectRef getCoordsObject();
    public void setCoordsObject(ObjectRef obj);
    public int getApplyToJoint();
    public void setApplyToJoint(int jointID);
    public String [] getValueNames();
    public double [] getDefaultGraphValues();
    public double[][] getValueRange();
    public ObjectInfo [] getDependencies();
    public void deleteDependencies(ObjectInfo obj);
    public void updateObjectReferences(Map<ObjectInfo, ObjectIn-
fo> objectMap);
    public void writeToStream(DataOutputStream out, Scene scene)
throws IOException;
    public void initFromStream(DataInputStream in, Scene scene)
throws IOException, InvalidObjectException;
    public void editKeyframe(LayoutWindow win, int which);
    public void edit(LayoutWindow win);
    public String getWindowTitle();
    public Object getPreview(ProcedureEditor editor);
    public void updatePreview(Object preview);
    public void disposePreview(Object preview);
    public boolean allowViewAngle();
    public boolean allowParameters();
    public boolean canEditName();
    public void acceptEdits(ProcedureEditor editor);
    public void editProperties(ProcedureEditor editor);
}
```

artofillusion.animation. ProceduralRotationTrack

This Track uses a procedure to rotate the object.

```
public class ProceduralRotationTrack extends Track implements
ProcedureOwner{
    public static final int ABSOLUTE;
    public static final int RELATIVE;

    public static final int WORLD;
```

```
    public static final int PARENT;
    public static final int OBJECT;
    public static final int LOCAL;

    public ProceduralRotationTrack(ObjectInfo info);
    public void apply(double time);
    public Track duplicate(Object obj);
    public void copy(Track tr);
    public double [] getKeyTimes();
    public Timecourse getTimecourse();
    public void setKeyframe(double time, Keyframe k,
Smoothness s);
    public Keyframe setKeyframe(double time, Scene sc);
    public int moveKeyframe(int which, double time);
    public void deleteKeyframe(int which);
    public boolean isNullTrack();
    public Track [] getSubtracks();
    public boolean canAcceptAsParent(Object obj);
    public Object getParent();
    public void setParent(Object obj);
    public int getSmoothingMethod();
    public void setSmoothingMethod(int method);
    public boolean isRelative();
    public void setRelative(boolean rel);
    public int getCoordinateSystem();
    public void setCoordinateSystem(int system);
    public ObjectRef getCoordsObject();
    public void setCoordsObject(ObjectRef obj);
    public int getApplyToJoint();
    public void setApplyToJoint(int jointID);
    public String [] getValueNames();
    public ObjectInfo [] getDependencies();
    public void deleteDependencies(ObjectInfo obj);
    public void updateObjectReferences(Map<ObjectInfo, ObjectIn-
fo> objectMap);
    public void writeToStream(DataOutputStream out, Scene scene)
throws IOException;
    public void initFromStream(DataInputStream in, Scene scene)
throws IOException, InvalidObjectException;
    public void editKeyframe(LayoutWindow win, int which);
    public void edit(LayoutWindow win);
    public String getWindowTitle();
    public Object getPreview(ProcedureEditor editor);
    public void updatePreview(Object preview);
    public void disposePreview(Object preview);
    public boolean allowViewAngle();
    public boolean allowParameters();
    public boolean canEditName();
    public void acceptEdits(ProcedureEditor editor);
    public void editProperties(ProcedureEditor editor);
}
```

artofillusion.animation. RotationKeyframe

This is a keyframe for the RotationTrack.

```
public class RotationKeyframe implements Keyframe{
  public double x, y, z;
  public RotationKeyframe(double xrot, double yrot, double zrot);
  public RotationKeyframe(CoordinateSystem coords);
  public void set(double xrot, double yrot, double zrot);
  public double [] getGraphValues();
  public void setGraphValues(double values[]);
  public boolean getUseQuaternion();
  public void setUseQuaternion(boolean use);
  public double [] getQuaternion();
  public void applyToCoordinates(CoordinateSystem coords,
double weight, Mat4 preTransform,
Mat4 postTransform, boolean relative, boolean enablex, boolean
enabley, boolean enablez);
  public Keyframe duplicate();
  public Keyframe duplicate(Object owner);
  public Keyframe blend(Keyframe o2, double weight1,
double weight2);
  public Keyframe blend(Keyframe o2, Keyframe o3,
double weight1, double weight2, double weight3);
  public Keyframe blend(Keyframe o2, Keyframe o3, Keyframe o4,
double weight1, double weight2, double weight3, double weight4);
  public boolean equals(Keyframe k);
  public void writeToStream(DataOutputStream out)
throws IOException;
  public RotationKeyframe(DataInputStream in, Object parent)
throws IOException;
}
```

artofillusion.animation.RotationTrack

This is the animation track that controls the rotation of an object.

```
public class RotationTrack extends Track{
  public static final int ABSOLUTE;
  public static final int RELATIVE;

  public static final int WORLD;
  public static final int PARENT;
  public static final int OBJECT;
  public static final int LOCAL;

  public RotationTrack(ObjectInfo info);
  public RotationTrack(ObjectInfo info, String name,
boolean useQuaternion, boolean affectX, boolean affectY,
```

```
    boolean affectZ);
    public void apply(double time);
    public Track duplicate(Object obj);
    public void copy(Track tr);
    public double [] getKeyTimes();
    public Timecourse getTimecourse();
    public void setKeyframe(double time, Keyframe k,
Smoothness s);
    public Keyframe setKeyframe(double time, Scene sc);
    public Keyframe setKeyframeIfModified(double time, Scene sc);
    public int moveKeyframe(int which, double time);
    public void deleteKeyframe(int which);
    public boolean isNullTrack();
    public boolean affectsX();
    public boolean affectsY();
    public boolean affectsZ();
    public Track [] getSubtracks();
    public boolean canAcceptAsParent(Object obj);
    public Object getParent();
    public void setParent(Object obj);
    public int getSmoothingMethod();
    public void setSmoothingMethod(int method);
    public boolean isRelative();
    public void setRelative(boolean rel);
    public boolean getUseQuaternion();
    public void setUseQuaternion(boolean use);
    public int getCoordinateSystem();
    public void setCoordinateSystem(int system);
    public ObjectRef getCoordsObject();
    public void setCoordsObject(ObjectRef obj);
    public int getApplyToJoint();
    public void setApplyToJoint(int jointID);
    public String [] getValueNames();
    public double [] getDefaultGraphValues();
    public double[][] getValueRange();
    public ObjectInfo [] getDependencies();
    public void deleteDependencies(ObjectInfo obj);
    public void updateObjectReferences(Map<ObjectInfo, ObjectIn-
fo> objectMap);
    public void writeToStream(DataOutputStream out, Scene scene)
throws IOException;
    public void initFromStream(DataInputStream in, Scene scene)
throws IOException, InvalidObjectException;
    public void editKeyframe(LayoutWindow win, int which);
    public void edit(LayoutWindow win);
}
```

artofillusion.animation. ScalarKeyframe

This class is a keyframe that stores a scalar of type double.

```
public class ScalarKeyframe implements Keyframe{
  public double val;

  public ScalarKeyframe(double d);
  public Keyframe duplicate();
  public Keyframe duplicate(Object owner);
  public double [] getGraphValues();
  public void setGraphValues(double values[]);
  public Keyframe blend(Keyframe o2, double weight1,
double weight2);
  public Keyframe blend(Keyframe o2, Keyframe o3,
double weight1, double weight2, double weight3);
  public Keyframe blend(Keyframe o2, Keyframe o3, Keyframe o4,
double weight1, double weight2, double weight3, double weight4);
  public boolean equals(Keyframe k);
  public void writeToStream(DataOutputStream out)
throws IOException;
  public ScalarKeyframe(DataInputStream in, Object parent)
throws IOException;
}
```

artofillusion.animation.Score

This is the component that displays the animation score that appears at the bottom of the Art of Illusion main window.

```
public class Score extends BorderContainer
implements EditingWindow, PopupMenuManager{
  public static final int TRACKS_MODE;
  public static final int SINGLE_GRAPH_MODE;
  public static final int MULTI_GRAPH_MODE;

  public static final int SELECT_AND_MOVE;
  public static final int SCROLL_AND_SCALE;

  public Score(LayoutWindow win);
  public void showPopupMenu(Widget w, int x, int y);
  public BPopupMenu getPopupMenu();
  public Dimension getMinimumSize();
  public Track [] getSelectedTracks();
  public SelectionInfo [] getSelectedKeyframes();
  public void setSelectedKeyframes(SelectionInfo sel[]);
  public void addSelectedKeyframes(SelectionInfo newsel[]);
  public void removeSelectedKeyframe(Keyframe key);
  public boolean isKeyframeSelected(Keyframe k);
  public boolean isKeyframeSelected(Keyframe k, int value);
  public void rebuildList();
  public double getStartTime();
  public void setStartTime(double time);
  public double getScale();
```

```
      public void setScale(double s);
      public void setTime(double time);
      public void startAnimating();
      public void stopAnimating();
      public boolean getAnimating();
      public double getPlaybackSpeed();
      public void setPlaybackSeed(double speed);
      public void tracksModified(boolean updateScene);
      public void repaintGraphs();
      public void repaintAll();
      public void setScrollPosition(int pos);
      public void markerMoved(Marker m, boolean intermediate);
      public void layoutChildren();
      public void editSelectedTrack();
      public void finishEditingTrack(Track tr);
      public void setTracksEnabled(boolean enable);
      public void keyframeSelectedTracks();
      public void keyframeModifiedTracks();
      public void duplicateSelectedTracks();
      public void deleteSelectedTracks();
      public void selectAllTracks();
      public void addTrack(Object obj[], Class trackClass,
Object extraArgs[], boolean deselectOthers);
      public void editSelectedKeyframe();
      public void deleteSelectedKeyframes();
      public boolean confirmClose();
      public ToolPalette getToolPalette();
      public void setTool(EditingTool tool);
      public void setHelpText(String text);
      public BFrame getFrame();
      public void updateImage();
      public void updateMenus();
      public void setUndoRecord(UndoRecord command);
      public void setModified();
      public Scene getScene();
      public ViewerCanvas getView();
      }
```

artofillusion.animation.SelectionInfo

This object holds information about the selected keyframe.

```
public class SelectionInfo{
  public Track track;
  public Keyframe key;
  public int keyIndex;
  public boolean selected[];

  public SelectionInfo(Track tr, Keyframe k);
}
```

artofillusion.animation.Skeleton

A skeleton defines a framework that can be used to reshape an object as if the object has bones and joints.

```
public class Skeleton{
  public Skeleton();
  public Skeleton duplicate();
  public void copy(Skeleton s);
  public boolean equals(Object o);
  public void addJoint(Joint j, int parentID);
  public void deleteJoint(int id);
  public void addAllJoints(Skeleton s);
  public void setJointParent(Joint j, Joint parent);
  public int findJointIndex(int id);
  public Joint getJoint(int id);
  public Joint [] getJoints();
  public int getNumJoints();
  public int getNextJointID();
  public void scale(double x, double y, double z);
  public void blend(Skeleton average, Skeleton s[],
double weight[]);
  public void draw(MeshViewer view, boolean enabled);
  public static void adjustMesh(Mesh oldMesh, Mesh newMesh);
  public void writeToStream(DataOutputStream out)
throws IOException;
  public Skeleton(DataInputStream in) throws IOException,
InvalidObjectException;
}
```

artofillusion.animation.SkeletonTool

This is the tool for editing skeletons.

```
public class SkeletonTool extends EditingTool
{
  public SkeletonTool(MeshEditorWindow fr, boolean
allowCreating);
  public void activate();
  public int whichClicks();
  public String getToolTipText();
  public void drawOverlay(ViewerCanvas view);
  public void mousePressed(WidgetMouseEvent e,
ViewerCanvas view);
  public void mouseDragged(final WidgetMouseEvent e,
ViewerCanvas view);
  public void mouseReleased(WidgetMouseEvent e,
ViewerCanvas view);
  public void iconDoubleClicked();
  protected void adjustMesh(Mesh newMesh);
```

}

artofillusion.animation.Smoothness

This class stores the smoothness information for a Keyframe. The smoothness can be set as one value for all or with a value for left and a value for right, indicating the value coming in and the value leaving the Keyframe.

```
public class Smoothness{
  public Smoothness();
  public Smoothness(double s);
  public Smoothness duplicate();
  public double getLeftSmoothness();
  public double getRightSmoothness();
  public void setSmoothness(double s);
  public void setSmoothness(double left, double right);
  public boolean isForceSame();
  public Smoothness getSmoother();
  public void writeToStream(DataOutputStream out)
throws IOException;
  public Smoothness(DataInputStream in) throws IOException;
}
```

animation

artofillusion.animation.TextureTrack

The is the track used for animating texture parameters.

```
public class TextureTrack extends Track{
  public TextureTrack(ObjectInfo info);
  public void apply(double time);
  public Track duplicate(Object obj);
  public void copy(Track tr);
  public double [] getKeyTimes();
  public Timecourse getTimecourse();
  public void setKeyframe(double time, Keyframe k,
Smoothness s);
  public Keyframe setKeyframe(double time, Scene sc);
  public Keyframe setKeyframeIfModified(double time, Scene sc);
  public int moveKeyframe(int which, double time);
  public void deleteKeyframe(int which);
  public boolean isNullTrack();
  public Track [] getSubtracks();
  public boolean canAcceptAsParent(Object obj);
  public Object getParent();
  public void setParent(Object obj);
  public int getSmoothingMethod();
  public void setSmoothingMethod(int method);
```

```
    public String [] getValueNames();
    public double [] getDefaultGraphValues();
    public double[][] getValueRange();
    public ObjectInfo [] getDependencies();
    public void deleteDependencies(ObjectInfo obj);
    public void parametersChanged();
    public void writeToStream(DataOutputStream out, Scene scene)
throws IOException;
    public void initFromStream(DataInputStream in, Scene scene)
throws IOException, InvalidObjectException;
    public void editKeyframe(LayoutWindow win, int which);
    public void edit(LayoutWindow win);
}
```

artofillusion.animation.TimeAxis

This is a component that is used to display a time axis.

```
public class TimeAxis extends CustomWidget{
    public TimeAxis(int subdivisions, double scale, Score sc);
    public double getStartTime();
    public void setStartTime(double time);
    public double getScale();
    public void setScale(double s);
    public void setSubdivisions(int s);
    public void addMarker(Marker m);
    public Dimension getPreferredSize();
}
```

artofillusion.animation.Timecourse

A Timecourse is a quantity that changes as a function of time. A series of time points define the transition.

```
public class Timecourse{
    public static final int DISCONTINUOUS;
    public static final int LINEAR;
    public static final int INTERPOLATING;
    public static final int APPROXIMATING;

    public Timecourse(Keyframe value[], double time[],
Smoothness smoothness[]);
    public void setTimepoints(Keyframe value[], double time[],
Smoothness smoothness[]);
    public int addTimepoint(Keyframe v, double t, Smoothness s);
    public void removeTimepoint(double t);
    public void removeTimepoint(int which);
    public void removeAllTimepoints();
    public int moveTimepoint(int which, double t);
```

```
public double [] getTimes();
public Keyframe [] getValues();
public Smoothness [] getSmoothness();
public boolean getSubdivideAdaptively();
public void setSubdivideAdaptively(boolean adaptive);
public Timecourse duplicate(Object owner);
public Timecourse subdivide(int method);
public Keyframe evaluate(double t, int method);
}
```

artofillusion.animation.Track

This is the abstract class that defines an animation track.

```
public abstract class Track{
  protected String name;
  protected boolean enabled = true, quantized = true;

  protected Track();
  public Track(String name);
  public String getName();
  public void setName(String name);
  public boolean isEnabled();
  public void setEnabled(boolean enable);
  public boolean isQuantized();
  public void setQuantized(boolean quantize);
  public String [] getValueNames();
  public double [] getGraphValues(Keyframe key);
  public double [] getDefaultGraphValues();
  public double[][] getValueRange();
  public abstract void edit(LayoutWindow win);
  public void editKeyframe(LayoutWindow win, int which);
  public abstract void apply(double time);
  public abstract Track duplicate(Object parent);
  public abstract void copy(Track tr);
  public abstract double [] getKeyTimes();
  public Timecourse getTimecourse();
  public int getSmoothingMethod();
  public void setKeyframe(double time, Keyframe k,
Smoothness s);
  public Keyframe setKeyframe(double time, Scene sc);
  public Keyframe setKeyframeIfModified(double time, Scene sc);
  public abstract int moveKeyframe(int which, double time);
  public abstract void deleteKeyframe(int which);
  public abstract boolean isNullTrack();
  public Track [] getSubtracks();
  public boolean canAcceptAsParent(Object obj);
  public Object getParent();
  public void setParent(Object obj);
  public ObjectInfo [] getDependencies();
  public void deleteDependencies(ObjectInfo obj);
```

```
   public void updateObjectReferences(Map<ObjectInfo, ObjectIn-
fo> objectMap);
   public abstract void writeToStream(DataOutputStream out,
Scene scene) throws IOException;
   public abstract void initFromStream(DataInputStream in, Scene
scene) throws IOException, InvalidObjectException;
}
```

artofillusion.animation.TrackDisplay

This is the interface for a component that is used in the Score to display the contents of Tracks.

```
public interface TrackDisplay{
   public void setStartTime(double time);
   public void setScale(double s);
   public void setSubdivisions(int s);
   public void setYOffset(int offset);
   public void addMarker(Marker m);
   public void setMode(int m);
}
```

artofillusion.animation.TrackGraph

This is a graph for displaying and editing keyframe values.

```
public class TrackGraph extends CustomWidget implements
TrackDisplay{
   public static final int HANDLE_SIZE;
   public static final int TICK_SIZE;
   public static final Color LINE_COLOR[], LIGHT_LINE_COLOR[],
SELECTED_VALUE_COLOR, SELECTED_KEY_COLOR;

   public TrackGraph(LayoutWindow win, Score sc, TimeAxis ta);
   public void setStartTime(double time);
   public void setScale(double s);
   public void setSubdivisions(int s);
   public void setYOffset(int offset);
   public void addMarker(Marker m);
   public void setMode(int m);
   public VerticalAxis getAxis();
   public void setTracks(Track t[]);
   public void showLineAtBottom(boolean show);
   public void tracksModified();
   public void selectionChanged();
}
```

artofillusion.animation.TracksPanel

This is the panel that displays all of the tracks in the Score.

```
public class TracksPanel extends CustomWidget implements
TrackDisplay{
  public TracksPanel(LayoutWindow win, TreeList list, Score sc,
int subdivisions, double scale);
  public void setStartTime(double time);
  public void setScale(double s);
  public void setSubdivisions(int s);
  public void setYOffset(int offset);
  public void addMarker(Marker m);
  public void setMode(int m);
}
```

artofillusion.animation. TrackTreeElement

This class represents a Track in the Score's TreeList.

```
public class TrackTreeElement extends TreeElement{
  public TrackTreeElement(Track tr, TreeElement parent, TreeList
tree);
  public String getLabel();
  public boolean canAcceptAsParent(TreeElement el);
  public void addChild(TreeElement el, int position);
  public void removeChild(Object object);
  public Object getObject();
  public boolean isGray();
}
```

artofillusion.animation. VectorKeyframe

This keyframe stores a vector value.

```
public class VectorKeyframe extends Vec3 implements Keyframe{
  public VectorKeyframe();
  public VectorKeyframe(double xval, double yval, double zval);
  public VectorKeyframe(Vec3 v);
  public Keyframe duplicate(Object owner);
  public Keyframe duplicate();
  public double [] getGraphValues();
  public void setGraphValues(double values[]);
  public Keyframe blend(Keyframe o2, double weight1,
double weight2);
```

```
    public Keyframe blend(Keyframe o2, Keyframe o3, double
weight1, double weight2, double weight3);
    public Keyframe blend(Keyframe o2, Keyframe o3, Keyframe o4,
double weight1, double weight2, double weight3, double weight4);
    public boolean equals(Keyframe k);
    public void writeToStream(DataOutputStream out)
throws IOException;
    public VectorKeyframe(DataInputStream in, Object parent)
throws IOException;
}
```

artofillusion.animation.VerticalAxis

This class draws the vertical axis on keyframe graphs.

```
public class VerticalAxis extends CustomWidget{
    public static final int TICK_SIZE;

    public VerticalAxis();
    public void setGraphRange(double min, double max);
    public void showLineAtBottom(boolean show);
}
```

artofillusion.animation.VisibilityTrack

This is the track for animating the visibility of objects.

```
public class VisibilityTrack extends Track{
    public VisibilityTrack(ObjectInfo info);
    public void apply(double time);
    public Track duplicate(Object obj);
    public void copy(Track tr);
    public double [] getKeyTimes();
    public Timecourse getTimecourse();
    public void setKeyframe(double time, Keyframe k,
Smoothness s);
    public Keyframe setKeyframe(double time, Scene sc);
    public Keyframe setKeyframeIfModified(double time, Scene sc);
    public int moveKeyframe(int which, double time);
    public void deleteKeyframe(int which);
    public boolean isNullTrack();
    public boolean canAcceptAsParent(Object obj);
    public Object getParent();
    public void setParent(Object obj);
    public String [] getValueNames();
    public double [] getDefaultGraphValues();
    public double[][] getValueRange();
    public void writeToStream(DataOutputStream out, Scene scene)
throws IOException;
```

```
        public void initFromStream(DataInputStream in, Scene scene)
     throws IOException, InvalidObjectException;
        public void editKeyframe(LayoutWindow win, int which);
        public void edit(LayoutWindow win);
     }
```

artofillusion.animation.WeightTrack

This track controls how much weight is given to the parent track.

```
     public class WeightTrack extends Track{
        public WeightTrack(Track parent);
        public double getWeight(double time);
        public void apply(double time);
        public Track duplicate(Object parent);
        public void copy(Track tr);
        public Timecourse getTimecourse();
        public void setTimecourse(Timecourse t);
        public int getSmoothingMethod();
        public void setSmoothingMethod(int method);
        public double [] getKeyTimes();
        public void setKeyframe(double time, Keyframe k,
     Smoothness s);
        public Keyframe setKeyframe(double time, Scene sc);
        public int moveKeyframe(int which, double time);
        public void deleteKeyframe(int which);
        public boolean isNullTrack();
        public Object getParent();
        public String [] getValueNames();
        public double [] getDefaultGraphValues();
        public double[][] getValueRange();
        public void writeToStream(DataOutputStream out, Scene scene)
     throws IOException;
        public void initFromStream(DataInputStream in, Scene scene)
     throws IOException, InvalidObjectException;
        public void editKeyframe(LayoutWindow win, int which);
        public void edit(LayoutWindow win);
     }
```

Chapter 13

The artofillusion.animation.distortion Package

Distortions are a type of animation that reshape or distort the object. They are used when the goal is to animate the vertices of the object, rather than the position and rotation of the object. Art of Illusion has several distortions built into it. A couple of the more visually interesting distortions are the TwistDistortion, which causes the animated object to look like someone is twisting it like a rag, and the ShatterDistortion, which causes the object to look like it has broken into many triangles that are spinning out into space away from the object (Essentially, a quick way to model an explosion.). Art of Illusion does not currently have this capability, but if someone were to develop a cloth simulation for it, it would likely be done as a distortion.

Most of the objects in this package come in pairs. There is a distortion object, which defines the transformation and there is the track, which is used to apply the transformation to the object during animation.

artofillusion.animation.distortion. BendDistortion

This distortion bends an object.

```
public class BendDistortion extends Distortion{
    public static final int POS_X;
    public static final int NEG_X;
    public static final int POS_Y;
    public static final int NEG_Y;
    public static final int POS_Z;
    public static final int NEG_Z;

    public static final int X_AXIS;
    public static final int Y_AXIS;
    public static final int Z_AXIS;

    public BendDistortion(int axis, int direction, double angle,
boolean forward, Mat4 preTransform, Mat4 postTransform);
    public boolean isIdenticalTo(Distortion d);
    public Distortion duplicate();
    public Mesh transform(Mesh obj);
}
```

artofillusion.animation.distortion. BendTrack

This is the animation track for the BendDistortion.

```
public class BendTrack extends Track{
    public BendTrack(ObjectInfo info);
    public void apply(double time);
    public Track duplicate(Object obj);
    public void copy(Track tr);
    public double [] getKeyTimes();
    public Timecourse getTimecourse();
    public void setKeyframe(double time, Keyframe k,
Smoothness s);
    public Keyframe setKeyframe(double time, Scene sc);
    public int moveKeyframe(int which, double time);
    public void deleteKeyframe(int which);
    public boolean isNullTrack();
    public Track [] getSubtracks();
    public boolean canAcceptAsParent(Object obj);
    public Object getParent();
    public void setParent(Object obj);
    public int getSmoothingMethod();
    public void setSmoothingMethod(int method);
    public String [] getValueNames();
    public double [] getDefaultGraphValues();
    public double[][] getValueRange();
```

```
    public ObjectInfo [] getDependencies();
    public void deleteDependencies(ObjectInfo obj);
    public void writeToStream(DataOutputStream out, Scene scene)
throws IOException;
    public void initFromStream(DataInputStream in, Scene scene)
throws IOException, InvalidObjectException;
    public void editKeyframe(LayoutWindow win, int which);
    public void edit(LayoutWindow win);
}
```

artofillusion.animation.distortion. CustomDistortion

This is a distortion that the user can define through the use of a procedure.

```
public class CustomDistortion extends Distortion{
    public CustomDistortion(Procedure proc, int procVersion,
PointInfo point, double weight, Mat4 preTransform,
Mat4 postTransform);
    public boolean isIdenticalTo(Distortion d);
    public Distortion duplicate();
    public Mesh transform(Mesh obj);
}
```

artofillusion.animation.distortion. CustomDistortionTrack

This is the animation track for the CustomDistortion.

```
public class CustomDistortionTrack extends Track implements
ProcedureOwner{
    public CustomDistortionTrack(ObjectInfo info);
    public void apply(double time);
    public Track duplicate(Object obj);
    public void copy(Track tr);
    public double [] getKeyTimes();
    public Timecourse getTimecourse();
    public void setKeyframe(double time, Keyframe k,
Smoothness s);
    public Keyframe setKeyframe(double time, Scene sc);
    public int moveKeyframe(int which, double time);
    public void deleteKeyframe(int which);
    public boolean isNullTrack();
    public Track [] getSubtracks();
    public boolean canAcceptAsParent(Object obj);
    public Object getParent();
    public void setParent(Object obj);
    public int getSmoothingMethod();
```

distortion

```
   public void setSmoothingMethod(int method);
   public String [] getValueNames();
   public double [] getDefaultGraphValues();
   public double[][] getValueRange();
   public ObjectInfo [] getDependencies();
   public void deleteDependencies(ObjectInfo obj);
   public void writeToStream(DataOutputStream out, Scene scene)
throws IOException;
   public void initFromStream(DataInputStream in, Scene scene)
throws IOException, InvalidObjectException;
   public void editKeyframe(LayoutWindow win, int which);
   public void edit(LayoutWindow win);
   public String getWindowTitle();
   public Object getPreview(ProcedureEditor editor);
   public void updatePreview(Object preview);
   public void disposePreview(Object preview);
   public boolean allowParameters();
   public boolean allowViewAngle();
   public boolean canEditName();
   public void acceptEdits(ProcedureEditor editor);
   public void editProperties(ProcedureEditor editor);
}
```

artofillusion.animation.distortion. Distortion

This is the interface that defines the methods that all Distortions must have. The method setPreviousDistortion is used to chain distortions together. The transform method takes the Mesh passed in and outputs a different mesh that has the transformation applied to it.

```
public abstract class Distortion{
   public void setPreviousDistortion(Distortion previous);
   public Distortion getPreviousDistortion();
   public abstract boolean isIdenticalTo(Distortion d);
   public abstract Distortion duplicate();
   public abstract Mesh transform(Mesh obj);
}
```

artofillusion.animation.distortion. IKDistortion

This is a distortion that is applied through the use of inverse kinematics (motions necessary to achieve a desired position). It makes use of the artofillusion.animation.IKSolver.

```
public class IKDistortion extends Distortion{
    public IKDistortion(boolean locked[], Vec3 target[], double weight,
Actor actor);
    public boolean isIdenticalTo(Distortion d);
    public Distortion duplicate();
    public Mesh transform(Mesh obj);
}
```

artofillusion.animation.distortion. PoseDistortion

This Distortion poses an object.

```
public class PoseDistortion extends Distortion{
    public PoseDistortion(double weight, Keyframe pose, Actor
actor, boolean relative);
    public boolean isIdenticalTo(Distortion d);
    public Distortion duplicate();
    public Mesh transform(Mesh obj);
}
```

artofillusion.animation.distortion. ScaleDistortion

This Distortion scales an object.

```
public class ScaleDistortion extends Distortion{
    public ScaleDistortion(double xscale, double yscale, double
zscale, Mat4 preTransform, Mat4 postTransform);
    public boolean isIdenticalTo(Distortion d);
    public Distortion duplicate();
    public Mesh transform(Mesh obj);
}
```

artofillusion.animation.distortion. ScaleTrack

This is the animation track for the ScaleDistortion.

```
public class ScaleTrack extends Track{
    public ScaleTrack(ObjectInfo info);
    public void apply(double time);
    public Track duplicate(Object obj);
    public void copy(Track tr);
    public double [] getKeyTimes();
    public Timecourse getTimecourse();
```

```
    public void setKeyframe(double time, Keyframe k,
Smoothness s);
    public Keyframe setKeyframe(double time, Scene sc);
    public int moveKeyframe(int which, double time);
    public void deleteKeyframe(int which);
    public boolean isNullTrack();
    public Track [] getSubtracks();
    public boolean canAcceptAsParent(Object obj);
    public Object getParent();
    public void setParent(Object obj);
    public int getSmoothingMethod();
    public void setSmoothingMethod(int method);
    public String [] getValueNames();
    public double [] getDefaultGraphValues();
    public double[][] getValueRange();
    public ObjectInfo [] getDependencies();
    public void deleteDependencies(ObjectInfo obj);
    public void writeToStream(DataOutputStream out, Scene scene)
throws IOException;
    public void initFromStream(DataInputStream in, Scene scene)
throws IOException, InvalidObjectException;
    public void editKeyframe(LayoutWindow win, int which);
    public void edit(LayoutWindow win);
}
```

artofillusion.animation.distortion. ShatterDistortion

The ShatterDistortion breaks the Mesh into many pieces as if it had exploded and the pieces are traveling away from the center through animation time.

```
public class ShatterDistortion extends Distortion{
    public static final int X_AXIS;
    public static final int Y_AXIS;
    public static final int Z_AXIS;

    public ShatterDistortion(double time, double size, double speed,
double randomness, double gravity, double spin, double
disappear, int gravityAxis, Mat4 gravityDirTransform);
    public boolean isIdenticalTo(Distortion d);
    public Distortion duplicate();
    public Mesh transform(Mesh obj);
}
```

artofillusion.animation.distortion. ShatterTrack

This is the animation track for the ShatterDistortion.

```
public class ShatterTrack extends Track{
  public ShatterTrack(ObjectInfo info);
  public void apply(double time);
  public Track duplicate(Object obj);
  public void copy(Track tr);
  public double [] getKeyTimes();
  public int moveKeyframe(int which, double time);
  public void deleteKeyframe(int which);
  public boolean isNullTrack();
  public boolean canAcceptAsParent(Object obj);
  public Object getParent();
  public void setParent(Object obj);
  public void writeToStream(DataOutputStream out, Scene scene)
throws IOException;
  public void initFromStream(DataInputStream in, Scene scene)
throws IOException, InvalidObjectException;
  public void edit(LayoutWindow win);
}
```

artofillusion.animation.distortion. SkeletonShapeDistortion

This Distortion reshapes the Skeleton of the object.

```
public class SkeletonShapeDistortion extends Distortion{
  public SkeletonShapeDistortion(Skeleton skeleton, double
weight, Actor actor);
  public boolean isIdenticalTo(Distortion d);
  public Distortion duplicate();
  public Mesh transform(Mesh obj);
}
```

artofillusion.animation.distortion. SkeletonShapeEditorWindow

This is a window for editing SkeletonShape keyframes.

```
public class SkeletonShapeEditorWindow extends
MeshEditorWindow implements MeshEditController{
  public SkeletonShapeEditorWindow(EditingWindow parent, String
title, SkeletonShapeTrack track, int keyIndex, Runnable onClose);
  public void updateMenus();
  public ObjectInfo getObject();
  public void setObject(Object3D obj);
  public void setMesh(Mesh mesh);
  public int getSelectionMode();
  public void setSelectionMode(int mode);
  public boolean [] getSelection();
```

```
    public void setSelection(boolean selected[]);
    public int[] getSelectionDistance();
    protected void doOk();
    protected void doCancel();
    protected void resetCommand();
    protected void createFromGesturesCommand();
    protected void editProperties();
    public void adjustDeltas(Vec3 delta[]);
    public void deleteCommand();
}
```

artofillusion.animation.distortion. SkeletonShapeKeyframe

This is a keyframe for the SkeletonShapeTrack.

```
public class SkeletonShapeKeyframe implements Keyframe{
    public SkeletonShapeKeyframe(Object3D owner, Skeleton s);
    public Object3D getObject();
    public Skeleton getSkeleton();
    public Keyframe duplicate();
    public Keyframe duplicate(Object owner);
    public double [] getGraphValues();
    public void setGraphValues(double values[]);
    public Keyframe blend(Keyframe o2, double weight1, double
weight2);
    public Keyframe blend(Keyframe o2, Keyframe o3, double
weight1, double weight2, double weight3);
    public Keyframe blend(Keyframe o2, Keyframe o3, Keyframe o4,
double weight1, double weight2, double weight3, double weight4);
    public boolean equals(Keyframe k);
    public void writeToStream(DataOutputStream out) throws
IOException;
    public SkeletonShapeKeyframe(DataInputStream in, Object
parent) throws IOException;
}
```

artofillusion.animation.distortion. SkeletonShapeTrack

This is the animation track for the SkeletonShapeDistortion.

```
public class SkeletonShapeTrack extends Track{
    public SkeletonShapeTrack(ObjectInfo info);
    public boolean getUseGestures();
    public void setUseGestures(boolean use);
    public void apply(double time);
    public Track duplicate(Object obj);
    public void copy(Track tr);
```

```
public double [] getKeyTimes();
public Timecourse getTimecourse();
public void setKeyframe(double time, Keyframe k, Smoothness
s);
public Keyframe setKeyframe(double time, Scene sc);
public int moveKeyframe(int which, double time);
public void deleteKeyframe(int which);
public boolean isNullTrack();
public Track [] getSubtracks();
public boolean canAcceptAsParent(Object obj);
public Object getParent();
public void setParent(Object obj);
public int getSmoothingMethod();
public void setSmoothingMethod(int method);
public String [] getValueNames();
public double [] getDefaultGraphValues();
public double[][] getValueRange();
public ObjectInfo [] getDependencies();
public void deleteDependencies(ObjectInfo obj);
public void writeToStream(DataOutputStream out, Scene scene)
throws IOException;
public void initFromStream(DataInputStream in, Scene scene)
throws IOException, InvalidObjectException;
public void editKeyframe(final LayoutWindow win, int which);
public void edit(LayoutWindow win);
}
```

artofillusion.animation.distortion.Tran sformDistortion

This distortion applies a transformation matrix to each vertex of a mesh.

```
public class TransformDistortion extends Distortion{
public TransformDistortion(Mat4 transform);
public boolean isIdenticalTo(Distortion d);
public Distortion duplicate();
public Mesh transform(Mesh obj);
}
```

artofillusion.animation.distortion. TwistDistortion

This Distortion causes the object to look twisted.

```
public class TwistDistortion extends Distortion{
public static final int X_AXIS;
public static final int Y_AXIS;
public static final int Z_AXIS;
```

```
    public TwistDistortion(int axis, double angle, boolean forward,
Mat4 preTransform, Mat4 postTransform);
    public boolean isIdenticalTo(Distortion d);
    public Distortion duplicate();
    public Mesh transform(Mesh obj);
}
```

artofillusion.animation.distortion. TwistTrack

This is the animation track for the TwistDistortion.

```
public class TwistTrack extends Track{
    public TwistTrack(ObjectInfo info);
    public void apply(double time);
    public Track duplicate(Object obj);
    public void copy(Track tr);
    public double [] getKeyTimes();
    public Timecourse getTimecourse();
    public void setKeyframe(double time, Keyframe k, Smoothness
s);
    public Keyframe setKeyframe(double time, Scene sc);
    public int moveKeyframe(int which, double time);
    public void deleteKeyframe(int which);
    public boolean isNullTrack();
    public Track [] getSubtracks();
    public boolean canAcceptAsParent(Object obj);
    public Object getParent();
    public void setParent(Object obj);
    public int getSmoothingMethod();
    public void setSmoothingMethod(int method);
    public String [] getValueNames();
    public double [] getDefaultGraphValues();
    public double[][] getValueRange();
    public ObjectInfo [] getDependencies();
    public void deleteDependencies(ObjectInfo obj);
    public void writeToStream(DataOutputStream out, Scene scene)
throws IOException;
    public void initFromStream(DataInputStream in, Scene scene)
throws IOException, InvalidObjectException;
    public void editKeyframe(LayoutWindow win, int which);
    public void edit(LayoutWindow win);
}
```

Chapter 14

The artofillusion.image Package

The image package contains classes that Art of Illusion needs to work with the image file formats that it is able to save and/or read.

artofillusion.image.BMPEncoder

This class is for saving images in the BMP file format.

```
public class BMPEncoder{
  public static final int[] HEADER_PART1;
  public static final int[] HEADER_PART2;
  public static final int[] HEADER_PART3;
  public static final int IMAGE_WIDTH;
  public static final int IMAGE_LENGTH;
  public static final int IMAGE_START;

  public BMPEncoder(Image im) throws InterruptedException {
  protected static void writeIA(DataOutputStream out, int[] data)
    throws IOException;
  protected static int[] formatLittleEndian(int data);
  public void writeImage(DataOutputStream out)
    throws IOException;
}
```

artofillusion.image.ComplexImage

This class stores an image.

```
public class ComplexImage{
  public static final int BLUE;
  public static final int GREEN;
  public static final int RED;
```

```
public static final int ALPHA;
public static final int DEPTH;
public static final int OBJECT;
public static final int NOISE;

public ComplexImage(Image image);
public void setComponentValues(int component, float values[]);
public int getWidth();
public int getHeight();
public Image getImage();
public boolean hasFloatData(int component);
public float getPixelComponent(int x, int y, int component);
public ComplexImage duplicate();
public void rebuildImage();
}
```

artofillusion.image.HDRDecoder

This class is for loading HDR format files.

```
public class HDRDecoder{
  public static HDRImage createImage(File file)
    throws IOException;
}
```

artofillusion.image.HDREncoder

This class if for saving HDR format files.

```
public class HDREncoder{
  public static void writeImage(ComplexImage img, OutputStream
out) throws IOException;
}
```

artofillusion.image.HDRImage

HDRImage is an ImageMap subclass. It represents a high dynamic range image stored in Greg Ward's RGBE format, as described in "Graphics Gems IV", edited by James Arvo, Academic Press, 1994.

This class uses magic numbers for compents. The key for the components is RED: 0, GREEN: 1, BLUE: 2, ALPHA: 3.

Locations are given in x and y, with x and y being between 0.0 and 1.0.

```
public class HDRImage extends ImageMap{
```

```
public HDRImage(byte r[], byte g[], byte b[], byte e[], int xres, int
yres);
  public int getWidth();
  public int getHeight();
  public int getComponentCount();
  public float getComponent(int component, boolean wrapx,
boolean wrapy, double x, double y, double xsize, double ysize);
  public float getAverageComponent(int component);
  public void getColor(RGBColor theColor, boolean wrapx,
boolean wrapy, double x, double y, double xsize, double ysize);
  public void getGradient(Vec2 grad, int component, boolean
wrapx, boolean wrapy, double x, double y, double xsize, double
ysize);
  public Image getPreview();
  public HDRImage(DataInputStream in) throws IOException,
InvalidObjectException;
  public void writeToStream(DataOutputStream out) throws
IOException;
}
```

artofillusion.image.ImageAverager

This class calculates and average of a series of images. This is done by first adding images using addImage then when the call is made to getAverageImage, an image is created with each pixel being made up of the average of all pixels at that location across the images. The clear method resets the average for another set of images.

```
public class ImageAverager{
  public ImageAverager(int width, int height);
  public void addImage(Image im);
  public void addImage(ComplexImage img);
  public ComplexImage getAverageImage();
  public void clear();
}
```

artofillusion.image.ImageMap

An ImageMap is an image that can be used to texture an object. It provides preview capability that is a reduced resolution version of the image.

This class uses magic numbers for compents. The key for the components is RED: 0, GREEN: 1, BLUE: 2, ALPHA: 3.

Locations are given in x and y, with x and y being between 0.0 and 1.0.

```
public abstract class ImageMap{
  public ImageMap();
  public static ImageMap loadImage(File file) throws Exception;
  public abstract int getWidth();
  public abstract int getHeight();
  public abstract int getComponentCount();
  public abstract float getComponent(int component, boolean
wrapx, boolean wrapy, double x, double y, double xsize, double
ysize);
  public abstract float getAverageComponent(int component);
  public abstract void getColor(RGBColor theColor, boolean wrapx,
boolean wrapy, double x, double y, double xsize, double ysize);
  public abstract void getGradient(Vec2 grad, int component,
boolean wrapx, boolean wrapy, double x, double y, double xsize,
double ysize);
  public abstract Image getPreview();
  public int getID();
  public abstract void writeToStream(DataOutputStream out)
throws IOException;
}
```

artofillusion.image.ImageOrColor

This class does color multiplication between either a user specified color and another color or a user specified color and an ImageMap.

```
public class ImageOrColor{
  public ImageOrColor(RGBColor theColor);
  public ImageOrColor(RGBColor scaleColor, ImageMap theMap);
  public ImageMap getImage();
  public RGBColor getColor();
  public void getColor(RGBColor theColor, boolean wrapx,
boolean wrapy, double x, double y, double xsize, double ysize);
  public void getAverageColor(RGBColor theColor);
  public ImageOrColor duplicate();
  public void copy(ImageOrColor obj);
  public ImageOrColor(DataInputStream in, Scene theScene)
throws IOException;
  public void writeToFile(DataOutputStream out, Scene theScene)
throws IOException;
  public Widget getEditingPanel(final BFrame parent, final Scene
theScene);
}
```

artofillusion.image.ImageOrValue

This class is used to scale colors by a user specified amount.

This class uses magic numbers for compents. The key for the components is RED: 0, GREEN: 1, BLUE: 2, ALPHA: 3.

Locations are given in x and y, with x and y being between 0.0 and 1.0.

```
public class ImageOrValue{
  public ImageOrValue(float val);
  public ImageOrValue(float scale, ImageMap theMap, int
whichComponent);
  public ImageMap getImage();
  public int getComponent();
  public float getValue();
  public float getValue(boolean wrapx, boolean wrapy, double x,
double y, double xsize, double ysize);
  public void getGradient(Vec2 grad, boolean wrapx, boolean
wrapy, double x, double y, double xsize, double ysize);
  public float getAverageValue();
  public ImageOrValue duplicate();
  public void copy(ImageOrValue obj);
  public ImageOrValue(DataInputStream in, Scene theScene)
throws IOException;
  public void writeToFile(DataOutputStream out, Scene theScene)
throws IOException;
  public Widget getEditingPanel(BFrame parent, Scene theScene);
}
```

artofillusion.image.ImageSaver

This class is for saving rendered images to disk.

```
public class ImageSaver{
  public static final int FORMAT_JPEG;
  public static final int FORMAT_TIFF;
  public static final int FORMAT_PNG;
  public static final int FORMAT_BMP;
  public static final int FORMAT_HDR;
  public static final int FORMAT_QUICKTIME;

  public ImageSaver(BFrame parent);
  public ImageSaver(BFrame parent, int width, int height, int fps, int
startFrameNumber) throws IOException;
  public boolean clickedOk();
  public boolean saveImage(Image im) throws IOException;
```

```
    public boolean saveImage(ComplexImage img) throws IOExcep-
tion;
    public static boolean saveImage(Image im, File f, int format, int
quality) throws IOException, InterruptedException;
    public static boolean saveImage(ComplexImage img, File f, int
format, int quality) throws IOException, InterruptedException;
    public void lastMovieImage() throws IOException;
}
```

artofillusion.image.ImagesDialog

This dialog is for editing the list of image maps used in the scene.

```
public class ImagesDialog extends BDialog{
    public ImagesDialog(BFrame fr, Scene sc, ImageMap selected);
    public ImageMap getSelection();
}
```

artofillusion.image.MIPMappedImage

This is the class for a MIP mapped image.

This class uses magic numbers for compents. The key for the components is RED: 0, GREEN: 1, BLUE: 2, ALPHA: 3.

Locations are given in x and y, with x and y being between 0.0 and 1.0.

```
public class MIPMappedImage extends ImageMap{
    public MIPMappedImage(Image im) throws
InterruptedException;
    public MIPMappedImage(File file) throws InterruptedException;
    public int getWidth();
    public int getHeight();
    public int getComponentCount();
    public float getComponent(int component, boolean wrapx,
boolean wrapy, double x, double y, double xsize, double ysize);
    public float getAverageComponent(int component);
    public void getColor(RGBColor theColor, boolean wrapx,
boolean wrapy, double x, double y, double xsize, double ysize);
    public void getGradient(Vec2 grad, int component, boolean
wrapx, boolean wrapy, double x, double y, double xsize, double
ysize);
    public Image getPreview();
    public MIPMappedImage(DataInputStream in) throws
IOException, InvalidObjectException;
    public MIPMappedImage(DataInputStream in, short version)
throws IOException, InvalidObjectException;
    public void writeToStream(DataOutputStream out) throws
```

IOException;
}

artofillusion.image.TIFFEncoder

This class is for saving TIFF images.

```
public class TIFFEncoder{
  public static final int NEW_SUBFILE_TYPE;
  public static final int IMAGE_WIDTH;
  public static final int IMAGE_LENGTH;
  public static final int BITS_PER_SAMPLE;
  public static final int COMPRESSION;
  public static final int PHOTO_INTERP;
  public static final int IMAGE_DESCRIPTION;
  public static final int STRIP_OFFSETS;
  public static final int SAMPLES_PER_PIXEL;
  public static final int ROWS_PER_STRIP;
  public static final int STRIP_BYTE_COUNT;
  public static final int X_RESOLUTION;
  public static final int Y_RESOLUTION;
  public static final int PLANAR_CONFIGURATION;
  public static final int RESOLUTION_UNIT;
  public static final int SOFTWARE;
  public static final int DATE_TIME;
  public static final int COLOR_MAP;
  public static final int EXTRA_SAMPLES;
  public static final int SAMPLE_FORMAT;

  public TIFFEncoder(Image im) throws InterruptedException;
  public void writeImage(DataOutputStream out) throws
  IOException;
}
```

Chapter 15

The artofillusion.image.filter Package

This package contains ImageFilters. An ImageFilter is a class that are used for post-processing rendered images. They can be used for such things as changing the color saturation, or applying a blur. They can be combined for various effects. If used to their greatest advantage, they can reduce post-processing time by removing the need to process images with a tool like Photoshop or The Gimp. Art of Illusion does not have the full capability of those tools, but since the ImageFilter is one of the type of plugins that Art of Illusion adds automatically, adding capability is easily accomplished.

artofillusion.image.filter.BlurFilter

The blur filter softens the final image by blending neighboring pixels

```
public class BlurFilter extends ImageFilter{
  public BlurFilter();
  public String getName();
  public void filterImage(ComplexImage image, Scene scene,
SceneCamera camera, CoordinateSystem cameraPos);
  public Property[] getProperties();
  public void writeToStream(DataOutputStream out, Scene
theScene) throws IOException;
  public void initFromStream(DataInputStream in, Scene theScene)
throws IOException;
}
```

artofillusion.image.filter. BrightnessFilter

The BrightnessFilter changes the brightness of the final image.

```
public class BrightnessFilter extends ImageFilter{
  public BrightnessFilter();
  public String getName();
  public void filterImage(ComplexImage image, Scene scene,
SceneCamera camera, CoordinateSystem cameraPos);
  public Property[] getProperties();
  public void writeToStream(DataOutputStream out, Scene
theScene) throws IOException;
  public void initFromStream(DataInputStream in, Scene
theScene) throws IOException;
}
```

artofillusion.image.filter. DepthOfFieldFilter

This filter blurs part of the image to simulate depth of field.

```
public class DepthOfFieldFilter extends ImageFilter{
  public DepthOfFieldFilter();
  public String getName();
  public int getDesiredComponents();
  public void filterImage(ComplexImage image, Scene scene,
SceneCamera camera, CoordinateSystem cameraPos);
  public Property[] getProperties();
  public Widget getConfigPanel(Runnable changeCallback);
  public void writeToStream(DataOutputStream out, Scene
theScene) throws IOException;
  public void initFromStream(DataInputStream in, Scene
theScene) throws IOException;
}
```

artofillusion.image.filter. ExposureFilter

This filter changes the exposure of the final image.

```
public class ExposureFilter extends ImageFilter{
  public ExposureFilter();
  public String getName();
```

```
public void filterImage(ComplexImage image, Scene scene,
SceneCamera camera, CoordinateSystem cameraPos);
public Property[] getProperties();
public void writeToStream(DataOutputStream out, Scene
theScene) throws IOException;
public void initFromStream(DataInputStream in, Scene theScene)
throws IOException;
}
```

artofillusion.image.filter.GlowFilter

This filter adds a glow to the final image.

```
public class GlowFilter extends ImageFilter{
public static final String CROSSHAIR;
public static final String DIAGONAL;
public static final String STAR;
public static final String CIRCLE;

public GlowFilter();
public String getName();
public void filterImage(ComplexImage image, Scene scene,
SceneCamera camera, CoordinateSystem cameraPos);
public Property[] getProperties();
public void writeToStream(DataOutputStream out, Scene
theScene) throws IOException;
public void initFromStream(DataInputStream in, Scene theScene)
throws IOException;
}
```

artofillusion.image.filter.ImageFilter

This is the abstract interface for image filters.
Plugin classes that implement this interface will be
added to the list of ImageFilters by Art of Illusion.

```
public ImageFilter() {
public abstract String getName();
public int getDesiredComponents();
public abstract void filterImage(ComplexImage image, Scene
scene, SceneCamera camera, CoordinateSystem cameraPos);
public ImageFilter duplicate();
public void copy(ImageFilter f);
public TextureParameter [] getParameters();
public double [] getParameterValues();
public void setParameterValue(int index, double value);
public Property[] getProperties();
public Object getPropertyValue(int index);
public void setPropertyValue(int index, Object value);
public abstract void writeToStream(DataOutputStream out,
Scene theScene) throws IOException;
```

```
public abstract void initFromStream(DataInputStream in, Scene
theScene) throws IOException;
    public Widget getConfigPanel(final Runnable changeCallback);
}
```

artofillusion.image.filter. NoiseReductionFilter

This applys a filter that anisotropic diffusion filter to the final image.

```
public class NoiseReductionFilter extends ImageFilter{
    public NoiseReductionFilter();
    public String getName();
    public void filterImage(final ComplexImage image, Scene scene,
SceneCamera camera, CoordinateSystem cameraPos);
    public int getDesiredComponents();
    public Property[] getProperties();
    public void writeToStream(DataOutputStream out, Scene
theScene) throws IOException;
    public void initFromStream(DataInputStream in, Scene theScene)
throws IOException;
}
```

artofillusion.image.filter.OutlineFilter

This filter outlines the edges of the objects in the final image.

```
public class OutlineFilter extends ImageFilter{
    public OutlineFilter();
    public String getName()'
    public int getDesiredComponents();
    public void filterImage(ComplexImage image, Scene scene,
SceneCamera camera, CoordinateSystem cameraPos);
    public Property[] getProperties();
    public void writeToStream(DataOutputStream out, Scene
theScene) throws IOException;
    public void initFromStream(DataInputStream in, Scene theScene)
throws IOException;
}
```

artofillusion.image.filter. SaturationFilter

This filter adjusts the saturation of the final image.

```
public class SaturationFilter extends ImageFilter{
    public SaturationFilter();
```

```
    public String getName();
    public void filterImage(ComplexImage image, Scene scene,
SceneCamera camera, CoordinateSystem cameraPos);
    public TextureParameter [] getParameters();
    public Property[] getProperties();
    public void writeToStream(DataOutputStream out, Scene
theScene) throws IOException;
    public void initFromStream(DataInputStream in, Scene theScene)
throws IOException;
}
```

artofillusion.image.filter.TintFilter

This filter adjusts the tint of the final image by multiplying it by a color.

```
public class TintFilter extends ImageFilter{
    public TintFilter();
    public String getName();
    public void filterImage(ComplexImage image, Scene scene,
SceneCamera camera, CoordinateSystem cameraPos);
    public Property[] getProperties();
    public void writeToStream(DataOutputStream out, Scene
theScene) throws IOException;
    public void initFromStream(DataInputStream in, Scene theScene)
throws IOException;
}
```

filter

Chapter 16

The artofillusion.keystroke Package

The keystroke package contains the classes that are responsible for editing and maintaining the information about the keystroke short cuts that the user can create in Art of Illusion to speed up the editing process.

artofillusion.keystroke. KeystrokeEditor

This is the dialog for through which the user can edit a single keystroke record.

```
public class KeystrokeEditor extends BDialog{
  public static KeystrokeRecord showEditorDialog(KeystrokeRecord
record, WindowWidget parent);
}
```

artofillusion.keystroke. KeystrokeManager

This class maintains the list of keystrokes and executes there function when they are pressed.

```
public class KeystrokeManager{
  public static KeystrokeRecord[] getAllRecords();
  public static void setAllRecords(KeystrokeRecord allRecords[]);
  public static void addRecord(KeystrokeRecord record);
  public static void removeRecord(KeystrokeRecord record);
```

```
   public static void recordModified();
   public static void executeKeystrokes(KeyEvent event,
EditingWindow window);
   public static void addRecordsFromXML(InputStream in) throws
Exception;
   public static void saveRecords() throws Exception;
}
```

artofillusion.keystroke. KeystrokePreferencesPanel

This class is the panel that is allows the user to edit the list of keystrokes.

```
public class KeystrokePreferencesPanel extends FormContainer{
   public KeystrokePreferencesPanel();
   public void saveChanges();
}
```

artofillusion.keystroke. KeystrokeRecord

This class represents the individual record of a keystroke sequence.

```
public class KeystrokeRecord{
   public KeystrokeRecord(int keyCode, int modifiers, String name,
String script, String language);
   public KeystrokeRecord(int keyCode, int modifiers, String name,
String script);
   public int getKeyCode();
   public void setKeyCode(int keyCode);
   public int getModifiers();
   public void setModifiers(int modifiers);
   public String getName();
   public void setName(String name);
   public String getScript();
   public void setScript(String script);
   public String getLanguage();
   public void setLanguage(String language);
   public KeystrokeRecord duplicate();
}
```

Chapter 17

The artofillusion.material Package

The material package contains those classes that describe and map materials to objects. Materials are the physical properties of an object that can be modeled in Art of Illusion, primarily the internal color, transparency, and index of refraction of an object, as opposed to textures, which describe the surface of the object.

artofillusion.material. LinearMaterialMapping

This class represents the linear mapping between the material coordinates and the world coordinates.

```
public class LinearMaterialMapping extends MaterialMapping{
    protected CoordinateSystem coords;
    protected double ax, bx, cx, dx, ay, by, cy, dy, az, bz, cz, dz;
    protected double xscale, yscale, zscale;
    protected boolean scaleToObject;

    public LinearMaterialMapping(Object3D theObject, Material3D
theMaterial);
    public static String getName();
    public static boolean legalMapping(Object3D obj, Material mat);
    public Vec3 getCenter();
    public void setCenter(Vec3 center);
    public Vec3 getScale();
    public void setScale(Vec3 scale);
    public boolean isScaledToObject();
```

```
    public void setScaledToObject(boolean scaled);
    public Vec3 getRotations();
    public void setRotations(Vec3 angles);
    public double getStepSize();
    public void getMaterialSpec(Vec3 pos, MaterialSpec spec,
double size, double time);
    public MaterialMapping duplicate();
    public MaterialMapping duplicate(Object3D obj, Material mat);
    public void copy(MaterialMapping mapping);
    public Widget getEditingPanel(Object3D obj, MaterialPreviewer
preview);
    public LinearMaterialMapping(DataInputStream in, Object3D the-
Object, Material theMaterial) throws IOException,
InvalidObjectException;
    public void writeToFile(DataOutputStream out)
throws IOException;
}
```

artofillusion.material.Material

This class holds the information to describe a material that can be mapped to an object. The index of refraction defaults to 1.0;

```
public abstract class Material{
    protected String name;
    protected double refraction;
    protected int id;

    public static String getTypeName();
    public String getName();
    public void setName(String name);
    public double indexOfRefraction();
    public void setIndexOfRefraction(double n);
    public double getStepSize();
    public boolean usesImage(ImageMap image);
    public abstract boolean isScattering();
    public int getID();
    public void assignNewID();
    public void setID(int newid);
    public abstract MaterialMapping getDefaultMapping(Object3D
obj);
    public abstract Material duplicate();
    public abstract void edit(BFrame fr, Scene sc);
    public abstract void writeToFile(DataOutputStream out, Scene
theScene) throws IOException;
}
```

artofillusion.material.Material3D

This class is a material that is defined in three dimensions. Given a point (x, y, z), the class will return the properties at that location.

```
public abstract class Material3D extends Material{
  public abstract void getMaterialSpec(MaterialSpec spec, double
x, double y, double z, double xsize, double ysize, double zsize,
double t);
  public MaterialMapping getDefaultMapping(Object3D obj);
}
```

artofillusion.material.MaterialMapping

This class is the mapping of a material to the local coordinate system of the object.

```
public abstract class MaterialMapping{
  protected MaterialMapping(Object3D obj, Material mat);
  public abstract void writeToFile(DataOutputStream out) throws
IOException;
  public static String getName();
  public double indexOfRefraction();
  public abstract double getStepSize();
  public boolean isScattering();
  public boolean castsShadows();
  public Material getMaterial();
  public Object3D getObject();
  public abstract void getMaterialSpec(Vec3 pos, MaterialSpec
spec, double size, double t);
  public abstract MaterialMapping duplicate();
  public abstract MaterialMapping duplicate(Object3D obj, Material
mat);
  public abstract void copy(MaterialMapping map);
  public abstract Widget getEditingPanel(Object3D obj,
MaterialPreviewer preview);
}
```

artofillusion.material.MaterialSpec

This class represents the properties of a single point inside an object.

```
public class MaterialSpec{
  public RGBColor transparency, color, scattering;
  public double eccentricity;

  public MaterialSpec();
}
```

artofillusion.material. ProceduralMaterial3D

This class represents a Material3D with properties determined by a procedure.

```
public class ProceduralMaterial3D extends Material3D
implements ProcedureOwner{
    public ProceduralMaterial3D();
    public static String getTypeName();
    public double getStepSize();
    public void setStepSize(double step);
    public void getMaterialSpec(MaterialSpec spec, double x, double
y, double z, double xsize, double ysize, double zsize, double t);
    public boolean usesImage(ImageMap image);
    public boolean isScattering();
    public boolean castsShadows();
    public Material duplicate();
    public void edit(BFrame fr, Scene sc);
    public ProceduralMaterial3D(DataInputStream in, Scene
theScene) throws IOException, InvalidObjectException;
    public void writeToFile(DataOutputStream out, Scene theScene)
throws IOException;
    public String getWindowTitle();
    public Object getPreview(ProcedureEditor editor);
    public void updatePreview(Object preview);
    public void disposePreview(Object preview);
    public boolean allowViewAngle();
    public boolean allowParameters();
    public boolean canEditName();
    public void acceptEdits(ProcedureEditor editor);
    public void editProperties(ProcedureEditor editor);
}
```

artofillusion.material.UniformMaterial

This class represents a uniform material.

```
public class UniformMaterial extends Material{
    public UniformMaterial();
    public static String getTypeName();
    public boolean isScattering();
    public boolean castsShadows();
    public void getMaterialSpec(MaterialSpec spec);
    public MaterialMapping getDefaultMapping(Object3D obj);
    public Material duplicate();
    public void edit(final BFrame fr, Scene sc);
    public UniformMaterial(DataInputStream in, Scene theScene)
throws IOException, InvalidObjectException;
```

```
    public void writeToFile(DataOutputStream out, Scene theScene)
throws IOException;
    }
```

artofillusion.material.
UniformMaterialMapping

This is the mapping for a uniform material.

```
public class UniformMaterialMapping extends MaterialMapping{
    public UniformMaterialMapping(Object3D theObject, Material
theMaterial);
    public double getStepSize();
    public void getMaterialSpec(Vec3 pos, MaterialSpec spec,
double size, double t);
    public static boolean legalMapping(Object3D obj, Material mat);
    public MaterialMapping duplicate();
    public MaterialMapping duplicate(Object3D obj, Material mat);
    public void copy(MaterialMapping map);
    public Widget getEditingPanel(Object3D obj, MaterialPreviewer
preview);
    public UniformMaterialMapping(DataInputStream in, Object3D
theObject, Material theMaterial) throws IOException,
InvalidObjectException;
    public void writeToFile(DataOutputStream out)
throws IOException;
    }
```

Chapter 18

The artofillusion.math Package

The math package includes several classes that Art of Illusion uses for calculation it does with the objects.

artofillusion.math.BoundingBox

The BoundingBox marks the extremes of an object in the x, y, and z directions. A typical use of the BoundingBox is to eliminate objects from calculations. If the operation would not fall within the BoundingBox, then there is no reason to do a more detailed determination of whether it would fall within the object.

```
public class BoundingBox{
  public double minx, maxx, miny, maxy, minz, maxz;

  public BoundingBox(double x1, double x2, double y1, double y2,
double z1, double z2);
  public BoundingBox(Vec3 p1, Vec3 p2);
  public BoundingBox(BoundingBox b);
  public Vec3 getSize();
  public Vec3 getCenter();
  public Vec3 [] getCorners();
  public BoundingBox merge(BoundingBox b);
  public void extend(BoundingBox b);
  public final boolean contains(Vec3 p);
  public final boolean intersects(BoundingBox b);
  public final double distanceToPoint(Vec3 p);
  public final void outset(double dist);
  public final BoundingBox translate(double dx, double dy, double
dz);
  public final BoundingBox transformAndOutset(Mat4 m);
```

```
public String toString();
}
```

artofillusion.math.Cells

This class provides an implementation of Steven Worley's cellular texture basis function as described in Worley, S. "A Cellular Texture Basis Function." Siggraph Proceedings, pp. 291-294, 1996. This function scatters "feature points" at random locations throughout 3D space. At any point (x, y, z), it defines the function f1(x, y, z) to be the distance to the nearest feature point. It similarly defines f2(x, y, z) as the distance to the second nearest feature point, and similarly for f3(x, y, z), etc.

```
public class Cells{
  public static final int EUCLIDEAN;
  public static final int CITY_BLOCK;
  public static final int CHESS_BOARD;

  public Cells();
  public int getMetric();
  public void setMetric(int metric);
  public void calcFunctions(Vec3 p, double value[], Vec3 grad[], int
id[]);
}
```

artofillusion.math.CoordinateSystem

The CoordinateSystem class describes the position and orientation of one coordinate system relative to another one. It is defined by three vectors. orig defines the position of the origin of the new coordinate system, while zdir and updir define the directions of the z and y axes, respectively. (Note that the y axis will only be parallel to updir in the special case that zdir and updir are perpendicular to each other.)

Alternatively, the orientation can be represented by three rotation angles about the (global) x, y, and z axes. Both representations are maintained internally.

```
public class CoordinateSystem{
```

```
public CoordinateSystem();
public CoordinateSystem(Vec3 orig, Vec3 zdir, Vec3 updir);
public CoordinateSystem(Vec3 orig, double x, double y, double z);
public final CoordinateSystem duplicate();
public final void copyCoords(CoordinateSystem c);
public final boolean equals(Object coords);
public final void setOrigin(Vec3 orig);
public final void setOrientation(Vec3 zdir, Vec3 updir);
public final void setOrientation(double x, double y, double z);
public final Vec3 getOrigin();
public final Vec3 getZDirection();
public final Vec3 getUpDirection();
public final double [] getRotationAngles();
public final void transformAxes(Mat4 m);
public final void transformOrigin(Mat4 m);
public final void transformCoordinates(Mat4 m);
public final Mat4 fromLocal();
public final Mat4 toLocal();
public final double getAxisAngleRotation(Vec3 axis);
public CoordinateSystem(DataInputStream in) throws
IOException;
public void writeToFile(DataOutputStream out) throws
IOException;
}
```

artofillusion.math.FastMath

FastMath is a set of math functions that are faster than the standard Java versions. The are specialized to the task, so they may return different results than their Java counterparts.

```
public class FastMath{
  public static int floor(double d);
  public static int ceil(double d);
  public static int round(double d);
  public static double pow(double base, int exponent);
  public static double atan(double d);
}
```

artofillusion.math.FastRandom

This is a random number generator that is faster than java.util.Random.

```
public class FastRandom extends Random{
  public FastRandom(long seed);
  public void setSeed(long seed);
  protected int next(int bits);
}
```

artofillusion.math.Mat4

This class represents a 4x4 matrix.

```
public class Mat4{
    public final double m11, m12, m13, m14;
    public final double m21, m22, m23, m24;
    public final double m31, m32, m33, m34;
    public final double m41, m42, m43, m44;

    public Mat4 (double e11, double e12, double e13, double e14,
                 double e21, double e22, double e23, double e24,
                 double e31, double e32, double e33, double e34,
                 double e41, double e42, double e43, double e44);
    public final Mat4 times(Mat4 a);
    public final Vec3 times(Vec3 v);
    public final Vec3 timesDirection(Vec3 v);
    public final Vec2 timesXY(Vec3 v);
    public final Vec2 timesXY(Vec3 v, Vec2 result);
    public final double timesZ(Vec3 v);
    public final void transform(Vec3 v);
    public final void transformDirection(Vec3 v);
    public static Mat4 identity();
    public static Mat4 scale(double sx, double sy, double sz);
    public static Mat4 translation(double dx, double dy, double dz);
    public static Mat4 xrotation(double angle);
    public static Mat4 yrotation(double angle);
    public static Mat4 zrotation(double angle);
    public static Mat4 axisRotation(Vec3 axis, double angle);
    public static Mat4 viewTransform(Vec3 orig, Vec3 zdir, Vec3
updir);
    public static Mat4 objectTransform(Vec3 orig, Vec3 zdir, Vec3
updir);
    public static Mat4 perspective(double d);
    public String toString();
    public boolean equals(Object o);
    public int hashCode();
    public Mat4(DataInputStream in) throws IOException;
    public void writeToFile(DataOutputStream out) throws
IOException;
}
```

artofillusion.math.Noise

This class provides an interface for a 3D noise function.

```
public class Noise{
    public static double value(double x, double y, double z);
    public static void calcGradient(Vec3 gradient, double x, double y,
    double z);
```

```
  public static void calcVector(Vec3 v, double x, double y, double
z);
  public NoiseGenerator getGenerator();
  public void setGenerator(NoiseGenerator gen);
  public static interface NoiseGenerator
  {
    public double getValue(double x, double y, double z);
    public void getGradient(Vec3 gradient, double x, double y,
double z);
    public void getVector(Vec3 v, double x, double y, double z);
  }
}
```

artofillusion.math.PerlinNoise

This class provides an implementation of Ken Perlin's noise function.

```
public class PerlinNoise{
  public static double value(double x, double y, double z);
  public static void calcGradient(Vec3 gradient, double x, double y,
double z);
  public static void calcVector(Vec3 v, double x, double y, double
z);
}
```

math

artofillusion.math.RGBColor

The RGBColor class is used to represent a color. This class uses floating point numbers (usually between 0 and 1) to store the red, green, and blue components, in contrast to java.awt.Color which uses integers.

```
public class RGBColor{
  public float red, green, blue;

  public RGBColor();
  public RGBColor(float r, float g, float b);
  public RGBColor(double r, double g, double b);
  public final void setRGB(float r, float g, float b);
  public final void setRGB(double r, double g, double b);
  public final float getRed();
  public final float getGreen();
  public final float getBlue();
  public boolean equals(Object c);
  public int hashCode();
  public final RGBColor duplicate();
  public final void copy(RGBColor color);
  public final Color getColor();
```

```
    public Widget getSample(int width, int height);
    public final int getARGB();
    public final void setARGB(int color);
    public final void add(RGBColor color);
    public final void subtract(RGBColor color);
    public final void multiply(RGBColor color);
    public final void add(float r, float g, float b);
    public final void subtract(float r, float g, float b);
    public final void multiply(float r, float g, float b);
    public final void scale(float s);
    public final void scale(double s);
    public final void clip();
    public final float getBrightness();
    public final float getMaxComponent();
    public final void setHSV(float h, float s, float v);
    public final float[] getHSV();
    public final void setHLS(float h, float l, float s);
    public final float[] getHLS();
    public final int getERGB();
    public final void setERGB(int ergb);
    public final void setERGB(byte r, byte g, byte b, byte e);
    public final float[] getYCrCb() ;
    public final void setYCrCb (float Y, float Cr, float Cb);
    public RGBColor(DataInputStream in) throws IOException;
    public void writeToFile(DataOutputStream out) throws
IOException;
    public String toString();
}
```

artofillusion.math.SimplexNoise

This class implements Ken Perlin's Simplex Noise function.

```
public class SimplexNoise {
  public static void noiseGradient(Vec2 gradient, double xin,
double yin) ;
  public static double noise(double xin, double yin, double zin) ;
  public static void noiseGradient(Vec3 gradient, double xin,
double yin, double zin) ;
  public static void noiseVector(Vec3 v, double xin, double yin, dou-
ble zin) ;
  public static double noise(double x, double y, double z, double w)
}
```

artofillusion.math.SVD

The SVD class defines methods for solving sets of linear equations by singular value decomposition.

```
public class SVD{
```

```
public static void solve(double a[][], double b[]);
public static void solve(double a[][], double b[], double tol);
}
```

artofillusion.math.Vec2

This class represents a two dimensional vector.

```
public class Vec2{
  public double x, y;

  public Vec2();
  public Vec2(double xval, double yval);
  public Vec2(Vec2 v);
  public final void set(double xval, double yval);
  public final double dot(Vec2 v);
  public final double cross(Vec2 v);
  public final Vec2 plus(Vec2 v);
  public final Vec2 minus(Vec2 v);
  public final Vec2 times(double d);
  public final boolean equals(Object o);
  public int hashCode();
  public final double length();
  public final double length2();
  public final void add(Vec2 v);
  public final void subtract(Vec2 v);
  public final void scale(double d);
  public final double distance(Vec2 v);
  public final double distance2(Vec2 v);
  public final void normalize();
  public String toString();
  public static Vec2 vx();
  public static Vec2 vy();
  public Vec2(DataInputStream in) throws IOException;
  public void writeToFile(DataOutputStream out) throws
IOException;
}
```

artofillusion.math.Vec3

This class represents a three dimensional vector.

```
public class Vec3{
  public double x, y, z;

  public Vec3();
  public Vec3(double xval, double yval, double zval);
  public Vec3(Vec3 v);
  public final void set(double xval, double yval, double zval);
  public final void set(Vec3 v);
  public final double dot(Vec3 v);
  public final Vec3 cross(Vec3 v);
```

```
    public final Vec3 plus(Vec3 v);
    public final Vec3 minus(Vec3 v);
    public final Vec3 times(double d);
    public final boolean equals(Object o);
    public int hashCode();
    public final double length();
    public final double length2();
    public final void add(Vec3 v);
    public final void subtract(Vec3 v);
    public final void multiply(Vec3 v);
    public final void scale(double d);
    public final void normalize();
    public final double distance(Vec3 v);
    public final double distance2(Vec3 v);
    public final Vec2 dropAxis(int which);
    public String toString();
    public static Vec3 vx();
    public static Vec3 vy();
    public static Vec3 vz();
    public Vec3(DataInputStream in) throws IOException;
    public void writeToFile(DataOutputStream out) throws
    IOException;
}
```

Chapter 19

The artofillusion.object Package

The object package contains the object classes that are in Art of Illusion.

artofillusion.object.CompoundImplicit Object

This class is for an implicit object that contains other implicit objects.

```
public class CompoundImplicitObject extends ImplicitObject{
  public CompoundImplicitObject();
  public void addObject(ImplicitObject obj, CoordinateSystem
coords);
  public int getNumObjects();
  public ImplicitObject getObject(int index);
  public void setObject(int index, ImplicitObject obj);
  public CoordinateSystem getObjectCoordinates(int index);
  public void setObjectCoordinates(int index, CoordinateSystem
coords);
  public double getCutoff();
  public void setCutoff(double cutoff);
  public double getFieldValue(double x, double y, double z, double
size, double time);
  public void getFieldGradient(double x, double y, double z, double
size, double time, Vec3 grad);
  public boolean getPreferDirectRendering();
  public Object3D duplicate();
  public void copyObject(Object3D obj);
  public synchronized BoundingBox getBounds();
  public void setSize(double xsize, double ysize, double zsize);
  public boolean isEditable();
  public void edit(EditingWindow parent, ObjectInfo info, Runnable
cb);
```

```
public Keyframe getPoseKeyframe();
public void applyPoseKeyframe(Keyframe k);
public void editKeyframe(EditingWindow parent, final Keyframe k,
final ObjectInfo info)
{
    public void run();
}
public static class CompoundImplicitKeyframe implements
Keyframe{
    public Keyframe duplicate();
    public Keyframe duplicate(Object owner);
    public double [] getGraphValues();
    public void setGraphValues(double values[]);
    public Keyframe blend(Keyframe o2, double weight1, double
weight2);
    public Keyframe blend(Keyframe o2, Keyframe o3, double
weight1, double weight2, double weight3);
    public Keyframe blend(Keyframe o2, Keyframe o3, Keyframe
o4, double weight1, double weight2, double weight3, double
weight4);
    public boolean equals(Keyframe k);
    public void writeToStream(DataOutputStream out) throws IOEx-
ception;
    public CompoundImplicitKeyframe(DataInputStream in, Object
parent) throws IOException;
}
}
```

artofillusion.object.CSGModeller

This class performs the work of applying Boolean operations to create meshes based on objects.

```
public class CSGModeller{
    public CSGModeller(TriangleMesh obj1, TriangleMesh obj2,
CoordinateSystem coords1, CoordinateSystem coords2);
    public TriangleMesh getMesh(int op, Texture texture);
    public VertexInfo(Vec3 r, float smoothness, double param[], int
type);
}
```

artofillusion.object.CSGObject

This class represents two objects combined by Boolean operations.

```
public class CSGObject extends Object3D{
    public static final int UNION;
    public static final int INTERSECTION;
    public static final int DIFFERENCE12;
    public static final int DIFFERENCE21;
```

```
public CSGObject(ObjectInfo o1, ObjectInfo o2, int op);
public Object3D duplicate();
public void copyObject(Object3D obj);
public ObjectInfo getObject1();
public ObjectInfo getObject2();
public int getOperation();
public void setOperation(int op);
public void setComponentObjects(ObjectInfo o1, ObjectInfo o2);
public Vec3 centerObjects();
public BoundingBox getBounds();
void findBounds();
public void setSize(double xsize, double ysize, double zsize);
public int canConvertToTriangleMesh();
public boolean isClosed();
public TriangleMesh convertToTriangleMesh(double tol);
public boolean isEditable();
public void edit(EditingWindow parent, ObjectInfo info, Runnable
cb);
public void setTexture(Texture tex, TextureMapping mapping);
public void setMaterial(Material mat, MaterialMapping mapping);
public RenderingMesh getRenderingMesh(double tol, boolean
interactive, ObjectInfo info);
public WireframeMesh getWireframeMesh();
public void writeToFile(DataOutputStream out, Scene theScene)
throws IOException;
public CSGObject(DataInputStream in, Scene theScene) throws
IOException, InvalidObjectException;
public Keyframe getPoseKeyframe();
public void applyPoseKeyframe(Keyframe k);
public void editKeyframe(EditingWindow parent, final Keyframe k,
final ObjectInfo info);
public static class CSGKeyframe implements Keyframe
{
  public Keyframe key1, key2;
  public CoordinateSystem coords1, coords2;

  public CSGKeyframe(Keyframe key1, Keyframe key2,
CoordinateSystem coords1, CoordinateSystem coords2);
  public Keyframe duplicate();
  public Keyframe duplicate(Object owner);
  public double [] getGraphValues();
  public void setGraphValues(double values[]);
  public Keyframe blend(Keyframe o2, double weight1, double
weight2);
  public Keyframe blend(Keyframe o2, Keyframe o3, double
weight1, double weight2, double weight3);
  public Keyframe blend(Keyframe o2, Keyframe o3, Keyframe
o4, double weight1, double weight2, double weight3, double
weight4);
  public boolean equals(Keyframe k);
  public void writeToStream(DataOutputStream out) throws
IOException;
```

```
    public CSGKeyframe(DataInputStream in, Object parent) throws
IOException;
    }
}
```

artofillusion.object.Cube

This class represents a rectangular solid.

```
public class Cube extends Object3D{
    public Cube(double xsize, double ysize, double zsize);
    public Object3D duplicate();
    public void copyObject(Object3D obj);
    public BoundingBox getBounds();
    public void setSize(double xsize, double ysize, double zsize);
    public int canConvertToTriangleMesh();
    public TriangleMesh convertToTriangleMesh(double tol);
    public WireframeMesh getWireframeMesh();
    public RenderingMesh getRenderingMesh(double tol, boolean
interactive, ObjectInfo info);
    public void setTexture(Texture tex, TextureMapping mapping);
    public boolean isEditable();
    public void edit(EditingWindow parent, ObjectInfo info, Runnable
cb);
    public Cube(DataInputStream in, Scene theScene) throws
IOException, InvalidObjectException;
    public void writeToFile(DataOutputStream out, Scene theScene)
throws IOException;
    public Property[] getProperties();
    public Object getPropertyValue(int index);
    public void setPropertyValue(int index, Object value);
    public Keyframe getPoseKeyframe();
    public void applyPoseKeyframe(Keyframe k);
    public void configurePoseTrack(PoseTrack track);
    public void editKeyframe(EditingWindow parent, Keyframe k, Ob-
jectInfo info);
}
```

artofillusion.object.Cylinder

This is the class that Art of Illusion uses to represent cylinders and cones.

```
public class Cylinder extends Object3D{
    public Cylinder(double height, double xradius, double yradius,
double ratio);
    public Object3D duplicate();
    public void copyObject(Object3D obj);
    public double getRatio();
    public void setRatio(double ratio);
    public BoundingBox getBounds();
    public void setSize(double xsize, double ysize, double zsize);
```

```
    public WireframeMesh getWireframeMesh();
    public int canConvertToTriangleMesh();
    public TriangleMesh convertToTriangleMesh(double tol);
    public RenderingMesh getRenderingMesh(double tol, boolean
interactive, ObjectInfo info);
    public void setTexture(Texture tex, TextureMapping mapping);
    public boolean isEditable();
    public void edit(EditingWindow parent, ObjectInfo info, Runnable
cb);
    public Cylinder(DataInputStream in, Scene theScene) throws
IOException, InvalidObjectException;
    public void writeToFile(DataOutputStream out, Scene theScene)
throws IOException;
    public Property[] getProperties();
    public Object getPropertyValue(int index);
    public void setPropertyValue(int index, Object value);
    public Keyframe getPoseKeyframe();
    public void applyPoseKeyframe(Keyframe k);
    public void configurePoseTrack(PoseTrack track);
    public String [] getPoseValueNames();
    public double [] getDefaultPoseValues();
    public double[][] getPoseValueRange();
    public void editKeyframe(EditingWindow parent, Keyframe k,
ObjectInfo info);
    public static class CylinderKeyframe implements Keyframe
    {
    public double rx, ry, ratio, height;

    public CylinderKeyframe(double rx, double ry, double height,
double ratio);
    public Keyframe duplicate();
    public Keyframe duplicate(Object owner);
    public double [] getGraphValues();
    public void setGraphValues(double values[]);
    public Keyframe blend(Keyframe o2, double weight1, double
weight2);
    public Keyframe blend(Keyframe o2, Keyframe o3, double
weight1, double weight2, double weight3);
    public boolean equals(Keyframe k);
    public void writeToStream(DataOutputStream out) throws
IOException;
    }
}
```

artofillusion.object.DirectionalLight

A directional light represents a distant light source that, like the Sun, emits light from one direction with the rays parallel to each other.

```
public class DirectionalLight extends Light{
    public DirectionalLight(RGBColor theColor, float theIntensity);
```

```
public DirectionalLight(RGBColor theColor, float theIntensity,
double theRadius);
public Object3D duplicate();
public void copyObject(Object3D obj);
public BoundingBox getBounds();
public void setSize(double xsize, double ysize, double zsize);
public double getRadius();
public void setRadius(double r);
public void getLight(RGBColor light, Vec3 position);
public boolean canSetTexture();
public WireframeMesh getWireframeMesh();
public boolean isEditable();
public DirectionalLight(DataInputStream in, Scene theScene)
throws IOException, InvalidObjectException;
public void writeToFile(DataOutputStream out, Scene theScene)
throws IOException;
public void edit(EditingWindow parent, ObjectInfo info, Runnable
cb);
public Property[] getProperties();
public Object getPropertyValue(int index);
public void setPropertyValue(int index, Object value);
public Keyframe getPoseKeyframe();
public void applyPoseKeyframe(Keyframe k);
public void configurePoseTrack(PoseTrack track);
public void editKeyframe(EditingWindow parent, Keyframe k,
ObjectInfo info);
public static class DirectionalLightKeyframe implements
Keyframe
{
  public RGBColor color;
  public float intensity;
  public double radius;

  public DirectionalLightKeyframe(RGBColor color, float intensity,
double radius);
  public Keyframe duplicate();
  public Keyframe duplicate(Object owner);
  public double [] getGraphValues();
  public void setGraphValues(double values[]);
  public Keyframe blend(Keyframe o2, double weight1, double
weight2);
  public Keyframe blend(Keyframe o2, Keyframe o3, double
weight1, double weight2, double weight3);
  public Keyframe blend(Keyframe o2, Keyframe o3, Keyframe
o4, double weight1, double weight2, double weight3, double
weight4);
  public boolean equals(Keyframe k);
  public void writeToStream(DataOutputStream out) throws
IOException;
  public DirectionalLightKeyframe(DataInputStream in, Object
parent) throws IOException;
}
}
```

artofillusion.object.ExternalObject

This class represents an object that is stored in an external file.

```
public class ExternalObject extends ObjectWrapper{
  public ExternalObject(File file, String name);
  public String getExternalObjectName();
  public void setExternalObjectName(String name);
  public int getExternalObjectId();
  public void setExternalObjectId(int id);
  public boolean getIncludeChildren();
  public void setIncludeChildren(boolean include);
  public File getExternalSceneFile();
  public void setExternalSceneFile(File file);
  public String getLoadingError();
  public void reloadObject();
  public Object3D duplicate();
  public void copyObject(Object3D obj);
  public void setSize(double xsize, double ysize, double zsize);
  public boolean isEditable();
  public void edit(EditingWindow parent, ObjectInfo info, Runnable
cb);
  public boolean canSetTexture();
  public boolean canSetMaterial();
  public boolean canConvertToActor();
  public void writeToFile(DataOutputStream out, Scene theScene)
throws IOException;
  public ExternalObject(DataInputStream in, Scene theScene)
throws IOException, InvalidObjectException;
}
```

artofillusion.object.FacetedMesh

This class represents a mesh made up of polygon faces.

```
public interface FacetedMesh extends Mesh{
  int getFaceCount();
  int getFaceVertexCount(int face);
  int getFaceVertexIndex(int face, int vertex);
}
```

artofillusion.object.ImplicitObject

This abstract class represents an object whose surface is defined as an isosurface of a 3D field function.

```
public abstract class ImplicitObject extends Object3D{
```

```
    public abstract double getFieldValue(double x, double y, double
z, double size, double time);
    public void getFieldGradient(double x, double y, double z, double
size, double time, Vec3 grad);
    public double getMaxGradient();
    public double getCutoff();
    public abstract boolean getPreferDirectRendering();
    public ImplicitObject();
    public ImplicitObject(DataInputStream in, Scene theScene)
throws IOException, InvalidObjectException;
    public void writeToFile(DataOutputStream out, Scene theScene)
throws IOException;
    public int canConvertToTriangleMesh();
    public TriangleMesh convertToTriangleMesh(double tol);
    public RenderingMesh getRenderingMesh(double tol, boolean
interactive, ObjectInfo info);
    public WireframeMesh getWireframeMesh();
    protected void clearCachedMesh();
    public void sceneChanged(ObjectInfo info, Scene scene);
    public void generateMesh(double tol, List<Vec3> vertices,
List<int[]> faces);
}
```

artofillusion.object.ImplicitSphere

This object is a spherical implicit object (i.e. a metaball). It is characterized by two numbers: a radius, which is the radius of the sphere it creates in isolation, and an "influence radius", which is the distance it extends outward before the implicit function becomes zero. The influence radius **must** be larger than the radius, or the behavior becomes undefined. This class is generally not useful on its own, but collections of ImplicitSpheres are useful for many sorts of effects where balls should smoothly merge together when they come close.

```
public class ImplicitSphere extends ImplicitObject{
    public ImplicitSphere(double radius, double influenceRadius);
    public double getRadius();
    public void setRadius(double radius);
    public double getInfluenceRadius();
    public void setInfluenceRadius(double influenceRadius);
    public double getCutoff();
    public boolean getPreferDirectRendering();
    public double getFieldValue(double x, double y, double z, double
size, double time);
    public void getFieldGradient(double x, double y, double z, double
size, double time, Vec3 grad);
    public void applyPoseKeyframe(Keyframe k);
```

```
public void configurePoseTrack(PoseTrack track);
public String [] getPoseValueNames();
public double [] getDefaultPoseValues();
public Object3D duplicate();
public void copyObject(Object3D obj);
public BoundingBox getBounds();
public void setSize(double xsize, double ysize, double zsize);
public WireframeMesh getWireframeMesh();
public RenderingMesh getRenderingMesh(double tol, boolean
interactive, ObjectInfo info);
public Keyframe getPoseKeyframe();
public Property[] getProperties();
public Object getPropertyValue(int index);
public void setPropertyValue(int index, Object value);
public void setTexture(Texture tex, TextureMapping mapping);
public void setMaterial(Material mat, MaterialMapping map);
public boolean isEditable();
public void edit(EditingWindow parent, ObjectInfo info, Runnable
cb);
public ImplicitSphere(DataInputStream in, Scene theScene)
throws IOException, InvalidObjectException;
public void writeToFile(DataOutputStream out, Scene theScene)
throws IOException;
public void editKeyframe(EditingWindow parent, Keyframe k,
ObjectInfo info);
public static class ImplicitSphereKeyframe implements Keyframe{
    public double radius, influenceRadius;
    public ImplicitSphereKeyframe(double radius, double influenc-
eRadius);
    public Keyframe duplicate();
    public Keyframe duplicate(Object owner);
    public double [] getGraphValues();
    public void setGraphValues(double values[]);
    public Keyframe blend(Keyframe o2, double weight1, double
weight2);
    public Keyframe blend(Keyframe o2, Keyframe o3, double
weight1, double weight2, double weight3);
    public Keyframe blend(Keyframe o2, Keyframe o3, Keyframe
o4, double weight1, double weight2, double weight3, double
weight4);
    public boolean equals(Keyframe k);
    public void writeToStream(DataOutputStream out) throws IOEx-
ception;
    public ImplicitSphereKeyframe(DataInputStream in, Object par-
ent) throws IOException;
    }
}
```

artofillusion.object.Light

This object is the abstract representation of a light
source for the scene.

```
public abstract class Light extends Object3D{
  protected RGBColor color;
  protected float intensity, decayRate;
  protected int type = TYPE_NORMAL;

  public static final int TYPE_SHADOWLESS;
  public static final int TYPE_AMBIENT;

  public Light();
  public Light(DataInputStream in, Scene theScene) throws
IOException, InvalidObjectException;
  public void setParameters(RGBColor color, float intensity, int
type, float decayRate);
  public RGBColor getColor();
  public void setColor(RGBColor color);
  public float getIntensity();
  public void setIntensity(float intensity);
  public abstract void getLight(RGBColor light, Vec3 position);
  public float getDecayRate();
  public void setDecayRate(float rate);
  public int getType();
  public void setType(int type);
}
```

artofillusion.object.Mesh

This interface describes an object that is represented by vertices.

```
public interface Mesh{
  public static final int NO_SMOOTHING;
  public static final int SMOOTH_SHADING;
  public static final int INTERPOLATING;
  public static final int APPROXIMATING;

  public MeshVertex[] getVertices();
  public Vec3 [] getVertexPositions();
  public void setVertexPositions(Vec3 v[]);
  public BoundingBox getBounds();
  public Vec3 [] getNormals();
  public TextureParameter [] getParameters();
  public ParameterValue [] getParameterValues();
  public abstract Object3D duplicate();
  public abstract void copyObject(Object3D obj);
  public Skeleton getSkeleton();
  public void setSkeleton(Skeleton s);
  public MeshViewer createMeshViewer(MeshEditController
controller, RowContainer options);
}
```

artofillusion.object.MeshVertex

This class represents a vertex in a mesh.

```
public class MeshVertex{
  public Vec3 r;
  public int ikJoint;
  public double ikWeight;

  public MeshVertex(Vec3 p);
  public MeshVertex(MeshVertex v);
  public static MeshVertex blend(MeshVertex v1, MeshVertex v2,
double w1, double w2);
}
```

artofillusion.object.NullObject

A NullObject has no effect on the rendered scene. It is typically used for grouping objects and changing the center of rotation of an object.

```
public class NullObject extends Object3D{
  public NullObject();
  public Object3D duplicate();
  public void copyObject(Object3D obj);
  public BoundingBox getBounds();
  public void setSize(double xsize, double ysize, double zsize);
  public boolean canSetTexture();
  public WireframeMesh getWireframeMesh();
  public boolean isEditable();
  public NullObject(DataInputStream in, Scene theScene) throws
IOException, InvalidObjectException;
  public void writeToFile(DataOutputStream out, Scene theScene)
throws IOException;
  public Keyframe getPoseKeyframe();
  public void applyPoseKeyframe(Keyframe k);
}
```

artofillusion.object.Object3D

All objects that can be placed into a scene extend this class.

```
public abstract class Object3D{
  protected Texture theTexture;
  protected Material theMaterial;
  protected TextureMapping texMapping;
  protected MaterialMapping matMapping;
  protected TextureParameter texParam[];
  protected ParameterValue paramValue[];
```

```java
    protected boolean parametersChanged;

    public static final int CANT_CONVERT;
    public static final int EXACTLY;
    public static final int APPROXIMATELY;

    public Object3D();
    public abstract Object3D duplicate();
    public abstract void copyObject(Object3D obj);
    public abstract BoundingBox getBounds();
    public abstract void setSize(double xsize, double ysize, double
zsize);
    public boolean isClosed();
    public int canConvertToTriangleMesh();
    public TriangleMesh convertToTriangleMesh(double tol);
    public void sceneChanged(ObjectInfo info, Scene scene);
    public boolean isEditable();
    public void edit(EditingWindow parent, ObjectInfo info, Runnable
cb);
    public void editGesture(EditingWindow parent, ObjectInfo info,
Runnable cb, ObjectInfo realObject);
    public boolean canSetTexture();
    public boolean canSetMaterial();
    public void setTexture(Texture tex, TextureMapping map);
    public Texture getTexture();
    public TextureMapping getTextureMapping();
    public void setMaterial(Material mat, MaterialMapping map);
    public Material getMaterial();
    public MaterialMapping getMaterialMapping();
    public TextureParameter [] getParameters();
    public void setParameters(TextureParameter param[]);
    public ParameterValue [] getParameterValues();
    public void setParameterValues(ParameterValue val[]);
    public ParameterValue getParameterValue(TextureParameter
param);
    public void setParameterValue(TextureParameter param,
ParameterValue val);
    public void copyTextureAndMaterial(Object3D obj);
    public Skeleton getSkeleton();
    public RenderingMesh getRenderingMesh(double tol, boolean
interactive, ObjectInfo info);
    public abstract WireframeMesh getWireframeMesh();
    public void renderObject(ObjectInfo obj, ViewerCanvas canvas,
Vec3 viewDir);
    public void writeToFile(DataOutputStream out, Scene theScene)
throws IOException;
    public Object3D(DataInputStream in, Scene theScene) throws
IOException, InvalidObjectException;
    public static ParameterValue readParameterValue
(DataInputStream in) throws IOException;
    public Property[] getProperties();
    public Object getPropertyValue(int index);
    public void setPropertyValue(int index, Object value);
    public abstract Keyframe getPoseKeyframe();;
```

```
    public abstract void applyPoseKeyframe(Keyframe k);
    public void configurePoseTrack(PoseTrack track);
    public void editKeyframe(EditingWindow parent, Keyframe k, Ob-
jectInfo info);
    public boolean canConvertToActor();
    public Object3D getPosableObject();
}
```

artofillusion.object.ObjectCollection

An ObjectCollection is an Object3D that is made up of a collection of objects.

```
public abstract class ObjectCollection extends Object3D{
    protected Vector<ObjectInfo> cachedObjects;
    protected BoundingBox cachedBounds;
    protected double lastTime;
    protected CoordinateSystem lastCoords;
    protected Scene lastScene;
    protected ObjectInfo lastInfo;
    protected boolean usesTime, usesCoords;
    protected Distortion previousDistortion;

    public ObjectCollection();
    public ObjectCollection(DataInputStream in, Scene theScene)
throws IOException, InvalidObjectException;
    public synchronized Enumeration<ObjectInfo> getObjects
(ObjectInfo info, boolean interactive, Scene scene);
    protected abstract Enumeration<ObjectInfo> enumerateObjects
(ObjectInfo info, boolean interactive, Scene scene);
    public BoundingBox getBounds();
    public void setUsesTime(boolean b);
    public void setUsesCoords(boolean b);
    public boolean isClosed();
    public boolean canSetMaterial();
    public RenderingMesh getRenderingMesh(double tol, boolean
interactive, ObjectInfo info);
    public WireframeMesh getWireframeMesh();
    public void renderObject(ObjectInfo obj, ViewerCanvas canvas,
Vec3 viewDir);
    public int canConvertToTriangleMesh();
    public TriangleMesh convertToTriangleMesh(double tol);
    public void sceneChanged(ObjectInfo info, Scene scene);
}
```

artofillusion.object.ObjectInfo

The ObjectInfo class wraps an Object3D object to provide additional information. The ObjectInfo class is usually passed to Art of Illusion methods rather than the Object3D class because the information is needed.

If two ObjectInfo classes reference the same Object3D object, they are considered live duplicates of each other.

```
public class ObjectInfo{
  public Object3D object;
  public CoordinateSystem coords;
  public String name;
  public boolean visible, selected, parentSelected;
  public ObjectInfo parent, children[];
  public Track tracks[];
  public Keyframe pose;
  public int id;

  public ObjectInfo(Object3D obj, CoordinateSystem c, String
name);
  public ObjectInfo duplicate();
  public ObjectInfo duplicate(Object3D obj);
  public static ObjectInfo [] duplicateAll(ObjectInfo info[]);
  public void copyInfo(ObjectInfo info);
  public void addChild(ObjectInfo info, int position);
  public void removeChild(ObjectInfo info);
  public void removeChild(int which);
  public void addTrack(Track tr, int position);
  public void removeTrack(Track tr);
  public void removeTrack(int which);
  public void setTexture(Texture tex, TextureMapping map);
  public void setMaterial(Material mat, MaterialMapping map);
  public void clearDistortion();
  public void addDistortion(Distortion d);
  public Distortion getDistortion();
  public boolean isDistorted();
  public void setDistortion(Distortion d);
  public Object3D getDistortedObject(double tol);
  public RenderingMesh getRenderingMesh(double tol);
  public RenderingMesh getPreviewMesh();
  public WireframeMesh getWireframePreview();
  public BoundingBox getBounds();
  public void clearCachedMeshes();
  public Skeleton getSkeleton();
  public Object3D getObject();
  public void setObject(Object3D object);
  public CoordinateSystem getCoords();
  public void setCoords(CoordinateSystem coords);
  public String getName();
  public void setName(String name);
  public boolean isVisible();
  public void setVisible(boolean visible);
  public boolean isLocked();
  public void setLocked(boolean locked);
  public ObjectInfo getParent();
  public void setParent(ObjectInfo parent);
```

```
public Keyframe getPose();
public void setPose(Keyframe pose);
public int getId();
public void setId(int id);
public ObjectInfo[] getChildren();
public Track[] getTracks();
}
```

artofillusion.object.ObjectWrapper

This class is an abstract class that defines classes that wrap another object.

```
public abstract class ObjectWrapper extends Object3D{
protected Object3D theObject;

public ObjectWrapper();
public ObjectWrapper(DataInputStream in, Scene theScene)
throws IOException, InvalidObjectException;
public Object3D getWrappedObject();
public BoundingBox getBounds();
public boolean isClosed();
public int canConvertToTriangleMesh();
public TriangleMesh convertToTriangleMesh(double tol);
public void sceneChanged(ObjectInfo info, Scene scene);
public void editGesture(EditingWindow parent, ObjectInfo info,
Runnable cb, ObjectInfo realObject);
public Texture getTexture();
public TextureMapping getTextureMapping();
public Material getMaterial();
public MaterialMapping getMaterialMapping();
public TextureParameter [] getParameters();
public void setParameters(TextureParameter param[]);
public ParameterValue [] getParameterValues();
public double [] getAverageParameterValues();
public void setParameterValues(ParameterValue val[]);
public ParameterValue getParameterValue(TextureParameter
param);
public void setParameterValue(TextureParameter param,
ParameterValue val);
public Skeleton getSkeleton();
public RenderingMesh getRenderingMesh(double tol, boolean
interactive, ObjectInfo info);
public WireframeMesh getWireframeMesh();
public void renderObject(ObjectInfo obj, ViewerCanvas canvas,
Vec3 viewDir);
public Keyframe getPoseKeyframe();
public void applyPoseKeyframe(Keyframe k);
public void configurePoseTrack(PoseTrack track);
public void editKeyframe(EditingWindow parent, Keyframe k,
ObjectInfo info);
}
```

artofillusion.object.PointLight

A PointLight is a Light that emits light in all directions.

```
public class PointLight extends Light{
    public PointLight(RGBColor theColor, float theIntensity, double theRadius);
    public PointLight(RGBColor theColor, float theIntensity, double theRadius, int type, float decay);
    public double getRadius();
    public void setRadius(double r);
    public void getLight(RGBColor light, Vec3 position);
    public Object3D duplicate();
    public void copyObject(Object3D obj);
    public BoundingBox getBounds();
    public void setSize(double xsize, double ysize, double zsize);
    public boolean canSetTexture();
    public WireframeMesh getWireframeMesh();
    public boolean isEditable();
    public void edit(EditingWindow parent, ObjectInfo info, Runnable cb);
    public PointLight(DataInputStream in, Scene theScene) throws IOException, InvalidObjectException;
    public void writeToFile(DataOutputStream out, Scene theScene) throws IOException;
    public Property[] getProperties();
    public Object getPropertyValue(int index);
    public void setPropertyValue(int index, Object value);
    public Keyframe getPoseKeyframe();
    public void applyPoseKeyframe(Keyframe k);
    public void configurePoseTrack(PoseTrack track);
    public void editKeyframe(EditingWindow parent, Keyframe k, ObjectInfo info);
    public static class PointLightKeyframe implements Keyframe
    {
    public RGBColor color;
    public float intensity, decayRate;
    public double radius;

    public PointLightKeyframe(RGBColor color, float intensity, float decayRate, double radius);
    public Keyframe duplicate();
    public Keyframe duplicate(Object owner);
    public double [] getGraphValues();
    public void setGraphValues(double values[]);
    public Keyframe blend(Keyframe o2, double weight1, double weight2);
    public Keyframe blend(Keyframe o2, Keyframe o3, double weight1, double weight2, double weight3);
    public Keyframe blend(Keyframe o2, Keyframe o3, Keyframe o4, double weight1, double weight2, double weight3, double weight4);
    public boolean equals(Keyframe k);
```

```
    public void writeToStream(DataOutputStream out) throws
IOException;
    }
}
```

artofillusion.object.
ProceduralDirectionalLight

This is a directional light that is controlled by a procedure.

```
public class ProceduralDirectionalLight extends DirectionalLight{
    public ProceduralDirectionalLight(double theRadius);
    public Object3D duplicate();
    public void copyObject(Object3D obj);
    public void sceneChanged(ObjectInfo info, Scene scene);
    public void getLight(RGBColor light, Vec3 position);
    public ProceduralDirectionalLight(DataInputStream in, Scene
theScene) throws IOException;
    public void writeToFile(DataOutputStream out, Scene theScene)
throws IOException;
    public void edit(EditingWindow parent, ObjectInfo info, Runnable
cb);
    public Property[] getProperties();
    public Object getPropertyValue(int index);
    public void setPropertyValue(int index, Object value);
    public Keyframe getPoseKeyframe();
    public void applyPoseKeyframe(Keyframe k);
    public void configurePoseTrack(PoseTrack track);
    public void editKeyframe(EditingWindow parent, Keyframe k,
ObjectInfo info);
    public static class ProceduralLightKeyframe implements
Keyframe
    {
    public HashMap<TextureParameter, Double> paramValues;
    public double radius;

    public ProceduralLightKeyframe(ProceduralDirectionalLight
light);
    public Keyframe duplicate();
    public Keyframe duplicate(Object owner);
    public double [] getGraphValues();
    public void setGraphValues(double values[]);
    public Keyframe blend(Keyframe o2, double weight1, double
weight2);
    public Keyframe blend(Keyframe o2, Keyframe o3, double
weight1, double weight2, double weight3);
    public Keyframe blend(Keyframe o2, Keyframe o3, Keyframe
o4, double weight1, double weight2, double weight3, double
weight4);
    public boolean equals(Keyframe k);
    public void writeToStream(DataOutputStream out) throws
```

IOException;
    public ProceduralLightKeyframe(DataInputStream in, Object parent) throws IOException;
    }
}

artofillusion.object.
ProceduralPointLight

This is a point light that is controlled by a procedure.

```
public class ProceduralPointLight extends PointLight{
    public ProceduralPointLight(double theRadius);
    public Object3D duplicate();
    public void copyObject(Object3D obj);
    public void sceneChanged(ObjectInfo info, Scene scene);
    public void getLight(RGBColor light, Vec3 position);
    public ProceduralPointLight(DataInputStream in, Scene theScene) throws IOException;
    public void writeToFile(DataOutputStream out, Scene theScene) throws IOException;
    public void edit(EditingWindow parent, ObjectInfo info, Runnable cb);
    public Property[] getProperties();
    public Object getPropertyValue(int index);
    public void setPropertyValue(int index, Object value);
    public Keyframe getPoseKeyframe();
    public void applyPoseKeyframe(Keyframe k);
    public void configurePoseTrack(PoseTrack track);
    public void editKeyframe(EditingWindow parent, Keyframe k, ObjectInfo info);
    public static class ProceduralLightKeyframe implements Keyframe
    {
    public HashMap<TextureParameter, Double> paramValues;
    public double radius;

    public ProceduralLightKeyframe(ProceduralPointLight light);
    public Keyframe duplicate();
    public Keyframe duplicate(Object owner);
    public double [] getGraphValues();
    public void setGraphValues(double values[]);
    public Keyframe blend(Keyframe o2, double weight1, double weight2);
    public Keyframe blend(Keyframe o2, Keyframe o3, double weight1, double weight2, double weight3);
    public Keyframe blend(Keyframe o2, Keyframe o3, Keyframe o4, double weight1, double weight2, double weight3, double weight4);
    public boolean equals(Keyframe k);
    public void writeToStream(DataOutputStream out) throws
```

```
IOException;
    public ProceduralLightKeyframe(DataInputStream in, Object
parent) throws IOException;
    }
}
```

artofillusion.object.ReferenceImage

A ReferenceImage is a 2D image that is used for reference during 3D modeling. It is a rectangle with an image mapped to it.

```
public class ReferenceImage extends Object3D{
    public ReferenceImage();
    public ReferenceImage(Image image);
    public Image getImage();
    public void setImage(Image image);
    public boolean canSetTexture();
    public Object3D duplicate();
    public void copyObject(Object3D obj);
    public BoundingBox getBounds();
    public void setSize(double xsize, double ysize, double zsize);
    public WireframeMesh getWireframeMesh();
    public Keyframe getPoseKeyframe();
    public void applyPoseKeyframe(Keyframe k);
    public void renderObject(ObjectInfo obj, ViewerCanvas canvas,
Vec3 viewDir);
    public ReferenceImage(DataInputStream in, Scene theScene)
throws IOException;
    public void writeToFile(DataOutputStream out, Scene theScene)
throws IOException;
    }
```

artofillusion.object.SceneCamera

A SceneCamera is the camera object that can be moved around the scene, the view of which can be rendered.

```
public class SceneCamera extends Object3D{
    public SceneCamera();
    public double getFieldOfView();
    public void setFieldOfView(double fieldOfView);
    public double getDepthOfField();
    public void setDepthOfField(double dof);
    public double getFocalDistance();
    public void setFocalDistance(double dist);
    public boolean isPerspective();
    public void setPerspective(boolean perspective);
    public ImageFilter [] getImageFilters();
```

```
public void setImageFilters(ImageFilter filters[]);
public int getExtraRequiredComponents();
public void setExtraRequiredComponents(int components);
public int getComponentsForFilters();
public void applyImageFilters(ComplexImage image, Scene
scene, CoordinateSystem coords);
public Mat4 getScreenTransform(int width, int height);
public void getRayFromCamera(double x, double y, double dof1,
double dof2, Vec3 origin, Vec3 direction);
public SceneCamera duplicate();
public void copyObject(Object3D obj);
public BoundingBox getBounds();
public void setSize(double xsize, double ysize, double zsize);
public boolean canSetTexture();
public WireframeMesh getWireframeMesh();
public Camera createCamera(int width, int height,
CoordinateSystem coords);
public ComplexImage renderScene(Scene theScene, int width, int
height, Renderer rend, CoordinateSystem cameraPos);
public boolean isEditable();
public void edit(final EditingWindow parent, final ObjectInfo info,
Runnable cb);
public SceneCamera(DataInputStream in, Scene theScene)
throws IOException, InvalidObjectException;
public void writeToFile(DataOutputStream out, Scene theScene)
throws IOException;
public Property[] getProperties();
public Object getPropertyValue(int index);
public void setPropertyValue(int index, Object value);
public Keyframe getPoseKeyframe();
public void applyPoseKeyframe(Keyframe k);
public void configurePoseTrack(PoseTrack track);
public void editKeyframe(EditingWindow parent, Keyframe k, Ob-
jectInfo info);
public static class CameraKeyframe implements Keyframe
{
   public double fov, depthOfField, focalDist;

   public CameraKeyframe(double fov, double depthOfField,
double focalDist);
   public Keyframe duplicate();
   public Keyframe duplicate(Object owner);
   public double [] getGraphValues();
   public void setGraphValues(double values[]);
   public Keyframe blend(Keyframe o2, double weight1, double
weight2);
   public Keyframe blend(Keyframe o2, Keyframe o3, double
weight1, double weight2, double weight3);
   public Keyframe blend(Keyframe o2, Keyframe o3, Keyframe o4,
double weight1, double weight2, double weight3, double weight4);
   public boolean equals(Keyframe k);
   public void writeToStream(DataOutputStream out) throws
IOException;
```

```
    public CameraKeyframe(DataInputStream in, Object parent)
throws IOException;
    }
}
```

artofillusion.object.Sphere

This is the sphere object that can be added to Art of Illusion scenes.

```
public class Sphere extends Object3D{
    public Sphere(double xradius, double yradius, double zradius);
    public Object3D duplicate();
    public void copyObject(Object3D obj);
    public BoundingBox getBounds();
    public void setSize(double xsize, double ysize, double zsize);
    public Vec3 getRadii();
    public WireframeMesh getWireframeMesh();
    public int canConvertToTriangleMesh();
    public TriangleMesh convertToTriangleMesh(double tol);
    public void setTexture(Texture tex, TextureMapping mapping);
    Vec3 [] subdivideSphere(int index[][], double tol);
    double faceError(Vec3 v1, Vec3 v2, Vec3 v3);
    Vec3 newVertex(Vec3 v);
    Vec3 [] findNormals(Vec3 v[]);
    public boolean isEditable();
    public void edit(EditingWindow parent, ObjectInfo info, Runnable
cb);
    public Sphere(DataInputStream in, Scene theScene) throws
IOException, InvalidObjectException;
    public void writeToFile(DataOutputStream out, Scene theScene)
throws IOException;
    public Property[] getProperties();
    public Object getPropertyValue(int index);
    public void setPropertyValue(int index, Object value);
    public Keyframe getPoseKeyframe();
    public void applyPoseKeyframe(Keyframe k);
    public void configurePoseTrack(PoseTrack track);
    public void editKeyframe(EditingWindow parent, Keyframe k,
ObjectInfo info);
}
```

artofillusion.object.SplineMesh

This object represents a spline mesh.

```
public class SplineMesh extends Object3D implements Mesh{
    public SplineMesh(Vec3 v[][], float usmoothness[], float
vsmoothness[], int smoothingMethod, boolean uclosed, boolean
vclosed);
    protected SplineMesh();
    public Object3D duplicate();
```

```
public void copyObject(Object3D obj);
public BoundingBox getBounds();
public MeshVertex[] getVertices();
public final MeshVertex getVertex(int u, int v);
public final int getUSize();
public final int getVSize();
public int getSmoothingMethod();
public float [] getUSmoothness();
public float [] getVSmoothness();
public Vec3 [] getVertexPositions();
public void setVertexPositions(Vec3 v[]);
public void setSmoothingMethod(int method);
public void setSmoothness(float usmoothness[], float
vsmoothness[]);
public void setShape(MeshVertex v[][], float usmoothness[], float
vsmoothness[]);
public boolean isUClosed();
public boolean isVClosed();
public boolean isClosed();
public void setClosed(boolean u, boolean v);
public void setSize(double xsize, double ysize, double zsize);
public boolean isEditable();
public void edit(EditingWindow parent, ObjectInfo info, Runnable
cb);
public void editGesture(final EditingWindow parent, ObjectInfo
info, Runnable cb, ObjectInfo realObject);
public MeshViewer createMeshViewer(MeshEditController
controller, RowContainer options);
public static SplineMesh subdivideMesh(SplineMesh mesh,
double tol);
public static MeshVertex calcInterpPoint(MeshVertex v[], float s[],
double oldParam[][], double newParam[], int i, int j, int k, int m);
public static MeshVertex calcApproxPoint(MeshVertex v[], float
s[], double oldParam[][], double newParam[], int i, int j, int k);
public WireframeMesh getWireframeMesh();
public RenderingMesh getRenderingMesh(double tol, boolean
interactive, ObjectInfo info);
public int canConvertToTriangleMesh();
public TriangleMesh convertToTriangleMesh(double tol);
public void setTexture(Texture tex, TextureMapping mapping);
public void setParameterValues(ParameterValue val[]);
public void setParameterValue(TextureParameter param,
ParameterValue val);
public Skeleton getSkeleton();
public void setSkeleton(Skeleton s);
public SplineMesh(DataInputStream in, Scene theScene) throws
IOException, InvalidObjectException;
public void writeToFile(DataOutputStream out, Scene theScene)
throws IOException;
public void makeRightSideOut();
public void reverseOrientation();
public Vec3 [] getNormals();
public Property[] getProperties();
public Object getPropertyValue(int index);
```

```
public void setPropertyValue(int index, Object value);
public Keyframe getPoseKeyframe();
public void applyPoseKeyframe(Keyframe k);
public boolean canConvertToActor();
public Object3D getPosableObject();
public static class SplineMeshKeyframe extends MeshGesture
{
  public SplineMeshKeyframe(SplineMesh mesh);
  protected Mesh getMesh();
  protected Vec3 [] getVertexPositions();
  protected void setVertexPositions(Vec3 pos[]);
  public Skeleton getSkeleton();
  public void setSkeleton(Skeleton s);
  public Keyframe duplicate();
  public Keyframe duplicate(Object owner);
  public double [] getGraphValues();
  public void setGraphValues(double values[]);
  public Keyframe blend(Keyframe o2, double weight1, double
weight2);
  public Keyframe blend(Keyframe o2, Keyframe o3, double
weight1, double weight2, double weight3);
  public Keyframe blend(Keyframe o2, Keyframe o3, Keyframe
o4, double weight1, double weight2, double weight3, double
weight4);
  public void blendSurface(MeshGesture average, MeshGesture p
[], double weight[]);
  public void textureChanged(TextureParameter oldParams[],
TextureParameter newParams[]);
  public ParameterValue getTextureParameter(TextureParameter
p);
  public void writeToStream(DataOutputStream out) throws
IOException;
  public SplineMeshKeyframe(DataInputStream in, Object parent)
throws IOException, InvalidObjectException;
  }
}
```

artofillusion.object.SpotLight

This object is a light source that models a spotlight.
Light comes from one location an expands out at and
angle.

```
public class SpotLight extends Light {
  public SpotLight(RGBColor theColor, float theIntensity, double
theAngle, double falloffRate, double theRadius);
  public SpotLight(RGBColor theColor, float theIntensity, double
theAngle, double falloffRate, double theRadius, int type, float
decay);
  public double getRadius();
  public void setRadius(double r);
  public double getAngle();
```

```java
    public void setAngle(double a);
    public double getFalloff();
    public void setFalloff(double f);
    public double getAngleCosine();
    public double getExponent();
    public void getLight(RGBColor light, Vec3 position);
    public Object3D duplicate();
    public void copyObject(Object3D obj);
    public BoundingBox getBounds();
    public void setSize(double xsize, double ysize, double zsize);
    public boolean canSetTexture();
    public WireframeMesh getWireframeMesh();
    public boolean isEditable();
    public SpotLight(DataInputStream in, Scene theScene) throws
IOException, InvalidObjectException;
    public void writeToFile(DataOutputStream out, Scene theScene)
throws IOException;
    public void edit(EditingWindow parent, ObjectInfo info, final
Runnable cb);
    public Property[] getProperties();
    public Object getPropertyValue(int index);
    public void setPropertyValue(int index, Object value);
    public Keyframe getPoseKeyframe();
    public void applyPoseKeyframe(Keyframe k);
    public void configurePoseTrack(PoseTrack track);
    public void editKeyframe(EditingWindow parent, Keyframe k,
ObjectInfo info);
    public static class SpotLightKeyframe implements Keyframe
    {
    public RGBColor color;
    public float intensity, decayRate;
    public double radius, angle, falloff;

    public SpotLightKeyframe(RGBColor color, float intensity, float
decayRate, double radius, double angle, double falloff);
    public Keyframe duplicate();
    public Keyframe duplicate(Object owner);
    public double [] getGraphValues();
    public void setGraphValues(double values[]);
    public Keyframe blend(Keyframe o2, double weight1, double
weight2);
    public Keyframe blend(Keyframe o2, Keyframe o3, double
weight1, double weight2, double weight3);
    public Keyframe blend(Keyframe o2, Keyframe o3, Keyframe
o4, double weight1, double weight2, double weight3, double
weight4);
    public boolean equals(Keyframe k);
    public void writeToStream(DataOutputStream out) throws
IOException;
    public SpotLightKeyframe(DataInputStream in, Object parent)
throws IOException;
    }
}
```

artofillusion.object.TriangleMesh

This object represents a triangle mesh.

```
public class TriangleMesh extends Object3D implements
FacetedMesh{
  public class Vertex extends MeshVertex {
    public int edges, firstEdge;
    public float smoothness;

    public Vertex(Vec3 p);
    public Vertex(Vertex v);
    public void copy(Vertex v);
    public void scale(double d);
    public void clear();
    public int[] getEdges();
    public boolean clockwise();
  }

  public class Edge {
    public int v1, v2, f1, f2;
    public float smoothness;

    public Edge(int vertex1, int vertex2, int face1);
  }

  public class Face {
    public int v1, v2, v3, e1, e2, e3;

    public Face(int vertex1, int vertex2, int vertex3, int edge1, int
edge2, int edge3);
    public int getSharedFace(Face f);
  }

  public TriangleMesh(Vec3 v[], int faces[][]);
  public TriangleMesh(Vertex v[], int faces[][]);
  protected TriangleMesh();
  public Object3D duplicate();
  public void copyObject(Object3D obj);
  void findEdges(int faces[][]);
  public BoundingBox getBounds();
  public MeshVertex[] getVertices();
  public Vertex getVertex(int i);
  public Edge[] getEdges();
  public Face[] getFaces();
  public int getSmoothingMethod();
  public Vec3 [] getVertexPositions();
  public void setVertexPositions(Vec3 v[]);
  public void setSmoothingMethod(int method);
  public void setShape(Vertex v[], int faces[][]);
  public boolean isClosed();
  public void setSize(double xsize, double ysize, double zsize);
  public int [][] findBoundaryEdges();
```

```
public boolean isEditable();
public void edit(final EditingWindow parent, ObjectInfo info,
Runnable cb);
public void editGesture(final EditingWindow parent, ObjectInfo
info, Runnable cb, ObjectInfo realObject);
public MeshViewer createMeshViewer(MeshEditController
controller, RowContainer options);
public int canConvertToTriangleMesh();
public TriangleMesh convertToTriangleMesh(double tol);
public WireframeMesh getWireframeMesh();
public RenderingMesh getRenderingMesh(double tol, boolean
interactive, ObjectInfo info);
public void setTexture(Texture tex, TextureMapping mapping);
public void setParameterValues(ParameterValue val[]);
public void setParameterValue(TextureParameter param,
ParameterValue val);
public Skeleton getSkeleton();
public void setSkeleton(Skeleton s);
public static TriangleMesh subdivideEdges(TriangleMesh mesh,
boolean splitEdge[], double tol);
public static TriangleMesh subdivideLinear(TriangleMesh mesh,
boolean split[]);
public static TriangleMesh subdivideLoop(TriangleMesh mesh,
boolean refineEdge[], double tol);
public static TriangleMesh subdivideButterfly(TriangleMesh
mesh, boolean refineEdge[], double tol);
public static TriangleMesh subdivideFaces(TriangleMesh mesh,
boolean split[]);
public TriangleMesh subdivideToLimit(double tol);
public TriangleMesh getDisplacedMesh(double tol, double time);
public void makeRightSideOut();
public void reverseNormals();
public Vec3 [] getNormals();
public int getFaceCount();
public int getFaceVertexCount(int faceIndex);
public int getFaceVertexIndex(int faceIndex, int vertexIndex);
public static TriangleMesh optimizeMesh(TriangleMesh mesh);
public void autosmoothMeshEdges(double angle);
public TriangleMesh(DataInputStream in, Scene theScene)
throws IOException, InvalidObjectException;
public void writeToFile(DataOutputStream out, Scene theScene)
throws IOException;
public Property[] getProperties();
public Object getPropertyValue(int index);
public void setPropertyValue(int index, Object value);
public Keyframe getPoseKeyframe();
public void applyPoseKeyframe(Keyframe k);
public boolean canConvertToActor();
public Object3D getPosableObject();
public static class TriangleMeshKeyframe extends MeshGesture{
    public TriangleMeshKeyframe(TriangleMesh mesh);
    protected Mesh getMesh();
    protected Vec3 [] getVertexPositions();
    protected void setVertexPositions(Vec3 pos[]);
```

```
    public Skeleton getSkeleton();
    public void setSkeleton(Skeleton s);
    public Keyframe duplicate();
    public Keyframe duplicate(Object owner);
    public double [] getGraphValues();
    public void setGraphValues(double values[]);
    public Keyframe blend(Keyframe o2, double weight1, double
weight2);
    public Keyframe blend(Keyframe o2, Keyframe o3, double
weight1, double weight2, double weight3);
    public Keyframe blend(Keyframe o2, Keyframe o3, Keyframe o4,
double weight1, double weight2, double weight3, double weight4);
    public void blendSurface(MeshGesture average, MeshGesture p
[], double weight[]);
    public boolean equals(Keyframe k);
    public void textureChanged(TextureParameter oldParams[], Tex-
tureParameter newParams[]);
    public ParameterValue getTextureParameter(TextureParameter
p);
    public void setTextureParameter(TextureParameter p,
ParameterValue value);
    public void writeToStream(DataOutputStream out) throws
IOException;
    public TriangleMeshKeyframe(DataInputStream in, Object
parent) throws IOException, InvalidObjectException;
    }
}
```

artofillusion.object.Tube

A Tube is a Curve that has an extruded surface
along its shape.

```
public class Tube extends Curve{
    public static final int OPEN_ENDS;
    public static final int CLOSED_ENDS;
    public static final int FLAT_ENDS;

    public Tube(Vec3 v[], float smoothness[], double thickness[], int
smoothingMethod, int endsStyle);
    public Tube(MeshVertex v[], float smoothness[], double
thickness[], int smoothingMethod, int endsStyle);
    public Tube(Curve c, double thickness[], int endsStyle);
    public Tube(Vec3 v[], double thickness, int smoothingMethod, int
endsStyle);
    public Object3D duplicate();
    public void copyObject(Object3D obj);
    public double [] getThickness();
    public void setThickness(double thickness[]);
    public void setShape(MeshVertex v[], float smoothness[], double
thickness[]);
    public int getEndsStyle();
    public void setEndsStyle(int style);
```

```
public boolean isClosed();
public void setClosed(boolean isClosed);
protected void clearCachedMesh();
public Tube subdivideTube(double tol);
public static double calcInterpThickness(double t[], float s[], int i,
int j, int k, int m);
public static double calcApproxThickness(double t[], float s[], int i,
int j, int k);
public boolean canSetTexture();
public int canConvertToTriangleMesh();
public RenderingMesh getRenderingMesh(double tol, boolean
interactive, ObjectInfo info);
public void setTexture(Texture tex, TextureMapping mapping);
public WireframeMesh getWireframeMesh();
public TriangleMesh convertToTriangleMesh(double tol);
public void edit(EditingWindow parent, ObjectInfo info, Runnable
cb);
public void editGesture(final EditingWindow parent, ObjectInfo
info, Runnable cb, ObjectInfo realObject);
public MeshViewer createMeshViewer(MeshEditController
controller, RowContainer options);
public Tube(DataInputStream in, Scene theScene) throws
IOException, InvalidObjectException;
public void writeToFile(DataOutputStream out, Scene theScene)
throws IOException;
public Property[] getProperties();
public Object getPropertyValue(int index);
public void setPropertyValue(int index, Object value);
public Keyframe getPoseKeyframe();
public void applyPoseKeyframe(Keyframe k);
public boolean canConvertToActor();
public Object3D getPosableObject();
public static class TubeKeyframe extends MeshGesture  {
public TubeKeyframe(Tube tube);
protected Mesh getMesh();
protected Vec3 [] getVertexPositions();
protected void setVertexPositions(Vec3 pos[]);
public Skeleton getSkeleton();
public void setSkeleton(Skeleton s);
public Keyframe duplicate();
public Keyframe duplicate(Object owner);
public double [] getGraphValues();
public void setGraphValues(double values[]);
public Keyframe blend(Keyframe o2, double weight1, double
weight2);
public Keyframe blend(Keyframe o2, Keyframe o3, double
weight1, double weight2, double weight3);
public Keyframe blend(Keyframe o2, Keyframe o3, Keyframe
o4, double weight1, double weight2, double weight3, double
weight4);
public void blendSurface(MeshGesture average, MeshGesture
p[], double weight[]);
public boolean equals(Keyframe k);
public void textureChanged(TextureParameter oldParams[],
```

```
TextureParameter newParams[]);
    public ParameterValue getTextureParameter(TextureParameter
p);
    public void setTextureParameter(TextureParameter p,
ParameterValue value);
    public void writeToStream(DataOutputStream out) throws
IOException;
    public TubeKeyframe(DataInputStream in, Object parent)
throws IOException, InvalidObjectException;
  }
}
```

object

Chapter 20

The artofillusion.procedural Package

The procedural package contains the classes for the modules that are available for use when the user is defining the procedural textures and materials.

artofillusion.procedural.AbsModule

The output of this module is the absolute value of the number that is input.

```
public class AbsModule extends Module{
  public AbsModule(Point position);
  public void init(PointInfo p);
  public double getAverageValue(int which, double blur);
  public double getValueError(int which, double blur);
  public void getValueGradient(int which, Vec3 grad, double blur);
}
```

artofillusion.procedural.BiasModule

The output of this module is from Perlin's Bias function.

```
public class BiasModule extends Module{
  public BiasModule(Point position);
  public void init(PointInfo p);
  public double getAverageValue(int which, double blur);
  public double getValueError(int which, double blur);
  public void getValueGradient(int which, Vec3 grad, double blur);
}
```

artofillusion.procedural.BlendModule

This module outputs a weighted average of two colors. This is based on the value of the number passed in, making it possible for the number passed in to represent a pattern, which the BlendModule will add color to.

```
public class BlendModule extends Module{
  public BlendModule(Point position);
  public void init(PointInfo p);
  public void getColor(int which, RGBColor c, double blur);
}
```

artofillusion.procedural.BlurModule

This module Blurs the input.

```
public class BlurModule extends Module{
  public BlurModule(Point position);
  public void init(PointInfo p);
  public double getAverageValue(int which, double blur);
  public double getValueError(int which, double blur);
  public void getValueGradient(int which, Vec3 grad, double blur);
}
```

artofillusion.procedural.BrickModule

This module outputs a brick pattern.

```
public class BrickModule extends Module{
  public BrickModule(Point position);
  public double getBrickHeight();
  public void setBrickHeight(double h);
  public double getGap();
  public void setGap(double g);
  public double getOffset();
  public void setOffset(double o);
  public void init(PointInfo p);
  public double getAverageValue(int which, double blur);
  public double getValueError(int which, double blur);
  public void getValueGradient(int which, Vec3 grad, double blur);
  public boolean edit(BFrame fr, Scene theScene);
  public Module duplicate();
  public void writeToStream(DataOutputStream out, Scene
theScene) throws IOException;
  public void readFromStream(DataInputStream in, Scene
theScene) throws IOException;
}
```

artofillusion.procedural.CellsModule

This module generates a cellular pattern.

```
public class CellsModule extends Module{
  public CellsModule(Point position);
  public int getMetric();
  public void setMetric(int m);
  public void init(PointInfo p);
  public double getAverageValue(int which, double blur);
  public double getValueError(int which, double blur);
  public void getValueGradient(int which, Vec3 grad, double blur);
  public boolean edit(BFrame fr, Scene theScene);
  public Module duplicate();
  public void writeToStream(DataOutputStream out, Scene
theScene) throws IOException;
  public void readFromStream(DataInputStream in, Scene
theScene) throws IOException;
}
```

artofillusion.procedural. CheckerModule

This module generates a checkerboard pattern.

```
public class CheckerModule extends Module{
  public CheckerModule(Point position);
  public void init(PointInfo p);
  public double getAverageValue(int which, double blur);
  public double getValueError(int which, double blur);
  public void getValueGradient(int which, Vec3 grad, double blur);
}
```

artofillusion.procedural.ClipModule

This module confines the output to a range by clipping the input.

```
public class ClipModule extends Module{
  public ClipModule(Point position);
  public double getMinimum();
  public void setMinimum(double m);
  public double getMaximum();
  public void setMaximum(double m);
  public double getAverageValue(int which, double blur);
  public double getValueError(int which, double blur);
  public void getValueGradient(int which, Vec3 grad, double blur);
  public boolean edit(BFrame fr, Scene theScene);
  public Module duplicate();
```

```
    public void writeToStream(DataOutputStream out, Scene
theScene) throws IOException;
    public void readFromStream(DataInputStream in, Scene
theScene) throws IOException;
}
```

artofillusion.procedural.
ColorDarkenModule

This module outputs the darker color.

```
public class ColorDarkenModule extends Module{
    public ColorDarkenModule(Point position);
    public void init(PointInfo p);
    public void getColor(int which, RGBColor c, double blur);
}
```

artofillusion.procedural.
ColorDifferenceModule

This module outputs the difference between two colors.

```
public class ColorDifferenceModule extends Module{
    public ColorDifferenceModule(Point position);
    public void init(PointInfo p);
    public void getColor(int which, RGBColor c, double blur);
}
```

artofillusion.procedural.
ColorLightenModule

This module outputs the lighter color.

```
public class ColorLightenModule extends Module{
    public ColorLightenModule(Point position);
    public void init(PointInfo p);
    public void getColor(int which, RGBColor c, double blur);
}
```

artofillusion.procedural.ColorModule

This module outputs a color.

```
public class ColorModule extends Module{
    public ColorModule(Point position);
    public ColorModule(Point position, RGBColor color);
    public RGBColor getColor();
```

```
    public void setColor(RGBColor c);
    public boolean edit(BFrame fr, Scene theScene);
    public void getColor(int which, RGBColor c, double blur);
    public void calcSize();
    protected void drawContents(Graphics2D g);
    public Module duplicate();
    public void writeToStream(DataOutputStream out, Scene
theScene) throws IOException;
    public void readFromStream(DataInputStream in, Scene
theScene) throws IOException;
    }
```

artofillusion.procedural.
ColorProductModule

This module outputs the product of two colors.

```
public class ColorProductModule extends Module{
    public ColorProductModule(Point position);
    public void init(PointInfo p);
    public void getColor(int which, RGBColor c, double blur);
    }
```

procedural

artofillusion.procedural.
ColorScaleModule

This module outputs the product of a color and a number.

```
public class ColorScaleModule extends Module{
    public ColorScaleModule(Point position);
    public void init(PointInfo p);
    public void getColor(int which, RGBColor c, double blur);
    }
```

artofillusion.procedural.
ColorSumModule

This module outputs the sum of two colors.

```
public class ColorSumModule extends Module{
    public ColorSumModule(Point position);
    public void init(PointInfo p);
    public void getColor(int which, RGBColor c, double blur);
    }
```

artofillusion.procedural. CommentModule

This module provides a means to display a comment in the procedural window, but otherwise has no effect.

```
public class CommentModule extends Module{
    public CommentModule(Point position);
    public CommentModule(Point position, String text) ;
    public boolean edit(BFrame fr, Scene theScene);
    public Module duplicate();
    public void writeToStream(DataOutputStream out, Scene
theScene) throws IOException;
    public void readFromStream(DataInputStream in, Scene
theScene) throws IOException;
    public void calcSize();
    protected void drawContents(Graphics2D g);
}
```

artofillusion.procedural. CompareModule

This module compares two numbers and outputs either 0 or 1.

```
public class CompareModule extends Module{
    public CompareModule(Point position);
    public void init(PointInfo p);
    public double getAverageValue(int which, double blur);
    public double getValueError(int which, double blur);
    public void getValueGradient(int which, Vec3 grad, double blur);
}
```

artofillusion.procedural. CoordinateModule

This module outputs one of the four coordinates (x, y, z, or t). The class constants are used to specify which of the coordinates is intended.

```
public class CoordinateModule extends Module{
    public static final int X;
    public static final int Y;
    public static final int Z;
    public static final int T;
    public static final String COORD_NAME[];
```

```
   public CoordinateModule(Point position);
   public CoordinateModule(Point position, int coordinate);
   public void setCoordinate(int coordinate);
   public void init(PointInfo p);
   public double getAverageValue(int which, double blur);
   public double getValueError(int which, double blur);
   public void getValueGradient(int which, Vec3 grad, double blur);
   public Module duplicate();
   public void writeToStream(DataOutputStream out, Scene
theScene) throws IOException;
   public void readFromStream(DataInputStream in, Scene
theScene) throws IOException;
}
```

artofillusion.procedural. CosineModule

This module outputs the cosine of a number.

```
public class CosineModule extends Module{
   public CosineModule(Point position);
   public void init(PointInfo p);
   public double getAverageValue(int which, double blur);
   public double getValueError(int which, double blur);
   public void getValueGradient(int which, Vec3 grad, double blur);
}
```

artofillusion.procedural. DifferenceModule

This module outputs the difference between two numbers.

```
public class DifferenceModule extends Module{
   public DifferenceModule(Point position);
   public double getAverageValue(int which, double blur);
   public double getValueError(int which, double blur);
   public void getValueGradient(int which, Vec3 grad, double blur);
}
```

artofillusion.procedural.ExpModule

This module returns the exponential of a number.

```
public class ExpModule extends Module{
   public ExpModule(Point position);
   public void init(PointInfo p);
   public double getAverageValue(int which, double blur);
   public double getValueError(int which, double blur);
```

```
  public void getValueGradient(int which, Vec3 grad, double blur);
}
```

artofillusion.procedural.ExprModule

This module outputs an expression applied to three numbers.

```
public class ExprModule extends Module {
  public ExprModule(Point position);
  public final void init(PointInfo p);
  public final double getValueError (int which, double blur);
  public void setInput(IOPort which, IOPort port);
  public boolean edit(BFrame fr, Scene theScene);
  public Module duplicate();
  public void writeToStream(DataOutputStream out, Scene
theScene) throws IOException;
  public void setExpr (String e);
  public void readFromStream(DataInputStream in, Scene
theScene) throws IOException;
  public final boolean isCompiled ();
}
```

artofillusion.procedural.
FunctionModule

This is a Module which outputs a user defined function of its input, $y = f(x)$. It is defined by a set of points (x,y). For other values of x, the output is determined by interpolation.

```
public class FunctionModule extends Module{
  public static final short LINEAR;
  public static final short SMOOTH_INTERPOLATE;

  public FunctionModule(Point position);
  public double [] getX();
  public double [] getY();
  public void setFunction(double x[], double y[]);
  public boolean getRepeat();
  public void setRepeat(boolean repeat);
  public short getMethod();
  public void setMethod(short method);
  public void init(PointInfo p);
  public double getAverageValue(int which, double blur);
  public double getValueError(int which, double blur);
  public void getValueGradient(int which, Vec3 grad, double blur);
  public void calcSize();
  protected void drawContents(Graphics2D g);
  public Module duplicate();
```

```
public void writeToStream(DataOutputStream out, Scene
theScene) throws IOException;
   public void readFromStream(DataInputStream in, Scene
theScene) throws IOException;
   public boolean edit(BFrame fr, Scene theScene);
}
```

artofillusion.procedural.GainModule

This module calculates Perlin's gain function.

```
public class GainModule extends Module{
   public GainModule(Point position);
   public void init(PointInfo p);
   public double getAverageValue(int which, double blur);
   public double getValueError(int which, double blur);
   public void getValueGradient(int which, Vec3 grad, double blur);
}
```

artofillusion.procedural.GridModule

This module generates a grid of dots.

```
public class GridModule extends Module{
   public GridModule(Point position);
   public double getXSpacing();
   public void setXSpacing(double space);
   public double getYSpacing();
   public void setYSpacing(double space);
   public double getZSpacing();
   public void setZSpacing(double space);
   public void init(PointInfo p);
   public double getAverageValue(int which, double blur);
   public double getValueError(int which, double blur);
   public void getValueGradient(int which, Vec3 grad, double blur);
   public boolean edit(BFrame fr, Scene theScene);
   public Module duplicate();
   public void writeToStream(DataOutputStream out, Scene
theScene) throws IOException;
   public void readFromStream(DataInputStream in, Scene
theScene) throws IOException;
}
```

artofillusion.procedural.HLSModule

This module takes three numbers as inputs and uses them to define Hue, Lightness, and Saturation for the color output.

```
public class HLSModule extends Module{
   public HLSModule(Point position);
```

```
public void init(PointInfo p);
public void getColor(int which, RGBColor c, double blur);
}
```

artofillusion.procedural.HSVModule

This module takes three numbers as inputs and uses them to define a color based on Hue, Saturation, and Value.

```
public class HSVModule extends Module{
    public HSVModule(Point position);
    public void init(PointInfo p);
    public void getColor(int which, RGBColor c, double blur);
}
```

artofillusion.procedural.ImageModule

This module outputs an image from an Image-Map.

```
public class ImageModule extends Module{
    public static final int RGB_MODEL;
    public static final int HSV_MODEL;
    public static final int HLS_MODEL;

    public ImageModule(Point position);
    public ImageMap getMap();
    public void setMap(ImageMap map);
    public double getXScale();
    public void setXScale(double scale);
    public double getYScale();
    public void setYScale(double scale);
    public boolean getTileX();
    public void setTileX(boolean b);
    public boolean getTileY();
    public void setTileY(boolean b);
    public boolean getMirrorX();
    public void setMirrorX(boolean b);
    public boolean getMirrorY();
    public void setMirrorY(boolean b);
    public int getColorModel();
    public void setColorModel(int model);
    public void init(PointInfo p);
    public void getColor(int which, RGBColor c, double blur);
    public double getAverageValue(int which, double blur);
    public void getValueGradient(int which, Vec3 grad, double blur);
    public void calcSize();
    protected void drawContents(Graphics2D g);
    public Module duplicate();
    public boolean edit(final BFrame fr, final Scene theScene);
```

```
    public void writeToStream(DataOutputStream out, Scene
theScene) throws IOException;
    public void readFromStream(DataInputStream in, Scene
theScene) throws IOException;
    }
```

artofillusion.procedural.InfoBox

This class displays helpful information about the
module ports when the user clicks them.

```
public class InfoBox{
    public InfoBox();
    public void setText(String text[]);
    public void setPosition(int x, int y);
    public Rectangle getBounds();
    public void draw(Graphics g);
    }
```

artofillusion.procedural.InterpModule

This module interpolates between two numbers.

```
public class InterpModule extends Module{
    public InterpModule(Point position);
    public void init(PointInfo p);
    public double getAverageValue(int which, double blur);
    public double getValueError(int which, double blur);
    public void getValueGradient(int which, Vec3 grad, double blur);
    }
```

artofillusion.procedural.IOPort

This class provides the graphical repretation of a
module port for the user interface.

```
public class IOPort{
    public static final int INPUT;
    public static final int OUTPUT;
    public static final int NUMBER;
    public static final int COLOR;
    public static final int TOP;
    public static final int BOTTOM;
    public static final int LEFT;
    public static final int RIGHT;
    public static final int SIZE;

    public IOPort(int valueType, int type, int location, String descrip-
tion[]);
    public Point getPosition();
    public void setPosition(int x, int y);
```

```
    public int getValueType();
    public int getType();
    public int getLocation();
    public Module getModule();
    public void setModule(Module mod);
    public int getIndex();
    public boolean contains(Point p);
    public String [] getDescription();
    public void setDescription(String desc[]);
    public void draw(Graphics g);
}
```

artofillusion.procedural.JitterModule

This module randomizes the input by displacing the coordinate system randomly.

```
public class JitterModule extends Module{
    public JitterModule(Point position);
    public double getXScale();
    public void setXScale(double scale);
    public double getYScale();
    public void setYScale(double scale);
    public double getZScale();
    public void setZScale(double scale);
    public double getXAmplitude();
    public void setXAmplitude(double amp);
    public double getYAmplitude();
    public void setYAmplitude(double amp);
    public double getZAmplitude();
    public void setZAmplitude(double amp);
    public void init(PointInfo p);
    public double getAverageValue(int which, double blur);
    public double getValueError(int which, double blur);
    public void getValueGradient(int which, Vec3 grad, double blur);
    public boolean edit(BFrame fr, Scene theScene);
    public Module duplicate();
    public void writeToStream(DataOutputStream out, Scene
theScene) throws IOException;
    public void readFromStream(DataInputStream in, Scene
theScene) throws IOException;
}
```

artofillusion.procedural.Link

This class defines the link between two ports.

```
public class Link{
    public IOPort from, to;

    public Link(IOPort from, IOPort to);
    public int getFromPortIndex();
```

```
    public int getToPortIndex();
}
```

artofillusion.procedural.LogModule

This module outputs the natural log of a number.

```
public class LogModule extends Module{
  public LogModule(Point position);
  public void init(PointInfo p);
  public double getAverageValue(int which, double blur);
  public double getValueError(int which, double blur);
  public void getValueGradient(int which, Vec3 grad, double blur);
}
```

artofillusion.procedural.MarbleModule

This module produces a marble pattern.

```
public class MarbleModule extends Module{
  public MarbleModule(Point position);
  public int getOctaves();
  public void setOctaves(int o);
  public double getAmplitude();
  public void setAmplitude(double a);
  public double getSpacing();
  public void setSpacing(double s);
  public void init(PointInfo p);
  public double getAverageValue(int which, double blur);
  public double getValueError(int which, double blur);
  public void getValueGradient(int which, Vec3 grad, double blur);
  public boolean edit(BFrame fr, Scene theScene);
  public Module duplicate();
  public void writeToStream(DataOutputStream out, Scene
theScene) throws IOException;
  public void readFromStream(DataInputStream in, Scene
theScene) throws IOException;
}
```

artofillusion.procedural.MaxModule

This module returns the maximum of two numbers.

```
public class MaxModule extends Module{
  public MaxModule(Point position);
  public void init(PointInfo p);
  public double getAverageValue(int which, double blur);
  public double getValueError(int which, double blur);
  public void getValueGradient(int which, Vec3 grad, double blur);
}
```

artofillusion.procedural.MinModule

This module returns the minimum of two numbers.

```
public class MinModule extends Module{
  public MinModule(Point position);
  public void init(PointInfo p);
  public double getAverageValue(int which, double blur);
  public double getValueError(int which, double blur);
  public void getValueGradient(int which, Vec3 grad, double blur);
}
```

artofillusion.procedural.ModModule

This module returns the modulo of a number.

```
public class ModModule extends Module{
  public ModModule(Point position);
  public void init(PointInfo p);
  public double getAverageValue(int which, double blur);
  public double getValueError(int which, double blur);
  public void getValueGradient(int which, Vec3 grad, double blur);
}
```

artofillusion.procedural.Module

This is the abstract parent of all modules that can be used in a procedure.

```
public class Module{
  protected IOPort input[], output[];
  public Module linkFrom[];
  public int linkFromIndex[];
  protected String name;
  protected Rectangle bounds;
  protected boolean checked;

  protected static final Font defaultFont;
  protected static final Stroke contourStroke;
  protected final Color selectedColor;
  protected static final FontMetrics defaultMetrics;

  public Module(String name, IOPort input[], IOPort output[], Point
  position);
  public String getName();
  public Rectangle getBounds();
  public void setPosition(int x, int y);
  public IOPort [] getInputPorts();
  public IOPort [] getOutputPorts();
```

```
    public int getInputIndex(IOPort port);
    public int getOutputIndex(IOPort port);
    public boolean inputConnected(int which);
    public IOPort getClickedPort(Point pos);
    public void setInput(IOPort which, IOPort port);
    public void calcSize();
    public void layout();
    public void draw(Graphics2D g, boolean selected);
    protected void drawContents(Graphics2D g);
    public boolean checkFeedback();
    public boolean edit(BFrame fr, Scene theScene);
    public void init(PointInfo p);
    public double getAverageValue(int which, double blur);
    public double getValueError(int which, double blur);
    public void getValueGradient(int which, Vec3 grad, double blur);
    public void getColor(int which, RGBColor color, double blur);
    public Module duplicate();
    public void writeToStream(DataOutputStream out, Scene
theScene) throws IOException;
    public void readFromStream(DataInputStream out, Scene
theScene) throws IOException;
    }
```

artofillusion.procedural.NoiseModule

This module generates fractal noise using Perlin's noise function.

```
public class NoiseModule extends Module{
    public NoiseModule(Point position);
    public int getOctaves();
    public void setOctaves(int o);
    public double getAmplitude();
    public void setAmplitude(double a);
    public void init(PointInfo p);
    public double getAverageValue(int which, double blur);
    public double getValueError(int which, double blur);
    public void getValueGradient(int which, Vec3 grad, double blur);
    public boolean edit(BFrame fr, Scene theScene);
    public Module duplicate();
    public void writeToStream(DataOutputStream out, Scene
theScene) throws IOException;
    public void readFromStream(DataInputStream in, Scene
theScene) throws IOException;
    }
```

artofillusion.procedural.
NumberModule

This module outputs a number.

```
public class NumberModule extends Module{
  public NumberModule(Point position);
  public NumberModule(Point position, double v);
  public double getValue();
  public void setValue(double v);
  public boolean edit(BFrame fr, Scene theScene);
  public double getAverageValue(int which, double blur);
  public void getValueGradient(Vec3 grad, double blur);
  public Module duplicate();
  public void writeToStream(DataOutputStream out, Scene
theScene) throws IOException;
  public void readFromStream(DataInputStream in, Scene
theScene) throws IOException;
}
```

artofillusion.procedural.OutputModule

This module represents one of the output values of a procedure.

```
public class OutputModule extends Module{
  public OutputModule(String name, String defaultLabel, double
defaultValue, RGBColor defaultColor, int type);
  public void setWidth(int w);
  public void calcSize();
  public double getAverageValue(int which, double blur);
  public void getValueGradient(int which, Vec3 grad, double blur);
  public void getColor(int which, RGBColor color, double blur);
}
```

artofillusion.procedural. ParameterModule

This module outputs a per-vertex texture parameter.

```
public class ParameterModule extends Module{
  public ParameterModule(Point position);
  public String getParameterName();
  public void setParameterName(String name);
  public double getMinimum();
  public void setMinimum(double val);
  public double getMaximum();
  public void setMaximum(double val);
  public double getDefaultValue();
  public void setDefaultValue(double val);
  public void init(PointInfo p);
  public double getAverageValue(int which, double blur);
  public void setIndex(int index);
  public TextureParameter getParameter(Object owner);
  public boolean edit(BFrame fr, Scene theScene);
```

```
  public Module duplicate();
  public void writeToStream(DataOutputStream out, Scene
theScene) throws IOException;
  public void readFromStream(DataInputStream in, Scene
theScene) throws IOException;
}
```

artofillusion.procedural.PointInfo

This class stores information about a point.

```
public class PointInfo{
  public double x, y, z, xsize, ysize, zsize, viewangle, t, param[];

  public PointInfo();
}
```

artofillusion.procedural.PolarModule

This module converts from rectangular to polar coordinates.

```
public class PolarModule extends Module{
  public PolarModule(Point position);
  public void init(PointInfo p);
  public double getAverageValue(int which, double blur);
  public double getValueError(int which, double blur);
  public void getValueGradient(int which, Vec3 grad, double blur);
}
```

artofillusion.procedural.PowerModule

This module raises a number by a power.

```
public class PowerModule extends Module{
  public PowerModule(Point position);
  public void init(PointInfo p);
  public double getAverageValue(int which, double blur);
  public double getValueError(int which, double blur);
  public void getValueGradient(int which, Vec3 grad, double blur);
}
```

artofillusion.procedural.Procedure

This class is the foundation class for a procedure, on which the modules are added. The procedure is formed by modules with defined links and connected to outputs.

```
public class Procedure{
  public Procedure(OutputModule output[]);
  public OutputModule [] getOutputModules();
  public Module [] getModules();
  public int getModuleIndex(Module mod);
  public int getOutputIndex(Module mod);
  public void addModule(Module mod);
  public void deleteModule(int which);
  public Link [] getLinks();
  public void addLink(Link ln);
  public void deleteLink(int which);
  public boolean checkFeedback();
  public void initForPoint(PointInfo p);
  public double getOutputValue(int which);
  public void getOutputGradient(int which, Vec3 grad);
  public void getOutputColor(int which, RGBColor color);
  public void copy(Procedure proc);
  public void writeToStream(DataOutputStream out, Scene
theScene) throws IOException;
  public void readFromStream(DataInputStream in, Scene
theScene) throws IOException, InvalidObjectException;
}
```

artofillusion.procedural. ProcedureEditor

This class is the component for editing a procedure.

```
public class ProcedureEditor extends CustomWidget{
  public ProcedureEditor(Procedure proc, ProcedureOwner owner,
Scene scene);
  public BFrame getParentFrame();
  public Scene getScene();
  public void setEditingWindow(EditingWindow window);
  public EditingWindow getEditingWindow();
  public Dimension getPreferredSize();
  public void saveState(boolean redo);
  public void updatePreview();
  public boolean isFocusTraversable();
  public Rectangle getRectangle(Point p1, Point p2);
}
```

artofillusion.procedure. ProcedureOwner

This is the interface for classes that own a procedure.

```
public interface ProcedureOwner{
  public String getWindowTitle();
  public Object getPreview(ProcedureEditor editor);
  public void updatePreview(Object preview);
  public void disposePreview(Object preview);
  public boolean allowParameters();
  public boolean allowViewAngle();
  public boolean canEditName();
  public String getName();
  public void setName(String name);
  public void acceptEdits(ProcedureEditor editor);
  public void editProperties(ProcedureEditor editor);
}
```

artofillusion.procedure. ProductModule

This module outputs the product of two numbers.

```
public class ProductModule extends Module{
  public ProductModule(Point position);
  public void init(PointInfo p);
  public double getAverageValue(int which, double blur);
  public double getValueError(int which, double blur);
  public void getValueGradient(int which, Vec3 grad, double blur);
}
```

artofillusion.procedure. RandomModule

This module outputs a random function of its input.

```
public class RandomModule extends Module{
  public RandomModule(Point position);
  public int getOctaves();
  public void setOctaves(int o);
  public double getAmplitude();
  public void setAmplitude(double a);
  public void init(PointInfo p);
  public double getAverageValue(int which, double blur);
  public double getValueError(int which, double blur);
  public void getValueGradient(int which, Vec3 grad, double blur);
  public Module duplicate();
  public void writeToStream(DataOutputStream out, Scene
theScene) throws IOException;
  public void readFromStream(DataInputStream in, Scene
theScene) throws IOException;
  public boolean edit(BFrame fr, Scene theScene);
}
```

artofillusion.procedure.RatioModule

This module outputs the ratio of two numbers.

```
public class RatioModule extends Module{
    public RatioModule(Point position);
    public void init(PointInfo p);
    public double getAverageValue(int which, double blur);
    public double getValueError(int which, double blur);
    public void getValueGradient(int which, Vec3 grad, double blur);
}
```

artofillusion.procedure.RGBModule

This module constructs a color from three values that specify Red, Green, and Blue.

```
public class RGBModule extends Module{
    public RGBModule(Point position);
    public void init(PointInfo p);
    public void getColor(int which, RGBColor c, double blur);
}
```

artofillusion.procedure. ScaleShiftModule

This module scales and shifts the input.

```
public class ScaleShiftModule extends Module{
    public ScaleShiftModule(Point position);
    public double getScale();
    public void setScale(double val);
    public double getShift();
    public void setShift(double val);
    public double getAverageValue(int which, double blur);
    public double getValueError(int which, double blur);
    public void getValueGradient(int which, Vec3 grad, double blur);
    public boolean edit(BFrame fr, Scene theScene);
    public Module duplicate();
    public void writeToStream(DataOutputStream out, Scene
theScene) throws IOException;
    public void readFromStream(DataInputStream in, Scene
theScene) throws IOException;
}
```

artofillusion.procedure.SineModule

This module outputs the sine of the input.

```
public class SineModule extends Module{
```

```
public SineModule(Point position);
public void init(PointInfo p);
public double getAverageValue(int which, double blur);
public double getValueError(int which, double blur);
public void getValueGradient(int which, Vec3 grad, double blur);
}
```

artofillusion.procedure. SpectrumModule

This module maps numbers to colors.

```
public class SpectrumModule extends Module{
  public SpectrumModule(Point position);
  public RGBColor [] getColors();
  public double [] getColorPositions();
  public void setColors(RGBColor color[], double position[]);
  public boolean getRepeat();
  public void setRepeat(boolean repeat);
  public void init(PointInfo p);
  public Module duplicate();
  public void writeToStream(DataOutputStream out, Scene
theScene) throws IOException;
  public void readFromStream(DataInputStream in, Scene
theScene) throws IOException;
  public void calcSize();
  protected void drawContents(Graphics2D g);
  public boolean edit(BFrame fr, Scene theScene);
}
```

artofillusion.procedure. SphericalModule

This converts from rectangular to spherical coordinates.

```
public class SphericalModule extends Module{
  public SphericalModule(Point position);
  public void init(PointInfo p);
  public double getAverageValue(int which, double blur);
  public double getValueError(int which, double blur);
  public void getValueGradient(int which, Vec3 grad, double blur);
}
```

artofillusion.procedure.SqrtModule

This module outputs the square root of the input.

```
public class SqrtModule extends Module{
  public SqrtModule(Point position);
```

```
    public void init(PointInfo p);
    public double getAverageValue(int which, double blur);
    public double getValueError(int which, double blur);
    public void getValueGradient(int which, Vec3 grad, double blur);
}
```

artofillusion.procedure.SumModule

This module sums two numbers.

```
public class SumModule extends Module{
    public SumModule(Point position);
    public double getAverageValue(int which, double blur);
    public double getValueError(int which, double blur);
    public void getValueGradient(int which, Vec3 grad, double blur);
}
```

artofillusion.procedure. TransformModule

This module performs a linear 3D coordinate transform.

```
public class TransformModule extends Module{
    public TransformModule(Point position);
    public CoordinateSystem getCoordinates();
    public void setCoordinates(CoordinateSystem coords);
    public double getXScale();
    public void setXScale(double scale);
    public double getYScale();
    public void setYScale(double scale);
    public double getZScale();
    public void setZScale(double scale);
    public void init(PointInfo p);
    public double getAverageValue(int which, double blur);
    public double getValueError(int which, double blur);
    public void getValueGradient(int which, Vec3 grad, double blur);
    public boolean edit(BFrame fr, Scene theScene);
    public Module duplicate();
    public void writeToStream(DataOutputStream out, Scene
theScene) throws IOException;
    public void readFromStream(DataInputStream in, Scene
theScene) throws IOException;
}
```

artofillusion.procedure. TurbulenceModule

This module generates fractal turbulence based on Perlin's algorithm.

```
public class TurbulenceModule extends Module{
  public TurbulenceModule(Point position);
  public int getOctaves();
  public void setOctaves(int o);
  public double getAmplitude();
  public void setAmplitude(double a);
  public void init(PointInfo p);
  public double getAverageValue(int which, double blur);
  public double getValueError(int which, double blur);
  public void getValueGradient(int which, Vec3 grad, double blur);
  public boolean edit(BFrame fr, Scene theScene);
  public Module duplicate();
  public void writeToStream(DataOutputStream out, Scene
theScene) throws IOException;
  public void readFromStream(DataInputStream in, Scene
theScene) throws IOException;
}
```

artofillusion.procedure. ViewAngleModule

This module outputs the viewing angle.

```
public class ViewAngleModule extends Module{
  public ViewAngleModule(Point position);
  public void init(PointInfo p);
  public double getAverageValue(int which, double blur);
  public double getValueError(int which, double blur);
  public void getValueGradient(int which, Vec3 grad, double blur);
  public Module duplicate();
  public boolean edit(BFrame fr, Scene theScene);
  public void writeToStream(DataOutputStream out, Scene
theScene) throws IOException;
  public void readFromStream(DataInputStream in, Scene
theScene) throws IOException;
}
```

artofillusion.procedure.WoodModule

This module generates a wood pattern.

```
public class WoodModule extends Module{
  public WoodModule(Point position);
  public int getOctaves();
  public void setOctaves(int o);
  public double getAmplitude();
  public void setAmplitude(double a);
  public double getSpacing();
  public void setSpacing(double s);
  public void init(PointInfo p);
```

```
public double getAverageValue(int which, double blur);
public double getValueError(int which, double blur);
public void getValueGradient(int which, Vec3 grad, double blur);
public boolean edit(BFrame fr, Scene theScene);
public Module duplicate();
public void writeToStream(DataOutputStream out, Scene
theScene) throws IOException;
  public void readFromStream(DataInputStream in, Scene
theScene) throws IOException;
}
```

Chapter 21

The artofillusion.script Package

The script package contains the classes that provide the mechanism for Art of Illusion to create and run scripts.

artofillusion.script. BeanshellScriptEngine

This class implements the BeanShell scripting language.

```
public class BeanshellScriptEngine implements ScriptEngine
{
  public BeanshellScriptEngine(ClassLoader parent);
  public String getName();
  public String getFilenameExtension();
  public void setOutput(PrintStream out);
  public void addImport(String packageOrClass) throws Exception;
  public void executeScript(String script, Map<String, Object> variables) throws ScriptException;
  public ToolScript createToolScript(String script) throws ScriptException;
  public ObjectScript createObjectScript(String script) throws ScriptException;
}
```

artofillusion.script. ExecuteScriptWindow

This is the user interface window in which the user can run scripts.

```
public class ExecuteScriptWindow extends BFrame{
  public ExecuteScriptWindow(LayoutWindow win);
}
```

artofillusion.script. GroovyScriptEngine

This class implements the Groovy scripting language.

```
public class GroovyScriptEngine implements ScriptEngine
{
  public GroovyScriptEngine(ClassLoader parent);
  public String getName();
  public String getFilenameExtension();
  public void setOutput(PrintStream out);
  public void addImport(String packageOrClass) throws Exception;
  public void executeScript(String script, Map<String, Object> variables) throws ScriptException;
  public ToolScript createToolScript(String script) throws ScriptException;
  public ObjectScript createObjectScript(String script) throws ScriptException;
}
```

artofillusion.script.ObjectScript

This is the interface for a parsed object script.

```
public interface ObjectScript{
  public void execute(ScriptedObjectController script) throws ScriptException;
}
```

artofillusion.script.ScriptEditor

This is the text area where the user may edit a script.

```
public class ScriptEditor extends BTextArea{
  public ScriptEditor(String text);
  public WidgetContainer createContainer();
}
```

artofillusion.script.ScriptedObject

This class represents an object that is controlled by a script.

```
public class ScriptedObject extends ObjectCollection{
  public ScriptedObject(String scriptText);
  public ScriptedObject(String scriptText);
  public String getScript();
  public void setScript(String scriptText);
  public String getLanguage();
  public void setLanguage(String language);
  public ObjectScript getObjectScript() throws EvalError;
  public final int getNumParameters();
  public final String getParameterName(int i);
  public final double getParameterValue(int i);
  public void setParameterName(int i, String name);
  public void setParameterValue(int i, double value);
  public void setParameters(String names[], double values[]);
  protected Enumeration<ObjectInfo> enumerateObjects
(ObjectInfo info, boolean interactive, Scene scene);
  public Object3D duplicate();
  public void copyObject(Object3D obj);
  public void setSize(double xsize, double ysize, double zsize);
  public Property[] getProperties();
  public Object getPropertyValue(int index);
  public void setPropertyValue(int index, Object value);
  public Keyframe getPoseKeyframe();
  public void applyPoseKeyframe(Keyframe k);
  public String [] getPoseValueNames();
  public double [] getDefaultPoseValues();
  public void configurePoseTrack(PoseTrack track);
  public void editKeyframe(EditingWindow parent, Keyframe k,
ObjectInfo info);
  public boolean isEditable();
  public void edit(EditingWindow parent, ObjectInfo info, Runnable
cb);
  public ScriptedObject(DataInputStream in, Scene theScene)
throws IOException, InvalidObjectException;
  public void writeToFile(DataOutputStream out, Scene theScene)
throws IOException;
  public static class ScriptedObjectKeyframe implements Keyframe
{
    public Hashtable<String, Double> valueTable;

    public ScriptedObjectKeyframe(ScriptedObject object, String
names[], double values[]);
    public Keyframe duplicate();
    public Keyframe duplicate(Object owner);
    public double [] getGraphValues();
    public void setGraphValues(double values[]);
    public Keyframe blend(Keyframe o2, double weight1, double
weight2);
```

```
    public Keyframe blend(Keyframe o2, Keyframe o3, double
weight1, double weight2, double weight3);
    public Keyframe blend(Keyframe o2, Keyframe o3, Keyframe
o4, double weight1, double weight2, double weight3, double
weight4);
    public boolean equals(Keyframe k);
    public void writeToStream(DataOutputStream out) throws
IOException;
    public ScriptedObjectKeyframe(DataInputStream in,
Object parent) throws IOException;
    }
}
```

artofillusion.script. ScriptedObjectController

This class mediates interactions between an ObjectScript and the rest of the program.

```
public class ScriptedObjectController{
  ScriptedObjectController(ObjectInfo obj,
ScriptedObjectEnumeration objectEnum, boolean interactive,
Scene sc);
  public final CoordinateSystem getCoordinates();
  public final double getTime();
  public final Scene getScene();
  public final boolean isPreview();
  public final double getParameter(String name) throws
IllegalArgumentException;
  public final void addObject(ObjectInfo info);
  public final void addObject(Object3D obj, CoordinateSystem
coords);
}
```

artofillusion.script. ScriptedObjectEditorWindow

This is the window to edit scripted objects.

```
public class ScriptedObjectEditorWindow extends BFrame{
  public ScriptedObjectEditorWindow(EditingWindow parent,
ObjectInfo obj, Runnable onClose);
}
```

artofillusion.script. ScriptedObjectEnumeration

This class enumerates the objects defined by a ScriptedObject.

```
public class ScriptedObjectEnumeration implements Enumeration{
  ScriptedObjectEnumeration(ObjectInfo obj, boolean interactive,
Scene sc);
  public synchronized void addObject(ObjectInfo info);
  public synchronized void executionComplete();
  public synchronized boolean hasMoreElements();
  public synchronized ObjectInfo nextElement();
}
```

artofillusion.script.ScriptEngine

This interface represents an engine that can compile and execute scripts. There are no public or protected members, package visibility only.

```
public interface ScriptEngine{}
```

artofillusion.script.ScriptException

This class is the exception thrown by the ScriptEngine interface.

```
public class ScriptException extends Exception{
  public ScriptException(String message, int lineNumber);
  public ScriptException(String message, int lineNumber, Throwable cause);
  public int getLineNumber();
}
```

artofillusion.script. ScriptOutputWindow

This is the window for displaying output from scripts.

```
public class ScriptOutputWindow extends OutputStream{
  public void write(final int b);
  public void write(byte b[], final int off, final int len);
}
```

artofillusion.script.ScriptRunner

This class executes the scripts. Only BeanShell and Groovy are supported at this time. Outside of the need of it in the internal workings of Art of Illusion the most helpful functions in this class are getLanguageForFilename() and getFilenameExtension(). These functions return the language name for a given file and return the default extension for a language, respectively.

```
public class ScriptRunner{
  public static final String LANGUAGES[] = {"Groovy",
"BeanShell"};
  public static ScriptEngine getScriptEngine(String language);
  public static void executeScript(String language, String script,
Map<String, Object> variables);
  public static ToolScript parseToolScript(String language, String
script) throws Exception;
  public static ObjectScript parseObjectScript(String language,
String script) throws Exception;
  public static int displayError(String language, Exception ex);
  public static String getLanguageForFilename(String filename);
  public static String getFilenameExtension(String language);
}
```

artofillusion.script.ToolScript

This is the interface for a parsed Tool Script.

```
public interface ToolScript{
  public void execute(LayoutWindow window) throws ScriptException;
}
```

Chapter 22

The artofillusion.texture Package

The texture package includes the classes that are used to texture objects. Textures define the appearance of the surface of objects. Textures do not define the interior properties of objects. Those are defined by the classes in the material package.

artofillusion.texture. ConstantParameterValue

This class defines a scalar parameter which is constant over the surface of a mesh.

```
public class ConstantParameterValue implements
ParameterValue{
  public ConstantParameterValue(double val);
  public double getValue();
  public void setValue(double val);
  public double getValue(int tri, int v1, int v2, int v3, double u,
double v, double w);
  public double getAverageValue();
  public ParameterValue duplicate();
  public boolean equals(Object o);
  public void writeToStream(DataOutputStream out) throws
IOException;
  public ConstantParameterValue(DataInputStream in) throws
IOException;
}
```

artofillusion.texture. CylindricalMapping

This class maps a texture to a cylinder.

```
public class CylindricalMapping extends NonlinearMapping2D{
    public CylindricalMapping(Object3D obj, Texture theTexture);
    public static String getName();
    public Vec2 getScale();
    public void setScale(Vec2 scale);
    public Vec3 getRotations();
    public void setRotations(Vec3 angles);
    public double getOffset();
    public void setOffset(double dist);
    public RenderingTriangle mapTriangle(int v1, int v2, int v3, int n1,
    int n2, int n3, Vec3 vert[]);
    public void setParameters(RenderingTriangle tri, double p1[],
    double p2[], double p3[], RenderingMesh mesh);
    public void getTextureSpec(Vec3 pos, TextureSpec spec, double
    angle, double size, double t, double param[]);
    public void getTransparency(Vec3 pos, RGBColor trans, double
    angle, double size, double t, double param[]);
    public double getDisplacement(Vec3 pos, double size, double t,
    double param[]);
    public Mat4 getPreTransform();
    public void getSpecIntermed(TextureSpec spec, double x,
    double y, double z, double size, double angle, double t, double
    param[]);
    public void getTransIntermed(RGBColor trans, double x, double
    y, double z, double size, double angle, double t, double param[]);
    public double getDisplaceIntermed(double x, double y, double z,
    double size, double t, double param[]);
    public Vec2 [] findTextureCoordinates(Mesh mesh);
    public TextureMapping duplicate();
    public TextureMapping duplicate(Object3D obj, Texture tex);
    public void copy(TextureMapping mapping);
    public TextureParameter [] getParameters();
    public Widget getEditingPanel(Object3D obj, MaterialPreviewer
    preview);
    public CylindricalMapping(DataInputStream in, Object3D obj,
    Texture theTexture) throws IOException, InvalidObjectException;
    public void writeToFile(DataOutputStream out) throws
    IOException;
}
```

artofillusion.texture. FaceParameterValue

This class defines a scalar parameter who value is defined on each face of a mesh.

```
public class FaceParameterValue implements ParameterValue{
  public FaceParameterValue(double val[]);
  public FaceParameterValue(FacetedMesh mesh,
TextureParameter param);
  public double [] getValue();
  public void setValue(double val[]);
  public double getValue(int tri, int v1, int v2, int v3, double u,
double v, double w);
  public double getAverageValue();
  public ParameterValue duplicate();
  public boolean equals(Object o);
  public void writeToStream(DataOutputStream out) throws
IOException;
  public FaceParameterValue(DataInputStream in) throws
IOException;
}
```

artofillusion.texture. FaceVertexParameterValue

This class defines a scalar parameter whose value is defined at each vertex of each face of a mesh.

```
public class FaceVertexParameterValue implements
ParameterValue{
  public FaceVertexParameterValue(double val[][]);
  public FaceVertexParameterValue(FacetedMesh mesh,
TextureParameter param);
  public void setValue(double val[][]);
  public double getValue(int faceIndex, int vertIndex);
  public void setValue(int faceIndex, int vertIndex, double
newValue);
  public double getValue(int faceIndex, int v1, int v2, int v3, double
u, double v, double w);
  public int getFaceCount();
  public int getFaceVertexCount(int faceIndex);
  public double getAverageValue();
  public ParameterValue duplicate();
  public boolean equals(Object o);
  public void writeToStream(DataOutputStream out) throws
IOException;
  public FaceVertexParameterValue(DataInputStream in) throws
IOException;
}
```

artofillusion.texture.ImageMapTexture

ImageMapTexture represents a texture whose properties are defined by images.

```
public class ImageMapTexture extends Texture2D{
    public ImageOrColor diffuseColor, specularColor,
transparentColor, emissiveColor;
    public ImageOrValue roughness, cloudiness, transparency,
specularity, shininess, bump, displacement;
    public boolean tileX, tileY, mirrorX, mirrorY;

    public ImageMapTexture();
    public static String getTypeName();
    public void getTextureSpec(TextureSpec spec, double x, double
y, double xsize, double ysize, double angle, double t, double
param[]);
    public void getTransparency(RGBColor trans, double x, double y,
double xsize, double ysize, double angle, double t, double param
[]);
    public double getDisplacement(double x, double y, double xsize,
double ysize, double t, double param[]);
    public void getAverageSpec(TextureSpec spec, double time,
double param[]);
    public boolean usesImage(ImageMap image);
    public Texture duplicate();
    public boolean hasComponent(int component);
    public void edit(BFrame fr, Scene sc);
    public ImageMapTexture(DataInputStream in, Scene theScene)
throws IOException, InvalidObjectException;
    public void writeToFile(DataOutputStream out, Scene theScene)
throws IOException;
}
```

artofillusion.texture.LayeredMapping

LayeredMapping is the TextureMapping
corresponding to LayeredTextures. It allows multiple
textures to be layered on top of each other. Most of
the actual work is done by this class, rather than
LayeredTexture.

```
public class LayeredMapping extends TextureMapping{
    public static final int BLEND;
    public static final int OVERLAY_BLEND_BUMPS;
    public static final int OVERLAY_ADD_BUMPS;

    public LayeredMapping(Object3D obj, Texture tex);
    public int getNumLayers();
    public Texture [] getLayers();
    public Texture getLayer(int which);
    public void setLayer(int which, Texture tex);
    public TextureMapping getLayerMapping(int which);
    public void setLayerMapping(int which, TextureMapping map);
    public int getLayerMode(int which);
```

```
    public void setLayerMode(int which, int mode);
    public TextureParameter[] getParameters();
    public TextureParameter [] getLayerParameters(int which);
    public TextureParameter getLayerBlendingParameter(int layer);
    public TextureParameter getParameterForLayer
(TextureParameter parameter, int layer);
    public void addLayer(Texture tex);
    public void addLayer(int index, Texture tex, TextureMapping map,
int mode);
    public void deleteLayer(int which);
    public void moveLayer(int which, int pos);
    public void readFromFile(DataInputStream in, Scene theScene)
throws IOException, InvalidObjectException;
    public void writeToFile(DataOutputStream out, Scene theScene)
throws IOException;
    public void writeToFile(DataOutputStream out) throws
IOException;
    public static String getName();
    public RenderingTriangle mapTriangle(int v1, int v2, int v3, int n1,
int n2, int n3, Vec3 vert[]);
    public void setParameters(RenderingTriangle tri, double p1[],
double p2[], double p3[], RenderingMesh mesh);
    public void getTextureSpec(Vec3 pos, TextureSpec spec, double
angle, double size, double t, double param[]);
    public void getAverageSpec(TextureSpec spec, double time, dou-
ble param[]);
    public void getTransparency(Vec3 pos, RGBColor trans, double
angle, double size, double t, double param[]);
    public double getDisplacement(Vec3 pos, double size, double t,
double param[]);
    public Texture getTexture();
    public Object3D getObject();
    public TextureMapping duplicate();
    public TextureMapping duplicate(Object3D obj, Texture tex);
    public void copy(TextureMapping theMap);
    public Widget getEditingPanel(Object3D obj, MaterialPreviewer
preview);
}
```

artofillusion.texture.LayeredTexture

LayeredTexture represents a texture which is composed of other textures layered on top of each other. This class serves mainly as a placeholder - most of the real work is done by LayeredMapping.

```
public class LayeredTexture extends Texture{
    public LayeredTexture(Object3D obj);
    public LayeredTexture(LayeredMapping map);
    public boolean usesImage(ImageMap image);
    public void getAverageSpec(TextureSpec spec, double time,
double param[]);
```

```
    public TextureMapping getDefaultMapping(Object3D object);
    public void setMapping(LayeredMapping map);
    public Texture duplicate();
    public boolean hasComponent(int component);
    public void edit(BFrame fr, Scene sc);
    public LayeredTexture(DataInputStream in, Scene theScene)
throws IOException, InvalidObjectException;
    public void writeToFile(DataOutputStream out, Scene theScene)
throws IOException;
}
```

artofillusion.texture.LayeredTriangle

LayeredTriangle is a subclass of RenderingTriangle, which represents a triangle whose properties are described by a LayeredMapping.

```
public class LayeredTriangle extends RenderingTriangle{
    public LayeredTriangle(int v1, int v2, int v3, int n1, int n2, int n3,
    double t1x, double t1y, double t1z, double t2x, double t2y, double
    t2z, double t3x, double t3y, double t3z, LayeredMapping
    theMapping, LayeredTexture theTexture, Vec3 vert[]);
    public void getTextureSpec(TextureSpec spec, double angle,
    double u, double v, double w, double size, double time);
    public void getTransparency(RGBColor trans, double angle,
    double u, double v, double w, double size, double time);
    public double getDisplacement(double u, double v, double w,
    double size, double time);
    public void setMesh(RenderingMesh mesh, TextureMapping
    map, int index);
}
```

artofillusion.texture.Linear2DTriangle

Linear2DTriangle is a subclass of RenderingTriangle, which represents a triangle whose properties are defined by a linear mapping of a Texture2D.

```
public class Linear2DTriangle extends RenderingTriangle{
    public Linear2DTriangle(int v1, int v2, int v3, int n1, int n2, int n3,
        double t1x, double t1y, double t2x, double t2y, double t3x,
        double t3y);
    public void setMesh(RenderingMesh mesh, TextureMapping
    map, int index);
    public void getTextureSpec(TextureSpec spec, double angle,
    double u, double v, double w, double size, double time);
    public void getTransparency(RGBColor trans, double angle,
    double u, double v, double w, double size, double time);
    public double getDisplacement(double u, double v, double w,
    double size, double time);
```

}

artofillusion.texture.Linear3DTriangle

Linear3DTriangle is a subclass of RenderingTriangle, which represents a triangle whose properties are defined by a linear mapping of a Texture3D.

```
public class Linear3DTriangle extends RenderingTriangle{
    public Linear3DTriangle(int v1, int v2, int v3, int n1, int n2, int n3,
        double t1x, double t1y, double t1z, double t2x, double t2y,
double t2z,
        double t3x, double t3y, double t3z);
    public void setMesh(RenderingMesh mesh, TextureMapping
map, int index);
    public void getTextureSpec(TextureSpec spec, double angle,
double u, double v, double w, double size, double time);
    public void getTransparency(RGBColor trans, double angle,
double u, double v, double w, double size, double time);
    public double getDisplacement(double u, double v, double w,
double size, double time);
}
```

artofillusion.texture.LinearMapping3D

LinearMapping3D is a Mapping3D which represents a linear mapping (this includes rotations, translations, and scalings) between texture coordinates and world coordinates.

```
public class LinearMapping3D extends Mapping3D{
    protected CoordinateSystem coords;
    protected double ax, bx, cx, dx, ay, by, cy, dy, az, bz, cz, dz;
    protected double xscale, yscale, zscale;
    protected Mat4 fromLocal;
    protected boolean transform, coordsFromParams,
scaleToObject;
    protected int numTextureParams;
    protected TextureParameter xparam, yparam, zparam;

    public LinearMapping3D(Object3D obj, Texture theTexture);
    public static String getName();
    public Vec3 getCenter();
    public void setCenter(Vec3 center);
    public Vec3 getScale();
    public void setScale(Vec3 scale);
    public Vec3 getRotations();
    public void setRotations(Vec3 angles);
    public boolean isBoundToSurface();
    public void setBoundToSurface(boolean bound);
```

```
    public boolean isScaledToObject();
    public void setScaledToObject(boolean scaled);
    public RenderingTriangle mapTriangle(int v1, int v2, int v3, int n1,
int n2, int n3, Vec3 vert[]);
    public void setParameters(RenderingTriangle tri, double p1[],
double p2[], double p3[], RenderingMesh mesh);
    public void getTextureSpec(Vec3 pos, TextureSpec spec, double
angle, double size, double time, double param[]);
    public void getTransparency(Vec3 pos, RGBColor trans, double
angle, double size, double time, double param[]);
    public double getDisplacement(Vec3 pos, double size, double
time, double param[]);
    public TextureMapping duplicate();
    public TextureMapping duplicate(Object3D obj, Texture tex);
    public void copy(TextureMapping mapping);
    public TextureParameter [] getParameters();
    public Widget getEditingPanel(Object3D obj, MaterialPreviewer
preview);
    public LinearMapping3D(DataInputStream in, Object3D obj,
Texture theTexture) throws IOException, InvalidObjectException;
    public void writeToFile(DataOutputStream out) throws
IOException;
}
```

artofillusion.texture.Mapping2D

Mapping2D is an abstract class describing a linear mapping between 2D texture coordinates and 3D space.

```
public abstract class Mapping2D extends TextureMapping{
    public Mapping2D(Object3D theObject, Texture theTexture);
    public Texture getTexture();
    public Object3D getObject();
    public static boolean legalMapping(Object3D obj, Texture tex);
    public abstract Vec2 [] findTextureCoordinates(Mesh mesh);
}
```

artofillusion.texture.Mapping3D

Mapping3D is an abstract class describing a linear mapping between 3D texture coordinates and 3D space.

```
public abstract class Mapping3D extends TextureMapping{
    public Mapping3D(Object3D theObject, Texture theTexture);
    public Texture getTexture();
    public Object3D getObject();
    public static boolean legalMapping(Object3D obj, Texture tex);
}
```

artofillusion.texture.MoveUVViewTool

MoveUVViewTool is an EditingTool used for moving the viewpoint in the UV editing window.

```
public class MoveUVViewTool extends EditingTool{
  public MoveUVViewTool(EditingWindow fr);
  public void activate();
  public int whichClicks();
  public boolean hilightSelection();
  public String getToolTipText();
  public void mousePressed(WidgetMouseEvent e, ViewerCanvas
view);
  public void mouseDragged(WidgetMouseEvent e, ViewerCanvas
view);
  public void mouseReleased(WidgetMouseEvent e, ViewerCanvas
view);
}
```

artofillusion.texture.
Nonlinear2DTriangle

Nonlinear2DTriangle is a subclass of RenderingTriangle, which represents a triangle whose properties are defined by a nonlinear mapping of a Texture2D. It stores a 3D "intermediate texture coordinate" for each vertex. To find the surface properties at a given point, it linearly interpolates to find the intermediate texture coordinate at that point, then calls the NonlinearMapping2D object to determine the final 2D texture coordinate and get the surface spec.

```
public class Nonlinear2DTriangle extends RenderingTriangle{
  public Nonlinear2DTriangle(int v1, int v2, int v3, int n1, int n2, int
n3, Vec3 t1, Vec3 t2, Vec3 t3);
  public void setParameters(double p1[], double p2[], double p3[],
RenderingMesh mesh);
  public void setMesh(RenderingMesh mesh, TextureMapping
map, int index);
  public void getTextureSpec(TextureSpec spec, double angle,
double u, double v, double w, double size, double t);
  public void getTransparency(RGBColor trans, double angle,
double u, double v, double w, double size, double t);
  public double getDisplacement(double u, double v, double w,
double size, double t);
}
```

artofillusion.texture. NonlinearMapping2D

NonlinearMapping2D is an abstract class describing a nonlinear mapping between 2D texture coordinates and 3D space. When called on to map a triangle, it first performs any initial linear transformations on the triangle vertices to yield 3Dimensional intermediate texture coordinates." It then provides a callback function which takes an intermediate texture coordinate and performs the final nonlinear mapping to yield a 2D texture coordinate.

```
public abstract class NonlinearMapping2D extends Mapping2D{
  public NonlinearMapping2D(Object3D theObject, Texture theTexture);
  public abstract Mat4 getPreTransform();
  public abstract void getSpecIntermed(TextureSpec spec, double x, double y, double z, double size, double angle, double t, double param[]);
  public abstract void getTransIntermed(RGBColor trans, double x, double y, double z, double size, double angle, double t, double param[]);
  public abstract double getDisplaceIntermed(double x, double y, double z, double size, double t, double param[]);
  public boolean isBoundToSurface();
  public void setBoundToSurface(boolean bound);
}
```

artofillusion.texture.ParameterValue

This interface represents a class that defines the value of a scalar parameter over the surface of a mesh.

```
public interface ParameterValue{
  public double getValue(int tri, int v1, int v2, int v3, double u, double v, double w);
  public double getAverageValue();
  public ParameterValue duplicate();
  public void writeToStream(DataOutputStream out) throws IOException;
}
```

artofillusion.texture. ProceduralTexture2D

This is a Texture2D which uses a Procedure to calculate its properties.

```
public class ProceduralTexture2D extends Texture2D implements
ProcedureOwner{
  public ProceduralTexture2D();
  public static String getTypeName();
  public void getAverageSpec(TextureSpec spec, double time,
double param[]);
  public void getTextureSpec(TextureSpec spec, double x, double
y, double xsize, double ysize, double angle, double t, double
param[]);
  public void getTransparency(RGBColor trans, double x, double y,
double xsize, double ysize, double angle, double t, double
param[]);
  public Procedure getProcedure();
  public boolean usesImage(ImageMap image);
  public double getDisplacement(double x, double y, double xsize,
double ysize, double t, double param[]);
  public Texture duplicate();
  public TextureParameter[] getParameters();
  public boolean hasComponent(int component);
  public void edit(BFrame fr, Scene sc);
  public ProceduralTexture2D(DataInputStream in, Scene
theScene) throws IOException, InvalidObjectException;
  public void writeToFile(DataOutputStream out, Scene theScene)
throws IOException;
  public String getWindowTitle();
  public Object getPreview(ProcedureEditor editor);
  public void updatePreview(Object preview);
  public void disposePreview(Object preview);
  public boolean allowParameters();
  public boolean allowViewAngle();
  public boolean canEditName();
  public void acceptEdits(ProcedureEditor editor);
  public void editProperties(ProcedureEditor editor);
}
```

artofillusion.texture. ProceduralTexture3D

This is a Texture3D which uses a Procedure to calculate its properties.

```
public class ProceduralTexture3D extends Texture3D implements
ProcedureOwner{
  public ProceduralTexture3D();
  public static String getTypeName();
```

```java
    public void getAverageSpec(TextureSpec spec, double time,
double param[]);
    public void getTextureSpec(TextureSpec spec, double x, double
y, double z, double xsize, double ysize, double zsize, double
angle, double t, double param[]);
    public void getTransparency(RGBColor trans, double x, double y,
double z, double xsize, double ysize, double zsize, double
angle, double t, double param[]);
    public Procedure getProcedure();
    public boolean usesImage(ImageMap image);
    public double getDisplacement(double x, double y, double z,
double xsize, double ysize, double zsize, double t, double param[]);
    public TextureParameter[] getParameters();
    public Texture duplicate();
    public boolean hasComponent(int component);
    public void edit(BFrame fr, Scene sc);
    public ProceduralTexture3D(DataInputStream in, Scene
theScene) throws IOException, InvalidObjectException;
    public void writeToFile(DataOutputStream out, Scene theScene)
throws IOException;
    public String getWindowTitle();
    public Object getPreview(ProcedureEditor editor);
    public void updatePreview(Object preview);
    public void disposePreview(Object preview);
    public boolean allowViewAngle();
    public boolean allowParameters();
    public boolean canEditName();
    public void acceptEdits(ProcedureEditor editor);
    public void editProperties(ProcedureEditor editor);
}
```

artofillusion.texture. ProjectionMapping

ProjectionMapping is a Mapping2D which projects the texture along a specified direction.

```java
public class ProjectionMapping extends Mapping2D{
    protected CoordinateSystem coords;
    protected double ax, bx, cx, dx, ay, by, cy, dy;
    protected double xscale, yscale;
    protected boolean coordsFromParams, scaleToObject;
    protected int numTextureParams;
    protected TextureParameter xparam, yparam, zparam;

    public ProjectionMapping(Object3D theObject, Texture
theTexture);
    public static String getName();
    public Vec2 getCenter();
    public void setCenter(Vec2 center);
    public Vec2 getScale();
    public void setScale(Vec2 scale);
```

```
    public Vec3 getRotations();
    public void setRotations(Vec3 angles);
    public boolean isBoundToSurface();
    public void setBoundToSurface(boolean bound);
    public boolean isScaledToObject();
    public void setScaledToObject(boolean scaled);
    public Mat4 getTransform();
    public RenderingTriangle mapTriangle(int v1, int v2, int v3, int n1,
int n2, int n3, Vec3 vert[]);
    public void setParameters(RenderingTriangle tri, double p1[],
double p2[], double p3[], RenderingMesh mesh);
    public void getTextureSpec(Vec3 pos, TextureSpec spec, double
angle, double size, double time, double param[]);
    public void getTransparency(Vec3 pos, RGBColor trans, double
angle, double size, double time, double param[]);
    public double getDisplacement(Vec3 pos, double size, double
time, double param[]);
    public Vec2 [] findTextureCoordinates(Mesh mesh);
    public TextureMapping duplicate();
    public TextureMapping duplicate(Object3D obj, Texture tex);
    public void copy(TextureMapping mapping);
    public TextureParameter [] getParameters();
    public Widget getEditingPanel(Object3D obj, MaterialPreviewer
preview);
    public ProjectionMapping(DataInputStream in, Object3D the-
Object, Texture theTexture) throws IOException,
InvalidObjectException;
    public void writeToFile(DataOutputStream out) throws
IOException;
}
```

artofillusion.texture.SphericalMapping

SphericalMapping is a Mapping2D which wraps
the texture around a sphere.

```
public class SphericalMapping extends NonlinearMapping2D{
    public SphericalMapping(Object3D theObject, Texture
theTexture);
    public static String getName();
    public Vec2 getScale();
    public void setScale(Vec2 scale);
    public Vec3 getRotations();
    public void setRotations(Vec3 angles);
    public double getOffset();
    public void setOffset(double degrees);
    public RenderingTriangle mapTriangle(int v1, int v2, int v3, int n1,
int n2, int n3, Vec3 vert[]);
    public void setParameters(RenderingTriangle tri, double p1[],
double p2[], double p3[], RenderingMesh mesh);
    public void getTextureSpec(Vec3 pos, TextureSpec spec, double
angle, double size, double time, double param[]);
```

```
    public double getDisplacement(Vec3 pos, double size, double
time, double param[]);
    public void getTransparency(Vec3 pos, RGBColor trans, double
angle, double size, double time, double param[]);
    public Mat4 getPreTransform();
    public void getSpecIntermed(TextureSpec spec, double x,
double y, double z, double size, double angle, double time, double
param[]);
    public void getTransIntermed(RGBColor trans, double x, double
y, double z, double size, double angle, double time, double param
[]);
    public double getDisplaceIntermed(double x, double y, double z,
double size, double time, double param[]);
    public Vec2 [] findTextureCoordinates(Mesh mesh);
    public TextureMapping duplicate();
    public TextureMapping duplicate(Object3D obj, Texture tex);
    public void copy(TextureMapping mapping);
    public TextureParameter [] getParameters();
    public Widget getEditingPanel(Object3D obj, MaterialPreviewer
preview);
    public SphericalMapping(DataInputStream in, Object3D
theObject, Texture theTexture) throws IOException,
InvalidObjectException;
    public void writeToFile(DataOutputStream out) throws
IOException;
}
```

artofillusion.texture.Texture

A Texture represents a description of the surface properties of an object: color, transparency, displacement, etc. This is distinct from the interior bulk properties, which are described by a Material object.

```
public abstract class Texture{
  protected String name;
  protected int id = nextID++;

  public static final int DIFFUSE_COLOR_COMPONENT;
  public static final int SPECULAR_COLOR_COMPONENT;
  public static final int TRANSPARENT_COLOR_COMPONENT;
  public static final int HILIGHT_COLOR_COMPONENT;
  public static final int EMISSIVE_COLOR_COMPONENT;
  public static final int BUMP_COMPONENT;
  public static final int DISPLACEMENT_COMPONENT;

  public static String getTypeName();
  public String getName();
  public void setName(String name);
  public abstract boolean hasComponent(int component);
  public TextureParameter[] getParameters();
```

```
    public boolean usesImage(ImageMap image);
    public int getID();
    public void assignNewID();
    public void setID(int newid);
    public abstract void getAverageSpec(TextureSpec spec, double
time, double param[]);
    public abstract TextureMapping getDefaultMapping(Object3D
object);
    public abstract Texture duplicate();
    public abstract void edit(BFrame fr, Scene sc);
    public abstract void writeToFile(DataOutputStream out, Scene
theScene) throws IOException;
}
```

artofillusion.texture.Texture2D

Texture2D represents a Texture whose surface properties are defined in 2D. This 2D surface can be mapped onto a 3D object by a variety of different mappings.

```
public abstract class Texture2D extends Texture{
    public abstract void getTextureSpec(TextureSpec spec, double x,
double y, double xsize, double ysize, double angle, double t,
double param[]);
    public abstract void getTransparency(RGBColor trans, double x,
double y, double xsize, double ysize, double angle, double t,
double param[]);
    public TextureMapping getDefaultMapping(Object3D object);
    public double getDisplacement(double x, double y, double xsize,
double ysize, double t, double param[]);
    public boolean displacementMapped();
    public Image createComponentImage(final double minu, double
maxu, double minv, final double maxv, final int width, final int
height, final int component, final double time, final double
param[]);
}
```

artofillusion.texture.Texture3D

Texture3D represents a Texture whose surface properties are defined in 3D.

```
public abstract class Texture3D extends Texture{
    public abstract void getTextureSpec(TextureSpec spec, double x,
double y, double z, double xsize, double ysize, double zsize,
double angle, double t, double param[]);
    public abstract void getTransparency(RGBColor trans, double x,
double y, double z, double xsize, double ysize, double zsize,
double angle, double t, double param[]);
    public TextureMapping getDefaultMapping(Object3D object);
```

```
    public double getDisplacement(double x, double y, double z,
double xsize, double ysize, double zsize, double t, double
param[]);
    public boolean displacementMapped();
}
```

artofillusion.texture.TextureMapping

A TextureMapping describes the mapping of a Texture's texture coordinates to points on the surface of an object. It operates in two ways. First, it generates RenderingTriangles which contain the necessary information to be rendered. Second, since some renderers can directly render certain objects without ever breaking them into triangles, it must be able to directly calculate the material properties for a point in space.

This is an abstract class. Its subclasses describe various types of mappings which are appropriate for various types of objects and materials.

```
public abstract class TextureMapping{
  public static final short FRONT_AND_BACK;
  public static final short FRONT_ONLY;
  public static final short BACK_ONLY;

  public abstract void writeToFile(DataOutputStream out) throws
IOException;
  public abstract Texture getTexture();
  public abstract Object3D getObject();
  public static String getName();
  public RenderingTriangle mapTriangle(int v1, int v2, int v3, int n1,
int n2, int n3, Vec3 vert[]);
  public void setParameters(RenderingTriangle tri, double p1[],
double p2[], double p3[], RenderingMesh mesh);
  public abstract void getTextureSpec(Vec3 pos, TextureSpec
spec, double angle, double size, double t, double param[]);
  public abstract void getTransparency(Vec3 pos, RGBColor trans,
double angle, double size, double t, double param[]);
  public abstract double getDisplacement(Vec3 pos, double size,
double t, double param[]);
  public abstract TextureMapping duplicate();
  public abstract TextureMapping duplicate(Object3D obj, Texture
tex);
  public abstract void copy(TextureMapping map);
  public TextureParameter [] getParameters();
  public short appliesTo();
  public final boolean appliesToFace(boolean front);
```

```
public void setAppliesTo(short whichFaces);
public abstract Widget getEditingPanel(Object3D obj,
MaterialPreviewer preview);
}
```

artofillusion.texture.TextureSpec

TextureSpec describes the properties of a point on the surface of an object.

```
public class TextureSpec{
  public final RGBColor diffuse, specular, transparent, emissive,
hilight;
  public double roughness, cloudiness;
  public final Vec3 bumpGrad;

  public TextureSpec();
}
```

artofillusion.texture.UniformMapping

UniformMapping is the TextureMapping for UniformTextures.

```
public class UniformMapping extends TextureMapping{
  public UniformMapping(Object3D theObject, Texture
theTexture);
  public Texture getTexture();
  public Object3D getObject();
  public RenderingTriangle mapTriangle(int v1, int v2, int v3, int n1,
int n2, int n3, Vec3 vert[]);
  public void getTextureSpec(Vec3 pos, TextureSpec spec, double
angle, double size, double t, double param[]);
  public void getTransparency(Vec3 pos, RGBColor trans, double
angle, double size, double t, double param[]);
  public double getDisplacement(Vec3 pos, double size, double t,
double param[]);
  public static boolean legalMapping(Object3D obj, Texture tex);
  public TextureMapping duplicate();
  public TextureMapping duplicate(Object3D obj, Texture tex);
  public void copy(TextureMapping map);
  public Widget getEditingPanel(Object3D obj, final
MaterialPreviewer preview);
  public UniformMapping(DataInputStream in, Object3D theObject,
Texture theTexture) throws IOException, InvalidObjectException;
  public void writeToFile(DataOutputStream out) throws
IOException;
}
```

artofillusion.texture.UniformTexture

UniformMaterial represents a material whose properties do not vary with position.

```
public class UniformTexture extends Texture{
  public RGBColor diffuseColor, specularColor, transparentColor,
emissiveColor;
  public double roughness, cloudiness;
  public float transparency, specularity, shininess;

  public UniformTexture();
  public static UniformTexture invisibleTexture();
  public static String getTypeName();
  public void getTextureSpec(TextureSpec spec);
  public void getTransparency(RGBColor trans);
  public void getAverageSpec(TextureSpec spec, double time,
double param[]);
  public TextureMapping getDefaultMapping(Object3D object);
  public Texture duplicate();
  public boolean hasComponent(int component);
  public void edit(final BFrame fr, Scene sc);
  public UniformTexture(DataInputStream in, Scene theScene)
throws IOException, InvalidObjectException;
  public void writeToFile(DataOutputStream out, Scene theScene)
throws IOException;
}
```

artofillusion.texture.UniformTriangle

UniformTriangle is a subclass of RenderingTriangle, which represents a triangle whose properties are uniform over the entire triangle.

```
public class UniformTriangle extends RenderingTriangle{
  public UniformTriangle(int v1, int v2, int v3, int n1, int n2, int n3);
  public void setMesh(RenderingMesh mesh, TextureMapping
map, int index);
  public void getTextureSpec(TextureSpec spec, double angle,
double u, double v, double w, double size, double t);
  public void getTransparency(RGBColor trans, double angle,
double u, double v, double w, double size, double t);
  public double getDisplacement(double u, double v, double w,
double size, double t);
}
```

artofillusion.texture. UVMappedTriangle

UVMappedTriangle is a subclass of RenderingTriangle, which represents a triangle whose 2D texture coordinates are explicitly specified at each vertex.

```
public class UVMappedTriangle extends RenderingTriangle{
  public UVMappedTriangle(int v1, int v2, int v3, int n1, int n2, int n3);
  public void setMesh(RenderingMesh mesh, TextureMapping map, int index);
  public void setTextureCoordinates(float s1, float t1, float s2, float t2, float s3, float t3, Vec3 vert1, Vec3 vert2, Vec3 vert3);
  public void getTextureSpec(TextureSpec spec, double angle, double u, double v, double w, double size, double time);
  public void getTransparency(RGBColor trans, double angle, double u, double v, double w, double size, double time);
  public double getDisplacement(double u, double v, double w, double size, double time);
}
```

artofillusion.texture.UVMapping

UVMapping is a Mapping2D which allows the user to specify the texture coordinates of each vertex by hand.

```
public class UVMapping extends Mapping2D{
  public UVMapping(Object3D theObject, Texture theTexture);
  public static String getName();
  public TextureParameter getUParameter();
  public TextureParameter getVParameter();
  public static boolean legalMapping(Object3D obj, Texture tex);
  public RenderingTriangle mapTriangle(int v1, int v2, int v3, int n1, int n2, int n3, Vec3 vert[]);
  public void setParameters(RenderingTriangle tri, double p1[], double p2[], double p3[], RenderingMesh mesh);
  public void getTextureSpec(Vec3 pos, TextureSpec spec, double angle, double size, double time, double param[]);
  public void getTransparency(Vec3 pos, RGBColor trans, double angle, double size, double time, double param[]);
  public double getDisplacement(Vec3 pos, double size, double time, double param[]);
  public Vec2 [] findTextureCoordinates(Mesh mesh);
  public Vec2 [][] findFaceTextureCoordinates(FacetedMesh mesh);
  public void setTextureCoordinates(Object3D obj, Vec2 uv[]);
  public void setTextureCoordinates(Object3D obj, Vec2 uv[],
```

```
TextureParameter uParameter, TextureParameter vParameter);
    public void setFaceTextureCoordinates(Object3D obj, Vec2
uv[][]);
    public void setFaceTextureCoordinates(Object3D obj, Vec2
uv[][], TextureParameter uParameter, TextureParameter
vParameter);
    public boolean isPerFaceVertex(FacetedMesh mesh);
    public TextureMapping duplicate();
    public TextureMapping duplicate(Object3D obj, Texture tex);
    public void copy(TextureMapping mapping);
    public TextureParameter [] getParameters();
    public Widget getEditingPanel(Object3D obj, MaterialPreviewer
preview);
    public UVMapping(DataInputStream in, Object3D theObject,
Texture theTexture) throws IOException, InvalidObjectException;
    public void writeToFile(DataOutputStream out) throws
IOException;
}
```

artofillusion.texture.
UVMappingViewer

UVMappingViewer appears in the UVMappingWindow, and is used for editing the UV texture coordinates at each vertex of a mesh.

```
public class UVMappingViewer extends MeshViewer{
    public UVMappingViewer(Texture2D tex, UVMappingWindow
window, double minu, double maxu, double minv, double maxv, int
component, int sampling, double time, double param[]);
    public MeshEditController getController();
    public void setParameters(double minu, double maxu, double
minv, double maxv);
    public void setParameters(double minu, double maxu, double
minv, double maxv, int component, int sampling);
    public double[] estimateDepthRange();
    public synchronized void updateImage();
    protected void drawObject();
    public boolean [] getSelection();
    public void setMesh(Mesh mesh);
    public void setDisplayedVertices(Vec2 coord[], boolean
display[]);
    public void updateVertexPositions(Vec2 coord[]);
    public double getMinU();
    public double getMaxU();
    public double getMinV();
    public double getMaxV();
    public boolean isDragInProgress();
    public void objectChanged();
    protected void mousePressed(WidgetMouseEvent e);
    protected void mouseDragged(WidgetMouseEvent e);
    protected void mouseReleased(WidgetMouseEvent e);
```

```
    protected void processMouseScrolled(MouseScrolledEvent ev);
}
```

artofillusion.texture. UVMappingWindow

UVMappingWindow is a window for editing the UV texture coordinates at each vertex of a mesh.

```
public class UVMappingWindow extends BDialog implements
MeshEditController, EditingWindow{
  public UVMappingWindow(BDialog parent, Object3D obj,
UVMapping map);
  public ObjectInfo getObject();
  public void setMesh(Mesh mesh);
  public int getSelectionMode();
  public void setSelectionMode(int mode);
  public boolean[] getSelection();
  public void setSelection(boolean selected[]);
  public int[] getSelectionDistance();
  public double getMeshTension();
  public int getTensionDistance();
  public void objectChanged();
  public void displayRangeChanged();
  public void setTextureCoords(Vec2 coords[]);
  public ToolPalette getToolPalette();
  public void setTool(EditingTool tool);
  public void setHelpText(String text);
  public BFrame getFrame();
  public void updateImage();
  public void updateMenus();
  public void updateTextFields();
  public void setUndoRecord(UndoRecord command);
  public void setModified();
  public Scene getScene();
  public ViewerCanvas getView();
  public boolean confirmClose();
}
```

artofillusion.texture. UVWMappedTriangle

UVWMappedTriangle is a subclass of RenderingTriangle, which represents a triangle whose 3D texture coordinates are explicitly specified at each vertex.

```
public class UVWMappedTriangle extends RenderingTriangle{
  public UVWMappedTriangle(int v1, int v2, int v3, int n1, int n2, int
n3);
```

```
public void setMesh(RenderingMesh mesh, TextureMapping
map, int index);
    public void setTextureCoordinates(float r1, float s1, float t1, float
r2, float s2, float t2,
        float r3, float s3, float t3, Vec3 vert1, Vec3 vert2, Vec3 vert3);
    public void getTextureSpec(TextureSpec spec, double angle,
double u, double v, double w, double size, double time);
    public void getTransparency(RGBColor trans, double angle,
double u, double v, double w, double size, double time);
    public double getDisplacement(double u, double v, double w,
double size, double time);
}

/** This class defines a scalar parameter who value is defined at
each vertex of a mesh. */

public class VertexParameterValue implements ParameterValue{
    public VertexParameterValue(double val[]);
    public VertexParameterValue(Mesh mesh, TextureParameter
param);
    public double [] getValue();
    public void setValue(double val[]);
    public double getValue(int tri, int v1, int v2, int v3, double u,
double v, double w);
    public double getAverageValue();
    public ParameterValue duplicate();
    public boolean equals(Object o);
    public void writeToStream(DataOutputStream out) throws
IOException;
    public VertexParameterValue(DataInputStream in) throws
IOException;
}
```

Chapter 23

The artofillusion.ui Package

The UI package contains the classes that are needed for the Art of Illusion user interface.

artofillusion.ui.ActionProcessor

This class processes "discardable" events. This is typically used for mouse-moved or mouse-dragged events, where significant time is needed to process each event, and they might be delivered faster than they can be processed.

Callback objects corresponding to particular events are passed to addEvent() as they occur. They are called one at a time. If several new events are delivered before the last one has been finished, all but the most recent one are discarded.

This class is not thread safe. addEvent() and stopProcessing() should only ever be

invoked from the event dispatch thread. In turn, all processing of events is guaranteed to be done on the event dispatch thread.

```
public class ActionProcessor{
  public ActionProcessor();
  public synchronized void addEvent(Runnable event);
  public void stopProcessing();
  public boolean hasBeenStopped();
```

```
public boolean hasEvent();
}
```

artofillusion.ui.AutoScroller

This class is attached to a scroll pane. It causes the scroll pane to automatically scroll whenever the mouse is dragged beyond the edge of it.

```
public class AutoScroller implements Runnable{
  protected BScrollPane sp;
  protected Thread scrollThread;
  protected int x, y, xinc, yinc, delay;

  public AutoScroller(BScrollPane pane, int xincrement, int yincrement);
  public void run();
  protected void scrollWhileDragging(Dimension scrollSize, Point scrollPos);
}
```

artofillusion.ui.ColorChooser

ColorChooser is a BDialog in which the user can edit an RGBColor object. It allows the color to be specified using the RGB, HSV, or HLS color models.

```
public class ColorChooser extends BDialog{
  public ColorChooser(BFrame parent, String title, RGBColor c);
}
```

artofillusion.ui.ComponentsDialog

A ComponentsDialog is a modal dialog containing a line of text, and one or more Widgets for the user to edit. Each Widget has a label next to it. At the bottom are two buttons labeled OK and Cancel.

```
public class ComponentsDialog extends BDialog{
  public ComponentsDialog(WindowWidget parent, String prompt,
Widget components[], String labels[]);
  public ComponentsDialog(WindowWidget parent, String prompt,
Widget components[], String labels[], Runnable onOK, Runnable
onCancel);
  public boolean clickedOk();
  public void setOkEnabled(boolean enabled);
}
```

artofillusion.ui. Compound3DManipulator

This class displays a set of curves and handles around a selection in a ViewerCanvas. It processes mouse clicks on them, and translates them into higher level events which are dispatched for further processing, most often by an EditingTool. It presents a composite user interface for performing moving, scaling, and rotating operations.

```
public class Compound3DManipulator extends EventSource
implements Manipulator{
  public final static ViewMode XYZ_MODE;
  public final static ViewMode UV_MODE;
  public final static ViewMode NPQ_MODE;
  public final static short X_MOVE_INDEX;
  public final static short X_SCALE_INDEX;
  public final static short Y_MOVE_INDEX;
  public final static short Y_SCALE_INDEX;
  public final static short Z_MOVE_INDEX;
  public final static short Z_SCALE_INDEX;
  public final static short CENTER_INDEX;
  public final static short ROTATE_INDEX;
  public final static short TOOL_HANDLE;
  public final static short UV_EXTRA_INDEX;
  public static final Axis X;
  public static final Axis Y;
  public static final Axis Z;
  public static final Axis U;
  public static final Axis V;
  public static final Axis W;
  public static final Axis UV;
  public static final Axis N;
  public static final Axis P;
  public static final Axis Q;
  public static final Axis ALL;
  public static final HandleType MOVE;
  public static final HandleType ROTATE;
  public static final HandleType SCALE;

  public Compound3DManipulator();
  public ViewMode getViewMode();
  public void setViewMode(ViewMode mode);
  public boolean getRotateAroundSelectionCenter();
  public void setRotateAroundSelectionCenter(boolean
rotateAroundSelectionCenter);
  public void setNPQAxes(Vec3 nDir, Vec3 pDir, Vec3 qDir);
  public Vec3 getAxisDirection(Axis axis, ViewerCanvas view);
```

```
    public HandleType getHandleTypeAtLocation(Point location,
ViewerCanvas view, BoundingBox selectionBounds);
    public void draw(ViewerCanvas view, BoundingBox
selectionBounds);
    public boolean mousePressed(WidgetMouseEvent ev,
ViewerCanvas view, BoundingBox selectionBounds);
    public void mousePressedOnHandle(WidgetMouseEvent ev,
ViewerCanvas view, BoundingBox selectionBounds, Vec3
handleLocation);
    public void mouseDragged(WidgetMouseEvent ev,
ViewerCanvas view);
    public void mouseReleased(WidgetMouseEvent ev,
ViewerCanvas view);
    public Rectangle findScreenBounds(BoundingBox b, Camera
cam);
    public static class ViewMode  {  }
    public static class Axis  {
      public String getName();
    }
    public static class HandleType  {  }
    public class HandleEvent  {
      public ViewerCanvas getView();
      public HandleType getHandleType();
      public Axis getAxis();
      public Rectangle getScreenBounds();
      public BoundingBox getSelectionBounds();
      public WidgetMouseEvent getMouseEvent();
      public Compound3DManipulator getManipulator();
    }
    public class HandlePressedEvent extends HandleEvent  {
      public HandlePressedEvent(ViewerCanvas view, HandleType
handleType, Axis axis, Rectangle screenBounds, BoundingBox
selectionBounds, WidgetMouseEvent event);
    }
    public class HandleDraggedEvent extends HandleEvent  {
      public HandleDraggedEvent(ViewerCanvas view, HandleType
handleType, Axis axis, Rectangle screenBounds, BoundingBox
selectionBounds, WidgetMouseEvent event, Mat4 transform);
      public HandleDraggedEvent(ViewerCanvas view, HandleType
handleType, Axis axis, Rectangle screenBounds, BoundingBox
selectionBounds, WidgetMouseEvent event, Mat4 transform,
double angle);
      public HandleDraggedEvent(ViewerCanvas view, HandleType
handleType, Axis axis, Rectangle screenBounds, BoundingBox
selectionBounds, WidgetMouseEvent event, Mat4 transform,
double scale1, double scale2);
      public Mat4 getTransform();
      public double getRotationAngle();
      public double getPrimaryScale();
      public double getSecondaryScale();
    }
    public class HandleReleasedEvent extends HandleEvent  {
```

```
public HandleReleasedEvent(ViewerCanvas view, HandleType
handleType, Axis axis, Rectangle screenBounds, BoundingBox
selectionBounds, WidgetMouseEvent event);
  }
}
```

artofillusion.ui.
DefaultDockableWidget

This is a DockableWidget subclass that paints its border using colors obtained from ThemeManager.

```
public class DefaultDockableWidget extends DockableWidget{
  public DefaultDockableWidget();
  public DefaultDockableWidget(Widget content, String label);
  protected void paintBorder(Graphics2D g);
}
```

artofillusion.ui.DefaultToolButton

This ToolButton is the classic button with one icon for standard representation and another one for selected state.

```
public class DefaultToolButton extends ToolButton{
  protected Image icon;
  protected Image selectedIcon;

  public DefaultToolButton(Object owner, ImageIcon image);
  public DefaultToolButton(Object owner, ImageIcon icon,
ImageIcon selectedIcon);
  public void paint(Graphics2D g);
  public Image applyStyle(ThemeManager.ButtonStyle style, String
type, Object owner, ImageIcon image)
  throws Exception;
}
```

artofillusion.ui.EditingTool

EditingTool is the superclass of tools for editing objects or scenes. An EditingTool has an image which appears in a tool palette, allowing the tool to be selected. When selected, the editing tool responds to events in the scene or object viewer.

An EditingTool specifies what types of mouse clicks it wants to receive by the value it returns from its whichClicks() method. This should be a sum of the constants OBJECT_CLICKS (for mouse clicks on objects), HANDLE_CLICKS (for mouse clicks on handles), and ALL_CLICKS (for all mouse clicks regardless of what they are on). The exact definition of an "object" or "handle" is not specified. It is up to the ViewerCanvas generating the events to decide what constitutes an object or handle.

An EditingTool may also specify whether the current selection may be changed while that tool is active by the value it returns from its allowSelectionChanges() method. This method is always called *after* mousePressed(), allowing the tool to first determine what was clicked on before deciding whether to allow the selection to change in response to the click.

More precisely, here is the sequence of actions a ViewerCanvas performs when the mouse is pressed:

- If the active EditingTool has requested ALL_CLICKS, its mousePressed() method is invoked.
- The ViewerCanvas determines what was clicked on.
- The active EditingTool's allowSelectionChanges() method is invoked and, if it returns true, the selection is updated in response to the click.
- If the click was on a handle and the active EditingTool has requested HANDLE_CLICKS, its mousePressedOnHandle() method is invoked.
- Otherwise, if the click was on an object and the active EditingTool has requested OBJECT_CLICKS, its mousePressedOnObject() method is invoked.

```
public abstract class EditingTool{
  protected EditingWindow theWindow;
  protected BFrame theFrame;
  protected ToolButton button;
```

```
    public EditingTool(EditingWindow win);
    public EditingWindow getWindow();
    public ToolButton getButton();
    protected void initButton(String name);
    public String getToolTipText();

    public static final int ALL_CLICKS;
    public static final int OBJECT_CLICKS;
    public static final int HANDLE_CLICKS;

    public int whichClicks();
    public boolean allowSelectionChanges();
    public boolean hilightSelection();
    public void drawOverlay(ViewerCanvas view);
    public void mousePressed(WidgetMouseEvent e, ViewerCanvas
view);
    public void mousePressedOnObject(WidgetMouseEvent e,
ViewerCanvas view, int obj);
    public void mousePressedOnHandle(WidgetMouseEvent e,
ViewerCanvas view, int obj, int handle);
    public void mouseReleased(WidgetMouseEvent e, ViewerCanvas
view);
    public void mouseDragged(WidgetMouseEvent e, ViewerCanvas
view);
    public void mouseMoved(WidgetMouseEvent e, ViewerCanvas
view);
    public void keyPressed(KeyPressedEvent e, ViewerCanvas
view);
    public void activate();
    public void deactivate();
    public boolean isEditable();
    public void iconDoubleClicked();
}
```

artofillusion.ui.EditingWindow

EditingWindow represents a window used for editing an object or scene.

```
public interface EditingWindow{
    public ToolPalette getToolPalette();
    public void setTool(EditingTool tool);
    public void setHelpText(String text);
    public BFrame getFrame();
    public void updateImage();
    public void updateMenus();
    public void setUndoRecord(UndoRecord command);
    public void setModified();
    public Scene getScene();
    public ViewerCanvas getView();
    public boolean confirmClose();
}
```

artofillusion.ui.FloatingDialog

This class is a dialog which "floats" above its parent window whenever it is set to be non-modal. That is, it is drawn above its parent, but always makes sure that the parent has focus so that it will respond to key-presses.

```
public class FloatingDialog extends BDialog{
  public FloatingDialog(WindowWidget parent);
  public FloatingDialog(WindowWidget parent, boolean modal);
  public FloatingDialog(WindowWidget parent, String title);
  public FloatingDialog(WindowWidget parent, String title, boolean modal);
}
```

artofillusion.ui.GenericTool

GenericTool is an EditingTool which performs no operations. It is generally used simply as a button, for allowing the user to select various options. The constructor takes the name of an image file, which is used as the tool's icon.

```
public class GenericTool extends EditingTool{
  public GenericTool(EditingWindow fr, String imageName, String tipText);
  public void activate();
  public int whichClicks();
  public String getToolTipText();
}
```

artofillusion.ui.GenericTreeElement

This class is a generic TreeElement which can represent any object, but not does need any special behavior.

```
public class GenericTreeElement extends TreeElement{
  public GenericTreeElement(String label, Object obj, TreeElement parent, TreeList tree, Vector children);
  public String getLabel();
  public boolean canAcceptAsParent(TreeElement el);
  public void addChild(TreeElement el, int position);
  public void removeChild(Object object);
  public Object getObject();
  public boolean isGray();
}
```

artofillusion.ui.ImageFileChooser

This is a BFileChooser for selecting image files to load. It displays a preview of the currently selected image.

```
public class ImageFileChooser extends BFileChooser{
  public ImageFileChooser(String title);
  public boolean showDialog(Widget parent);
}
```

artofillusion.ui.InfiniteDragListener

This class implements "infinite" mouse drags, which are not restricted by the boundaries of the screen. It is useful when you want to use mouse drags to control something other than the cursor position. It accomplishes this by repeatedly moving the cursor back to the original click position, while generating its own MouseDraggedEvents and MouseReleasedEvents as if the cursor were freely moving over an unbounded screen.

```
public class InfiniteDragListener extends EventSource{
  public InfiniteDragListener(Widget source);
  public void setEnabled(boolean enabled);
  public boolean isEnabled();
}
```

artofillusion.ui.Manipulator

A Manipulator is a class which presents a user interface in a ViewerCanvas. It is typically used by an EditingTool.

```
public interface Manipulator{
  void draw(ViewerCanvas view, BoundingBox selectionBounds);
  boolean mousePressed(WidgetMouseEvent ev, ViewerCanvas
view, BoundingBox selectionBounds);
  void mouseDragged(WidgetMouseEvent ev, ViewerCanvas
view);
  void mouseReleased(WidgetMouseEvent ev, ViewerCanvas
view);
}
```

artofillusion.ui.MeshEditController

This interface represents an object which coordinates the editing of a mesh.

```
public interface MeshEditController{
    public static final int POINT_MODE;
    public static final int EDGE_MODE;
    public static final int FACE_MODE;

    public ObjectInfo getObject();
    public void setMesh(Mesh mesh);
    public void objectChanged();
    public int getSelectionMode();
    public void setSelectionMode(int mode);
    public boolean[] getSelection();
    public void setSelection(boolean selected[]);
    public int[] getSelectionDistance();
    public double getMeshTension();
    public int getTensionDistance();
}
```

artofillusion.ui.MeshEditingTool

This is a subclass of EditingTool for tools which edit Mesh objects. It contains common features used by many tools.

```
public abstract class MeshEditingTool extends EditingTool{
    protected MeshEditController controller;

    public MeshEditingTool(EditingWindow fr, MeshEditController controller);
    protected BoundingBox findSelectionBounds(Camera cam);
}
```

artofillusion.ui.MessageDialog

A MessageDialog is a modal dialog containing one or more lines of text, and one or more buttons for the user to select from. Clicking any of the buttons dismisses the dialog.

This class is provided mainly for backward compatibility. In most cases, it is better to use a BStandardDialog, since that will have the correct platform-specific appearance. This class does have two advantages over BStandardDialog, however: it can display an arbitrary number of custom buttons, and it automatically breaks text into multiple lines.

```
public class MessageDialog extends BDialog{
  public MessageDialog(WindowWidget parent, String message);
  public MessageDialog(WindowWidget parent, String message,
String[] choices);
  public MessageDialog(WindowWidget parent, String[] message);
  public MessageDialog(WindowWidget parent, String[] message,
String[] choices);
  public int getChoice();
}
```

artofillusion.ui.NinePointManipulator

This class displays a set of handles around a selection in a ViewerCanvas. It processes mouse clicks on them, and translates them into higher level events which are dispatched for further processing, most often by an EditingTool. As the name suggests, this manipulator can display up to nine handles, corresponding to the eight compass points plus center.

```
public class NinePointManipulator extends EventSource
implements Manipulator{
  public static final Image ARROWS_N_S;
  public static final Image ARROWS_E_W;
  public static final Image ARROWS_NW_SE;
  public static final Image ARROWS_NE_SW;
  public static final Image ARROWS_N_W;
  public static final Image ARROWS_N_E;
  public static final Image ARROWS_S_W;
  public static final Image ARROWS_S_E;
  public static final Image ARROWS_ALL;

  public static final Image ROTATE_TOP;
  public static final Image ROTATE_BOTTOM;
  public static final Image ROTATE_LEFT;
  public static final Image ROTATE_RIGHT;
  public static final Image ROTATE_TOPLEFT;
  public static final Image ROTATE_TOPRIGHT;
  public static final Image ROTATE_BOTTOMLEFT;
  public static final Image ROTATE_BOTTOMRIGHT;

  public static final HandlePosition NW;
  public static final HandlePosition N;
  public static final HandlePosition NE;
```

```
  public static final HandlePosition W;
  public static final HandlePosition CENTER;
  public static final HandlePosition E;
  public static final HandlePosition SW;
  public static final HandlePosition S;
  public static final HandlePosition SE;

  public NinePointManipulator(Image images[]);
  public void draw(ViewerCanvas view, BoundingBox
selectionBounds);
  public boolean mousePressed(WidgetMouseEvent ev,
ViewerCanvas view, BoundingBox selectionBounds);
  public void mouseDragged(WidgetMouseEvent ev,
ViewerCanvas view);
  public void mouseReleased(WidgetMouseEvent ev,
ViewerCanvas view);
  public static class HandlePosition{
    public boolean isWest();
    public boolean isEast();
    public boolean isNorth();
    public boolean isSouth();
  }
  public class HandleEvent{
    public ViewerCanvas getView();
    public HandlePosition getHandle();
    public Rectangle getScreenBounds();
    public BoundingBox getSelectionBounds();
    public WidgetMouseEvent getMouseEvent();
    public NinePointManipulator getManipulator();
  }
  public class HandlePressedEvent extends HandleEvent { }
  public class HandleDraggedEvent extends HandleEvent { }
  public class HandleReleasedEvent extends HandleEvent { }
}
```

artofillusion.ui.ObjectTreeElement

This class represents an object in the tree of objects in a scene.

```
public class ObjectTreeElement extends TreeElement{
  protected ObjectInfo info;

  public ObjectTreeElement(ObjectInfo info, TreeList tree);
  public ObjectTreeElement(ObjectInfo info, TreeElement parent,
TreeList tree, boolean addChildren);
  public String getLabel();
  public Icon getIcon();
  public boolean canAcceptAsParent(TreeElement el);
  public void addChild(TreeElement el, int position);
  public void removeChild(Object object);
  public Object getObject();
  public boolean isGray();
```

```
  public void addTracks();
}
```

artofillusion.ui.PanelDialog

A PanelDialog is a modal dialog containing a line of text at the top, and a single Widget (usually a container with other Widgets). At the bottom are two buttons labeled OK and Cancel.

```
public class PanelDialog extends BDialog{
  public PanelDialog(WindowWidget parent, String prompt, Widget
thePanel);
  public boolean clickedOk();
}
```

artofillusion.ui.PopupMenuManager

This interface represents an object which creates and manages a popup menu for some other component.

```
public interface PopupMenuManager{
  public void showPopupMenu(Widget w, int x, int y);
}
```

artofillusion.ui.PropertyEditor

This class presents a user interface for editing the value of a Property. Given a Property object, it constructs an appropriate Widget based on the type of value it represents and the allowed values. The Widget dispatches a ValueChangedEvent whenever its value changes.

```
public class PropertyEditor{
  public PropertyEditor(Property property, Object value);
  public Property getProperty();
  public Widget getWidget();
  public String getLabel();
  public Object getValue();
  public void setValue(Object value);
}
```

artofillusion.ui.Spacer

This is a Widget which acts as a spacer. It displays a blank background, and copies its width and height from specified other Widgets.

```
public class Spacer extends CustomWidget{
    public Spacer(Widget copyHoriz, Widget copyVert);
    public Dimension getPreferredSize();
}
```

artofillusion.ui.ThemeManager

This class holds GUI customization information. Customization consists of various colors used in AoI GUI as well as the look and feel of some GUI elements (eg buttons). In this respect, the theme manager is thus a factory of GUI elements.

```
public class ThemeManager {
    public static class ColorSet {
        public final Color appBackground;
        public final Color paletteBackground;
        public final Color viewerBackground;
        public final Color viewerLine;
        public final Color viewerHandle;
        public final Color viewerHighlight;
        public final Color viewerSpecialHighlight;
        public final Color viewerDisabled;
        public final Color viewerSurface;
        public final Color viewerTransparent;
        public final Color viewerLowValue;
        public final Color viewerHighValue;
        public final Color dockableBarColor1;
        public final Color dockableBarColor2;
        public final Color dockableTitleColor;
        public final Color textColor;

        public String getName();
    }

    public static class ThemeInfo {
        public final String author;
        public final String description;
        public final Class buttonClass;
        public final Object buttonProperties;
        public final int buttonMargin;
        public final int paletteMargin;
        public final boolean classicToolBarButtons;
```

```java
    public final PluginRegistry.PluginResource resource;
    public final ClassLoader loader;
    public final boolean selectable;
    protected ButtonStyle buttonStyles;

    public String getName();
    public ColorSet[] getColorSets();
}
  public static class ButtonStyle  {
    protected Class ownerType;
    protected int width;
    protected int height;
    protected HashMap<String, String> attributes;
    protected ButtonStyle next;

    public ButtonStyle(Node node);
    protected void add(Node node);
    public ButtonStyle getStyle(Object owner);
    public String getAttribute(String name);
}
  public static ThemeInfo getSelectedTheme();
  public static void setSelectedTheme(ThemeInfo theme);
  public static ColorSet getSelectedColorSet();
  public static void setSelectedColorSet(ColorSet colorSet);
  public static List getThemes();
  public static ThemeInfo getDefaultTheme();
  public static URL getNotFoundURL(Object owner);
  public static ImageIcon getNotFoundIcon(Object owner);
  public static ToolButton getToolButton(Object owner, String
iconName, String selectedIconName);
  public static ToolButton getToolButton(Object owner, String
iconName);
  public static ImageIcon getIcon(String iconName);
  public static Color getAppBackgroundColor();
  public static Color getPaletteBackgroundColor();
  public static Color getDockableBarColor1();
  public static Color getDockableBarColor2();
  public static Color getDockableTitleColor();
  public static Color getTextColor();
  public static void initThemes();
  public static int getPaletteMargin();
  public static int getButtonMargin();
  public static ButtonStyle getButtonStyle(Object owner);
}
```

artofillusion.ui.ToolButton

A ToolButton provides the user interface for an
EditingTool in a ToolPalette. This is an abstract class.
Subclasses implement java.awt.Graphics2D.paint() to
determine the appearance of the button.
DefaultToolButton is the standard implementation

which is used by default, but themes may define their own subclasses to customize the appearance and behavior of buttons.

A ToolButton is not a widget. Most often it is used inside a ToolPalette, which handles events, layout, and so on for the ToolButtons it contains. If you want to display a ToolButton as an independent widget, you can do that with the ToolButtonWidget class.

```
public abstract class ToolButton {
  protected int height;
  protected int width;
  protected int state;
  protected Point position;
  protected Object owner;
  public static final int NORMAL_STATE;
  public static final int SELECTED_STATE;
  public static final int HIGHLIGHTED_STATE;

  public ToolButton(Object owner);
  public int getHeight();
  public int getWidth();
  public Dimension getSize();
  public int getState();
  public void setSelected(boolean selected);
  public void setHighlighted(boolean highlighted);
  public boolean isSelected();
  public boolean isHighlighted();
  public abstract void paint(Graphics2D g);
  public void setPosition(int x, int y);
  public Point getPosition();
}
```

artofillusion.ui.ToolBarButton

A ToolBarButton is a simple button that relies on a ToolButton for graphic representation.

```
public class ToolButtonWidget extends CustomWidget {
  public ToolButtonWidget(ToolButton button);
  public Dimension getMinimumSize();
  public Dimension getPreferredSize();
  public void setSelected(boolean selected);
  public boolean isSelected();
  public void paint(RepaintEvent ev);
}
```

artofillusion.ui.ToolPalette

A ToolPalette is drawn as a grid of images, one for each EditingTool that is added to the palette. It allows a single tool to be selected at any time.

```
public class ToolPalette extends CustomWidget{
    public ToolPalette(int w, int h);
    public void addTool(EditingTool t);
    public void addTool(int position, EditingTool t);
    public int getNumTools();
    public EditingTool getTool(int index);
    public EditingTool getDefaultTool();
    public void setDefaultTool(EditingTool t);
    public int getSelection();
    public EditingTool getSelectedTool();
    public Dimension getPreferredSize();
    public Dimension getMinimumSize();
    public void selectTool(EditingTool which);
    public void keyPressed(KeyPressedEvent ev);
    public void toggleDefaultTool();
}
```

artofillusion.ui.Translate

This class provides utilities for localizing text so that it can be translated into different languages. It does this by loading strings from a resource bundle, and using them to create properly localized widgets.

```
public class Translate{
    public static void setLocale(Locale l);
    public static Locale getLocale();
    public static Locale [] getAvailableLocales();
    public static BMenu menu(String name);
    public static BMenuItem menuItem(String name, Object listener,
String method);
    public static BMenuItem menuItem(String name, Object listener,
String method, Shortcut shortcut);
    public static BCheckBoxMenuItem checkboxMenuItem(String
name, Object listener, String method, boolean state);
    public static BButton button(String name, Object listener, String
method);
    public static BButton button(String name, String suffix, Object
listener, String method);
    public static BLabel label(String name);
    public static BLabel label(String name, String suffix);
    public static String text(String name);
    public static String text(String name, Object arg1);
    public static String text(String name, Object arg1, Object arg2);
    public static String text(String name, Object args[]);
```

}

artofillusion.ui.TreeElement

This is an abstract class representing an element in a tree.

```
public abstract class TreeElement{
  protected boolean selected, expanded, selectable;
  protected Vector<TreeElement> children;
  protected TreeElement parent;
  protected TreeList tree;

  public abstract String getLabel();
  public Icon getIcon();
  public boolean isSelected();
  public void setSelected(boolean selected);
  public boolean isExpanded();
  public void setExpanded(boolean expanded);
  public boolean isSelectable();
  public void setSelectable(boolean selectable);
  public boolean selectWithParent();
  public TreeElement getParent();
  public int getNumChildren();
  public TreeElement getChild(int which);
  public abstract boolean canAcceptAsParent(TreeElement el);
  public abstract void addChild(TreeElement el, int position);
  public abstract void removeChild(Object obj);
  public abstract Object getObject();
  public abstract boolean isGray();
}
```

artofillusion.ui.TreeList

This is a Widget which displays a hierarchy of objects. It provides functionality for opening and closing parts of the hierarchy, selecting elements, and moving elements around.

```
public class TreeList extends CustomWidget{
  protected UndoRecord undo;

  public TreeList(EditingWindow win);
  public Dimension getPreferredSize();
  public Dimension getMinimumSize();
  public void setAllowMultiple(boolean allow);
  public void setUpdateEnabled(boolean enabled);
  public void addElement(TreeElement el);
  public void addElement(TreeElement el, int position);
```

```
public TreeElement findElement(Object obj);
public void removeObject(Object obj);
public void removeAllElements();
public TreeElement [] getElements();
public Object [] getSelectedObjects();
public void deselectAll();
public Object [] getVisibleObjects();
public int getRowHeight();
public void setSelected(Object obj, boolean selected);
public void expandToShowObject(Object obj);
public void setYOffset(int offset);
public void setPopupMenuManager(PopupMenuManager
manager);
public class TreeElementEvent implements WidgetEvent{
  public TreeElement getElement();
  public Widget getWidget();
}
public class ElementMovedEvent extends TreeElementEvent { }
public class ElementExpandedEvent
extends TreeElementEvent { }
public class ElementDoubleClickedEvent
extends TreeElementEvent { }
}
```

artofillusion.ui.UIUtilities

This class provides a variety of static methods for performing useful UI related operations.

```
public class UIUtilities{
  public static void centerWindow(WindowWidget win);
  public static void centerDialog(BDialog dlg, WindowWidget
parent);
  public static void fitWindowToScreen(WindowWidget win);
  public static Font getDefaultFont();
  public static void setDefaultFont(Font font);
  public static int getStandardDialogInsets();
  public static void setStandardDialogInsets(int pixels);
  public static void applyDefaultFont(Widget w);
  public static void applyDefaultBackground(Widget w);
  public static void applyBackground(Widget w, Color color);
  public static void applyTextColor(Widget w, Color color);
  public static WidgetContainer createScrollingList(BList list);
  public static WindowWidget findWindow(Widget w);
  public static BFrame findFrame(Widget w);
  public static String [] breakString(String s);
  public static void setEnabled(Widget w, boolean enabled);
  public static List<Widget> findAllChildren(Widget w);
}
```

artofillusion.ui.ValueChecker

A ValueChecker determines whether a value is valid under an arbitrary set of criteria. It is used by ValueField.

```
public interface ValueChecker{
  public boolean isValid(double val);
}
```

artofillusion.ui.ValueField

A ValueField is a BTextField used for entering a numerical value. Constraints can be specified for the value, for example, that it must be positive. If an illegal value is entered into the text field, the text turns red to indicate this.

```
public class ValueField extends BTextField{
  public static final int NONE;
  public static final int NONNEGATIVE;
  public static final int NONZERO;
  public static final int POSITIVE;
  public static final int INTEGER;

  public ValueField(double value, int constraints);
  public ValueField(float value, int constraints);
  public ValueField(float value, int constraints, int columns);
  public ValueField(double value, int constraints, int columns);
  public void setValueChecker(ValueChecker vc);
  public ValueChecker getValueChecker();
  public boolean isTextValid();
  public boolean isValid(double val);
  public void checkIfValid();
  protected void textChanged();
  public double getValue();
  public void setValue(double val);
  public void setMinDecimalPlaces(int decimals);
  public void sendValidEventsOnly(boolean validOnly);
}
```

artofillusion.ui.ValueSelector

This class is used for selecting a numeric value within a (possibly unbounded) range. The user may edit the value either by typing into a text field, or by clicking and dragging on an "adjuster" Widget. This class is similar to JSlider, but it can be used when the permitted values are not restricted to a finite range.

```
public class ValueSelector extends RowContainer{
  public ValueSelector(double value, double min, double max,
  double increment);
  public double getValue();
  public void setValue(double value);
  public double getMinimumValue();
  public void setMinimumValue(double min);
  public double getMaximumValue();
  public void setMaximumValue(double max);
  public void setEnabled(boolean enabled);
}
```

artofillusion.ui.ValueSlider

A ValueSlider contains a BTextField and a BSlider which are together used for choosing a value. Editing either one causes the other to change automatically. If an illegal value is entered into the BTextField, the text turns red to indicate this.

```
public class ValueSlider extends WidgetContainer{
  public ValueSlider(double min, double max, int increments,
  double value);
  public void setForceInteger(boolean force);
  public void textChanged(ValueChangedEvent ev);
  public double getValue();
  public void setValue(double val);
  public double getMinimumValue();
  public double getMaximumValue();
  public void setMaximumValue(double max);
  public void setEnabled(boolean enabled);
  public int getChildCount();
  public Collection getChildren();
  public void layoutChildren();
  public synchronized void remove(Widget widget);
  public synchronized void removeAll();
  public Dimension getMinimumSize();
  public Dimension getPreferredSize();
}
```

Chapter 24

The artofillusion.unwrap Package

The unwrap package contains the SeamFinder class.

artofillusion.unwrap.SeamFinder

The SeamFind class associates with a TriangleMesh upon construction and provides a public member function, getSeamEdges(), that will return a list representing the seams it found in the mesh.

```
public class SeamFinder{
  public SeamFinder(TriangleMesh mesh);
  public List<Integer> getSeamEdges();
}
```

Chapter 25

The artofillusion.util Package

The util package contains some utility classes that Art of Illusion needs.

artofillusion.util.IconGenerator

The IconGenerator provides editing and compositing features for icon images.

```
public class IconGenerator{
  public static final byte FEATHER_OUT_DIR;
  public static final byte FEATHER_IN_DIR;
  protected Instruction program;
  protected int imageWidth, imageHeight;
  protected String[] delims;
  protected static final byte ARG_LIST;
  protected static final byte ARG_RESOLVE;
  protected static final byte ARG_NUMBER;
  protected static final byte OP_NONE;
  protected static final byte OP_COMPOSIT;
  protected static final byte OP_OVERLAY;
  protected static final byte OP_ADD;
  protected static final byte OP_SUBTRACT;
  protected static final byte OP_MULTIPLY;
  protected static final byte OP_ASSIGN;
  protected static final byte OP_SCALE;
  protected static final byte OP_FEATHER;
  protected static final byte OP_POSITION;
  protected static final byte OP_RESIZE;
  protected static final byte OP_CALL;
  protected static final byte OP_COLOR;
  protected static final byte OP_ARG;
  protected static final byte OP_LIST;
  protected static final byte OP_RESOLVE;
```

```java
    protected static final byte OP_NUMBER;
    protected static final int OPS;
    protected static final int ARG_DELIMS;
    protected static final int OPEN_CLOSE;
    protected static final String[] DEFAULT_DELIMS;
    protected static final String QUOTES;
    protected static final String WHITESPACE;
    protected static final String DEFAULT_TARGET;
    protected static final float SCALE_DOWN;
    protected static final Class[] NULL_SIG;
    protected static final Object[] NULL_ARGS;

    public IconGenerator(String macro)
    throws Exception;
    public IconGenerator(String macro, String[] delims)
    throws Exception;
    public void compile(String macro)
    throws Exception;
    public void setSize(int width, int height);
    public Image execute(Map<String, Object> namespace,
    ClassLoader loader)
    throws Exception;
    public static Image apply(String macro, String[] delims,
    Map<String, Object> namespace, ClassLoader loader, int width,
    int height)
    throws Exception;
    public static Image apply(String macro, String[] delims,
    Map<String, Object> namespace, ClassLoader loader)
    throws Exception;
    public static Image apply(String macro, Map<String,
    Object> namespace, ClassLoader loader)
    throws Exception;
    public static BufferedImage copy(Image orig);
    public static BufferedImage copy(Image orig, int width, int height,
    float scale);
    public static void bevel3D(BufferedImage image, int depth);
    public static void bevel3D(BufferedImage image, int depth,
    Rectangle clip);
    public static void add(BufferedImage image, int red, int green, int
    blue);
    public static void add(BufferedImage image, int red, int green, int
    blue, Rectangle clip);
    public static void subtract(BufferedImage image, int red, int
    green, int blue);
    public static void subtract(BufferedImage image, int red, int
    green, int blue, Rectangle clip);
    public static void multiply(BufferedImage image, float alpha, float
    red, float green, float blue);
    public static void multiply(BufferedImage image, float alpha, float
    red, float green, float blue, Rectangle clip);
    public static void assign(BufferedImage image, int alpha, int red,
    int green, int blue);
    public static void assign(BufferedImage image, int alpha, int red,
    int green, int blue, Rectangle clip);
```

```java
    public static void overlay(BufferedImage image, int alpha, int red,
int green, int blue);
    public static void overlay(BufferedImage image, int alpha, int red,
int green, int blue, Rectangle clip);
    public static void overlay(BufferedImage image, Image overlay);
    public static void overlay(BufferedImage image, Image overlay,
Rectangle clip);
    public static void antialias(BufferedImage image, float dark);
    public static void antialias(BufferedImage image, float alpha, float
attenuate, Rectangle clip);
    public static void feather(BufferedImage image, int xsize, int
ysize, byte dir);
    public static void feather(BufferedImage image, int xsize, int
ysize, byte dir, Rectangle clip);
    protected static class Instruction  {
    public Instruction();
    public Instruction(int width, int height);
    public void setSize(int width, int height);
    public Instruction compileNext(String[] delims)
throws Exception;
    public void compile(String macro, int pos, String[] delims)
throws Exception;
    public BufferedImage execute(BufferedImage lhs, Map<String,
Object> namespace, ClassLoader loader)
throws Exception;
    protected void error(String message, int pos)
throws Exception;
    protected ArgList parseArgs(ArgList vec, int maxArgs, int first,
int last);
    protected BufferedImage getImage(String name, int width, int
height, Map<String, Object> namespace, ClassLoader loader)
throws IOException;
    protected Object resolve(String target, List method, Map
namespace)
throws Exception;
    protected int parseToken(String macro, int pos);
    protected int skip(String macro, int start, int end, String
skipchars);
    protected int find(String macro, int start, int end, String
findchars);
    protected class ArgList {
    protected void parse(int maxArgs, String macro, int start, int
end);
    protected int getInt(int index);
    protected int getFloat(int index);
    protected int calc(int lhs, int index);
    protected float calc(float lhs, int index);
    }
  }
}
```

artofillusion.util. SearchlistClassLoader

The SearchlistClassLoader class loader loads classes using a search list.

```
public class SearchlistClassLoader extends ClassLoader{
  protected Vector list, search;
  protected Hashtable cache;
  protected Loader content;
  protected byte searchMode;
  protected int divide;
  public static final byte SHARED;
  public static final byte NONSHARED;
  public static final byte ORDERED;
  protected static final URL EMPTY_URL[];

  public SearchlistClassLoader();
  public SearchlistClassLoader(ClassLoader parent);
  public SearchlistClassLoader(URL url[]);
  public SearchlistClassLoader(URL url[], ClassLoader parent);
  public void setSearchMode(byte mode);
  public void add(ClassLoader loader);
  public void add(URL url);
  public URL[] getURLs();
  public URL[] getSearchPath();
  public Class loadLocalClass(String name)
  throws ClassNotFoundException;
  public URL getLocalResource(String name);
  public Class findClass(String name)
  throws ClassNotFoundException;
  public URL findResource(String path);
  public String findLibrary(String libname);
  protected Loader getLoader(int index, byte mode);
  protected byte[] loadClassData(ClassLoader cl, String name);
  public static String translate(String str, String match, String
replace);
  protected static class Loader  {
    Loader(ClassLoader loader, boolean shared);
  }
}
```

artofillusion.util.ThreadManager

This class coordinates threads for multi-threaded operations. The execution model provided by this class is a single "task" (e.g. tracing a ray through a single pixel) which must be executed many times. The task is parameterized by a single index (e.g. the column containing the pixel).

To use this class, pass it an object which implements the Task interface. It automatically creates an appropriate number of threads based on the number of available processors. When you call run(), the task is repeatedly executed by the worker threads, with the index running over the desired range. You may invoke run() any number of times (e.g. once for each row of the image). Finally, call finish() to clean up the worker threads.

```
public class ThreadManager{
  public ThreadManager();
  public ThreadManager(int numIndices, Task task);
  public void setNumIndices(int numIndices);
  public void setTask(Task task);
  public void setMaxThreads(int maxThreads);
  public void run();
  public void cancel();
  public void finish();
  public static interface Task{
    public void execute(int index);
    public void cleanup();
  }
}
```

util

Chapter 26

The artofillusion.view Package

The view package contains the classes that Art of Illusion uses to display the scene in the view ports.

artofillusion.view.CanvasDrawer

This interface defines an object which renders the content of a ViewerCanvas.

```
public interface CanvasDrawer{
  public void setTemplateImage(Image im);
  public void drawDraggedShape(Shape shape);
  public void drawBorder();
  public void drawHRule(int y, Color color);
  public void drawVRule(int x, Color color);
  public void drawBox(int x, int y, int width, int height, Color color);
  public void drawBoxes(java.util.List<Rectangle> box, Color
color);
  public void renderBox(int x, int y, int width, int height, double
depth, Color color);
  public void renderBoxes(java.util.List<Rectangle> box,
java.util.List<Double>depth, Color color);
  public void drawLine(Point p1, Point p2, Color color);
  public void renderLine(Vec3 p1, Vec3 p2, Camera cam, Color
color);
  public void renderLine(Vec2 p1, double zf1, Vec2 p2, double zf2,
Camera cam, Color color);
  public void renderWireframe(WireframeMesh mesh, Camera cam,
Color color);
  public void renderMeshTransparent(RenderingMesh mesh,
VertexShader shader, Camera cam, Vec3 viewDir, boolean
hideFace[]);
```

```
public void renderMesh(RenderingMesh mesh, VertexShader
shader, Camera cam, boolean closed, boolean hideFace[]);
   public void drawString(String text, int x, int y, Color color);
   public void drawImage(Image image, int x, int y);
   public void renderImage(Image image, Vec3 p1, Vec3 p2, Vec3
p3, Vec3 p4, Camera camera);
   public void drawShape(Shape shape, Color color);
   public void fillShape(Shape shape, Color color);
}
```

artofillusion.view. ConstantVertexShader

This is a VertexShader which renders the entire surface in a constant color, independent of orientation.

```
public class ConstantVertexShader implements VertexShader{
   public ConstantVertexShader(RGBColor color);
   public void getColor(int face, int vertex, RGBColor color);
   public boolean isUniformFace(int face);
   public boolean isUniformTexture();
   public void getTextureSpec(TextureSpec spec);
}
```

artofillusion.view.FlatVertexShader

This is a VertexShader which renders a mesh in a solid color with flat shading.

```
public class FlatVertexShader implements VertexShader{
   public FlatVertexShader(RenderingMesh mesh, Object3D object,
double time, Vec3 viewDir);
   public FlatVertexShader(RenderingMesh mesh, RGBColor color,
Vec3 viewDir);
   public void getColor(int face, int vertex, RGBColor color);
   public boolean isUniformFace(int face);
   public boolean isUniformTexture();
   public void getTextureSpec(TextureSpec spec);
}
```

artofillusion.view.GLCanvasDrawer

This is a CanvasDrawer which uses OpenGL to render the contents of a ViewerCanvas.

```
public class GLCanvasDrawer implements CanvasDrawer{
   public GLCanvasDrawer(ViewerCanvas view);
   public Component getGLCanvas();
   public void setTemplateImage(Image im);
   public void drawDraggedShape(Shape shape);
   public void drawBorder();
```

```
public void drawHRule(int y, Color color);
public void drawVRule(int x, Color color);
public void drawBox(int x, int y, int width, int height, Color color);
public void drawBoxes(java.util.List<Rectangle> box, Color
color);
public void renderBox(int x, int y, int width, int height, double
depth, Color color);
public void renderBoxes(java.util.List<Rectangle> box,
java.util.List<Double>depth, Color color);
public void drawLine(Point p1, Point p2, Color color);
public void renderLine(Vec3 p1, Vec3 p2, Camera cam, Color
color);
public void renderLine(Vec2 p1, double zf1, Vec2 p2, double zf2,
Camera cam, Color color);
public void renderWireframe(WireframeMesh mesh, Camera
cam, Color color);
public void renderMeshTransparent(RenderingMesh mesh,
VertexShader shader, Camera cam, Vec3 viewDir, boolean
hideFace[]);
public void renderMesh(RenderingMesh mesh, VertexShader
shader, Camera cam, boolean closed, boolean hideFace[]);
public void drawString(String text, int x, int y, Color color);
public void drawImage(Image image, int x, int y);
public void renderImage(Image image, Vec3 p1, Vec3 p2, Vec3
p3, Vec3 p4, Camera camera);
public void drawShape(Shape shape, Color color);
public void fillShape(Shape shape, Color color);
public void drawShape(Shape shape, Color color, int mode);
}
```

view

artofillusion.view. ParameterVertexShader

This is a VertexShader which colors the surface
based on the value of a TextureParameter.

```
public class ParameterVertexShader implements VertexShader{
public ParameterVertexShader(RenderingMesh mesh,
ParameterValue param, RGBColor lowColor, RGBColor
highColor, double minValue, double maxValue, Vec3 viewDir);
public void getColor(int face, int vertex, RGBColor color);
public boolean isUniformFace(int face);
public boolean isUniformTexture();
public void getTextureSpec(TextureSpec spec);
}
```

artofillusion.view. SelectionVertexShader

This is a VertexShader which highlights selected faces. For unselected faces, it delegates to another shader to select the color.

```
public class SelectionVertexShader implements VertexShader{
  public SelectionVertexShader(RGBColor selectionColor,
VertexShader shader, int faceIndex[], boolean selected[]);
  public void getColor(int face, int vertex, RGBColor color);
  public boolean isUniformFace(int face);
  public boolean isUniformTexture();
  public void getTextureSpec(TextureSpec spec);
}
```

artofillusion.view. SmoothVertexShader

This is a VertexShader which renders a uniform colored mesh with smooth shading.

```
public class SmoothVertexShader implements VertexShader{
  public SmoothVertexShader(RenderingMesh mesh, Object3D
object, double time, Vec3 viewDir);
  public SmoothVertexShader(RenderingMesh mesh, RGBColor
color, Vec3 viewDir);
  public void getColor(int face, int vertex, RGBColor color);
  public boolean isUniformFace(int face);
  public boolean isUniformTexture();
  public void getTextureSpec(TextureSpec spec);
}
```

artofillusion.view. SoftwareCanvasDrawer

This is a CanvasDrawer which implements a software renderer for generating the contents of a ViewerCanvas.

```
public class SoftwareCanvasDrawer implements CanvasDrawer{
  protected ViewerCanvas view;
  protected BufferedImage theImage;
  protected Graphics2D imageGraphics;
  protected int pixel[], zbuffer[];
  protected boolean hideBackfaces;
  protected int templatePixel[];
  protected Rectangle bounds;
```

```
public SoftwareCanvasDrawer(ViewerCanvas view);
public void setTemplateImage(Image im);
public void drawDraggedShape(Shape shape);
public BufferedImage getImage();
public void paint(RepaintEvent ev);
public void drawBorder();
public void drawHRule(int y, Color color);
public void drawVRule(int x, Color color);
public void drawBox(int x, int y, int width, int height, Color color);
public void drawBoxes(java.util.List<Rectangle> box, Color
color);
public void renderBox(int x, int y, int width, int height, double
depth, Color color);
public void renderBoxes(java.util.List<Rectangle> box,
java.util.List<Double>depth, Color color);
public void drawLine(Point p1, Point p2, Color color);
public void renderLine(Vec3 p1, Vec3 p2, Camera cam, Color
color);
public void renderLine(Vec2 p1, double zf1, Vec2 p2, double zf2,
Camera cam, Color color);
public void renderWireframe(WireframeMesh mesh, Camera
cam, Color color);
public void renderMeshTransparent(RenderingMesh mesh,
VertexShader shader, Camera cam, Vec3 viewDir, boolean
hideFace[]);
public void renderMesh(RenderingMesh mesh, VertexShader
shader, Camera cam, boolean closed, boolean hideFace[]);
public void drawString(String text, int x, int y, Color color);
public void drawShape(Shape shape, Color color);
public void fillShape(Shape shape, Color color);
public void drawImage(Image image, int x, int y);
public void renderImage(Image image, Vec3 p1, Vec3 p2, Vec3
p3, Vec3 p4, Camera camera);
}
```

view

artofillusion.view.
TexturedVertexShader

This is a VertexShader which renders a textured
mesh with smooth shading.

```
public class TexturedVertexShader implements VertexShader{
  public TexturedVertexShader(RenderingMesh mesh, Object3D
object, double time, Vec3 viewDir);
  public VertexShader optimize();
  public void getColor(int face, int vertex, RGBColor color);
  public boolean isUniformFace(int face);
  public boolean isUniformTexture();
  public void getTextureSpec(TextureSpec spec);
  public static void clearCachedShaders(RenderingMesh mesh);
}
```

artofillusion.view.VertexShader

This interface defines an object which selects colors for vertices. Objects implementing this interface are passed to a ViewerCanvas to tell it how to render a surface interactively.

```
public interface VertexShader{
  public void getColor(int face, int vertex, RGBColor color);
  public boolean isUniformFace(int face);
  public boolean isUniformTexture();
  public void getTextureSpec(TextureSpec spec);
}
```

artofillusion.view.ViewChangedEvent

A ViewChangedEvent is dispatched by a ViewerCanvas to indicate that some element of the view settings has changed. This includes the camera position or orientation, the zoom level, the projection mode, etc.

```
public class ViewChangedEvent{
  public ViewChangedEvent(ViewerCanvas source);
  public ViewerCanvas getSource();
}
```

artofillusion.view.ViewerControl

A ViewerControl defines a Widget that is added to the toolbar at the top of each ViewerCanvas. After creating a ViewerControl, invoke ViewerCanvas.addViewerControl(ViewerControl) to register it. Every time a new ViewerCanvas is then created, createWidget(artofillusion.ViewerCanvas) will be invoked to create a control for that canvas.

```
public interface ViewerControl{
  Widget createWidget(ViewerCanvas view);
  String getName();
}
```

artofillusion.view. ViewerOrientationControl

This is a ViewerControl for adjusting the scale of the view.

```
public class ViewerOrientationControl implements ViewerControl{
  public Widget createWidget(final ViewerCanvas view);
  public String getName();

  public static class OrientationChoice extends BComboBox{
    public void rebuildCameraList();
  }
}
```

artofillusion.view. ViewerPerspectiveControl

This is a ViewerControl for setting whether a view uses perspective mode.

```
public class ViewerPerspectiveControl implements ViewerControl{
  public Widget createWidget(final ViewerCanvas view);
  public String getName();
}
```

artofillusion.view.ViewerScaleControl

This is a ViewerControl for adjusting the scale of the view.

```
public class ViewerScaleControl implements ViewerControl{
  public Widget createWidget(final ViewerCanvas view);
  public String getName();
}
```

Chapter 27

The buoy.event Package

The event package contains the classes that buoy defines for handling events. These events serve to pass state information from the operating system to classes that are using buoy for the user interface.

buoy.event.CellValueChangedEvent

A CellValueChangedEvent is generated when the user edits the value in a cell of a BTable.

```
public class CellValueChangedEvent extends EventObject
implements WidgetEvent{
  public CellValueChangedEvent(Widget widget, int row, int col);
  public Widget getWidget();
  public int getRow();
  public int getColumn();
}
```

buoy.event.CommandEvent

This event represents a user action that issues a command, such as pressing a button or selecting a menu item.

```
public class CommandEvent extends ActionEvent implements
WidgetEvent{
  public CommandEvent(Widget source, long when, int modifiers);
  public CommandEvent(Widget source, long when, int modifiers,
String command);
  public Widget getWidget();
```

}

buoy.event.DocumentLinkEvent

A DocumentLinkEvents is generated when the user clicks on a hyperlink inside a BDocumentViewer. It is a simple wrapper around a javax.swing.event.HyperlinkEvent object.

```
public class DocumentLinkEvent extends EventObject implements
WidgetEvent{
  public DocumentLinkEvent(Widget widget, HyperlinkEvent
event);
  public Widget getWidget();
  public URL getURL();
  public String getDescription();
  public HyperlinkEvent getEvent();
}
```

buoy.event.EventProcessor

This class allows you to use anonymous inner classes as event handlers in unsigned applets and other situations where a SecurityManager prevents use of the AccessibleObject API. If you are writing an application, a signed applet, or any other type of program which is not restricted by a security manager, you can ignore this class.

```
public abstract class EventProcessor{
  public void processEvent(Object event);
  public abstract void handleEvent(Object event);
}
```

buoy.event.EventSource

An EventSource is any object that can dispatch events. It maintains a list of "event links", which are methods to be called when specific types of events occur.

```
public class EventSource{
  protected ArrayList eventLinks;

  public EventSource();
  public void addEventLink(Class eventType, Object target);
```

```
    public void addEventLink(Class eventType, Object target, String
method);
    public void addEventLink(Class eventType, Object target,
Method method);
    public void removeEventLink(Class eventType, Object target);
    public void dispatchEvent(Object event);
}
```

buoy.event.FocusGainedEvent

This is an event corresponding to a Widget gaining keyboard focus.

```
public class FocusGainedEvent extends WidgetFocusEvent{
    public FocusGainedEvent(Widget source, boolean temporary);
}
```

buoy.event.FocusLostEvent

This is an event corresponding to a Widget losing keyboard focus.

```
public class FocusLostEvent extends WidgetFocusEvent{
    public FocusLostEvent(Widget source, boolean temporary);
}
```

buoy.event.KeyPressedEvent

This is an event corresponding to a key on the keyboard being pressed.

```
public class KeyPressedEvent extends WidgetKeyEvent{
    public KeyPressedEvent(Widget source, long when, int
modifiers, int keyCode);
}
```

event

buoy.event.KeyReleasedEvent

This is an event corresponding to a key on the keyboard being released.

```
public class KeyReleasedEvent extends WidgetKeyEvent{
    public KeyReleasedEvent(Widget source, long when, int
modifiers, int keyCode);
}
```

buoy.event.KeyTypedEvent

This is an event corresponding to a Unicode character being generated by the user interacting with the keyboard.

```
public class KeyTypedEvent extends WidgetKeyEvent{
  public KeyTypedEvent(Widget source, long when, int modifiers,
char keyChar);
}
```

buoy.event.MouseClickedEvent

This is an event corresponding to the mouse button being pressed and released.

```
public class MouseClickedEvent extends WidgetMouseEvent{
  public MouseClickedEvent(Widget source, long when, int
modifiers, int x, int y, int clickCount, boolean popupTrigger, int
button);
}
```

buoy.event.MouseDraggedEvent

This is an event corresponding to the mouse being dragged inside a Widget.

```
public class MouseDraggedEvent extends WidgetMouseEvent{
  public MouseDraggedEvent(Widget source, long when, int
modifiers, int x, int y);
}
```

buoy.event.MouseEnteredEvent

This is an event corresponding to the mouse entering a Widget.

```
public class MouseEnteredEvent extends WidgetMouseEvent{
  public MouseEnteredEvent(Widget source, long when, int
modifiers, int x, int y);
}
```

buoy.event.MouseExitedEvent

This is an event corresponding to the mouse exiting a Widget.

```
public class MouseExitedEvent extends WidgetMouseEvent{
  public MouseExitedEvent(Widget source, long when, int
```

```
modifiers, int x, int y);
}
```

buoy.event.MouseMovedEvent

This is an event corresponding to the mouse being moved inside a Widget.

```
public class MouseMovedEvent extends WidgetMouseEvent{
  public MouseMovedEvent(Widget source, long when, int
modifiers, int x, int y);
}
```

buoy.event.MousePressedEvent

This is an event corresponding to the mouse button being pressed.

```
public class MousePressedEvent extends WidgetMouseEvent{
  public MousePressedEvent(Widget source, long when, int
modifiers, int x, int y, int clickCount, boolean popupTrigger,
int button);
}
```

buoy.event.MouseReleasedEvent

This is an event corresponding to the mouse button being released.

```
public class MouseReleasedEvent extends WidgetMouseEvent{
  public MouseReleasedEvent(Widget source, long when, int
modifiers, int x, int y, int clickCount, boolean popupTrigger,
int button);
}
```

buoy.event.MouseScrolledEvent

This class defines an event caused by rotating the scroll wheel on a mouse.

```
public class MouseScrolledEvent extends MouseWheelEvent
implements WidgetEvent{
  public MouseScrolledEvent(Widget source, long when, int
modifiers, int x, int y, int scrollType, int scrollAmount, int
wheelRotation);
  public Object getSource();
  public Widget getWidget();
}
```

event

buoy.event.RepaintEvent

A RepaintEvent is generated by certain Widgets (including CustomWidgets and many WidgetContainers) whenever a portion of it needs to be repainted.

```
public class RepaintEvent extends EventObject implements
WidgetEvent{
  public RepaintEvent(Widget widget, Graphics2D graphics);
  public Widget getWidget();
  public Graphics2D getGraphics();
}
```

buoy.event.SelectionChangedEvent

SelectionChangedEvents are generated by Widgets that allow the user to select part of their contents, whenever the selection changes.

```
public class SelectionChangedEvent extends EventObject
implements WidgetEvent{
  public SelectionChangedEvent(Widget widget);
  public SelectionChangedEvent(Widget widget, boolean
inProgress);
  public Widget getWidget();
  public boolean isInProgress();
}
```

buoy.event.ToolTipEvent

This event indicates that the user has performed the series of actions which signal that a tool tip should be displayed. Generally, this involves placing the mouse pointer over a Widget and not moving it for a certain amount of time.

```
public class ToolTipEvent extends EventObject implements
WidgetEvent{
  public ToolTipEvent(Widget source, long when, Point pos, Point
tipPos);
  public Widget getWidget();
  public long getWhen();
  public Point getPoint();
  public Point getToolTipLocation();
}
```

buoy.event.ValueChangeEvent

ValueChangedEvents are generated by Widgets that allow the user to enter a value, whenever the value changes.

```
public class ValueChangedEvent extends EventObject
implements WidgetEvent{
  public ValueChangedEvent(Widget widget);
  public ValueChangedEvent(Widget widget, boolean inProgress);
  public Widget getWidget();
  public boolean isInProgress();
}
```

buoy.event.WidgetEvent

This interface defines an event generated by a Widget.

```
public interface WidgetEvent{
  public Widget getWidget();
}
```

buoy.event.WidgetFocusEvent

This class defines an event caused by a change in whether a Widget has keyboard focus. This is an abstract class, with subclasses for particular types of events.

```
public abstract class WidgetFocusEvent extends FocusEvent
implements WidgetEvent{
  protected WidgetFocusEvent(Widget source, int id, boolean
temporary);
  public Object getSource();
  public Widget getWidget();
}
```

buoy.event.WidgetKeyEvent

This class defines an event caused by a keyboard action. It is sent to the Widget that has keyboard focus. This is an abstract class, with subclasses for particular types of events.

```
public abstract class WidgetKeyEvent extends KeyEvent imple-
ments WidgetEvent{
```

```
   protected WidgetKeyEvent(Widget source, int id, long when, int
modifiers, int keyCode, char keyChar);
   public Object getSource();
   public Widget getWidget();
}
```

buoy.event.WidgetMouseEvent

This class defines an event caused by the mouse
interacting with a Widget. It is an abstract class, with
subclasses for specific types of events.

```
public abstract class WidgetMouseEvent extends MouseEvent
implements WidgetEvent{
   protected WidgetMouseEvent(Widget source, int id, long when,
int modifiers, int x, int y, int clickCount, boolean popupTrigger, int
button);
   public Object getSource();
   public Widget getWidget();
}
```

buoy.event.WidgetWindowEvent

This class defines an event caused by the user
interacting with a window. It is an abstract class, with
subclasses for specific types of events.

```
public abstract class WidgetWindowEvent extends WindowEvent
implements WidgetEvent{
   public WidgetWindowEvent(WindowWidget source, int id);
   public Object getSource();
   public Widget getWidget();
}
```

buoy.event.WindowActivatedEvent

This is an event corresponding to a window
becoming the active window.

```
public class WindowActivatedEvent extends WidgetWindowEvent{
   public WindowActivatedEvent(WindowWidget source);
}
```

buoy.event.WindowClosingEvent

This event indicates that the user is attempting to
close a window, such as by clicking on its close box.

```
public class WindowClosingEvent extends WidgetWindowEvent{
   public WindowClosingEvent(WindowWidget source);
```

}

buoy.event.WindowDeactivatedEvent

This is an event corresponding to a window ceasing to be the active window.

```
public class WindowDeactivatedEvent extends
WidgetWindowEvent{
  public WindowDeactivatedEvent(WindowWidget source);
}
```

buoy.event.WindowDeIconifiedEvent

This event indicates that a window has been deiconified by the user.

```
public class WindowDeiconifiedEvent extends
WidgetWindowEvent{
  public WindowDeiconifiedEvent(WindowWidget source);
}
```

buoy.event.WindowIconifiedEvent

This event indicates that a window has been iconified by the user.

```
public class WindowIconifiedEvent extends WidgetWindowEvent{
  public WindowIconifiedEvent(WindowWidget source);
}
```

buoy.event.WindowResizedEvent

This event indicates that a window has been resized by the user.

```
public class WindowResizedEvent extends WidgetWindowEvent{
  public WindowResizedEvent(WindowWidget source);
}
```

event

Chapter 28

The buoy.internal Package

The internal package contains classes that buoy needs for some of its internal operations.

buoy.internal.EventLinkAdapter

This class handles interaction with the AWT event model. Its job is to implement every listener interface, then generate and dispatch appropriate event objects.

```
public class EventLinkAdapter implements FocusListener,
KeyListener, MouseListener, MouseMotionListener,
MouseWheelListener, WindowListener{
  public EventLinkAdapter(Widget widget);
  public void newEventType(Class eventType);
  public void mousePressed(MouseEvent ev);
  public void mouseReleased(MouseEvent ev);
  public void mouseClicked(MouseEvent ev);
  public void mouseEntered(MouseEvent ev);
  public void mouseExited(MouseEvent ev);
  public void mouseMoved(MouseEvent ev);
  public void mouseDragged(MouseEvent ev);
  public void mouseWheelMoved(MouseWheelEvent ev);
  public void keyPressed(KeyEvent ev);
  public void keyReleased(KeyEvent ev);
  public void keyTyped(KeyEvent ev);
  public void focusGained(FocusEvent ev);
  public void focusLost(FocusEvent ev);
  public void windowActivated(WindowEvent ev);
  public void windowClosed(WindowEvent ev);
  public void windowClosing(WindowEvent ev);
  public void windowDeactivated(WindowEvent ev);
  public void windowDeiconified(WindowEvent ev);
  public void windowIconified(WindowEvent ev);
```

```
    public void windowOpened(WindowEvent ev);
}
```

buoy.internal.EventLinkRecord

This class stores a list of methods to be invoked whenever an Event of a particular class is generated by a Widget.

```
public class EventLinkRecord{
    public EventLinkRecord(Class eventType);
    public Class getEventType();
    public void addLink(Object target, Method method);
    public void removeLink(Object target);
    public void dispatchEvent(Object event);
}
```

buoy.internal.SingleWidgetPanel

This is a JPanel subclass, which is used internally by various WidgetContainers. It contains a single Widget, and matches its minimum, maximum, and preferred sizes to the Widget.

```
public class SingleWidgetPanel extends JPanel{
    protected Widget widget;

    public SingleWidgetPanel(Widget widget);
    public Dimension getMinimumSize();
    public Dimension getMaximumSize();
    public Dimension getPreferredSize();
}
```

buoy.internal.ToolTipMonitor

ToolTipMonitor receives mouse events from Widgets, and sends out ToolTipEvents whenever the appropriate trigger action occurs.

```
public class ToolTipMonitor{
    public static void processMouseEvent(WidgetMouseEvent ev);
}
```

buoy.internal.WidgetContainerPanel

This is a JPanel subclass, which is used as the Component for many different WidgetContainers. When paintComponent() is called, it optionally fills

itself with its background color then sends out a
RepaintEvent.

```
public class WidgetContainerPanel extends JPanel{
  public WidgetContainerPanel(WidgetContainer container);
  public void paintComponent(Graphics g);
  public boolean isOpaque();
}
```

Chapter 29

The buoy.widget Package

The widget package contains the sundry widgets that are available in buoy.

buoy.widget.AWTWidget

This class is used to create a Widget that is a thin wrapper around an arbitrary AWT/Swing component.

```
public class AWTWidget extends Widget{
  public AWTWidget(Component comp);
  public void invalidateSize();
}
```

buoy.widget.BButton

A BButton is a pushbutton Widget. Its appearance can be customized by setting the text and/or image which appears on it.

```
public class BButton extends Widget{
  public static final Position CENTER;
  public static final Position NORTH;
  public static final Position SOUTH;
  public static final Position WEST;
  public static final Position EAST;
  public static final Position NORTHEAST;
  public static final Position SOUTHEAST;
  public static final Position NORTHWEST;
  public static final Position SOUTHWEST;

  public BButton();
  public BButton(String text);
```

```
public BButton(Icon icon);
public BButton(String text, Icon icon);
protected JButton createComponent();
public JButton getComponent();
public String getText();
public void setText(String text);
public Icon getIcon();
public void setIcon(Icon icon);
public String getActionCommand();
public void setActionCommand(String command);
public Dimension getMaximumSize();
public Position getTextPosition();
public void setTextPosition(Position position);
public static class Position{
  protected int value;
}
}
```

buoy.widget.BCheckBox

A BCheckBox is a Widget for making simple boolean selections. Clicking it with the mouse toggles it on and off.

```
public class BCheckBox extends Widget{
  public BCheckBox();
  public BCheckBox(String text, boolean state);
  protected JCheckBox createComponent(String text, boolean state);
  public JCheckBox getComponent();
  public boolean getState();
  public void setState(boolean selected);
  public String getText();
  public void setText(String text);
  public Dimension getMaximumSize();
}
```

buoy.widget.BCheckBoxMenuItem

A BCheckBoxMenuItem is a menu item for making simple boolean selectons. Selecting it toggles it on and off.

```
public class BCheckBoxMenuItem extends BMenuItem{
  public BCheckBoxMenuItem();
  public BCheckBoxMenuItem(String text, boolean state);
  public BCheckBoxMenuItem(String text, Icon image, boolean state);
  public BCheckBoxMenuItem(String text, Shortcut shortcut, boolean state);
```

```
   public BCheckBoxMenuItem(String text, Shortcut shortcut, Icon
image, boolean state);
   protected JMenuItem createComponent();
   public JMenuItem getComponent();
   public boolean getState();
   public void setState(boolean selected);
}
```

buoy.widget.BColorChooser

A BColorChooser is a Widget that allows the user
to select a color. It has tabs which provide various
ways of choosing the color, such as selecting one from
a palette or specifying values for hue, saturation, and
brightness.

```
public class BColorChooser extends Widget{
   public BColorChooser();
   public BColorChooser(Color color, String title);
   protected JColorChooser createComponent();
   public JColorChooser getComponent();
   public String getTitle();
   public void setTitle(String title);
   public Color getColor();
   public void setColor(Color color);
   public boolean showDialog(Widget parent);
}
```

buoy.widget.BComboBox

A BComboBox is a Widget that displays a popup
menu with a list of objects for the user to select.

```
public class BComboBox extends Widget{
   public BComboBox();
   public BComboBox(Object contents[]);
   public BComboBox(Collection contents);
   public BComboBox(ComboBoxModel model);
   protected JComboBox createComponent();
   public JComboBox getComponent();
   public boolean isEditable();
   public void setEditable(boolean editable);
   public void setContents(Object o[]);
   public void setContents(Collection c);
   public ComboBoxModel getModel();
   public void setModel(ComboBoxModel model);
   public void add(Object o);
   public void add(int index, Object o);
   public void replace(int index, Object o);
   public void remove(int index);
   public void removeAll();
```

widget

```
public int getItemCount();
public Object getItem(int index);
public int getPreferredVisibleRows();
public void setPreferredVisibleRows(int rows);
public int getSelectedIndex();
public void setSelectedIndex(int index);
public Object getSelectedValue();
public void setSelectedValue(Object value);
}
```

buoy.widget.BDialog

A BDialog is a WidgetContainer corresponding to
a dialog window. It may contain up to two child
Widgets, a BMenuBar, and a single other Widget
(usually a WidgetContainer of some sort) which fills
the rest of the window.

```
public class BDialog extends WindowWidget{
  public BDialog();
  public BDialog(String title);
  public BDialog(WindowWidget parent, boolean modal);
  public BDialog(WindowWidget parent, String title, boolean
modal);
  protected JDialog createComponent(Window parent, String title,
boolean modal);
  public JDialog getComponent();
  public int getChildCount();
  public Collection<Widget> getChildren();
  public BMenuBar getMenuBar();
  public void setMenuBar(BMenuBar menus);
  public void remove(Widget widget);
  public void removeAll();
  public String getTitle();
  public void setTitle(String title);
  public void setModal(boolean modal);
  public boolean isModal();
  public boolean isResizable();
  public void setResizable(boolean resizable);
  public void pack();
  protected JRootPane getRootPane();
}
```

buoy.widget.BDocumentViewer

A BDocumentViewer is used for displaying
formatted text documents. The supported document
types include HTML, Rich Text Format (RTF), and

plain text. This class is most often used for displaying help screens or documentation within a program.

```
public class BDocumentViewer extends Widget{
    public BDocumentViewer();
    public BDocumentViewer(URL document) throws IOException;
    protected JEditorPane createComponent();
    public JEditorPane getComponent();
    public URL getDocument();
    public void setDocument(URL document) throws IOException;
    public void setDocument(String text, String type);
    public String getContentType();
    public void processLinkEvent(DocumentLinkEvent event) throws
IOException;
    protected void updateScrollPane();
}
```

buoy.widget.BFileChooser

A BFileChooser is a Widget that allows the user to select files or directories from the file system. It has modes for loading files, saving files, and choosing directories. It supports both single and multiple selection modes, and you can optionally restrict the list of files shown in the dialog by setting a FileFilter.

```
public class BFileChooser extends Widget{
    public static final SelectionMode OPEN_FILE;
    public static final SelectionMode SAVE_FILE;
    public static final SelectionMode SELECT_FOLDER;

    public BFileChooser();
    public BFileChooser(SelectionMode mode, String title);
    public BFileChooser(SelectionMode mode, String title, File
directory);
    protected JFileChooser createComponent();
    public JFileChooser getComponent();
    public String getTitle();
    public void setTitle(String title);
    public SelectionMode getMode();
    public void setMode(SelectionMode mode);
    public boolean isMultipleSelectionEnabled();
    public void setMultipleSelectionEnabled(boolean multiple);
    public FileFilter getFileFilter();
    public void setFileFilter(FileFilter filter);
    public File getDirectory();
    public void setDirectory(File directory);
    public File getSelectedFile();
    public void setSelectedFile(File file);
    public File [] getSelectedFiles();
```

widget

```
public void setSelectedFiles(File files[]) throws IllegalArgumen-
tException;
public boolean showDialog(Widget parent);
public static class SelectionMode{}
}
```

buoy.widget.BFrame

A BFrame is a WidgetContainer corresponding to a main window. It may contain up to two child Widgets, a BMenuBar, and a single other Widget (usually a WidgetContainer of some sort) which fills the rest of the window.

```
public class BFrame extends WindowWidget{
  public BFrame();
  public BFrame(String title);
  protected JFrame createComponent();
  public JFrame getComponent();
  public int getChildCount();
  public Collection<Widget> getChildren();
  public BMenuBar getMenuBar();
  public void setMenuBar(BMenuBar menus);
  public void remove(Widget widget);
  public void removeAll();
  public String getTitle();
  public void setTitle(String title);
  public boolean isResizable();
  public void setResizable(boolean resizable);
  public boolean isIconified();
  public void setIconified(boolean iconified);
  public ImageIcon getIcon();
  public void setIcon(ImageIcon icon);
  public boolean isMaximized();
  public void setMaximized(boolean maximized);
  protected JRootPane getRootPane();
  public static List<BFrame> getFrames();
}
```

buoy.widget.BLabel

A BLabel is a Widget that displays a text string, an image, or both. The text may be specified as HTML, allowing it to contain complex formatting, multiple fonts, etc.

```
public class BLabel extends Widget{
  public static final Position CENTER;
  public static final Position NORTH;
  public static final Position SOUTH;
```

```
public static final Position WEST;
public static final Position EAST;
public static final Position NORTHEAST;
public static final Position SOUTHEAST;
public static final Position NORTHWEST;
public static final Position SOUTHWEST;

public BLabel();
public BLabel(String text);
public BLabel(String text, Position align);
public BLabel(Icon image);
public BLabel(Icon image, Position align);
public BLabel(String text, Icon image, Position align, Position
textPos);
protected JLabel createComponent(String text, Icon image);
public JLabel getComponent();
public String getText();
public void setText(String text);
public Icon getIcon();
public void setIcon(Icon image);
public Dimension getMaximumSize();
public Position getAlignment();
public void setAlignment(Position alignment);
public Position getTextPosition();
public void setTextPosition(Position position);
public static class Position {
  protected int value;
}
}
```

buoy.widget.BList

A BList is a Widget that displays a list of objects
for the user to select. Typically the objects are Strings,
but other types of objects can be used as well. It
supports both single and multiple selection modes.
There are methods for adding and removing objects in
the list. Alternatively, you can set a ListModel to
provide more complex behaviors.

```
public class BList extends Widget{
  protected DefaultListModel defaultModel;

  public BList();
  public BList(Object contents[]);
  public BList(Collection contents);
  public BList(ListModel model);
  protected JList createComponent();
  public JList getComponent();
  public void setContents(Object o[]);
  public void setContents(Collection c);
```

```
    public void add(Object o);
    public void add(int index, Object o);
    public void replace(int index, Object o);
    public void remove(int index);
    public void removeAll();
    public ListModel getModel();
    public void setModel(ListModel model);
    public int getItemCount();
    public Object getItem(int index);
    public boolean isMultipleSelectionEnabled();
    public void setMultipleSelectionEnabled(boolean multiple);
    public int getPreferredVisibleRows();
    public void setPreferredVisibleRows(int rows);
    public boolean isSelected(int index);
    public int getSelectedIndex();
    public int [] getSelectedIndices();
    public Object getSelectedValue();
    public Object [] getSelectedValues();
    public void clearSelection();
    public void setSelected(int index, boolean selected);
    public void scrollToItem(int index);
    public Dimension getMaximumSize();
}
```

buoy.widget.BMenu

A BMenu is a WidgetContainer corresponding to a pulldown menu in the menu bar of a window.

```
public class BMenu extends WidgetContainer implements
MenuWidget{
    public BMenu();
    public BMenu(String title);
    protected JMenu createComponent();
    public JMenu getComponent();
    public String getText();
    public void setText(String title);
    public int getMnemonic();
    public void setMnemonic(int key);
    public void add(MenuWidget widget);
    public void add(MenuWidget widget, int index);
    public void addSeparator();
    public int getChildCount();
    public MenuWidget getChild(int i);
    public Collection<Widget> getChildren();
    public void remove(Widget widget);
    public void removeAll();
    public void layoutChildren();
}
```

buoy.widget.BMenuBar

A BMenuBar is a WidgetContainer corresponding to the menu bar of a window.

```
public class BMenuBar extends WidgetContainer{
  public BMenuBar();
  protected JMenuBar createComponent();
  public JMenuBar getComponent();
  public void add(BMenu menu);
  public void add(BMenu menu, int index);
  public int getChildCount();
  public BMenu getChild(int i);
  public Collection<Widget> getChildren();
  public void remove(Widget widget);
  public void removeAll();
  public void layoutChildren();
}
```

buoy.widget.BMenuItem

A BMenuItem is a Widget corresponding to an item in a pulldown menu. Each menu item typically represents a different command, which the user can issue by selecting it with the mouse.

```
public class BMenuItem extends Widget implements MenuWidget{
  public BMenuItem();
  public BMenuItem(String text);
  public BMenuItem(String text, Icon image);
  public BMenuItem(String text, Shortcut shortcut);
  public BMenuItem(String text, Shortcut shortcut, Icon image);
  protected JMenuItem createComponent();
  public JMenuItem getComponent();
  public String getText();
  public void setText(String title);
  public String getActionCommand();
  public void setActionCommand(String command);
  public Shortcut getShortcut();
  public void setShortcut(Shortcut shortcut);
  public int getMnemonic();
  public void setMnemonic(int key);
  public Icon getIcon();
  public void setIcon(Icon image);
}
```

widget

buoy.widget.BorderContainer

BorderContainer is a WidgetContainer which may have up to five children: one along each edge, and a fifth one in the center. When this container is resized, the center component grows to take up as much space as possible.

```
public class BorderContainer extends WidgetContainer{
    public static final Position CENTER;
    public static final Position NORTH;
    public static final Position EAST;
    public static final Position SOUTH;
    public static final Position WEST;

    public BorderContainer();
    public JPanel getComponent();
    public int getChildCount();
    public Collection<Widget> getChildren();
    public Widget getChild(Position where);
    public Position getChildPosition(Widget widget);
    public void layoutChildren();
    public void add(Widget widget, Position where);
    public void add(Widget widget, Position where, LayoutInfo
layout);
    public LayoutInfo getChildLayout(Position where);
    public void setChildLayout(Position where, LayoutInfo layout);
    public LayoutInfo getChildLayout(Widget widget);
    public void setChildLayout(Widget widget, LayoutInfo layout);
    public LayoutInfo getDefaultLayout();
    public void setDefaultLayout(LayoutInfo layout);
    public void remove(Widget widget);
    public void remove(Position where);
    public void removeAll();
    public boolean getCornersAreVertical();
    public void setCornersAreVertical(boolean vertical);
    public Dimension getMinimumSize();
    public Dimension getPreferredSize();
    public static class Position;
}
```

buoy.widget.BOutline

A BOutline is a WidgetContainer that draws an outline around another Widget. The appearance of the outline is determined by a javax.swing.border.Border object. There are static methods for creating several common types of outlines, or you can use a different type by providing your own Border object.

```
public class BOutline extends WidgetContainer{
    public BOutline();
    public BOutline(Widget content, Border border);
```

```
   public static BOutline createEmptyBorder(Widget content, int
thickness);
   public static BOutline createEtchedBorder(Widget content,
boolean raised);
   public static BOutline createBevelBorder(Widget content,
boolean raised);
   public static BOutline createLineBorder(Widget content, Color
color, int thickness);
   public Border getBorder();
   public void setBorder(Border border);
   public Widget getContent();
   public void setContent(Widget contentWidget);
   public int getChildCount();
   public Collection<Widget> getChildren();
   public void remove(Widget widget);
   public void removeAll();
   public void layoutChildren();
   public Dimension getMinimumSize();
   public Dimension getMaximumSize();
   public Dimension getPreferredSize();
}
```

buoy.widget.BPasswordField

A BPasswordField is a simple text entry box for typing passwords. It allows the user to enter a single line of text. The characters typed into the box are hidden, and an alternate echo character is displayed instead.

```
public class BPasswordField extends BTextField{
   public BPasswordField();
   public BPasswordField(String text);
   public BPasswordField(int columns);
   public BPasswordField(String text, int columns);
   protected JPasswordField createComponent();
   public JPasswordField getComponent();
   public char getEchoChar();
   public void setEchoChar(char c);
   public String getText();
}
```

buoy.widget.BPopupMenu

A BPopupMenu is a WidgetContainer corresponding to a popup menu. It is typically displayed in response to a buoy.event.WidgetMouseEvent whose isPopupTrigger() method returns true. The exact conditions which represent a popup trigger are platform specific.

```
public class BPopupMenu extends WidgetContainer implements
MenuWidget{
    public BPopupMenu();
    protected JPopupMenu createComponent();
    public JPopupMenu getComponent();
    public void show(Widget widget, int x, int y);
    public void show(WidgetMouseEvent event);
    public void add(MenuWidget widget);
    public void add(MenuWidget widget, int index);
    public void addSeparator();
    public int getChildCount();
    public MenuWidget getChild(int i);
    public Collection<Widget> getChildren();
    public void remove(Widget widget);
    public void removeAll();
    public void layoutChildren();
}
```

buoy.widget.BProgressBar

BProgressBar is a Widget that displays the status of some operation. It is a horizontal or vertical bar that gradually fills up to indicate what fraction of the operation is complete. It optionally can also display a line of text describing the current state of the operation.

```
public class BProgressBar extends Widget{
    public static final Orientation HORIZONTAL;
    public static final Orientation VERTICAL;

    public BProgressBar();
    public BProgressBar(int min, int max);
    public BProgressBar(Orientation orient, int min, int max);
    protected JProgressBar createComponent();
    public JProgressBar getComponent();
    public int getValue();
    public void setValue(int value);
    public int getMinimum();
    public void setMinimum(int min);
    public int getMaximum();
    public void setMaximum(int max);
    public Orientation getOrientation();
    public void setOrientation(Orientation orient);
    public boolean isIndeterminate();
    public void setIndeterminate(boolean indeterminate);
    public boolean getShowProgressText();
```

```
public void setShowProgressText(boolean show);
public String getProgressText();
public void setProgressText(String text);
public static class Orientation {
  protected int value;
}
}
```

buoy.widget.BRadioButton

A BRadioButton is a Widget for selecting between several options. It is normally used as part of a RadioButtonGroup. Each BRadioButton represents a single option. Clicking on it selects it, and deselects all other members of its RadioButtonGroup.

```
public class BRadioButton extends Widget{
  public BRadioButton(RadioButtonGroup group);
  public BRadioButton(String text, boolean state, Radio-
ButtonGroup group);
  protected JRadioButton createComponent(String text, boolean
state);
  public JRadioButton getComponent();
  public boolean getState();
  public void setState(boolean selected);
  public String getText();
  public void setText(String text);
  public RadioButtonGroup getGroup();
  public void setGroup(RadioButtonGroup newGroup);
  public Dimension getMaximumSize();
}
```

buoy.widget.BRadioButtonMenuItem

A BRadioButtonMenuItem is a menu item for selecting between several options. It is normally used as part of a RadioButtonGroup. Each BRadioButtonMenuItem represents a single option. Choosing it from the menu selects it, and deselects all other members of its RadioButtonGroup.

```
public class BRadioButtonMenuItem extends BMenuItem{
  public BRadioButtonMenuItem(RadioButtonGroup group);
  public BRadioButtonMenuItem(String text, boolean state,
RadioButtonGroup group);
  public BRadioButtonMenuItem(String text, Icon image, boolean
state, RadioButtonGroup group);
  public BRadioButtonMenuItem(String text, Shortcut shortcut,
boolean state, RadioButtonGroup group);
```

```
    public BRadioButtonMenuItem(String text, Shortcut shortcut, Icon
image, boolean state, RadioButtonGroup group);
    protected JRadioButtonMenuItem createComponent();
    public JRadioButtonMenuItem getComponent();
    public boolean getState();
    public void setState(boolean selected);
    public RadioButtonGroup getGroup();
    public void setGroup(RadioButtonGroup newGroup);
}
```

buoy.widget.BScrollBar

A BScrollBar is a Widget that allows the user to select a single value by dragging a "thumb" along a bar.

```
public class BScrollBar extends Widget{
  public static final Orientation HORIZONTAL;
  public static final Orientation VERTICAL;

  public BScrollBar();
  public BScrollBar(int value, int extent, int minimum, int maximum,
Orientation orientation);
  protected JScrollBar createComponent(Orientation orientation);
  public JScrollBar getComponent();
  public int getMinimum();
  public void setMinimum(int value);
  public int getMaximum();
  public void setMaximum(int value);
  public int getValue();
  public void setValue(int value);
  public int getExtent();
  public void setExtent(int value);
  public Orientation getOrientation();
  public void setOrientation(Orientation orientation);
  public int getUnitIncrement();
  protected int getUnitIncrement(int direction);
  public void setUnitIncrement(int increment);
  public int getBlockIncrement();
  protected int getBlockIncrement(int direction);
  public void setBlockIncrement(int increment);
  public static class Orientation {
    protected int value;
  }
}
```

buoy.widget.BScrollPane

A BScrollPane is a WidgetContainer with up to five children.

```
public class BScrollPane extends WidgetContainer{
```

```
    public static final ScrollbarPolicy SCROLLBAR_NEVER;
    public static final ScrollbarPolicy SCROLLBAR_AS_NEEDED;
    public static final ScrollbarPolicy SCROLLBAR_ALWAYS;

    public BScrollPane();
    public BScrollPane(Widget contentWidget);
    public BScrollPane(ScrollbarPolicy horizontalPolicy,
ScrollbarPolicy verticalPolicy);
    public BScrollPane(Widget contentWidget, ScrollbarPolicy
horizontalPolicy, ScrollbarPolicy verticalPolicy);
    protected JScrollPane createComponent();
    public JScrollPane getComponent();
    public Widget getContent();
    public void setContent(Widget widget);
    public Widget getRowHeader();
    public void setRowHeader(Widget widget);
    public Widget getColHeader();
    public void setColHeader(Widget widget);
    public BScrollBar getHorizontalScrollBar();
    public BScrollBar getVerticalScrollBar();
    public ScrollbarPolicy getHorizontalScrollbarPolicy();
    public void setHorizontalScrollbarPolicy(ScrollbarPolicy policy);
    public ScrollbarPolicy getVerticalScrollbarPolicy();
    public void setVerticalScrollbarPolicy(ScrollbarPolicy policy);
    public Dimension getPreferredViewSize();
    public void setPreferredViewSize(Dimension size);
    public Dimension getViewSize();
    public boolean getForceWidth();
    public void setForceWidth(boolean force);
    public boolean getForceHeight();
    public void setForceHeight(boolean force);
    public int getChildCount();
    public Collection<Widget> getChildren();
    public void remove(Widget widget);
    public void removeAll();
    public void layoutChildren();
    public Dimension getMinimumSize();
    public Dimension getPreferredSize();
    public void setBackground(Color background);
    protected void invalidateSize();
    public static class ScrollbarPolicy { }
}
```

buoy.widget.BSeparator

A BSeparator is a Widget corresponding to a divider line between parts of a container.

```
public class BSeparator extends Widget implements MenuWidget{
    public static final Orientation HORIZONTAL;
    public static final Orientation VERTICAL;

    public BSeparator();
```

```
    public BSeparator(Orientation orientation);
    protected JSeparator createComponent();
    public JSeparator getComponent();
    public Orientation getOrientation();
    public void setOrientation(Orientation orientation);
    public static class Orientation  { }
}
```

buoy.widget.BSlider

A BSlider is a Widget that allows the user to select a single value by dragging a "thumb" along a bar. It can optionally show tick marks, labels, or both along the bar.

```
public class BSlider extends Widget{
    public static final Orientation HORIZONTAL;
    public static final Orientation VERTICAL;

    public BSlider();
    public BSlider(int value, int minimum, int maximum, Orientation
orientation);
    protected JSlider createComponent(Orientation orientation);
    public JSlider getComponent();
    public int getMinimum();
    public void setMinimum(int value);
    public int getMaximum();
    public void setMaximum(int value);
    public int getValue();
    public void setValue(int value);
    public Orientation getOrientation();
    public void setOrientation(Orientation orientation);
    public int getMajorTickSpacing();
    public void setMajorTickSpacing(int spacing);
    public int getMinorTickSpacing();
    public void setMinorTickSpacing(int spacing);
    public boolean getShowTicks();
    public void setShowTicks(boolean show);
    public boolean getShowLabels();
    public void setShowLabels(boolean show);
    public boolean getSnapToTicks();
    public void setSnapToTicks(boolean snap);
    public static class Orientation  {
      protected int value;
    }
}
```

buoy.widget.BSpinner

A BSpinner is a Widget that allows the user to select a value from an ordered sequence. It allows the user to enter a value, and also provides a pair of arrows for stepping through the values in the sequence.

```
public class BSpinner extends Widget{
  public BSpinner();
  public BSpinner(SpinnerModel model);
  public BSpinner(int value, int min, int max, int step);
  public BSpinner(double value, double min, double max, double step);
  public BSpinner(Date date);
  public BSpinner(Object values[]);
  protected JSpinner createComponent();
  public JSpinner getComponent();
  public Object getValue();
  public void setValue(Object value);
  public void commitEdit() throws ParseException;
  public SpinnerModel getModel();
  public void setModel(SpinnerModel model);
}
```

buoy.widget.BSplitPane

BSplitPane is a WidgetContainer whose space is divided between two child Widgets. A drag bar is placed between them, which the user can move to change how much space is given to each child.

```
public class BSplitPane extends WidgetContainer{
  public static final Orientation HORIZONTAL;
  public static final Orientation VERTICAL;

  public BSplitPane();
  public BSplitPane(Orientation orient);
  public BSplitPane(Orientation orient, Widget child1, Widget child2);
  protected JSplitPane createComponent();
  public JSplitPane getComponent();
  public int getDividerLocation();
  public void setDividerLocation(int location);
  public void setDividerLocation(double location);
  public void resetToPreferredSizes();
  public Orientation getOrientation();
  public void setOrientation(Orientation orient);
  public boolean isContinuousLayout();
  public void setContinuousLayout(boolean continuous);
  public boolean isOneTouchExpandable();
  public void setOneTouchExpandable(boolean expandable);
  public double getResizeWeight();
  public void setResizeWeight(double weight);
  public int getChildCount();
```

widget

```
public Collection<Widget> getChildren();
public Widget getChild(int index);
public void layoutChildren();
public void add(Widget widget, int index);
public void remove(Widget widget);
public void remove(int index);
public void removeAll();
public Dimension getMinimumSize();
public Dimension getPreferredSize();
public static class Orientation{
   protected int value;
}
}
```

buoy.widget.BStandardDialog

BStandardDialog is used for displaying a variety of "standard" modal dialogs which display messages or ask for simple types of input. Most platforms define a standardized appearance for such dialogs (the layout, the use of particular icons, etc.), and this class will automatically create dialogs which look correct for the current platform.

```
public class BStandardDialog{
   public static final Style ERROR;
   public static final Style INFORMATION;
   public static final Style WARNING;
   public static final Style QUESTION;
   public static final Style PLAIN;

   public BStandardDialog();
   public BStandardDialog(String title, Object message, Style style);
   public String getTitle();
   public void setTitle(String title);
   public Object getMessage();
   public void setMessage(Object message);
   public Style getStyle();
   public void setStyle(Style style);
   public void showMessageDialog(Widget parent);
   public int showOptionDialog(Widget parent, String options[],
String defaultVal);
   public String showInputDialog(Widget parent, String options[],
String defaultVal);
   public static class Style  {
      public int value;
   }
}
```

buoy.widget.BTabbedPane

BTabbedPane is a WidgetContainer which arranges its child Widgets in a row.

```
public class BTabbedPane extends WidgetContainer{
  public static final TabPosition TOP;
  public static final TabPosition LEFT;
  public static final TabPosition BOTTOM;
  public static final TabPosition RIGHT;

  public BTabbedPane();
  public BTabbedPane(TabPosition pos);
  protected JTabbedPane createComponent(TabPosition pos);
  public JTabbedPane getComponent();
  public int getChildCount();
  public Widget getChild(int i);
  public Collection<Widget> getChildren();
  public void layoutChildren();
  public void add(Widget widget, String tabName);
  public void add(Widget widget, String tabName, Icon image);
  public void add(Widget widget, String tabName, Icon image, int index);
  public void remove(Widget widget);
  public void remove(int index);
  public void removeAll();
  public int getChildIndex(Widget widget);
  public TabPosition getTabPosition();
  public void setTabPosition(TabPosition pos);
  public String getTabName(int index);
  public void setTabName(int index, String name);
  public Icon getTabImage(int index);
  public void setTabImage(int index, Icon image);
  public int getSelectedTab();
  public void setSelectedTab(int index);
  public static class TabPosition {
    protected int value;
  }
}
```

buoy.widget.BTable

A BTable is a Widget that displays a grid of objects. Typically the objects are Strings, but other types of objects can be used as well. It optionally can allow the user to select rows, columns, or individual cells, and to edit the contents of cells. There are methods for adding and removing rows and columns, and for setting the contents of cells. Alternatively, you can set a TableModel to provide more complex behaviors.

```
public class BTable extends Widget{
  protected DefaultTableModel defaultModel;
  protected BTableHeader tableHeader;
  protected ArrayList<Boolean> columnEditable;

  public static final SelectionMode SELECT_NONE;
  public static final SelectionMode SELECT_ROWS;
  public static final SelectionMode SELECT_COLUMNS;
  public static final SelectionMode SELECT_CELLS;

  public BTable();
  public BTable(int rows, int cols);
  public BTable(Object cellData[][], Object columnTitle[]);
  public BTable(TableModel model);
  protected JTable createComponent();
  public JTable getComponent();
  public BTableHeader getTableHeader();
  public TableModel getModel();
  public void setModel(TableModel model);
  public void addColumn(Object columnTitle);
  public void addColumn(Object columnTitle, Object
columnData[]);
  public void removeColumn(int index);
  public void removeAllColumns();
  public void addRow(Object rowData[]);
  public void addRow(int index, Object rowData[]);
  public void removeRow(int index);
  public void removeAllRows();
  public int getRowCount();
  public int getColumnCount();
  public boolean isColumnEditable(int index);
  public void setColumnEditable(int index, boolean editable);
  public Object getCellValue(int row, int col);
  public void setCellValue(int row, int col, Object value);
  public Object getColumnHeader(int col);
  public void setColumnHeader(int col, Object value);
  public int getRowHeight(int row);
  public void setRowHeight(int row, int height);
  public int getColumnWidth(int col);
  public void setColumnWidth(int col, int width);
  public void sizeColumnToFit(int col);
  public boolean getColumnsResizable();
  public void setColumnsResizable(boolean resizable);
  public boolean getColumnsReorderable();
  public void setColumnsReorderable(boolean reorderable);
  public SelectionMode getSelectionMode();
  public void setSelectionMode(SelectionMode mode);
  public boolean isMultipleSelectionEnabled();
  public void setMultipleSelectionEnabled(boolean multiple);
  public boolean isRowSelected(int row);
```

```
public void setRowSelected(int row, boolean selected);
public int[] getSelectedRows();
public boolean isColumnSelected(int col);
public void setColumnSelected(int col, boolean selected);
public int[] getSelectedColumns();
public boolean isCellSelected(int row, int col);
public void setCellSelected(int row, int col, boolean selected);
public Point[] getSelectedCells();
public void clearSelection();
public int findRow(Point pos);
public int findColumn(Point pos);
public void editCellAt(int row, int col);
public boolean getShowHorizontalLines();
public void setShowHorizontalLines(boolean show);
public boolean getShowVerticalLines();
public void setShowVerticalLines(boolean show);
public void scrollToCell(int row, int col);
protected void setParent(WidgetContainer container);
public class BTableHeader extends Widget {
  public JTableHeader getComponent();
  public BTable getTable();
}
public static class SelectionMode { }
}
```

buoy.widget.BTextArea

A BTextArea is a multi-line text entry box. You can specify a preferred size for the text area in terms of rows and columns, but it automatically expands to be large enough to show all text contained in it.

```
public class BTextArea extends TextWidget{
  public static final WrapStyle WRAP_NONE;
  public static final WrapStyle WRAP_CHARACTER;
  public static final WrapStyle WRAP_WORD;

  public BTextArea();
  public BTextArea(String text);
  public BTextArea(int rows, int columns);
  public BTextArea(String text, int rows, int columns);
  protected JTextArea createComponent();
  public JTextArea getComponent();
  public int getRows();
  public void setRows(int rows);
  public int getColumns();
  public void setColumns(int columns);
  public int getLineCount();
  public WrapStyle getWrapStyle();
  public void setWrapStyle(WrapStyle style);
  public int getTabSize();
  public void setTabSize(int size);
```

```
public void append(String text);
public void insert(String text, int pos);
public void replaceRange(String text, int start, int end);
public Dimension getMinimumSize();
protected void textChanged();
public static class WrapStyle { }
}
```

buoy.widget.BTextField

A BTextField is a simple text entry box. It allows the user to enter a single line of text.

```
public class BTextField extends TextWidget{
    public BTextField();
    public BTextField(String text);
    public BTextField(int columns);
    public BTextField(String text, int columns);
    protected JTextField createComponent();
    public JTextField getComponent();
    public int getColumns();
    public void setColumns(int columns);
}
```

buoy.widget.BToolBar

A BToolBar is a WidgetContainer which displays a series of Widgets in a row or column.

```
public class BToolBar extends WidgetContainer{
    public static final Orientation HORIZONTAL;
    public static final Orientation VERTICAL;

    public BToolBar();
    public BToolBar(Orientation orientation);
    protected JToolBar createComponent();
    public JToolBar getComponent();
    public Orientation getOrientation();
    public void setOrientation(Orientation orientation);
    public void add(Widget widget);
    public void add(Widget widget, int index);
    public void addSeparator();
    public int getChildCount();
    public Widget getChild(int i);
    public Collection<Widget> getChildren();
    public void remove(Widget widget);
    public void removeAll();
    public int getChildIndex(Widget widget);
    public void layoutChildren();
    public static class Orientation { }
}
```

buoy.widget.BToolTip

A BToolTip is a small floating window that appears in front of another Widget. It contains a single line of text, and generally provides information about the function of the Widget it is displayed over.

```
public class BToolTip extends Widget{
  public BToolTip();
  public BToolTip(String text);
  protected JToolTip createComponent();
  public JToolTip getComponent();
  public String getText();
  public void setText(String text);
  public void show(Widget widget, Point where);
  public void processEvent(ToolTipEvent event);
  public static BToolTip getShowingToolTip();
  public static void hide();
}
```

buoy.widget.BTree

A BTree is a Widget that displays a hierarchical list of objects (or "nodes"). The user can collapse or expand particular nodes to hide or show their child nodes. It optionally can allow the user to select nodes from the tree, or to edit the contents of nodes.

```
public class BTree extends Widget{
  public BTree();
  public BTree(TreeNode root);
  public BTree(TreeModel model);
  protected JTree createComponent(TreeModel model);
  public JTree getComponent();
  public TreeModel getModel();
  public void setModel(TreeModel model);
  public TreePath getRootNode();
  public int getChildNodeCount(TreePath path);
  public TreePath getChildNode(TreePath path, int index);
  public TreePath getParentNode(TreePath path);
  public boolean isLeafNode(TreePath path);
  public TreePath addNode(TreePath parent, MutableTreeNode
node);
  public TreePath addNode(TreePath parent, MutableTreeNode
node, int index);
  public void removeNode(TreePath path);
  public boolean isSelectionEnabled();
  public void setSelectionEnabled(boolean enabled);
  public boolean isMultipleSelectionEnabled();
  public void setMultipleSelectionEnabled(boolean multiple);
```

```
  public int getSelectionCount();
  public TreePath getSelectedNode();
  public TreePath [] getSelectedNodes();
  public boolean isNodeSelected(TreePath path);
  public void setNodeSelected(TreePath path, boolean selected);
  public void clearSelection();
  public boolean isEditable();
  public void setEditable(boolean editable);
  public void editNode(TreePath path);
  public TreePath findNode(Point pos);
  public boolean isNodeExpanded(TreePath path);
  public void setNodeExpanded(TreePath path, boolean expand-
ed);
  public boolean isNodeVisible(TreePath path);
  public void makeNodeVisible(TreePath path);
  public void scrollToNode(TreePath path);
  public boolean isRootNodeShown();
  public void setRootNodeShown(boolean shown);
  public int getPreferredVisibleRows();
  public void setPreferredVisibleRows(int rows);
  public TreeCellRenderer getCellRenderer();
  public void setCellRenderer(TreeCellRenderer renderer);
}
```

buoy.widget.BuoyComponent

This class is a JPanel which contains a Widget. It
is used for embedding Buoy-based user interfaces into
Swing-based windows.

```
public class BuoyComponent extends SingleWidgetPanel{
  public BuoyComponent(Widget widget);
  public Widget getWidget();
  public void validate();
}
```

buoy.widget.BWindow

A BWindow is a WidgetContainer corresponding
to an undecorated window. It has no title bar or
pulldown menus. It may contain a single Widget
(usually a WidgetContainer of some sort) which fills
the window.

```
public class BWindow extends WindowWidget{
  public BWindow();
  protected JWindow createComponent();
  public JWindow getComponent();
  public int getChildCount();
  public Collection<Widget> getChildren();
```

```
public void remove(Widget widget);
public void removeAll();
protected JRootPane getRootPane();
}
```

buoy.widget.ColumnContainer

ColumnContainer is a WidgetContainer which arranges its child Widgets in a single column, from top to bottom.

```
public class ColumnContainer extends WidgetContainer{
  public ColumnContainer();
  public JPanel getComponent();
  public int getChildCount();
  public Widget getChild(int i);
  public Collection<Widget> getChildren();
  public void layoutChildren();
  public void add(Widget widget);
  public void add(Widget widget, LayoutInfo layout);
  public void add(Widget widget, int index, LayoutInfo layout);
  public LayoutInfo getChildLayout(int index);
  public void setChildLayout(int index, LayoutInfo layout);
  public LayoutInfo getChildLayout(Widget widget);
  public void setChildLayout(Widget widget, LayoutInfo layout);
  public LayoutInfo getDefaultLayout();
  public void setDefaultLayout(LayoutInfo layout);
  public void remove(Widget widget);
  public void remove(int index);
  public void removeAll();
  public int getChildIndex(Widget widget);
  public Dimension getMinimumSize();
  public Dimension getPreferredSize();
}
```

buoy.widget.CustomWidget

A CustomWidget is used for defining new graphical objects. It occupies a rectangular region of a window, and its preferred, minimum, and maximum sizes can all be modified.

```
public class CustomWidget extends Widget{
  public CustomWidget();
  public void setMinimumSize(Dimension size);
  public void setMaximumSize(Dimension size);
  public void setPreferredSize(Dimension size);
  public boolean isOpaque();
  public void setOpaque(boolean opaque);
}
```

widget

buoy.widget.ExplicitContainer

ExplicitContainer is a WidgetContainer which allows the sizes and positions of its children to be set explicitly.

```
public class ExplicitContainer extends WidgetContainer{
    public ExplicitContainer();
    public JPanel getComponent();
    public int getChildCount();
    public Widget getChild(int i);
    public Collection<Widget> getChildren();
    public void layoutChildren();
    public void add(Widget widget, Rectangle bounds);
    public int getChildIndex(Widget widget);
    public Rectangle getChildBounds(int index);
    public void setChildBounds(int index, Rectangle bounds);
    public Rectangle getChildBounds(Widget widget);
    public void setChildBounds(Widget widget, Rectangle bounds);
    public void remove(Widget widget);
    public void removeAll();
    public Dimension getMinimumSize();
    public Dimension getPreferredSize();
}
```

buoy.widget.FormContainer

FormContainer is a WidgetContainer which arranges its children in a grid. The width of each row and the height of each column may be different, and a single Widget may occupy a rectangular block of cells.

```
public class FormContainer extends WidgetContainer{
    public FormContainer(double colWeight[], double rowWeight[]);
    public JPanel getComponent();
    public FormContainer(int numCols, int numRows);
    public int getChildCount();
    public Widget getChild(int i);
    public Collection<Widget> getChildren();
    public int getRowCount();
    public int getColumnCount();
    public void setRowCount(int rows);
    public void setColumnCount(int columns);
    public double getRowWeight(int row);
    public double getColumnWeight(int col);
    public void setRowWeight(int row, double weight);
    public void setColumnWeight(int col, double weight);
    public void layoutChildren();
    public void add(Widget widget, int col, int row);
    public void add(Widget widget, int col, int row, LayoutInfo layout);
```

```
    public void add(Widget widget, int col, int row, int width, int
height);
    public void add(Widget widget, int col, int row, int width, int height,
LayoutInfo layout);
    public LayoutInfo getChildLayout(int index);
    public void setChildLayout(int index, LayoutInfo layout);
    public LayoutInfo getChildLayout(Widget widget);
    public void setChildLayout(Widget widget, LayoutInfo layout);
    public LayoutInfo getDefaultLayout();
    public void setDefaultLayout(LayoutInfo layout);
    public Rectangle getChildCells(int index);
    public void setChildCells(int index, Rectangle cells);
    public Rectangle getChildCells(Widget widget);
    public void setChildCells(Widget widget, Rectangle cells);
    public void remove(Widget widget);
    public void remove(int index);
    public void removeAll();
    public int getWidgetIndex(Widget widget);
    public Dimension getMinimumSize();
    public Dimension getPreferredSize();
    protected void invalidateSize();
}
```

buoy.widget.GridContainer

GridContainer is a WidgetContainer which
arranges its child Widgets in a uniform grid. Every
column is the same width, and every row is the same
height.

```
public class GridContainer extends WidgetContainer{
    public GridContainer(int cols, int rows);
    public JPanel getComponent();
    public int getChildCount();
    public Collection<Widget> getChildren();
    public Widget getChild(int col, int row);
    public void layoutChildren();
    public void add(Widget widget, int col, int row);
    public void add(Widget widget, int col, int row, LayoutInfo layout);
    public LayoutInfo getChildLayout(int col, int row);
    public void setChildLayout(int col, int row, LayoutInfo layout);
    public LayoutInfo getChildLayout(Widget widget);
    public void setChildLayout(Widget widget, LayoutInfo layout);
    public LayoutInfo getDefaultLayout();
    public void setDefaultLayout(LayoutInfo layout);
    public int getRowCount();
    public void setRowCount(int rows);
    public int getColumnCount();
    public void setColumnCount(int cols);
    public void remove(Widget widget);
    public void remove(int col, int row);
    public void removeAll();
```

```
    public Point getChildCell(Widget widget);
    public Dimension getMinimumSize();
    public Dimension getPreferredSize();
}
```

buoy.widget.LayoutInfo

A LayoutInfo object contains information about how a Widget should be layed out within the space provided by its WidgetContainer. Most containers allow you to specify a default LayoutInfo for all Widgets, and also to specify a different one for each Widget.

```
public class LayoutInfo implements Cloneable{
    public static final Alignment CENTER;
    public static final Alignment NORTH;
    public static final Alignment SOUTH;
    public static final Alignment WEST;
    public static final Alignment EAST;
    public static final Alignment NORTHEAST;
    public static final Alignment SOUTHEAST;
    public static final Alignment NORTHWEST;
    public static final Alignment SOUTHWEST;

    public static final FillType NONE;
    public static final FillType HORIZONTAL;
    public static final FillType VERTICAL;
    public static final FillType BOTH;

    public LayoutInfo();
    public LayoutInfo(Alignment align, FillType fill);
    public LayoutInfo(Alignment align, FillType fill, Insets insets,
Dimension padding);
    public Alignment getAlignment();
    public void setAlignment(Alignment align);
    public FillType getFill();
    public void setFill(FillType fill);
    public Insets getInsets();
    public void setInsets(Insets insets);
    public Dimension getPadding();
    public void setPadding(Dimension padding);
    public Object clone();
    public Dimension getPreferredSize(Widget widget);
    public Dimension getMaximumSize(Widget widget);
    public Rectangle getWidgetLayout(Widget widget, Rectangle
rect);
    public static class Alignment{
      protected int value;
    }
    public static class FillType{ }
```

}

buoy.widget.MenuWidget

This interface represents any Widget that can be a child of a BMenu.

```
public interface MenuWidget{ }
```

buoy.widget.OverlayContainer

OverlayContainer is a WidgetContainer which overlays its children on top of each other. Every child Widget is sized to fill the entire container, and the preferred size of the container is equal to the largest preferred size of any of its children.

```
public class OverlayContainer extends WidgetContainer{
    public OverlayContainer();
    public JPanel getComponent();
    public int getChildCount();
    public Widget getChild(int i);
    public Collection<Widget> getChildren();
    public int getChildIndex(Widget widget);
    public void layoutChildren();
    public void add(Widget widget, int index);
    public void add(Widget widget);
    public void remove(Widget widget);
    public void removeAll();
    public void setVisibleChild(int i);
    public void setVisibleChild(Widget child);
    public Dimension getMinimumSize();
    public Dimension getPreferredSize();
    protected void invalidateSize();
}
```

widget

buoy.widget.RadioButtonGroup

A RadioButtonGroup manages a set of BRadioButtons and BRadioButtonMenuItems. It ensures that only one member of the group is selected at any time. It provides methods for determining which member is currently selected, and for changing the selection.

```
public class RadioButtonGroup extends EventSource{
    public RadioButtonGroup();
    void add(BRadioButton button);
```

```
void add(BRadioButtonMenuItem item);
void remove(int i);
public Object getSelection();
public void setSelection(Object sel);
public Iterator getRadioButtons();
public int getRadioButtonCount();
public Object getRadioButton(int i);
}
```

buoy.widget.RowContainer

RowContainer is a WidgetContainer which arranges its child Widgets in a row, from left to right.

```
public class RowContainer extends WidgetContainer{
  public RowContainer();
  public JPanel getComponent();
  public int getChildCount();
  public Widget getChild(int i);
  public Collection<Widget> getChildren();
  public void layoutChildren();
  public void add(Widget widget);
  public void add(Widget widget, LayoutInfo layout);
  public void add(Widget widget, int index, LayoutInfo layout);
  public LayoutInfo getChildLayout(int index);
  public void setChildLayout(int index, LayoutInfo layout);
  public LayoutInfo getChildLayout(Widget widget);
  public void setChildLayout(Widget widget, LayoutInfo layout);
  public LayoutInfo getDefaultLayout();
  public void setDefaultLayout(LayoutInfo layout);
  public void remove(Widget widget);
  public void remove(int index);
  public void removeAll();
  public int getChildIndex(Widget widget);
  public Dimension getMinimumSize();
  public Dimension getPreferredSize();
}
```

buoy.widget.Shortcut

A Shortcut represents a keyboard shortcut that can be used for activating a menu item. It consists of a particular key that must be pressed, plus a set of modifier keys.

```
public class Shortcut{
  public static final int SHIFT_MASK;
  public static final int CTRL_MASK;
  public static final int META_MASK;
  public static final int ALT_MASK;
  public static final int DEFAULT_MASK;
```

```
public Shortcut(char c);
public Shortcut(int key);
public Shortcut(char c, int modifiers);
public Shortcut(int key, int modifiers);
public KeyStroke getKeyStroke();
public char getKeyChar();
public int getKeyCode();
public int getModifiers();
}
```

buoy.widget.TextWidget

A TextWidget is a Widget that allows the user to view and edit text. This is an abstract class.

```
public abstract class TextWidget extends Widget{
    protected CaretListener caretListener;
    protected DocumentListener documentListener;
    protected int suppressEvents;

    protected TextWidget();
    public JTextComponent getComponent();
    public String getText();
    public void setText(String text);
    public int getLength();
    public int getCaretPosition();
    public void setCaretPosition(int pos);
    public int getSelectionStart();
    public void setSelectionStart(int pos);
    public int getSelectionEnd();
    public void setSelectionEnd(int pos);
    public String getSelectedText();
    public boolean isEditable();
    protected void caretMoved();
    protected void textChanged();
}
```

buoy.widget.Widget

A Widget is a graphical object. It occupies a fixed region of the screen, and can respond to user actions. This is an abstract class.

```
public abstract class Widget extends EventSource{
    protected Component component;
    protected EventLinkAdapter eventAdapter;

    protected Widget();
    public Component getComponent();
    public WidgetContainer getParent();
    protected void setParent(WidgetContainer container);
```

```
    protected void invalidateSize();
    public Dimension getMinimumSize();
    public Dimension getMaximumSize();
    public Dimension getPreferredSize();
    public Rectangle getBounds();
    public void repaint();
    public boolean isVisible();
    public void setVisible(boolean visible);
    public boolean isEnabled();
    public void setEnabled(boolean enabled);
    public Cursor getCursor();
    public void setCursor(Cursor cursor);
    public Color getBackground();
    public void setBackground(Color background);
    public Font getFont();
    public void setFont(Font font);
    public boolean hasFocus();
    public void requestFocus();
    public boolean isFocusable();
    public void setFocusable(boolean focusable);
    public String getName();
    public void setName(String name);
    public void addEventLink(Class eventType, Object target, Method
method);
    public void dispatchEvent(Object event);
}
```

buoy.widget.WidgetContainer

A WidgetContainer is a Widget which contains other Widgets. It is responsible for arranging them on the screen. This is an abstract class.

```
public abstract class WidgetContainer extends Widget{
    protected boolean opaque;

    public WidgetContainer();
    public abstract int getChildCount();
    public abstract Collection<Widget> getChildren();
    public abstract void remove(Widget widget);
    public abstract void removeAll();
    protected void setAsParent(Widget widget);
    protected void removeAsParent(Widget widget);
    public abstract void layoutChildren();
    public boolean isOpaque();
    public void setOpaque(boolean opaque);
}
```

buoy.widget.WindowWidget

A WindowWidget is a WidgetContainer corresponding to a window. This is an abstract class.

```java
public abstract class WindowWidget extends WidgetContainer{
    protected Widget content;
    protected Dimension lastSize;

    public Window getComponent();
    public void setBounds(Rectangle bounds);
    public Widget getContent();
    public void setContent(Widget contentWidget);
    public void pack();
    public void layoutChildren();
    public void dispose();
    public void toFront();
    public void toBack();
    public boolean isVisible();
    public void setVisible(boolean visible);
    public BButton getDefaultButton();
    public void setDefaultButton(BButton button);
    protected abstract JRootPane getRootPane();
}
```

Chapter 30

The buoy.xml Package

The xml package contains classes that buoy uses to interact with XML files.

buoy.xml.IconResource

This is a subclass of ImageIcon which loads the image from the classpath by calling ClassLoader.getResource(). The main value of this class is that, unlike standard ImageIcons, it can be successfully serialized as XML by WidgetEncoder. Because the image is specified by a relative path, it will be found when the XML is decoded, regardless of where the application is stored on the computer.

```
public class IconResource extends ImageIcon{
  public IconResource(String resourceName);
  public IconResource(String resourceName, String description);
  public IconResource(String resourceName, ClassLoader
classloader);
  public String getResourceName();
}
```

buoy.xml.WidgetDecoder

This class is used for reconstructing user interfaces that were serialized as XML by WidgetDecoder.

```
public class WidgetDecoder{
  public WidgetDecoder(InputStream in);
```

```
public WidgetDecoder(InputStream in, ResourceBundle
resources);
    public WidgetDecoder(InputStream in, ExceptionListener
listener);
    public WidgetDecoder(InputStream in, ExceptionListener
listener, ResourceBundle resources);
    public Object getRootObject();
    public Object getObject(String name);
    public static void registerObject(String name, Object obj);
}
```

buoy.xml.WidgetEncoder

This class is used for serializing Widgets as XML. This allows user interfaces to be saved in a persistent form, then reconstructed using the WidgetDecoder class.

```
public class WidgetEncoder{
    public static void writeObject(Object obj, OutputStream out);
    public static void writeObject(Object obj, OutputStream out,
ExceptionListener listener);
    public static void setPersistenceDelegate(Class cls,
PersistenceDelegate delegate);
}
```

buoy.xml.WidgetLocalization

This class cooperates with WidgetEncoder and WidgetDecoder to localized the text stored in XML files. Rather than containing the actual text which will appear in the user interface, the XML file contains keys which are looked up from a ResourceBundle at decoding time. This class maintains a list of String objects which are to be localized at encoding time, and performs the actual substitution at decoding time.

```
public class WidgetLocalization{
    public static void addLocalizedString(String s);
    public static void removeLocalizedString(String s);
    public static boolean isLocalizedString(String s);
    public static String [] getAllLocalizedStrings();
    public static Object getLocalizedString(String key);
}
```

Chapter 31

The buoy.xml.delegate Package

The buoy.xml.delegate package contains the PersistanceDelegate classes the buoy uses to serialize components.

buoy.xml.delegate.BListDelegate

This class is a PersistenceDelegate for serializing BLists.

```
public class BListDelegate extends EventSourceDelegate{
    public BListDelegate();
    protected Expression instantiate(Object oldInstance, Encoder out);
}
```

buoy.xml.delegate. BorderContainerDelegate

This class is a PersistenceDelegate for serializing BorderContainers.

```
public class BorderContainerDelegate extends
EventSourceDelegate{
    public BorderContainerDelegate();
    protected void initialize(Class type, Object oldInstance, Object
newInstance, Encoder out);
}
```

buoy.xml.delegate. BSplitPanelDelegate

This class is a PersistenceDelegate for serializing BSplitPanes.

```
public class BSplitPaneDelegate extends EventSourceDelegate{
    public BSplitPaneDelegate();
    protected void initialize(Class type, Object oldInstance, Object
newInstance, Encoder out);
}
```

buoy.xml.delegate.BTableDelegate

This class is a PersistenceDelegate for serializing BTables.

```
public class BTableDelegate extends EventSourceDelegate{
    public BTableDelegate();
    protected Expression instantiate(Object oldInstance, Encoder
out);
    protected void initialize(Class type, Object oldInstance, Object
newInstance, Encoder out);
}
```

buoy.xml.delegate. BTableHeaderDelegate

This class is a PersistenceDelegate for serializing BTableHeaders.

```
public class BTableHeaderDelegate extends
EventSourceDelegate{
    public BTableHeaderDelegate();
    protected Expression instantiate(Object oldInstance, Encoder
out);
}
```

buoy.xml.delegate. EventSourceDelegate

This class is a PersistenceDelegate for serializing EventSources. It extends DefaultPersistenceDelegate to record the list of event links.

```
public class EventSourceDelegate extends
DefaultPersistenceDelegate{
    public EventSourceDelegate();
```

```
public EventSourceDelegate(String constructorPropertyNames[]);
protected void initialize(Class type, Object oldInstance, Object
newInstance, Encoder out);
protected void initializeEventLinks(Object oldInstance, Object
newInstance, Encoder out);
protected static Object getField(Object obj, String field);
}
```

buoy.xml.delegate. FormContainerDelegate

This class is a PersistenceDelegate for serializing FormContainers.

```
public class FormContainerDelegate extends
EventSourceDelegate{
public FormContainerDelegate();
protected void initialize(Class type, Object oldInstance, Object
newInstance, Encoder out);
}
```

buoy.xml.delegate. GridContainerDelegate

This class is a PersistenceDelegate for serializing GridContainers.

```
public class GridContainerDelegate extends
EventSourceDelegate{
public GridContainerDelegate();
protected void initialize(Class type, Object oldInstance, Object
newInstance, Encoder out);
}
```

buoy.xml.delegate. IndexedContainerDelegate

This class is a PersistenceDelegate for serializing a variety of WidgetContainers. It assumes the container has a list of children which are indexed by a single integer, and that children can be added to it by calling an "add" method.

```
public class IndexedContainerDelegate extends
EventSourceDelegate{
public IndexedContainerDelegate(String propertyMethods[]);
protected void initialize(Class type, Object oldInstance, Object
newInstance, Encoder out);
```

}

buoy.xml.delegate. OverlayContainerDelegate

This class is a PersistenceDelegate for serializing OverlayContainers.

```
public class OverlayContainerDelegate extends
EventSourceDelegate{
    public OverlayContainerDelegate();
    protected void initialize(Class type, Object oldInstance, Object
newInstance, Encoder out);
}
```

buoy.xml.delegate.ShortcutDelegate

This class is a PersistenceDelegate for serializing Shortcuts.

```
public class ShortcutDelegate extends
DefaultPersistenceDelegate{
    public ShortcutDelegate();
    protected Expression instantiate(Object oldInstance, Encoder
out);
}
```

buoy.xml.delegate.StaticFieldDelegate

This class is a PersistenceDelegate for serializing the values of static fields of classes. It is used when a class defines various constants, and the appropriate way to "instantiate" one of them is to get it from the appropriate static field.

```
public class StaticFieldDelegate extends PersistenceDelegate{
    public StaticFieldDelegate(Class cls);
    protected Expression instantiate(Object oldInstance, Encoder
out);
    protected boolean mutatesTo(Object oldInstance, Object
newInstance);
}
```

Chapter 32

Math Quick Reference

Computer graphics programming often requires the use of mathematical equations. The next few pages contain equations you may need while working with graphics. They are included here for your convenience. For proofs and detailed explanations, you should consult the appropriate mathematics textbook.

Triangle

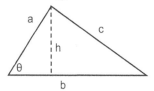

$$h = a \sin \theta$$

$$Area = \frac{1}{2}b * h$$

$$c^2 = a^2 + b^2 - 2ab \cos \theta$$

Right Triangle

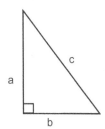

$$c^2 = a^2 + b^2$$

Equilateral Triangle

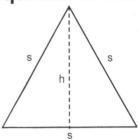

$$h = \frac{\sqrt{3} * s}{2}$$

$$Area = \frac{\sqrt{3} * s^2}{4}$$

Parallelogram

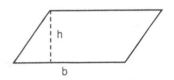

$$Area = bh$$

Trapezoid

$$Area = \frac{h}{2}(a+b)$$

Circle

$$Area = \pi r^2$$
$$Circ = 2\pi r$$

Sector of Circle

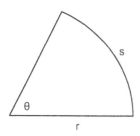

$$Area = \frac{\theta r^2}{2}$$

$$s = r\theta$$

Ellipse

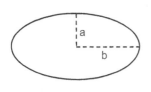

$$Area = \pi ab$$

$$Circ \approx 2\pi\sqrt{\frac{a^2 + b^2}{2}}$$

Trigonometric Identities

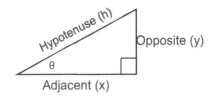

$$\sin\theta = \frac{y}{h} = \frac{1}{\csc\theta}$$

$$\cos\theta = \frac{x}{h} = \frac{1}{\sec\theta}$$

$$\tan\theta = \frac{y}{x} = \frac{\sin\theta}{\cos\theta}$$

$$\cot\theta = \frac{x}{y} = \frac{\cos\theta}{\sin\theta}$$

$$\sec\theta = \frac{h}{x} = \frac{1}{\cos\theta}$$

$$\csc\theta = \frac{h}{y} = \frac{1}{\sin\theta}$$

$$\sin^2\theta + \cos^2\theta = 1$$

$$\tan^2\theta + 1 = \sec^2\theta$$

$$\cot^2\theta + 1 = \csc^2\theta$$

$$\sin(\theta \pm \phi) = \sin\theta\cos\phi \pm \cos\theta\sin\phi$$

$$\cos(\theta \pm \phi) = \cos\theta\cos\phi \mp \sin\theta\sin\phi$$

$$\tan(\theta \pm \phi) = \frac{\tan\theta \pm \tan\phi}{1 \mp \tan\theta\tan\phi}$$

$$\sin 2\theta = 2\sin\theta\cos\theta$$

$$\cos 2\theta = 2\cos^2\theta - 1 = 1 - 2\sin^2\theta$$

$$\sin^2\theta = \tfrac{1}{2}(1 - \cos 2\theta)$$

$$\cos^2\theta = \tfrac{1}{2}(1 + \cos 2\theta)$$

$$\tan\frac{\theta}{2} = \frac{1 - \cos\theta}{\sin\theta} = \frac{\sin\theta}{1 + \cos\theta}$$

$$\sin(-\theta) = -\sin\theta$$
$$\cos(-\theta) = \cos\theta$$
$$\tan(-\theta) = -\tan\theta$$

$$\cot(-\theta) = -\cot\theta$$
$$\sec(-\theta) = \sec(\theta)$$
$$\csc(-\theta) = -\csc\theta$$

$$\sin\theta\sin\phi = \tfrac{1}{2}[\cos(\theta-\phi) - \cos(\theta+\phi)]$$

$$\cos\theta\cos\phi = \tfrac{1}{2}[\cos(\theta-\phi) + \cos(\theta+\phi)]$$

$$\sin\theta\cos\phi = \tfrac{1}{2}[\sin(\theta+\phi) + \sin(\theta-\phi)]$$

$$\cos\theta\sin\phi = \tfrac{1}{2}[\sin(\theta+\phi) - \sin(\theta-\phi)]$$

$$\sin^{-1}x = \frac{\pi}{2} - \cos^{-1}x = \tan^{-1}\frac{x}{\sqrt{1-x^2}}$$

$$\cos^{-1}x = \frac{\pi}{2} - \sin^{-1}x = \cot^{-1}\frac{x}{\sqrt{1-x^2}}$$

$$\tan^{-1}x = \frac{\pi}{2} - \cot^{-1}x = \sin^{-1}\frac{x}{\sqrt{1-x^2}}$$

$$\cot^{-1}x = \tan^{-1}\frac{1}{x}$$

$$\sec^{-1}x = \cos^{-1}\frac{1}{x}$$

$$\csc^{-1}x = \sin^{-1}\frac{1}{x}$$

Math

Vector Math

Given two n-dimensional vectors **v**=(v₁, v₂, ..., vₙ) and **w**=(w₁, w₂, ..., wₙ), the **dot product** is represented as d=**v·w**. It has the value:

$$d = v \cdot w = \sum_{i=1}^{n} v_i w_i$$

The dot product of two vectors results in a scalar value. The following are true of dot products:

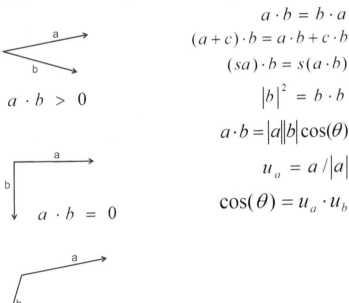

$$a \cdot b = b \cdot a$$
$$(a + c) \cdot b = a \cdot b + c \cdot b$$
$$(sa) \cdot b = s(a \cdot b)$$
$$|b|^2 = b \cdot b$$
$$a \cdot b = |a||b| \cos(\theta)$$
$$u_a = a / |a|$$
$$\cos(\theta) = u_a \cdot u_b$$

$a \cdot b > 0$

$a \cdot b = 0$

$a \cdot b < 0$

The **cross product** or **vector product** is a multiplication of vectors that results in another vector. The cross product is perpendicular to both of the original vectors. It can be used to find the normal of the plane the vectors are in. The following is the definition:

$$\mathbf{a} \times \mathbf{b} = (a_y b_z - a_z b_y)\mathbf{i} + (a_z b_x - a_x b_z)\mathbf{j} + (a_x b_y - a_y b_x)\mathbf{k}$$

It is frequently seen in the following form:

$$a \times b = \begin{vmatrix} i & j & k \\ a_x & a_y & a_z \\ b_x & b_y & b_z \end{vmatrix}$$

The following are true concerning cross products:

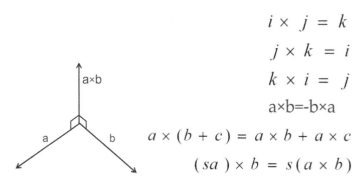

$$i \times j = k$$
$$j \times k = i$$
$$k \times i = j$$
$$a \times b = -b \times a$$
$$a \times (b + c) = a \times b + a \times c$$
$$(sa) \times b = s(a \times b)$$

Equation of a Line

The equation of a line takes on different forms. The slope-intercept form is given by:

$$y = mx + b$$

Here, m is the slope and b is the y-intercept.

A more useful equation for graphics is the parametric equation of a line. It is defined by two points on the line. Usually these are the two points at the ends of the line segment that we intend to draw. The value of t specifies where we are along the line. This equation is given by:

$$x = (1 - t)A_x + B_x$$
$$y = (1 - t)A_y + B_y$$
$$z = (1 - t)A_z + B_z$$

And the haft also went in after the blade; and the fat closed upon the blade, so that he could not draw the dagger out of his belly; and the dirt came out.

— *Judges 3:22*

Also Available

Church Website Design: A Step By Step Approach
(ISBN 1-4196-5971-5)

Mother Not Wanted
(ISBN 978-1-61295-000-6)
Searching For Mom
(ISBN 978-1-4196-7039-8)
How to Become a Bible Character
(ISBN 978-1-4196-8331-2)
For the Love of a Devil
(ISBN 978-1-4392-1425-1)
And Thy House
(ISBN 978-1-4392-6871-1)

About the Author

Timothy Fish began programming computers at an early age, beginning with a TRS-80, when he imagined the possibility of having the computer draw cartoon characters. He has received a BS in Computer Science/ Mathematics from Southeast Missouri State University and a MS in Computer Science from Nova Southeastern University. In his day job, he is a Software Engineer, but is able to use his limited free time for website development, computer generated artwork and writing novels.

About the Cover

The cover of this book was rendered using Art of Illusion. The objects were created in Art of Illusion, with the exception that some textures were edited using The Gimp. The cloth simulator described in Chapter 10 was used for the image on the back as well as two cloths that are lying on the table. Other items in the scene that make use of plugins from the book include the placement of the three objects in the center of the table, the tile on the floor, and the walls of the room. Though not visible, there is a Fan object that is a child of the fan that can be seen.